Presenting the

★PAST★

ESSAYS
on History
and the Public

EDITED BY
SUSAN PORTER BENSON,
STEPHEN BRIER,
AND ROY ROSENZWEIG

TEMPLE UNIVERSITY PRESS   *Philadelphia*

Temple University Press, Philadelphia 19122
Published 1986
Printed in the United States of America

Library of Congress Cataloging-in-Publication Data

Main entry under title:
Presenting the past.

1. United States—History—Study and teaching—Addresses, essays, lectures.
2. Public history—United States—Addresses, essays, lectures.
3. United States—Popular Culture—Historiography—Addresses, essays, lectures.
4. United States—Historiography—Addresses, essays, lectures.
I. Benson, Susan Porter, 1943–
II. Brier, Stephen.
III. Rosenzweig, Roy.
E175.8.P83 1986   73'.072   5-27648
ISBN 0-87722-406-4

Terence O'Donnell, "Pitfalls Along the Path of Public History," copyright 1982 by The Regents of the University of California. Reprinted from *The Public Historian*, vol. 4, no. 1, Winter 1982, pp. 65–72, by permission of the Regents.

Photo/Illustration Credits:
Page 3—© 1981, G. B. Trudeau. Reprinted by permission of Universal Press Syndicate. All rights reserved. Page 19—© 1959 by the New York Times Company. Reprinted by permission. Page 51—courtesy Joshua Brown. Page 65—© David Macauley, *Cathedral: The Story of Its Construction*, Boston: Houghton/Mifflin, 1973. Page 85—The Museum of Modern Art/Film Stills Archive. Reprinted by permission. Page 103—*The New York Times* (advertisement), Dec. 31, 1980. Page 119—H. W. Pierson, *In the Brush*, 1981. Page 135—courtesy Colonial Williamsburg Foundation. Page 163—*Historic Preservation*, Jan./Feb. 1985. Reprinted by permission. Page 201 (left)—photograph courtesy of The National Museum of American History, Smithsonian Institution. Page 201 (right)—courtesy of Mattel and Indiana State Museum. Page 223—*American Heritage* (advertisement), June/July 1985. Page 237—courtesy Jean-Christophe Agnew. Page 247—BNHP/Minnie Conn. Page 265—courtesy Scovill, Inc. Page 279—from the collection of the National Gay Archives, Hollywood, CA. Reprinted by permission. Page 291—Gordon Parks, "The Life and Times of Rosie the Riveter." Page 305—J. A. Rogers, *Your History: From the Beginning of Time to the Present*, Baltimore: Black Classic Press, 1983. Reprinted by permission. Page 337—*American Splendor* no. 8, © 1983 by Harvey Pekar. Reprinted by permission.

To the memory of
Herbert G. Gutman
(1928–1985)

★ Contents ★

★ Preface ★

A new generation of historians who were intellectually and politically shaped by the civil rights, antiwar, and feminist movements emerged in the 1970s and 1980s. This new generation advocates a "new" kind of history—one that explores long-neglected subjects like women, blacks, peasants, and workers; one that critically reexamines the centers of power and authority around the world; one that reaches beyond the confines of academe. To a remarkable degree these scholars have reshaped the practice of history in the United States and have won recognition and acceptance from the mainstream of the historical profession. A major voice of this new generation of historians and activists has been the *Radical History Review*. Begun in 1973 as the newsletter of the Mid-Atlantic Radical Historians Organization (MARHO), the collectively edited *Review* established itself by the late 1970s as an important historical and theoretical journal.

Critical Perspectives on the Past, the series of which this collection is the first volume, builds on the approaches and achievements of the *Radical History Review* but takes advantage of the greater flexibility and wider distribution of a book series. Following the *Review's* precedent, this series will often present collections of essays on a particular theme. But the book format will allow us to publish a much more comprehensive array of essays and make these volumes suitable for classroom use. In addition to collections of essays-—an anthology on the history of sexuality, for example, is already in the works—the series will also include monographs, particularly syntheses of the latest scholarship on important topics. Our goals for the series are large and ambitious: to present the latest work in the area; to break new empirical, methodological, and theoretical ground; to criticize historical orthodoxy; to connect the past and the present; to offer writing that is clear, lively, and accessible to a broad audience.

Like the series that this volume inaugurates, *Presenting the Past* emerges from the milieu of the *Radical History Review*. The *Review* was the first historical journal to take an active interest in how history was being presented in nonacademic settings, and it published preliminary versions of a number of the essays that appear in this book. Michael Wallace, the editorial secretary of the *Radical History Review* for the past several years, played a central role in encouraging the journal to move in this direction. In 1980 and 1981 Warren Goldstein worked with the three editors of this volume on a special issue of the *Review* that featured earlier versions of six of the essays included here. Since 1982 Jean-Christophe Agnew has shared with two of us the responsibility for coordinating the public history section of the *Review;* in that capacity he helped to solicit and edit some of the articles that appear here. Joshua Brown, the *Review's* art director, assisted us in shaping the design as well as the contents of this book. We would like to express our sincere thanks to Mike, Warren, Jean-Christophe, and Josh as well as to several other *Review* colleagues who made important contributions to the development and editing of this book: Betsy Blackmar, Barbara Melosh, Michael Merrill, Marjorie Murphy, Daniel J. Walkowitz, and Peter Weiler. We would also like to thank George Mason University's word processing center for help in typing some of the articles and our friends at Temple University Press, particularly our copy editor, Jane Barry, our editor, Janet Francendese, and the director, David Bartlett, for their strong encouragement of this book and the entire series.

Finally, we have dedicated this book to the memory of Herbert G. Gutman. Although Herb had little to do with the development or editing of this particular volume, he had a great deal to do with the larger context out of which it emerged. Both intellectually and personally, he nurtured and shaped the generation of historians who came of age in the 1960s, among them the editors of this volume. His energy, vision, and commitment sustained and inspired us and will continue to do so.

S. P. B.

S. B.

R. R.

Introduction

Introduction

"Our students will not recognize the urgency in Nicaragua," warns Education Secretary William J. Bennett, "if they cannot recognize the history that is threatening to repeat itself." According to Bennett, a knowledge of the Cuban missile crisis and the Monroe Doctrine would inevitably persuade young Americans to support Ronald Reagan's policy of subverting the Nicaraguan government. For conservative columnist William Safire, the relevant history may be different, but the lesson is the same: "if you believe that our attempt to save South Vietnam from Communist takeover was nobly motivated . . . then you stand with Ronald Reagan: You see the Managua Communists as the puppets of Havana and Moscow, and you are eager to supply the contras." But Safire also concedes the possibility of an alterative interpretation: "if you believe that Vietnam was an exercise in American imperialism, doomed from the start and needlessly prolonged, then . . . you equate the contras with the 'corrupt dictatorship in Saigon' and refuse them the guns they need."

These divergent understandings of the past are not the only forms of historical consciousness affecting Central America. In Nicaragua, the historical memory of the nationwide rebellion led by Augusto Sandino in the 1920s and 1930s against a quarter-century of U.S. Marine occupation helped sustain broad-based support for the Sandinista movement until it could re-emerge in the 1950s. The popular memory of Sandino—transmitted orally "through songs sung by parents to their children," according to one contemporary historian—powerfully shaped national political consciousness and continues to fuel support for the revolutionary government.

BY SUSAN PORTER BENSON, STEPHEN BRIER, AND ROY ROSENZWEIG

Conservatives like Bennett and Safire and revolutionaries like the Sand-
inistas can at least agree on one thing—history matters. Popular understandings of everything from global wars to local strikes to family migrations crucially affect how we behave in the present. For example, recollections of the
Great Depression as a time of personal failure, triumphant collective action,
or salvation through government intervention inform current attitudes toward
institutions as diverse as the family, trade unions, and the federal government.

Despite the impact of historical consciousness on popular perceptions of
contemporary events and institutions, professional historians have paid remarkably little attention to the presentation and perception of history outside
the classroom. Their debates, to a very large degree, have remained confined
within their discipline. They have argued fiercely over whether Carl Becker,
Bernard Bailyn, or Pauline Maier has "correctly" understood the American
Revolution. But they have generally ignored how Colonial Williamsburg,
American Heritage magazine, Twentieth Century–Fox, and Howard Fast
have interpreted the same events for a much larger audience. Similarly, most
academic historians have shown little interest in speaking directly to that
audience.

There are recent signs, however, that academic historians have begun to
remedy their neglect of popular history and the general public. In particular,
an emerging professional public history movement is training historians to
work in such diverse settings as the government bureaucracy, the corporate
board room, the local historical society, the national historical museum, the
film editing room, the union hall, and the senior citizen center. Within the
past decade we have seen the establishment of a professional journal (the
Public Historian), a professional organization (the National Council on Public
History), conferences, and numerous undergraduate and graduate courses and
degree programs (including doctorates in public history). This collection con-
tributes to the growing body of literature about public history, but it also
addresses broader and more analytical questions than much of the professional
writing in this vein: broader in that it examines the place of historical consciousness in American life and asks how ideas about history shape current
beliefs and actions; more analytical in that the essays in this collection go
beyond the "how-to-do-it" approach to public history to dissect the message
and the methods of popular historical presentations in the United States.

From this perspective, there are at least three identifiable varieties of public
history, each with quite different origins and goals. The first variant is the
most pervasive and influential in shaping popular historical consciousness.
Every day Americans confront a multitude of historical images and messages
in television docudramas, paperback potboilers, newspapers, movies, mu-

seums, and historic houses, and even on restaurant placemats and sugar packets. Usually serving dominant interests or reinforcing popular prejudices, this variant of public history can transform history into just another disposable and smartly packaged commodity. The historical "messages" embedded in these commercial forms have a profound impact on public consciousness because of their constant repetition and their slick and palatable presentations.

The second type, represented by the professional public history movement, has done the most to develop and defend the idea of public history. The newest of the three, it is based on a dissatisfaction with the narrowness of the academic audience as well as a desire to expand the job market for historians beyond colleges and universities. The practitioners of this "applied" history are served by the growing number of university-based programs providing "more" or "better" or "more professional" public history through a variety of practical programs on public policy, business history, editing and archival practices, local history, and historic preservation. Because these public history programs grow out of an effort to professionalize a new field, they exist uneasily between traditional academic historians and those who present commercialized or politicized versions of the past outside the university.

The third type of public history is commonly called "people's history." Although difficult to define, it generally refers to efforts to encourage a progressive, accessible, and frequently oppositional historical vision in a variety of community and organizational contexts. The earlier roots of people's history include such groups as the pre–World War I Socialist Party history clubs, but its more immediate origins lie in the political upheavals of the late 1960s and early 1970s. Convinced that the discovery and knowledge of one's own history can be personally empowering and a catalyst for social movements, the practitioners of people's history have often experimented with new media and explored topics ignored by mainstream academic historians. In addition, some people's historians have emphasized the *process* as well as the content of history, striving to make it a partnership between those with historical expertise and those with historical experience.

Presenting the Past proceeds from the assumption that all these aspects of public history must be taken seriously and viewed critically if we are to understand the evolution of popular historical consciousness. We offer neither superficial attacks on the history presented in commercial media nor uncritical celebrations of people's history. Public historians, whatever their political orientation, can learn from the successes and failures of both mainstream and left history.

We have organized this collection into three sections, focusing in turn on mass culture and popular historical consciousness, on professional public history or applied history, and on people's history projects. To some extent the divisions are artificial because both the varieties of public history and the articles resist easy classification. The case studies that make up most of this book demonstrate the complexity of specific projects and raise theoretical issues that cross the line between oppositional and mainstream public history. Moreover, the boundary between the two has been permeable: mainstream public history, in its desire to broaden its appeal, has incorporated some of the populist content of people's history; similarly, people's history, in its eagerness to make its perspective more accessible to the public, has adopted some of the sophistication of mainstream presentations.

Part I, "Packaging the Past: Mass Culture and Historical Consciousness," looks at the large-scale production and dissemination of historical knowledge, particularly in commercial media. These contributions explore the role of mass culture in perpetuating either historical amnesia or versions of the past that affirm dominant values and institutions. Michael H. Frisch notes both of these effects in confronting the largest theoretical issue facing public history —the nature of historical memory and consciousness in the United States. Distinguishing between history (what happened) and memory (how people remember what happened), Frisch argues that the disturbing content of the first is constantly being edited out by the second. The next five pieces in this section show how this process operates within specific commercial forms— historical magazines, popular fiction, children's books, Hollywood films, and television docudramas. Roy Rosenzweig, examining the history of *American Heritage* magazine, shows how it became in the 1950s and 1960s an alluring substitute for older communities of storytelling and remembrance that had decayed with the development of suburbia and post–World War II American life. Presenting history as a tidy and attractive package, it reinforced the perception of the past as fixed, closed, and seamless.

The historical fiction that fills the supermarket book racks—as we learn from Priscilla Murolo's analysis of the historical sagas of Howard Fast—is equally likely to distort the past. Fast in his recent sagas coopts challenges to the status quo with a political message denatured by a denial of irreconcilable social conflicts and a facile reliance on upper-class heroes and heroines. Similar problems can be found in the academically shunned literary ghetto of children's history books. There Joshua Brown finds an all-too-common focus on "Great Men" and a simplistic sentimentalism in both text and pictures.

The distortions of popular fiction are magnified and multiplied in filmed and televised historical epics. In his study of Twentieth Century–Fox's 1939 film, *Drums Along the Mohawk,* Edward Countryman shows how Hollywood transformed a subtle novel about revolutionary America into a love story grounded in reactionary conventions about women and Indians. The novel's intricate web of economic, racial, and gender conflicts was sacrificed to film-industry imperatives. Eric Breitbart's article on televised historical doc-udramas examines the cynical manipulations of the past justified as dramatic license but serving corporate profits. Surveying commercialized history extravaganzas since the panoramas of the late nineteenth century, he finds that the intentional distortion of history is not at all new; sophisticated technology, however, has provided contemporary docudramatists with an alarmingly expanded ability to produce convincing distortions of the past.

Although often sharp in their criticism, the authors of articles in this section make clear that products of the commercial culture are neither worthless nor indistinguishable from one another. Joshua Brown, for example, argues that some children's history books offer models worthy of imitation and provide a richly textured view of the past. Similarly, Roy Rosenzweig finds that *American Heritage* can teach historians about reaching and holding the interest of a large audience, particularly through the inventive use of graphics. Avoiding an approach that sees mass culture as purely manipulative, these pieces consider both the diversity among producers of popular history and the complex interplay between producers and their presumed audience. Yet, even granting the complexity of commercially produced public history, its overall tendency is to reinforce existing arrangements and points of view. These commercialized and commoditized images can crowd out alternative visions of the past, as Gertrude Fraser and Reginald Butler chillingly demonstrate. Their account of a confrontation between two self-serving racist versions of the past in a court case concerning the disposition of an abandoned Virginia graveyard shows that the historical consciousness of locally powerful whites, although divided, still effectively excluded blacks.

Although the purveyors of commercialized culture offer powerful images for public consumption, other groups now challenge their monopoly of public attention. The public or applied history movement, with its emphasis on non-academic arenas for history, has grown significantly. Non-university-based professional historians have increasingly shaped popular historical consciousness through their work in museums, historical societies, preservation agencies, and corporate archives and historical offices. Part II— "Professionalizing the Past: Reflections on Applied History"—examines some of the fruits of this public history movement. Looking first at the development of history museums, Michael Wallace traces the role of corporate leaders such as Henry Ford and John D. Rockefeller, Jr., in creating the institutional contexts in which museum professionals now work. Despite their differences, Rockefeller's Colonial Williamsburg and Ford's Greenfield Village provided historical oases for millions of visitors who found in them a virtuous and heroic past. In a second article on the historic preservation movement, Wallace finds patricians in control at first, later to be joined by other groups—local boosters, young urban professionals, real estate developers, and working-class urbanites— whose interests sometimes reinforced and sometimes challenged the intentions of the first preservationists. During the 1960s and 1970s, the historical museums and the historic preservation movement were forced to respond in spite of their origins to new trends in American historiography as well as progressive social movements: Colonial Williamsburg recognized, however imperfectly, the reality of slavery, while preservationists helped forge a short-lived alliance with minority and working-class constituents. Those moments, Wallace concludes, provide necessary and appropriate precedents for both movements to follow in the future if they are ever to serve other than elite interests.

In their discussion of the presentation of women's history in museums, Barbara Melosh and Christina Simmons find more dramatic evidence of the impact of social and historiographical changes on public historical presentations. For instance, they argue that exhibits at the Smithsonian's National Museum of American History evolved from presenting women as appendages of great men to a pluralist inclusion of women in the "big picture" to using gender as a basic category of historical analysis. Melosh and Simmons, like Wallace, shed light on the role of the public sector in shaping our understanding of the past, showing that federal, state, and local governments have both legitimated dominant views and allowed the intervention of alternative voices. Daniel J. Walkowitz, by contrast, finds corporate-sponsored history a far more monolithic and direct expression of powerful economic interests. Historians who work in corporations, he argues, serve their employers well, not simply because adherence to the company line is a condition of their jobs but because their own perspectives already coincide with the views of corporate America. Finally, Terence O'Donnell evaluates the contradictory practices of the professional public history movement. Criticizing practitioners of public history for claiming too much for their field while seeking too avidly to create jobs for unemployed historians, he urges public historians to accept a more modest role for themselves and their new field.

Part III, "Politicizing the Past: Toward A People's History," considers a variety of attempts to shape historical consciousness in ways that challenge the status quo. Articles about projects in Baltimore (by Linda Shopes), the Naugatuck Valley (by Jeremy Brecher), and Lynn, Lawrence, and Boston (by James R. Green) suggest the variety of local history efforts, ranging from multiyear, well-funded undertakings to largely volunteer efforts and one-shot events. In some cases, an occupational focus—on brass workers, shoe workers, or clerical workers—further defines the project. These community history projects share a desire not simply to recapture the past but to create new constituencies for and practitioners of history. All three authors probe the relationship between community historians and the people they study, noting the differences in the two groups' understandings of the meaning of the past.

Another set of articles focuses on efforts by specific groups to recapture a suppressed or ignored history and use it as a vehicle for developing group identity and pride. History's "gay ghetto," Lisa Duggan argues, benefits and suffers from the marginality of the homosexual community, much as Afro-Americans' and women's marginality spurred their historical consciousness a decade ago. Duggan stresses the enthusiasm that suffuses lesbian and gay community history projects, linking amateur and professional historians as well as historians and audiences in a mutual effort; at the same time, she notes divisions within the lesbian and gay communities and the tenuous nature of many of the projects. Sonya Michel looks at a small but influential corner of the public history of women, exploring the strengths and weaknesses of three well-known women's labor history films. Located at the juncture of oral history and feminist consciousness-raising, the films vary widely in their politics and aesthetics as well as in their success in developing an appropriate relationship between filmic form and historical content.

The long and little-known evolution of Afro-American public history comes to light in the sweeping survey by Jeffrey C. Stewart and Fath Davis Ruffins. Amateurs and professionals coexisted less easily in the Afro-American community, divided not only by professional status but also by class and political differences. Nonetheless, Stewart and Ruffins argue that for the last century and a half, Afro-American history has been an important and popularly recognized tool in the fight against racism. Despite the energy and activity of people's historians, their political impact is not always so easy to evaluate. James R. Green, while describing the products of the Massachusetts History Workshop, assesses that larger impact— actual and potential—in his survey of the evolution of people's history and in his comparison of the history workshop movements in England and the United States.

Although the writers of the essays in this volume adhere to no single perspective, most of the authors—as well as the editors— sympathize with the diverse and diffuse efforts to create a people's history and a critical historical consciousness in the United States. The essays in *Presenting the Past* document the substantial accomplishments and the subtler inroads made by these efforts. Thanks to the work of people's historians—and, of course, those laboring in more traditional settings—American history is no longer solely the story of the rich and powerful, of the white and male. And this more pluralistic version of the past has found its way, at least to a limited degree, into some of the commercial expressions of historical consciousness dissected in Part I of this volume. High school and college textbooks, television docudramas, and even theme park exhibits now include the experiences of Afro-Americans, Native Americans, and women.

Despite the successes of the 1960s and 1970s, the prospects for a more inclusive vision of history are growing dimmer in the 1980s. The more conservative political climate has legitimated simplistic patriotic celebrations of the past and encouraged elitism, racism, sexism, and homophobia in history as elsewhere. More specifically, it has reduced funding for people's history, not only curtailing such projects themselves but also threatening their role as a catalyst for change in other forms of public history. By the late 1970s people's history projects had become heavily dependent on funding from the National Endowment for the Humanities (NEH). With the election of Ronald Reagan in 1980 and his appointment of the conservative William Bennett as the Endowment's director in 1982, support for such projects began to dry up. The most expensive efforts, such as films and large-scale community and oral history projects, face an uncertain future without federal funding. A return to the more modest approaches of the 1960s—mimeographed pamphlets and slide shows, for example—may be necessary.

The funding problems facing people's history projects have been exacerbated by their tenuous connections to community institutions or organizations, as Linda Shopes makes clear in her essay on the Baltimore Neighborhood Heritage Project. Although labor unions were often willing to house labor history projects funded by the government, few have been interested in continuing to support them when outside funding disappeared. Many community history projects—linked to universities by the requirements of NEH funding—failed to build connections with local churches, community organizations, or social clubs that might have sustained them on a permanent basis. Nevertheless, the experiments of the Massachusetts History Workshop and some lesbian and gay history projects offer promising models for people's historians seeking to root their work within specific communities.

Even if the crisis of funding is resolved, these projects will have to confront other problems of historical and political analysis. People's history projects have generally drawn on a pluralist and populist rather than Marxist analysis of American history and have consequently avoided some difficult historical questions. For example, they have decried the oppression and exploitation of blacks, women, workers, and immigrants, but they have not adequately considered or presented the lines of tension and exploitation among these same groups. The film *With Babies and Banners,* for example, ended with a critique of the sexism of the United Automobile Workers, but projects have more frequently drawn back from considering the labor movement's racism and sexism. Similarly, people's history has tended to celebrate the struggles of oppressed groups without systematically analyzing why these groups have so often lost these struggles, in some cases simply turning the celebratory and chauvinistic history of the 1950s on its head.

At the same time that people's historians in the United States need to sharpen their modes of historical analysis, they also need to rethink their modes of historical work. Despite intentions to the contrary, most people's history projects have operated from the "top down." Experts or professionals prepared a product—whether film, play, exhibit, or pamphlet—for a largely passive audience. Although some promising exceptions are documented in this volume, people's history projects have not always embodied the democratic values that they have espoused. Their organizers have sometimes been too protective of their own status as "professionals" and have been reluctant to take up the difficult task of democratizing historical work as well as the historical record. But even the most determinedly democratic projects, as Shopes, Brecher, and Green all point out, have been pushed in more traditional directions by product-oriented funding agencies, which often insist on tight deadlines at the expense of widespread participation. The diffusion of the skills of writing history and the development of a more critical stance toward mass culture's views of history are formidable yet necessary goals of any effort to forge a truly inclusive historical vision.

Whether a nonhierarchical, democratic, and community-based historical practice can be merged with a theoretical understanding of class, racial, and sexual oppression depends only in part on the energy and vision of those committed to developing a people's history in the United States. As in the past, both the prospects and the potential of the people's history movement are closely tied to broader movements for social change. A revival of such movements in coming years will foster more sophisticated and useful public history efforts even as it will facilitate the incorporation of a broader historical vision into mass-cultural versions of history.

Yet even in their current form, people's history projects can be a potent force for sustaining a vision of social change that can, in turn, nurture and encourage these same social movements. History, we believe, can empower people, although not merely by celebrating the past or by suggesting "lessons" to apply to the present. History can be used to teach people that the social, political, economic, and cultural institutions that delimit contemporary life are not timeless but rather the products of human agency and historical choices. Grasping the contingent nature of the past can break the tyranny of the present; seeing how historical actors made and remade social life, we can gain a new vision of our own present and future. That is perhaps the most important lesson that historians can help people to draw from the past.

★ I ★
Packaging the Past:

Mass Culture and Historical Consciousness

DOONESBURY

The Memory of History

In the last few years, there has been an exponential increase in the number of people involved in what is coming to be called "public history." Often publicly funded, these individuals have been working on historical documentaries, oral histories, archival and bibliographic projects, neighborhood studies and exhibits, policy-related historical research in business and government, and so on. This has led to a flood of new kinds of historical products, generally meant for various public audiences, rather than the usual circle of professional academic specialists.

As both a participant in and observer of this phenomenon, I have become concerned about the relatively casual way in which the public history impulse has been discussed. Simply put, far more attention has been paid to the "how" than to the "why" of public history. The latter question has frequently been met through formulaic appeals to unexceptionable goals, such as encouraging a wider sharing of knowledge and a broader participation in the process of history-making; giving an empowering sense of their own history to groups denied this by the form, dissemination, and structural biases of conventional scholarship; and providing business or government with a sense of the recent past that is usable in complex policy analyses. But these all have the somewhat hollow ring of justification, begging what ought to be prior questions about the very nature of historical sensitivity and consciousness in American society today, and about how, why, and whether this ought to be, needs to be, and can be altered, and if so to what specific ends. These questions have been finessed in a great many public history efforts, including, sometimes especially, those developed in the interest of facilitating progressive social change. Whether top-down or bottom-up, most of the energy in public history

BY MICHAEL H. FRISCH

has been directed toward what could be called the "supply-side" dynamics of the presumably unbalanced market for historical intelligence.

The supply-side reference is only partially facetious. Efforts to supply more and better public history will be no more likely than Reaganomics to redress the inequities and distortions in our public culture unless they manage to address as well some fundamental paradoxes in the way Americans—in all their dominant and not-so-dominant cultures—have managed variously to invoke, revoke, and generally shrink from provoking a serious reckoning with their past.

To put the matter this way—to view the capacity to engage and make use of history as at once structured, variable, and problematic—is to suggest the centrality of the relationship between history and the process of memory, individual and collective. What matters is not so much the history that is placed before us, but rather what we are able to remember, and what role that knowledge plays in our lives. I will argue in this essay that the relationship between history and memory is peculiarly and perhaps uniquely fractured in contemporary American life, and that repairing it needs to be a major goal of a public history concerned with enhancing our ability to imagine and create a different future through a re-use of the past. To see why this is so requires some exploration of the problem of historical consciousness itself, an expedition that may help remove public history from the closed, neoclassical circle of supply and demand.[1]

Let me begin this excursion with two stories that are at first glance contradictory but on closer examination make the same point.

The first incident, involving a student who forgot who won and who lost the war in Vietnam, happened during a seminar several years ago. The class had read a good portion of Frances Fitzgerald's *Fire in the Lake*. They came in eager to discuss the book's chilling dissection of America's almost purposeful ethnocentrism as this had contributed to the devastation of Vietnam. None was more stirred than a student who expressed her particular shock at the cynicism with which American military and diplomatic personnel manipulated a succession of South Vietnamese governments. "That's just outrageous," she exclaimed. "Does that *still* go on there? Is our ambassador *still* giving them orders like that?"

There was a stunned silence from the other students; you did not then have to be over twenty or twenty-five to remember vividly the war's end in 1975. Somebody gently pointed out that we didn't have an ambassador there any more, that in fact we had no real influence at all, given that the North and the National Liberation Front had won and taken over. The student was embarrassed. Of course she knew that, and almost immediately she began to recall and display for the class a series of media images, as if to confirm her knowledge—the helicopter on the roof, the ambassador with the plastic-wrapped flag (an image transposed in memory from the fall of Cambodia), and so on. In the more serious discussion that followed, she noted that although she had followed the war closely while it was going on, on reflection it was clear that she had scarcely thought about it since the day it ended. It seemed important to her to point out that she really did know the history—it was just that her sense of it had become remote, inaccessible, and ultimately garbled. The lapse, she insisted, was only one of memory.

The second story comes from a 1977 television documentary by Bill Moyers, a powerful study of the CIA's secret war against Castro, which focused particularly on the Cuban-exile terrorists trained, financed, encouraged, and then suddenly abandoned by the CIA. The program included a long interview with a former high-ranking CIA official who had played a key policy-making role in these activities. With a liberal's sense of disbelief, Moyers asked him how it could have happened—the cloak-and-dagger Mafia connection, the comic-opera beard-powder operation, and the quite uncomical assassination plots. How could it conceivably be justified under any construction of U.S. policy, given our presumed values and beliefs?

Interestingly, the official—no Gordon Liddy, he—did not attempt to offer any justification. He nodded all through Moyers' litany of horrors, and then replied, in effect (I have no transcript at hand), "Well, it can't be justified or defended. But," he added, shaking his head sagely, "you've got to see it in the context of the period. People back then just had a thing about communism. They were willing to do anything. It was just, you know, the spirit of the times." This, from an official of an agency that had plotted to overthrow Salvador Allende only a few years previously, an agency (and a government) whose subsequent and ongoing response to what it presumes to be communism (especially in Latin America) demonstrates how little it has learned from the darkest days of the 1950s.

These are, then, opposite stories. In one the subject forgets; in the other he remembers well, setting his recollections in supposedly helpful historical perspective. But somehow the result is the same: in each, the past is almost entirely severed from the present, sealed in a kind of protective wrapping, either of forgetfulness or artificial distance. All this is hardly exceptional, of course. The most casual reflection locates these two anecdotes within a broad pattern that can be found extending from popular culture to professional scholarship, a pattern wherein selective amnesia and artificial distance can combine to render even last month's history a two-dimensional caricature. The result, far from coincidentally, is a present that seems to float in time—

unencumbered, unconstrained, and uninstructed by any active sense of how it came to be.

These stories from several years back suggest some of the dilemmas public history needs to be confronting now. Indeed, the problem of how the Vietnam War is coming to be remembered and understood as history is worth closer examination here. If so much that is threatening about this recent history can be blocked out now, with the evidence all around us and the experience still painfully fresh, how can we expect people to relate to the challenging but fragile visions of a more complex past, resurrected and presented by imaginative public history projects? Will they not be ignored, absorbed, deflected, or denatured even more easily, and at precisely the point where they threaten to make a real difference in contemporary life? If public history is to avoid this fate, we need to understand more clearly the processes of denial and disengagement that the current "digestion" of the Vietnam War shows to be well advanced politically, culturally, and intellectually.

In the political arena, for instance, where major conflicts in a democratic society are presumably engaged, the war and its roots were never legitimately discussable. At first these concerns were out of bounds because the war was still going on. Then they were out of bounds because the war was over and needed to be "put behind us." Neither the war nor the entire complex of historical questions it raised about the relationship of the United States to the forces of change in the Third World were directly engaged in any of the five or six presidential campaigns of this era, or in the ones immediately following.[2] They had to be forced to the surface by an extraordinary, extra-institutional mass movement and faded from view once its immediate objective was achieved. The subsequent invention of the "post-Vietnam syndrome" and, more recently, the posing of the question "Another Vietnam in Central America?"—a question at once imprecise and over-literal—show some of the consequences of this depoliticization of experience for both left and right.

Mass-mediated popular culture offers other insights into how complex historical experience is processed for acceptable public remembering. Films like *The Deerhunter* and *Apocalypse Now* said almost nothing about the real history and impact of the war. But they have an enormous amount to teach, in all their pretentious posturing, about how we have been encouraged to "deal with" such a traumatic collective experience. Each film is willfully and explicitly antihistorical; in a context where the forces of history virtually scream to be noticed, solitary individuals are the heroic focus, men kept deliberately isolated from that history, apparently so they can stand as metaphors for the human condition or some other abstraction the filmmakers imagined might be obscured by contact with the real world.

The means of denial in the world of scholarship are different, but already they have begun to exercise the same cauterizing, distancing influence. What the politicians ignore and the media abstract, the academics have begun to obliterate. A fine example of this is *America in Vietnam* by the political scientist Guenter Lewy, a book whose questions and answers—and even more the generally positive and respectful reception accorded them—say a great deal about the process of academic digestion.[3]

Lewy's book attempts to strip the war of all the pesky moral, political, and emotional questions that so complicate the study of history. In effect, the book tries to recapture within the narrow bounds of policy models and bureaucratic/military analysis a debate that began, so long ago, with the discovery of the fatal descriptive, predictive, and moral limitations of these bounds. The result, accordingly, is a return to where we were in 1965: we are offered as sober historical conclusions what were, in fact, that era's question-begging clichés: the armies of the South performed poorly because of deficient leadership, for example; and, Americans misjudged the nature of a civil war. These are now intoned in the dispassionate voice of social science, with hardly a "why?" or a "so what?" in sight. Handled in this fashion, Vietnam is remembered without any recourse to those insights into change and history that were forced to the surface by the extraordinary intensity of that era and, it was once hoped, left permanently on view for needed reflection. When all that is excluded as incompatible with the demands of cool, objective scholarship, history becomes as comfortable a shield for Lewy as it was for that retired CIA man helping Bill Moyers see things in a mature, historical perspective.

Recent documentary efforts to deal with Vietnam's passage into the historical dimension have been no more successful in preventing a momentarily glimpsed reality from slipping back behind a curtain of amnesia or receding into a blurry distance. I am thinking of perhaps the most important public historical effort in recent years, and certainly the most elaborate and expensive: the thirteen-segment "Vietnam: A Television History," produced by WGBH, Boston.

Most critics have had mixed reactions to the series: some of its features and episodes have been held powerful and striking; others have seemed to most observers wholly inadequate to the complexities under examination. But there is a general consensus that the effect of the series has been to depoliticize the war, to see it as a "tragedy" without winners or losers. In ways that will be discussed below, much of this depoliticization is rooted in the project's public-historical methodology. But surely there is a deeper dimension to the process of digestion, which has tended to make Vietnam, as it settles into historical memory, a vague symbol drained of much of the political and cultural content that once stood at the center of America's conflict over the war. The hollow media blitz of 1985 "remembering" the fall of Saigon ten years earlier only reinforces this point.

Indeed, the Vietnam example, however extreme, is neither isolated nor even special. To the extent that our public culture is characterized by a broad and seemingly willful disengagement from the past, it becomes crucial for public historians in particular to inquire into the sources of this phenomenon. If these are not clearly understood, it is hard to see how public history can have even a chance of reaching the ambitious goals toward which it has been directed.

The problem has a number of dimensions, all of them at least partially relevant to a satisfactory explanation of our uncertain relation to our own history. For a start, the dilemma of historical consciousness featured centrally in the old, sweeping debates about American "capital C" Culture. Conservatives have generally bemoaned our weak sense of historical interconnectedness, finding Americans insensitive to the presence of the past in their lives and institutions and disrespectful of the constraints fortuitously conferred by experience. Liberals have celebrated these same traits as sources of the energy needed to escape the dead hand of the past. Both, of course, are describing America in similar terms: a liberal culture born free of a connection with a slowly unfolding past, and hence free, or condemned, to create a culture based on dreams about individual freedom, rights, and opportunities, dreams presumably made tangible through pragmatic institutional improvisation.

All of this is not irrelevant to the problem at hand, but such cultural explanations are at once too absolute and too solipsistic to tell us very much. A wry comment by a Nigerian friend is particularly apt in this regard: "What's so mysterious?" he observed. "Why bother with history when you're rich and powerful? All it can do is tell you how you climbed to the top, which is a story it's probably best not to examine too closely. No, you don't need history. What you need is something more like a pretty carpet that can be rolled out on ceremonial occasions to cover all those bloodstains on the stairs. And, in fact, that's what you usually get from your historians." Then he went on more solemnly: "For the rest of us, it's a lot different. We don't have the luxury of ignoring history. History is a giant stone that lies on top of us; for us, history is something we have to struggle to get out from under."[4] To say that most of American history has been seen through the eyes of the powerful is a familiar criticism, but we rarely acknowledge, as my friend suggests, how profoundly power, privilege, and freedom from historical constraint have conditioned our basic relation to the past.

For all its insight, however, this structural dimension is an insufficient explanation for our sense of history, if only because the freedom has always been relative, the privilege contested at home and abroad, and the image of power accordingly somewhat deceptive. All this suggests that beyond cultural generalities and structural attributes lies a third dimension, one that might be called functional, which is responsive to the particular demands of historical conflict and struggle. Far from being merely cosmetic and aesthetic, the impulse to cover the bloodstains has been historically intentional—a deliberate if not necessarily conscious part of the process by which a not-so-solidly established power is maintained and shored up.

This helps to explain why the detachment from history seems to be widening especially now, when America is displaying a superficial political consensus seemingly premised on an almost total denial of Third World challenges to both the economic pillars and the ideological mystifications sustaining its power. Whatever its part in rationalizing and sustaining the expansion of this power, a self-serving history has been stretched vulnerably thin, like Napoleon's army, by its very success.

Given the difficulty of explaining now the reality of defeat, or at least the necessity of retreat, through the conventional manipulations of history, the United States has fallen back on a simple and desperate denial of memory, and hence responsibility. During the Angolan crisis, I recall seeing an African leader on "Meet the Press." After enduring much indignant badgering about the new government's "tilt" to the Soviets, he finally replied that after twenty years of Soviet support for the Popular Movement for the Liberation of Angola and twenty years of American loyalty to Portuguese colonialism, the Angolan posture should hardly need to be explained to Americans, and it certainly did not need to be justified. In this respect, more recently, the cynicism of the self-righteous American response to post-Somoza Nicaragua is virtually total. When the sky is dark with chickens coming back to the American roost, it would seem that the last line of defense is to slam the door of memory. It is, of course, a gravely dangerous response; the United States in such circumstances is a pitiful but far from helpless giant whose recklessness is only increased by an amnesia offering dubious refuge from the consequences of its own past acts.

These considerations bring us back to the problem I raised at the start: the limits of a simplistic, supply-side approach to public history and the need to see both its potential and its limitations as rooted in the more broadly problematic nature of historical consciousness in our culture. I have been suggesting that one way to approach this is to deal more frontally with the complex matter of historical memory.

Memory has always proven difficult for historians to confront, committed as they are to notions of objectivity beyond the definitive subjectivity of individual and collective recall. Usually, the evidence of memory is considered as an information source to be confirmed by scholarship, or, alternatively, as a way of getting a kind of impressionistic gestalt beyond accountability and testing. Both understandings miss the dimension I am getting at here: the process of historical memory itself as a subject for study, one capable of saying a great deal about how the past does or does not figure in our lives, and what this in turn tells us about both history and ourselves.

The point is perhaps made clearer by noticing a linguistic curiosity: in English we have no verb that readily corresponds to the noun history. We talk about doing history, or studying it, or reading and writing and teaching it, but there is no way to express concisely the activity of rendering the past comprehensible. With the phenomenon of memory, of course, this is not the case at all. Indeed, the relationship is virtually reversed: the noun, memory, presumes the active verb, to remember. Involved as well, by definition, is the leap across time from the then of happening to the now of recall. For all the dilemmas of subjectivity, then, the evidence of memory is indispensable for observing precisely the relationships and the process I am arguing we need to understand better.

There are a number of tools and methods for getting at this, of which oral history is certainly the most important. This is because it is unique in being a method that creates its own documents, documents that are by definition explicit dialogues about memory, with the speaker necessarily triangulated between past experiences and the present context of remembering. Unfortunately, oral history has become one of the best examples of the uncritical rush to the supply side, especially given the ease of entry and the assumed demand for its products. This has been particularly true of many self-consciously radical oral historians, who have tended to assume that once the people can be put in touch with their own history, the hegemonic dominant culture will be undermined and false consciousness dispelled.

The matter is hardly this simple, of course, as I learned at one symposium featuring remembrances of 1930s organizing at its most violent and militant. The radical historians present heard in the tapes evidence of pervasive class conflict and a call to militance based on labor's proud heritage of struggle. But many of the trade unionists present came away with a very different message: remembrance of the "bad old days" of strikes and conflict, they tended to say, made them appreciate how much progress—measured by their current no-strike contracts, grievance arbitration, and pension benefits—they had made since the 1930s. Significantly, the program offered no opportunity for collectively discussing, contrasting, and evaluating these different ways of recalling the past and connecting it to the present, which might have made for an important public-historical event. Instead, the oral history was simply presented for consumption, as if its meaning were self-evident.[5]

A similar casualness often characterizes the use of oral-historical evidence in documentaries. In "Vietnam: A Television History," for instance, it is the presentational strategy rather than the explicit interpretation that generates the effect noted above, the deflecting and defusing of political content in the history being presented to the public. Two attributes in particular illustrate this process.

The first is the tendency for interview subjects to be differentiated in terms of the type of statement the editors have chosen to include, and for this differentiation to follow closely lines of class and power. Thus, peasants, ground soldiers, and random individuals tend to be quoted as offering personal experiences, direct observations, and recalled feelings. The higher or more important the position of the subject, however, the more likely he or she is to be seen as offering historical judgments of a broader nature, sweeping evaluations of what an event meant, what caused it, or what the public felt. This correlation of interpretive power and social class position is neither coincidental nor without effect.

The second attribute involves the near-exclusive reliance of "Vietnam" on the recorded remembrances of those who "were there." This "pure" oral history strategy becomes especially problematic when the topic is a political or military decision or event, since those who "were there" tend to be at best prisoners of the framework we seek to place in perspective and at worst self-serving apologists for their own past actions. Many of the deepest problems of the documentary are rooted in this decision to grant "experience" sole interpretive authority, as if there were no other independent sources of knowledge useful for assessing historical truth. In combination, these two attributes make it virtually impossible for the documentary to place the past operations of power in critical perspective, since both nonprivileged reflection and informed but noncomplicit sources of knowledge are excluded, in effect, by oral-historical definition.[6]

There are, of course, many examples of more careful uses of oral history, and I am encouraged that many of the oral-historical efforts that have had the widest impact and public visibility are those that have engaged the dialogue between past and present most explicitly, or at least have given it a central place in the presentation of the historical information itself. I am thinking about books like *Hard Times, All God's Dangers,* and *Brass Valley,* for instance, or films like *Union Maids,* the *Good Fight,* and *Seeing Red.*[7]

Making memory the focus of critical attention in using oral history is a good bit harder than it sounds, however, regardless of the intentions or sensitivity of the historian. This is because audience response is itself such a complicating factor. Audiences used to viewing their history from a safe distance often resist attempts to close the gap, especially when that process collapses comfortable assumptions as well. I have written elsewhere about how the critical reception of Studs Terkel's *Hard Times* exemplified this problem. The book was so casually understood as a romantic evocation of "the way it was" that critics and presumably many readers managed to avoid its starker evidence about the Depression's role in people's memories and contemporary consciousness, evidence suggested by the dialogue between past and present that Terkel intended to be the focus of his pointedly labeled "memory book."[8] But a better and more current example would be the reception, here and abroad, of Marcel Ophuls' documentary films, a body of work that has tried with singular explicitness to force its audience into a confrontation not only with the past, but with what has been done to and with the memory of that past.

If readers evaded the most challenging aspects of *Hard Times* by gathering the book up in an affectionate, emotional embrace, they have frequently used the opposite strategy in dealing with Ophuls' disturbing films, but to the same effect. The films generated angry and shrill controversy, with the documentary methodology becoming so central to the debate that many overlooked completely the complex struggle with history that Ophuls had placed before them. *The Sorrow and the Pity* has been more controversial in France than in the United States, since its issues of occupation, domestic collaboration, and resistance are reasonably remote from recent American experience. It will accordingly be easier to illustrate my point by referring to a film that touches American values, presumptions, and concerns more directly, Ophuls' Nuremberg documentary, *The Memory of Justice*.

The film is not really a study of the trials themselves, though powerful use is made of documentary footage and vivid reminiscence. Instead, the central focus in every respect is Ophuls' exhaustive examination—over four-and-one-half hours' worth—of how the issues at Nuremberg appear, some thirty years later, to participants, observers, and later-born heirs to the history of the Nazi era. The film's title, then, expresses its subject quite precisely. Ophuls' context is the moral dilemma involved in the collision of unimaginable atrocity with the necessary but insufficient authority of law and morality, as represented by Nurembeg. But his deeper concern is with how these dilemmas have figured in people's lives as the atrocities and trials have faded into the past, and whether or not they have made a difference in how we make our way through our own present.

To get at this dimension, Ophuls pushes the documentary method far beyond conventional bounds. He includes a great deal of interview and documentary material that is not about Nuremberg at all, paying particular attention to the American experience in Vietnam and to the terrorism employed by the French in their struggle to hold Algeria. Sometimes this is included to set the necessary context for individual memoirs, since so many of the principals, like Telford Taylor, went on to have a major part in later controversies that have been informed by and are resonant with Nuremberg. But, generally, the contemporary exploration of these other themes is aimed toward a broader point.

Ophuls wants to examine, I think, whether and how the memory of Nuremberg explicitly affects our response to issues of war crimes and moral responsibility when they are raised today, and whether and how our way of framing and engaging such issues reveals the more implicit traces of the Nuremberg era. Even more, the non-Nuremberg portions of the film have the effect of dissolving the inevitable moral distance from which outsiders observe Germans confronting their Nazi past. The painful scenes of suburban Americans trying to avoid dealing with the immorality of our bombing in Vietnam are, in this sense, both a dramatic and a historical counterpoise to the famous scene of plump, pink, prosperous German youngsters lolling in the nude by an elegant sauna, agonizing over the degree of their responsibility for the Holocaust.

In many quarters, all this has not been well received, which is to say not well perceived. The film was savagely attacked by many American critics, particularly the self-appointed Jewish guardians of the Holocaust clustered around *Commentary* magazine. Harold Rosenberg's long, vicious polemic in the *New York Review of Books* was the most elaborate of these and bears special relevance to our discussion because of its fundamental misunderstanding of the role of memory in the film.[9]

Basically, such critics accused Ophuls of denying the evil of Nazism by presuming to compare it to other instances of supposed war crimes. The film, says Rosenberg, ends up in "a near-nihilistic bog, in which no one is guilty because all are guilty, and no one is qualified morally to judge." The focus on Vietnam was held a special abomination by these critics, who seemed to feel that it presented them with an intolerable choice: either Ophuls wants us to think the Nazis were no worse than us, or he believes that we are no better than they. In either case, Rosenberg condemned the analogy as the foulest ahistorical and antihistorical distortion.

In truth, the film makes no analogy. It is not the objective reality of Vietnam and the Nazi death camps that the film compares. Rather, it seeks the reverberation of the Nuremberg issues in a later history, which thankfully cannot replicate them in scale or meaning, but to which they are unfortunately not irrelevant, either. Rosenberg and many opponents of the film argue that any such attempt to use these reference points in our own time is to undercut the horrific exceptionalism of the Nazis. It is as if they want to preserve it as an example of ultimate evil, a moral yardstick that, like the Bureau of Standards' platinum foot, should be kept hermetically locked away in a vault and never actually employed to gauge the real world.

Such resistance to comparison and resonance may occasionally serve the ends of pure scholarship, though even this seems to me a curious notion. But clearly such an approach is totally alien to the processes of historical memory if these are to mean anything in public life. The truths of history and memory are in this sense distinct. Though obviously our memories ought to be informed by as much good history as we can produce, the Ophuls film helps to focus on the role of memory in a public history that will matter, a role that must be informed by a fundamental commitment to the importance of that verb at the heart of memory, making it something alive and active as we confront our own world. Through the use of historical documents and current interviews, the film creates a process that forces us to remember the past in the fullest and most difficult sense of the verb. This, it seems to me, is a considerable advance over the general tendency of public history to produce images of the past for our passive consumption.

This contrast has rarely been more important than now, though for the reasons touched on earlier we are unlikely to appreciate it without the help of the most powerful examples the best public history can provide. It is easier to say this, of course, and easier to underscore the importance of appreciating historical memory as a problematic dimension of our culture, than it is to define how public history ought specifically to engage the problem. Rather than offering any inevitably facile prescriptions in this regard, I prefer to close by pointing to a quality we might seek, one almost palpably evident in Ophuls' films and in the other works I mentioned above.

Here a final bit of word play, suggested by the debate about *The Memory of Justice,* may help. On reading Harold Rosenberg's malicious attack on the film, it struck me that the critique was ignorant in a special sense of the word, one recalling the active verb near *its* base. Rosenberg was ignorant not in what he did not know, but in what he chose or was driven to ignore in the film. I suspect that a good deal of historical ignorance involves this active dimension: *ignore-ance.* At the same time, the word that comes to mind when I reflect on the Ophuls' film and work like it is intelligence. *The Memory of Justice* is an intelligent film, not because of what it knows or says, but because of the care, the depth, the insight, and the sensitivity with which it reflects on and explores a profound problem. It reminds us that intelligence is most fundamentally a quality of vision and spirit.

This is a somewhat alien notion in American public life, where intelligence has come to be something to be produced by schools, marketed by business, and commodified in a way that requires no reading of Marx to understand. When events in Iran—the Shah's fall and later the taking of the hostages— caught Washington by surprise, officials immediately identified the cause as a failure in intelligence gathering, as if acorns of insight lie about in the forests of foreign policy, needing only to be scooped up. Intelligence gathering was also faulted after the serial car-bombings of U.S. facilities in Lebanon, and, more grandly, after the fall of China in 1949, Cuba in 1958, Vietnam in 1975, and Nicaragua in 1979. If this suggests a pattern, so does the characteristic response: allocating more money and power to the CIA to gather, cultivate, produce, or generate more and better intelligence. The metaphors for intelligence range from the primitive hunting and gathering to the elegantly postindustrial, but they are always economic, with intelligence pictured as a much-sought-after good that is in mysteriously short supply.

Public historians, I believe, must avoid this trap and not treat historical intelligence as a commodity whose supply they seek to replenish, whether by bringing down illuminating fire from elite heights or by gathering gold in mineshafts dug from the bottom up. Whether one is talking about the history of a war or the memories of old residents in a crumbling ethnic neighborhood, what we need are works that will search out the sources and consequences of our active ignore-ance. We need projects that will involve people in exploring what it means to remember, and what to do with memories to make them active and alive, as opposed to mere objects of collection. To the extent that this is done, we will be seizing an opportunity not nearly so accessible to conventional academic historical scholarship, whatever its virtues: the opportunity to help liberate for that active remembering all the intelligence, in the way I am using the word, of a people long kept separated from the sense of their own past.

"You can hardly expect them to have 'American Heritage' or 'Horizon' on the economy flight, dear."

Marketing the Past:

American Heritage *and Popular History in the United States*

In the spring of 1976, Francis M. Watson, Jr., a professional investigator of "red subversion," testified before a Senate Committee examining "The Attempt to Steal the Bicentennial." The group charged with this insidious plot, the Peoples Bicentennial Commission—"a propaganda and organizing tool of a small group of New Left political extremists," according to Watson—had produced a Bicentennial guide entitled *America's Birthday.* "There are authentic looking pictures in here of colonial America," Watson told the committee, "and some rather good art work, and there is a quotation from Thomas Jefferson. . . .If one of your kids brought it home and you just leafed through it, you would think, well, this is great. . . . It looks like something *American Heritage* might have done."[1]

To Watson, *American Heritage* was everything the Peoples Bicentennial Commission (PBC) was not: safe, acceptable, and divorced from current political controversies. In its twenty-two years of operation before Watson's testimony, *American Heritage,* with its smoothly written, lavishly illustrated, elegantly packaged stories of the American past, had become the easily recognized standard of popular history against which other efforts—whatever their political pedigree—might be measured. When Francis Watson wanted to describe the work of the PBC, he looked to "*The* Magazine of History," as *American Heritage* calls itself.

In the past thirty years, millions of Americans have also looked to *American Heritage.* The figures on its readership are staggering. Since its founding in 1954, the magazine has sold close to forty million copies. By 1968 its book division had already issued some two hundred titles with sales in excess of $33 million. Dozens more books have been published in joint ventures with

BY ROY ROSENZWEIG

21

other publishers, including a sixteen-volume history of the United States sold through supermarkets and a bestselling American history textbook. In the late 1950s Associated Press even syndicated condensed versions of *American Heritage* articles to more than seventy newspapers with a combined circulation of close to ninety million people. And *American Heritage* has not limited itself to print media: thousands have taken its historical tours or purchased historical "artifacts" from its gift catalog; millions have seen one or both of its television series.[2]

Although the audience for *American Heritage* must be measured in the millions, the number of professional historians who have given it even passing critical attention can be counted on the fingers of one hand.[3] Yet historians interested in communicating historical insights beyond their own ranks are ill-advised to dismiss *American Heritage* out of hand. As the most influential and successful post–World War II historical publication, *American Heritage* has shaped the historical consciousness of a large and crucial segment of the American public; it has given the public its *definition* as well as its *interpretation* of history. By looking between *Heritage*'s hard covers, we can better understand the perils and possibilities of popular history in both its commercial and noncommercial variants. The glossy, colorful pages of *American Heritage* constitute an important chapter in the largely untold story of popular history and mass historical consciousness in the United States.

I n 1938 Allan Nevins, a New York newspaperman turned Columbia University history professor, urged the creation of a "popular historical magazine, published monthly, written for the multitude and not the learned few and full of articles relating the past (particularly the American past) to the present." Nevins was legendary for his prodigious historical output (more than one hundred books and one thousand articles to his name) and his workaholic habits (colleagues remember him pounding away at his typewriter while his dinner guests enjoyed cocktails with his wife, Mary, and emerging from his study to greet them only when the first course was served). And he pursued his dream of a popular history magazine with some of the same zeal that he brought to his research and writing.[4]

Nevins envisioned a popular history magazine that would be printed and distributed by Condé Nast (publisher of *Vogue*) but would be published by a nonprofit corporation endorsed by the American Historical Association (AHA), a professional organization dominated by academic historians. The half-million dollars needed to finance the magazine was to be raised through private contributions, but the promoters saw the imprimatur of the AHA as crucial in obtaining the necessary contributions and subscriptions. With Nevins lobbying hard for the plan, the AHA Executive Committee quickly endorsed it with only one dissent.

The lone dissenter, Harvard professor Frederick Merk, was a formidable opponent. While the plan awaited final approval at the December annual meeting in Chicago, Merk circulated a ten-page memo charging that the Nevins plan was "a venture reckless in a business sense and ultimately hazardous to the good name of the A.H.A." According to Nevins, however, Merk and his allies really objected to the whole notion of a *popular* history magazine, regarding "it as downright discreditable for any professional historian to contribute a paper to . . . any . . . magazine of general circulation." In Nevins' recollection, Merk asserted "that if the association sponsored a popular magazine of history it must be prepared to see . . . Nevins [and other AHA leaders] make off illegally with the revenues that the magazine earned." Merk's anticommercial and antipopular strictures carried the day. The Business Meeting overrode the AHA Executive Committee and Council, rejecting the plan by a vote of 69 to 62.[5]

Nevins was not, however, easily thwarted. Riding the train home to New York, he outlined a plan for a new historical society that would unite popular and academic historians and sponsor a popular history magazine. Nevins launched the new group—soon called the Society of American Historians (SAH)—and vented his "indignation" over the AHA meeting in a vitriolic *Saturday Review* attack on the "pedants" and "Dryasdusts" of the historical profession, whom he blamed "for the present crippled gait of history in America." Nevins received numerous congratulatory letters on his blast— many from academic historians. But his charge that the AHA's official publication, the *American Historical Review,* contained the "worst examples of how history should never be written" and that "real history" was being written by "the men and women farthest removed from the deadly touch of the academic glossologists" closed the door on further cooperation with the AHA.[6]

It is easy to sympathize with Nevins in his struggle against the conservative doyens of the historical profession. Yet the clash between "popularizers" and "pendants" obscured more complicated questions about the purpose and prospective audience of the new magazine. Despite Merk's charges, Nevins acted primarily out of what one historian has called his passionate belief "that history should be a major part of every citizen's life." Nevins envisioned his popular magazine as the *Saturday Review* of history—a bridge between the academic specialist and the general reader and a form of cultural uplift and adult education for a "democratic public." Although Nevins' vision allowed for contending and controversial viewpoints, he assumed that it would not lead readers to question any fundamental tenets of the American system. Rather, he wrote in 1939, the magazine "would do much to educate Americans in the dignity and fascination of their own past." And by the time the magazine actually was underway some years later, he was even more direct about its affirmative purpose, declaring that "a review of our history" shows us that "[t]he American idea is as valid as ever."[7]

Despite his references to the popular history audience as the "multitude" or "the democratic public," Nevins apparently defined the magazine's prospective readership more narrowly than these terms suggest. In 1954, just after *American Heritage* appeared, Nevins admitted privately: "We had always hoped to reach the intelligent professional man and businessman and it became clear we were doing just that." Rhetoric aside, the magazine's projected ten-dollar subscription price circumscribed the "democratic public" in 1938, when factory workers made twenty-two dollars a week and *Life* magazine cost only a dime.[8] Such pricing should be contrasted with other 1930s efforts at presenting the past to a truly mass public through, for example, the Federal Theatre Project's low-priced plays or the historical murals painted on post office walls.

Operating in this populst context, the historian Carl Becker wrote in 1939 to Nevins and the AHA's executive secretary, Conyers Read, urging that the projected magazine "reach as wide a reading public as possible. To do this the journal should not be very expensive." Read, however, was not optimistic: "It so happens," he told Becker, "that the only printer who seems disposed to render the kind of business support that is essential leans to the snooty magazine type." Writing to another AHA leader, Read was even more direct: "The purpose, I am convinced, is a sound one; and though it is aimed at the rich, I suspect that the rich are more in need of historical-mindedness than the poor."[9]

Nevins thus envisioned a magazine that would be popular but not populist, readable and engaging but also serious and uplifting. Although many leading academic and popular historians supported his new venture, the project stalled for lack of funds and because Nevins soon turned his attention to the more pressing claims of World War II. By the late 1940s, however, Nevins and his associates had turned out a prospectus for "a magazine of world history" called *Milestones*. Working with *Saturday Review*'s editor, Henry Seidel Canby, and tapping various wealthy friends and acquaintances, Nevins collected about $60,000 for the project. With Canby's son Courtlandt as project director, they assembled a sample issue of the magazine (now called *History*), which was distinguished by a hard cover and an absence of advertisements—brilliant innovations that gave the magazine a "cultured" image, permitted a higher subscription price, and lowered start-up costs by avoiding the necessity of a guaranteed circulation base for advertisers. Yet they still failed to interest rich individuals or foundations in financing the project. Nevins urged that they go ahead on a limited budget of $30,000 (one-third of it to come from his own pocket), but the Canbys hesitated. Conventional wisdom held that new magazines required at least a half-million dollars in start-up capital.[10]

Meanwhile, a very different group, the American Association for State and Local History (AASLH), had already launched its own illustrated, popular American history magazine for a mere $2,000. Like Nevins' Society of American Historians, the AASLH had its roots in dissatisfaction with the AHA. In 1940 the AHA's Conference of State and Local Historical Societies, whose leaders believed that the academically oriented AHA was doing little for their organizations, disbanded and founded the AASLH as a separate organization. Although *American Heritage* (as the AASLH called the magazine it started in 1949) was novel in its heavily illustrated and full-color format, it drew on an older tradition of historical magazines issued by patriotic, genealogical, and historical societies and reflected as well the chauvinistic, localistic, and popular impulses of the local history movement.[11] Its opening issue announced its purposes in cold war and nationalistic terms: "What is needed in America today is a new appreciation and understanding of our American heritage and its advantages over the ways of totalitarianism and dictatorship." Not surprisingly, the editors saw grassroots history as the best "foundation for a stronger Americanism": "for local history is . . . close to the experience of our people. A deeper loyalty to our institutions and our way of life must rest upon a firm bedrock of love of our home communities."[12]

More prominent in the original *American Heritage* than cold war nationalism, however, was a grassroots and folksy approach to the past. Special issues of *American Heritage* featured specific communities or regions, ranging from the Champlain Valley to Minnesota to Hawaii. Articles typically covered such topics as "American Folk Heroes," "Colonial Craftsmen," and "The Franklin Stove." The magazine was pluralistic enough to include an article on the United Auto Workers (UAW) in its special issue on Detroit. Moreover, since the editors envisioned local historical society members as a crucial segment of their readership, they promoted active participation in researching and presenting the past. Articles reported on state and local historical societies and the restoration of historic sites; regular columns discussed pedagogy, antiques, and audiovisual materials.[13]

Despite a modest budget and a small staff (the editor, Earle W. Newton, and the contributors were unpaid), the magazine had attracted 17,000 subscribers by 1952 and even drawn some notice outside professional and amateur historical circles. One nonhistorian so attracted was James Parton, who in late 1953 spotted the magazine on the coffee table of the headmaster of the Loomis School, where he was a member of the board of trustees. The grandson of the famous nineteenth-century biographer, the Harvard-educated Parton had learned magazine journalism in Henry Luce's Time-Life empire. More recently, he had joined the magazine-consulting and book-packaging business of two former Time-Life colleagues, Joseph Thorndike and Oliver Jensen. The AASLH's homey *American Heritage* piqued Parton's interest, since the firm was looking for a magazine of its own to publish.[14]

From fellow Loomis trustee Winthrop Rockefeller Parton learned that the editing and distribution of the magazine were becoming increasingly burdensome for the small AASLH. Another elite connection pushed the project further along. Alexander Hehmeyer, counsel to Parton's firm as well as to Nevins' SAH, brought his two clients together. Parton now saw that he could combine "the grassroots historians on one side and the academic level on the other," and take advantage of the existing subscription base of *American Heritage* and the hardcover, adless format that Nevins and his colleagues had hit upon.[15]

By April 1954 the AASLH had agreed to turn over *American Heritage* to a new publishing company under Parton. The Nevins group, whose own fundraising had foundered, had little choice but to sign up as well. Although some of Nevins' colleagues grumbled about the "commercial character of the enterprise" and the slighting of the SAH, he threw himself behind the new plan with characteristic enthusiasm, investing some of his own money in the venture and helping to recruit the journalist-turned-historian Bruce Catton for the crucial post of editor. Despite Nevins' active participation, the reconstitution of *American Heritage* under the auspices of Parton's firm marked a crucial shift away from the Columbia professor's original vision of a popular history magazine as a vehicle for civic virtue and cultural uplift, or even the AASLH's notion of patriotism and grassroots participation. Commercial success was now the bottom line. Parton made this quite clear in his impatient response to Nevins' concern that they find an editor who would ensure a quality publication. It was "essentially promotional steps," he told Nevins, that would determine the success of the magazine, since "the public is going to have to buy the product we offer on faith. . . . [E]ven the ideal editor won't count for much if we don't launch the publication itself with the right ruffle of drums and unfurling of flags."[16]

The particular drums and flags that Parton rounded up to publicize *American Heritage* revealed just how far the undertaking had strayed from Nevins' earlier conception. A full-page advertisement in the October 17, 1954, *New York Times Book Review,* as well as promotional letters (accompanied, Parton noted, by a folder "printed in 4-color to accentuate the *popular* characteristic of the magazine"), emphasized that *American Heritage* would be—above all—*entertaining* to read. It would "bring to life again the vivid, exciting story of our country's past"—an "endlessly fascinating" and "vast and vivid" story that "is as exciting, as flamboyant, as filled with actions and thought and daring (and true purpose) as any citizens ever had." And the list of "What You Will Find in *American Heritage*" brought home the message that the magazine would be fun. Although the advertisement promised the reader "important things to think about," it gave much more space to previewing "fascinating things to look at" ("picture stories, often in color, on . . . houses and ships, soldiers and ladies"), "tales of adventure" ("girl captive of the Sioux"), "things to smile at," and "a good deal of nostalgia." The advertisement gave equal weight to the new magazine's packaging: its beautiful hard-cover binding, lack of advertising, "heavy, glossy paper," and profuse illustrations, "many in glorious color."[17]

This advertisement contrasts sharply with the one that Nevins and his associates had inserted (as a trial balloon) in the same publication for *History* three and a half years before. The earlier advertisement portrayed history as a duty and a responsibility "for people who want to grow as individuals and as citizens." Referring to both the magazine and the field of study, it proclaimed that "*History* is for . . . PUBLIC OFFICIALS, who seek knowledge to fulfill a public trust. BUSINESSMEN, who must chart a course among the larger events that now control their fortunes. LABOR LEADERS, who have a special responsibility as a new historical force. . . . COMMITTEE MEMBERS, who want their community activities to serve good ends effectively." The message was, in effect, nineteenth-century cultural uplift refracted through the lens of the cold war. The list of projected articles in a "typical issue" of *History* reinforced this serious tone: "The Failure of the League of Nations," "Behavior Under Stress: The American Soldier in World War II," "Stalin's Rise to Power," and "1848: The Backgrounds." Far from being a form of diversion or escape from the present, *History* would remind its readers of the problems of the day with "Behind the News" historical background articles.[18]

Nevins nursed private doubts about the Time-Life crew's commercial packaging of the past. He urged the editor, Bruce Catton, to "strike a distinctly literary and cultural note in the magazine." And he confided to his diary his criticisms of two major articles in the first issue: a "super-illustrated" nostalgic encomium to the "Old Fall River Line" by the associate editor, Oliver Jensen, and "a slick piece on New York clubs which was Superficiality itself." A few years later he worried (again privately) that "the multiplication of picture books about the Civil War and about American History in general is a bad token. People should read; they should read thoughtfully."[19]

But the success of the magazine appears to have submerged such doubts. As he noted in his diary, "dozens of New Yorkers spoke to me appreciatively" of Jensen's paean to the Old Fall River Line, and "even the anecdotal paper on clubs was deemed clever by many." Nevins, whose historical writings in the fifties celebrated the genius of American capitalism and berated other historians for showing "feminine idealism" in being too "apologetic" about "our love of the dollar," could hardly quarrel with commercial success. Indeed, he lavishly praised Parton's profit-making abilities and criticized himself for having "committed an egregious act of folly in [previously] taking the position that it should be a nonprofit magazine. . . . Too late I realized that we had been unworldly, impractical, and silly."[20]

Even the most cynical observer would have found it difficult to argue with the almost magical publishing formula that Parton and his partners had devised. Parton had raised only $64,000 for promoting and producing *American Heritage*. But he immediately sank almost all the money into a direct-mail campaign. And when prepaid subscriptions started flooding in at the rate of three hundred per day, he threw the money back into more—equally profitable—mailings. It was, a colleague later explained, like running a parlay at the track and "doubling each time." By the time the first issue appeared to rave reviews in December 1954, it had 40,000 subscribers—already close to the break-even point of 60,000. Within weeks the first issue sold out its entire 80,000-copy print run and became a collector's item. When the print run for the third issue reached 100,000, Parton, one of the heaviest investors in the magazine, opposed selling any more stock: "Let us keep the pot as sweet as possible," he told Nevins with a grin. Within five years the subscription list had tripled again, and *American Heritage* found itself more popular than such well-established publications as *Harper's, Atlantic,* and *Scientific American.* "We have had a gusher," Parton euphorically told one interviewer.[21]

The rich oil field that *American Heritage* had discovered turned out to be the postwar upper middle class. *American Heritage*'s expensive cover price ($2.95) and subscription rate ($12.00)—four times that of the old *American Heritage* and a good deal more than Carl Becker would have wanted—made it "the history minded man's *Fortune.*" Still, quite a few more people could afford $12.00 for a magazine subscription in 1954 than might have put out $10.00 back in 1938, when the Condé Nast project was first floated and factory wages were only one-third as high. Although *American Heritage* benefited from postwar affluence, the audience it attracted seems to have been considerably richer than the price alone would have dictated. The magazine's powerful appeal to the well-to-do surprised even its savvy promoters. Assessing *American Heritage*'s direct-mail promotional campaign in September 1954, Parton told Nevins that "the low-brow [mailing] lists proved no good at all. But our best lists, the Book of the Month and Atlantic Monthly lists, . . . were excellent."[22]

By 1959 there was firm statistical evidence that *American Heritage* had "found its broadest audience among America's upper-middle-class," as a promotional brochure put it. Its readers had a median income more than double the national median, and they were ten times more likely than the average American family to have incomes over $15,000 per year (the top 3 percent of the population). Uniformly white collar and well educated, 80 percent of *American Heritage* readers worked in what surveyors described as "executive-managerial-proprietor" positions, and 60 percent held at least a B.A. degree (more than seven times the national average). At a time when close to one-fifth of the population was still of immigrant stock, more than 90 percent of the magazine's readers traced their ancestry to nineteenth-century Americans, and more than half claimed "American heritages" going back to the eighteenth century or earlier. A contemporary cartoon nicely captured the magazine's "upscale" image. Set in an airplane, it shows a wife explaining to her irritated husband: "You can hardly expect them to have 'American Heritage' . . . on the economy flight, dear."[23]

What was it about *American Heritage* that attracted this "first-class" readership? Although Parton's brilliant promotional mailings won the magazine its first subscribers, there was obviously something about the magazine that retained their allegiance (*Heritage* proved to have one of the highest renewal rates in the publishing industry, with two-thirds of the original subscribers still with the magazine after five years) and brought in tens of thousands more upper-middle-class readers every year in the late 1950s.[24] To understand that appeal we need to look first at the magazine's creators and then at its contents, focusing initially on 1954 to 1969, the first half of the magazine's history.

E ven before the first issue of *American Heritage* was in the mail, the local historians of the AASLH had already been excluded from any serious role in the magazine they had founded. The Time-Life crowd apparently found the AASLH and its publication unsophisticated. Parton called them "humble-type historians who think the Conestoga wagon is very important," and Jensen felt that their articles reflected an interest in "antiquarianism" rather than "history." Nevins was even more contemptuous of the original *American Heritage*, despite his membership on its editorial board. He derided it as "a poor magazine from a literary or historical point of view" that "had never printed one really first-class article." The only issue that he thought "adequate" was the one on New York City for which he had been guest editor. Not surprisingly, neither the articles and personnel nor the localistic and participatory impulses—nor the three-dollar subscription price—of the old magazine survived the change in ownership. The new editors quickly discarded the backlog of articles that Newton had built up. The two columns they initially retained did not last out 1955. A few AASLH leaders joined the magazine's advisory board but had little impact on its operations.[25]

Although contractually the AASLH was given a much larger role in the refounding of *American Heritage* than Nevins' SAH, the latter had a much greater impact on the magazine. More precisely, Nevins himself played a significant role: recruiting his friends and students as authors, writing numerous reviews and articles himself (one on twenty-four hours' notice), suggesting story ideas, tracking down pictures and documents to publish, and regularly checking in at the magazine's Fifth Avenue offices.[26] The day-to-day running of the magazine, however, fell to Parton's crew of Time-Life veterans and editor Catton. Parton, the president of the company and the publisher of the magazine, devoted most of his energies to business and promotion. Joseph Thorndike, a Harvard and Time-Life graduate like Parton, took a more direct editorial hand in the new magazine. But he gradually shifted his energies to the company's new ventures: *Horizon,* the hardcover magazine of the arts, launched in 1958, and the highly profitable book division. Like his two partners, Oliver Jensen had moved from the Ivy League to Time-Life, where he worked under and roomed with Thorndike. A "brilliant editor," Jensen started out as *Heritage*'s associate editor. But in 1959 he replaced Catton (who became senior editor) and held the editorship until 1976.[27]

Besides Nevins, the only non-Time-Life veteran to take a major role in the magazine was Bruce Catton. Like Nevins, Catton had grown up in a religious family in the rural Midwest of the 1890s and started out as a newspaperman. During World War II he became information director for the War Production Board and later worked in a similar capacity under Henry Wallace in the Department of Commerce. Captivated by some old Union Army regimental histories that he ran across in a second-hand bookstore, Catton had meanwhile begun to write a trilogy on the Army of the Potomac. The third volume, *A Stillness at Appomattox,* won the 1954 Pulitzer Prize, established Catton as the nation's most popular Civil War historian, and made him a logical candidate for the job of editing the new history magazine. His journalistic background and vivid writing style appealed to the Time-Lifers; his Pulitzer Prize gave him sufficient credentials to satisfy the academic historians in the Nevins group.[28]

What sort of magazine came out of the collaboration of Nevins, Catton, and the Time-Life veterans? "Our beat," Catton told readers in the elegant editorial statement that introduced the December 1954 inaugural issue, "is anything that ever happened in America. Our principal question is: What did men *do* there?" In words that New Left historians might have borrowed fifteen years later, Catton explained that the magazine would be at least as interested in "the doings of wholly obscure people" as in "great men." "[T]he faith that moves us is, quite simply, the belief that our heritage is best understood by a study of things that the ordinary folk of America have done and thought and dreamed since first they began to live here." These words might seem surprising until we recall the populist—really Popular Front—language that Catton (a writer for the liberal *Nation* until 1954) had used in his first book, *The Warlords of Washington: The Inside Story of Big Business Versus the People in World II,* where he proclaimed that "democracy is The People . . . not just the people who own things and manage things and control things, but *all* the people." And in a watered-down form, such Capraesque sentiments even found expression in Catton's Civil War books, which emphasized the experience of the ordinary soldier.[29]

Yet Catton's populism was attenuated still further in the pages of *American Heritage.* Though the stories of "great men" never dominated the magazine, neither did those of truly "ordinary folk." To a remarkable degree, the magazine concentrated instead on a miscellaneous collection of people who might be called "characters"—adventurers, rogues, heroes, and oddballs. And rather than repeating well-worn stories of great men and great events, *American Heritage* featured curious, amusing, or charming "sidelights" to famous events or persons—the false teeth and loose-fitting clothes of artist Charles Wilson Peale rather than the cultural significance of his museum, or the "charming" picture letter Teddy Roosevelt sent to his son rather than his conduct of foreign policy. An editorial assistant who worked briefly at *American Heritage* in the early 1960s recalls overhearing a member of the promotion department loudly lamenting this vision of the past: "Jesus, here I am pitching the new *American Heritage* history of WWI and do I tell people about the thousands pointlessly slaughtered, about fucking Verdun—never! Instead I tell our fat readers that World War I gave us the wristwatch and 'three on a match' and other fun items."[30]

The magazine's promotional material most clearly highlights *American Heritage*'s penchant for light-hearted, amusing, or stirring sketches. In a 1958 subscription letter, for example, Parton aptly summarized the magazine's mix of articles in peculiarly appropriate language: "To list the contents on the box—as if it were a breakfast cereal—this magazine is full of loud explosions and quiet discoveries, of floods and ceremonies, of frauds and heroes, orators and artists, scientists and doctors, not to mention locomotives and carriages, fine glass and fast horses, low resorts and high aspirations—all that infinite kaleidoscope whose sum is the past and whose product is the present. No artificial coloring is added." Issues from the fifties and sixties fully bear out Parton's hype. Typical offerings included one or two adventure or military yarns (the heroism of "tough Henry Knox"; the cross-country balloon flight of "dauntless" John Wise; the "tragic story" of the "ne'er-do-wells and deserters" of the San Patricio Battalion, who "lived hard, fought hard—and died when they saw a flag go up"); two or three nostalgic reveries (an evocation of the "sumptuous . . . luxurious . . . romantic" Overland Limited railroad; an "affectionate memoir of rural life a century ago"); and one or two stories of bizarre or unusual "characters" (the "scandalous" and "promiscuous" William Byrd II; the "preposterous pathfinder" and "glorious misfit" Giacomo Beltrami).[31]

A commitment to the "human dimension" of the past—a commitment that Catton, Nevins, and the Time-Life crew shared—became, in practice, a predilection for the "human interest" story set in the past. Although both Catton and Nevins probably had more serious aspirations for their history, the notion of the "human interest" story could hardly have been foreign to two men trained in journalism, where that durable genre was born. Catton, in fact, preferred to call himself "a reporter, not a historian" and decreed that "whatever else it is, history ought to be a good yarn."[32] And the light human interest tale or character sketch was probably second nature to men like Jensen, Thorndike, and Parton, who had grown up journalistically on *Life* magazine. Jensen, after all, had written "breezy" profiles of Hollywood stars for *Life* and had edited its lighter features. "We thought that we could be interesting to a large audience," Jensen has recalled, "particularly if we approached history with some of the journalistic techniques we'd learned at *Time* and *Life*." Parton similarly celebrated *American Heritage* as the "lively offspring of the marriage" of history and journalism and defined it as a "newsmagazine of the past."[33]

If the background of the magazine's creators in part explains *American Heritage*'s preference for adventure, nostalgia, human interest, and character sketches, the appeal of these articles to the magazine's upper-middle-class readers is more difficult to fathom. The simplest explanation is that such pieces provided engagingly written, colorfully illustrated entertainment and escapism. This is no doubt true, but it begs the question. Why *this* form of entertainment?

One possible, though speculative, line of explanation would be to link *Heritage*'s popularity in the postwar period to the gradual destruction of older, local, regional, ethnic, and family oral historical traditions in the same era. The upper-middle-class readers of *American Heritage* in the fifties and sixties, living in big cities or newly built suburbs, working in large corporations, and spending increasing amounts of their leisure time in front of the television set, had become severed from oral, family, and local historical traditions—the funny, touching, unusual *stories* that had been familiar to their grandparents, parents, and even to themselves in their childhoods. Both Catton and Nevins, for example, later recalled the stories told by Civil War veterans in their midwestern childhood homes. "When I was growing up in northern Michigan," Catton reminisced, "all the old men in the town were Civil War veterans. We boys used to sit around and listen to their yarns, and see them parading in Fourth of July celebrations." Such communal celebrations and recollections became increasingly rare after World War II, not simply because the "old soldiers" of the Civil War had faded away, but even more because such activities found little place in the corporate and suburban world of the upper-middle-class manager or professional. Perhaps Conyers Read's half-serious comment that "the rich are more in need of historical-mindedness than the poor" had some truth in it.[34]

Just as Catton's Civil War books provided a purchasable substitute for the "yarns" he had heard as a youngster, so did the magazine he edited offer a commercial product that could replace waning local traditions, legends, and stories with polished and packaged national tales and sketches. Indeed, the very first paragraph of the advertisements *American Heritage* ran in 1954 linked the magazine to oral traditions that potential readers may have sensed were slipping away: "The stories of your family history—the day grandfather enlisted under Grant; that rugged first winter on the homestead; the always miraculous accidents which brought your varied ancestors together—these you rightly treasure and re-tell. They highlight your heritage, your sense of roots and place, your invaluable legacy."[35]

American Heritage, then, offered its readers a commercial substitute for the traditional stories that found little place in the home and office of the "organization man." Yet although the magazine built on regret about, and possibly even resistance to, the disappearance of older forms of transmitting history, it was also an important agent in fostering that change. *American Heritage* may have implicitly promised the "stories of your family history," but the stories that it actually served up were quite different. They were national rather than local, they were written rather than told, they lacked particularistic contexts and meanings—and, most important, they were sold rather than passed on.

The magazine's form, too, simultaneously resisted and embraced change. *American Heritage*'s lack of advertisements, its hard-cover format, and its editorial content allied it with tradition, with a conservative and seemingly uncommercial past. But in its aggressive mass marketing and packaging of history, it embraced and encouraged a highly commercial and untraditional future. Actually, its readers may have themselves embodied the same contradiction: as members of the postwar upper middle class, they were agents of revolutionary social and economic changes, of the penetration of the market into previously private corners of everyday life; as readers of *American Heritage,* they expressed their nostalgia for a world that they had not just "lost" but had actually helped destroy.

These contradictions may explain why the magazine's content reflected nostalgia for the past, while its tone reflected the self-confidence of the present. Perhaps influenced by the cosmopolitan culture of New York publishing in which its editors operated, *American Heritage* generally avoided the language of shrill, cold war nationalism or even localistic patriotism that would have been familiar to readers of the AASLH version of the magazine. At the same time, the magazine's mood or tone, which is best characterized as an upbeat, confident optimism, was very much in step with the dominant "liberal consensus" ideology of the period. Like the most famous exponent of that world view, John F. Kennedy, *American Heritage* exuded confidence about what Americans had done in the past—and implicitly could do in the future. In the face of the "ominous sounds" of the present, Catton wrote in a 1959 magazine promotion, we gain "understanding—and confidence" from the "clear voice" of the past. "For it becomes clear that the best that we have done—and some of that has been very good indeed—was made possible by the hope and the courage and the undying tenacity of the people themselves."[36] The *American Heritage* version of the past almost always had a happy ending, and, by implication, so would the future.

Stories of human interest and inspiring characters—*American Heritage*'s dominant motif—were, of course, not the only sort of articles that appeared in the fifties and sixties. The magazine included at least one or two more serious or "weighty" articles, often by Nevins' friends or students, in each issue. Such articles were more in line with Nevins' original vision of the magazine as a vehicle of cultural uplift. At the same time, they reinforced the image of serious purpose mixed with good clean fun that the magazine sought to convey and market. As one astute critic noted in the mid-1950s, *American Heritage* and similar publications served as "respectable substitutes for the historical novel."[37] The inclusion of more serious articles furthered the magazine's appeal to its upper-middle-class and professional readers, many of whom intended the magazine to provide a healthy, but palatable, dose of "culture" for their baby-boom offspring. Not surprisingly for the period, *American Heritage* subscribers of the 1950s averaged better than two children per household. And in 1956 when the magazine asked its subscribers why they read *American Heritage,* 6 percent volunteered "value for my children" as their chief explanation, even though that was not one of the choices offered on the survey form.[38]

Since these "serious articles" generally came from the pens of the period's leading historians, they usually offered popularizations of the consensus historiography that then dominated the discipline. The attacks on economic interpretations of the Constitution, denunciations of Radical Reconstruction, celebrations of big business, and appreciations of Wilsonian internationalism found in the textbooks and professional journals of the day had their popular counterparts in *American Heritage* articles.[39]

The first issue of the magazine, for example, included a classic tract from Nevins' own crusade to transform the "robber baron" into the "industrial statesman." Striking a typical 1950s pose of "balance," Nevins titled the article "Henry Ford: A Complex Man." On the one hand, he forthrightly acknowledged Ford's "repugnant acts" and his "strong inclination to prejudice," while he avoided giving any concrete examples of these faults. On the other—much heavier—hand, he presented Ford's "quick brain," "courageous innovation," "warm love of nature," "frontiersman instinct," and "plain living" through colorful and vivid anecdotes. The illustrations (a crucial ingredient in *American Heritage*) emphasized even more strongly the folksy and humane Ford: they portray Ford sitting with a group of children (Ford "could hold a group of children enthralled," said the caption) and dressed as a Western badman (Ford "had a mischievous sense of humor"). And in the article's last paragraph, Nevins looks down from on high and finds Ford good: "As the years pass and as we gain perspective . . . his social primitivism will seem more a part of the general ignorance and gullibility of our adolescent American civilization. His great achievement . . . will loom up as the really significant fact of his career. . . . Of few of the industrial path-hewers of his time can it be said that they produced so much that is permanently and profitably usable."[40]

One would have to look hard to find a better example of what one leading historian called in 1957 (without a hint of criticism) "The Age of Balanced Appreciation—one that realizes the weaknesses of our great men but says that they were great all the same, that their virtues outweighed their defects."

American Heritage, which was much more likely to tell readers how the rich
had given away their money than how they had made it, joined in this rush to
replace the old "bum and strumpet" school with a more affirmative "drum
and trumpet" approach.[41] A celebratory, affirmative, uncritical tone—though
one that was a bit less shrill than some other academic and popular voices of
the day—was at least part of *American Heritage*'s success formula.

The foregoing account hardly exhausts the range of articles or topics covered in *American Heritage* during its first fifteen years. Among other things,
this brief survey slights some of the magazine's most praiseworthy features—
its recovery and presentation, for example, of lost, forgotten, or previously
unavailable historical documents, especially such visual documents as Lewis
Miller's Central Park sketchbook or Frederick Lewis Allen's family albums.[42] Yet if it is impossible to discuss each of the one thousand articles
(about five million words) that *American Heritage* published in these years, it
is equally impossible to fully understand the magazine without a consideration
of what it did *not* publish.

In the 1950s and 1960s, serious treatments of Afro-Americans, women,
workers, strikes, and social conflict were all but absent from *American
Heritage*'s pages. The magazine's index for its first ten years provides a rough
quantitative measure of this selectivity. On the one hand, the index yields the
following references to minorities, radicals, and conflicts: Negroes (20),
Frederick Douglass (2), Italian Americans (1), poverty (3), abolitionists (6),
Socialist Party (2), Industrial Workers of the World (2), pacifism (2), strikes
(6), race riots (1), Ku Klux Klan (6). Many similar topics—unemployment,
domestic servants, lynching, Marcus Garvey, W. E. B. DuBois, and Polish
Americans—received no mention at all in the first sixty issues of *American
Heritage*. On the other hand, consider the coverage of these colorful, nostalgic, or elite topics: P. T. Barnum (12), Christmas (13), ships and shipping
(50), Mark Twain (34), railroads (170), Theodore Roosevelt (88), Jay Gould
(11), Rockefeller family and foundation (19), Vanderbilt family (20), Astor
family (15).

When *American Heritage* did turn its attention to women and minorities in
these years, it simply repeated the era's clichés. Women—including those
well known for public accomplishments—are presented almost exclusively as
characters in historical romances. Blacks lack even the "charm" or "scandal"
of romantic affairs to give them the dubious visibility of women in *American
Heritage*. The only article—out of more than eighty—in the magazine's first
year of publication that discussed an Afro-American was on "Crazy Bill Free-
man," an insane murderer described in the article as a "lazy," "crazy colored
fellow."[43]

In part, these biases and silences simply reflected (but also fostered) those of American society and the historical profession in the 1950s and 1960s. Yet the effort to sell history to an upper-middle-class white audience also shaped what *American Heritage* did and did not publish. *American Heritage* readers were not very likely to complain about the magazine's neglect of South Carolina slaves, Polish coal miners, or Texas populist farmers, since so few of them came from even remotely similar backgrounds. These were not the "stories of your family history" that the magazine's advertisements evoked. Furthermore, certain topics and historical experiences were excluded because they did not fit the magazine's smooth, optimistic tone. Stories about the sexual exploitation of slaves or the mangling of legs and arms in early factories, for example, were not the sort of thing that you would want to publish in a "family" magazine. The same impulse that led the outdoor museum at Colonial Williamsburg, as one critic noted, to focus on the more "pleasing aspects of colonial life," and to exclude the "smells, flies, pigs, dirt and slave quarters," also operated at *American Heritage*.[44] Those who marketed history to middle-class "tourists" in the 1950s sought to guarantee that their history journeys—whether to eighteenth-century Virginia or through the pages of *American Heritage*—would be smooth, pleasant, and entertaining.

Only once did poverty rear its ugly head in *American Heritage*'s entire first year of publication. And this intrusion was the result of an unintentional wrong turn by editor Bruce Catton. Reviewing E. J. Kahn's "entertaining story" about the song-and-dance team Harrigan and Hart (*The Merry Partners*), Catton was seemingly shocked by Kahn's detailed description of the New York Irish slums of Ned Harrigan's youth, with their "vicious medley of misery, vice, crime and poverty." But lest Catton's readers leave Hell's Kitchen with the feeling that "American society had gone down a dead-end street from which it could not conceivably extract itself," he quickly reassured them of America's "fantastic, self-rectifying resilience." "The imperfections in American society can exact a frightful human cost, on occasion, but we do seem to work our way out of them," Catton concluded cheerfully.[45] There was no reason to let the unpleasantness of Irish immigrant life disturb your faith in American society—or your leisure-time reading of *American Heritage*.

These same commercial pressures kept *American Heritage* free not just of unpleasant topics but of those that might be deemed controversial or contemporary. Jensen, for example, thought that controversies over "the business of whether or not we should have gotten into the War of 1812" were fine. "However, when you get up closer to modern times—for example, the career of Franklin Roosevelt, the New Deal, the policies of the Truman Administration—it seems to me that such matters are still in political controversy. . . . [H]istory ends where unsettled modern political struggles begin." Parton explicitly linked the avoidance of controversy to the magazine's marketing strategy: "We're deliberately avoiding taking sides or positions, because this is something which is being done by everybody else. For example, if we start taking argumentative positions on contemporary subjects, it would militate against the permanence which is our chief stock in trade."[46]

It might also, Parton did not need to add, lose them readers. In August 1954 Upton Close, a member of Nevins' SAH as well as a right-wing critic of U.S. foreign policy in Asia, expressed his concern that the new publication not "reflect the heretofore all too overwhelming left-wingism of the most vocal of [SAH] . . . members" and proposed that he contribute an article on "what Communist frontism has done to the standing of America and Western civilization." But Catton reassured Close: "this publication will reflect no left wing tendencies whatever and will confine itself as far as possible to straight forward presentations of various aspects of the American past." As for Close's proposed article, "the difficulty is that it would fall more in the field of current history than in the field of the more distant American past which is what we are trying to cultivate. It is probably true that history broadly speaking includes anything that happened prior to this week, but we are going to try to stay a little further away from the immediate past than your projected article would suggest."[47]

Keeping *American Heritage* firmly in the "more distant American past" was obviously the most prudent course if the magazine wanted to avoid offending potential readers like Upton Close. With the exception of Jensen (who was quite conservative), the magazine's cosmopolitan staff, and especially Catton, probably stood to the left of its readers. An adherence to "straight" and noncontemporary history, in effect, broadened *Heritage*'s appeal. Whatever the reasons, the result was the same: a politically bland tone, an evasion of the contemporary implications of U.S. history, and a tacit repudiation of Nevins' original goal of educating Americans "in the historical backgrounds of many a world problem of today."[48]

To talk only about the textual content of *American Heritage* is to miss its most distinctive and appealing feature—its elegant format and lavish use of pictures. "The key to our quick growth," Parton explained in 1959, "is illustration, particularly in color. . . . [T]he pictures are what lure people into the magazine." Certainly, very few readers had previously seen so much of the American past in so many stunning colors. With great resourcefulness, the art director, Irwin Glusker, and a team of production consultants developed new techniques for publishing a 112-page hardbound magazine with close to

40 pages of color pictures at a relatively modest price.[49] Equal care was devoted to locating the interesting and often previously unpublished pictures that illustrated the articles.

Form more than content often absorbed the attention and energies of the magazine's creators and editors. A former staff member vividly recalls the tremendous commitment to physical layout—"the design of each two-page spread: where the pictures went, how the text was arranged, the measurements of each caption." (Another former staff member working in the book division remembers painstaking efforts to ensure that the captions were squared off with four lines of precisely 67 or 59 or 24 characters.) Similarly, the editors' two chief concerns in selecting and editing articles were "good writing" (like Nevins, they were openly contemptuous of academic history writing by "the professors") and "fact checking" (in order to avoid letters from hundreds of history buffs pointing out an incorrect detail).[50]

Content and interpretation thus took a backseat to form and style. Such priorities reflect the editors' background as professional journalists or magazine people (and extremely talented ones at that) rather than professional historians. Their professional identity was wrapped up in producing an innovative and polished magazine, not innovative and polished historical interpretations. "What we've done," explained Thorndike, "is to apply pictorial journalism tenchniques to history." The result—"*Life* magazine meets the American past"—was a revolutionary departure in the visual presentation of American history. To a large degree, the current visual look of American history picture books and textbooks—lavish, colorful, picturesque, with lots of high art and classic illustration—derives from *American Heritage*. Indeed, the connection is quite direct. In the early 1960s *American Heritage* joined Harper & Row in producing a U.S. history textbook, for which the magazine provided the illustrations. Up to that time, no textbooks included color pictures, but the resulting text, John A. Garraty's *The American Nation* (1966), was so successful that the color format became standard for major college texts.[51]

Because of its commitment to visualizing U.S. history, *American Heritage* has recovered and published a vast number of otherwise unavailable documents of the American past—an invaluable resource for those interested in the visual documentation of American history. Yet the quality and quantity of the pictures should not blind us to the ways illustrations are used in the magazine. The photographs, paintings, and drawings that fill *American Heritage* are almost always treated as "facts" rather than interpretations. Only rarely do the captions or text indicate that the artist was expressing a particular view of events. And more often than not, the visual perspective that is offered—but not analyzed—is sentimental, nostalgic, or romantic. A 1955 article—atypical only in its proletarian subject matter—presented (possibly for the first time) Nicolino Calyo's mid-nineteenth-century watercolors of rosy-cheeked, colorfully dressed New York City street vendors. Yet the value of these fascinating visual documents would surely have been enhanced if the editors had used other words besides "charming" to describe Calyo's highly romanticized portraits of these often desperately poor peddlers. Just two months earlier the editors had chosen—even more inappropriately—the same word to caption the lead illustration in an article on Eli Whitney: "Legendary even before the war, the charm of an old-time cotton plantation shows through this Currier and Ives print."[51]

Almost as disturbing has been the magazine's tendency to present paintings or drawings done many years after the events depicted without indicating this time disparity. In the fities and sixties *American Heritage* published eight Alonzo Chappell illustrations of late eighteenth- or early nineteenth-century events or people. Only two are dated. Even these do not emphasize that Chappell was actually a mid- to late nineteenth-century illustrator of historical books and not a contemporary of his visual subjects.[53] That illustrations do not have to be used in uncritical, nostalgic, or careless ways is demonstrated in Maxine Hong Kingston's brilliant photo essay on Chinatown, which *American Heritage* itself published in 1978—one of the finest articles ever to appear in the magazine. In captions and text Kingston provides an acute commentary on the selectivity and distortions of Arnold Genthe's early twentieth-century San Francisco Chinatown photographs: their exclusion of white faces and westernized Chinese in order to create the "spell of a self-contained mythical Cathay"; their depiction of large numbers of children without any hint that children were tragically rare in the bachelor society brought about by the Chinese Exclusion Acts.[54]

Kingston's essay, alas, is the exception and not the rule. Most often *American Heritage*'s illustrations have reinforced—and to some extent have created—the messages of optimism, nostalgia, and adventure that are found in the articles. The magazine's hard covers (at least between 1954 and 1969) told a similar story. The front covers generally featured ships, battles, military officers, frontiersmen, Indians, and "classic" American art by Peale and Trumbull. On the average only one cover a year dated from after the Civil War. The back covers, by contrast, emphasized the sentimental and nostalgic side of the "American heritage": hobby horses, dolls, wooden Santas, cigar boxes, theater posters, and Currier and Ives prints. The pictures and covers were thus part of a unified package that reiterated the magazine's verbal text. In effect, as a product, *American Heritage* conveyed the same elegance, drama, and "colorfulness" that it recalled in the past—no sordid advertisements, no cheap paperback covers, only high-quality paper and beautiful pictures, agreeably wrapped between a tasteful eighteenth-century painting and a cheerful Currier and Ives print. Readers surveyed in 1979 spoke repeatedly of the magazine's "feel of quality," "class," "elegance," "format and grade of paper," and "no advertising" in explaining its appeal.[55] Here was a smartly packaged substitute for (or companion to) the old family photograph album, which you could display proudly, not just on any coffee table, but even on a coffee table in one of the "colonial style" living rooms so popular in the 1950s.

Wittingly or not, *American Heritage* encouraged readers to see history as precisely that—a tidy package. There are no loose ends in the *Heritage* of the fifties and sixties or in its vision of the past. An occasional interpretive dispute may surface in the magazine, but on most big questions the past is settled and done with. Readers had no reason to assume that the past had any bearing on what they did today or would do tomorrow. Nor would they be likely to assume—as did the editors of the original *American Heritage*—that history is something that ordinary people could research, write, or even question critically. It is just something that you consume every two months and then place neatly on your shelf.

R egular readers of the pleasant, uncontroversial, nostalgic magazine that I have been describing were probably more than a little surprised to unwrap their December 1969 issue. Rather than the usual reassuring eighteenth- or early nineteenth-century painting on the cover, they found a photograph of a garish neon-lit strip, in Brooklyn of all places. A headline on the cover—a feature the genteel bimonthly had never tried before—warned the reader: "The American Land: A Heritage in Peril." A look inside would have only momentarily quieted the reader's concern. The magazine *did* contain many of the familiar types of articles that its readers had grown to expect: a story on the "gallantry" of the World War II cargo vessel crew; a selection from the journal of a "high-spirited" volunteer flier in World War I; a long, nostalgic review of the "hopeful world" of 1857 by editor Jensen.

But the same issue of *American Heritage* also launched a new section devoted to "conservation," a striking departure from the magazine's previous fifteen years of publishing. It was almost as if someone had flung a molotov cocktail into the magazine's usually quiet pages. An article by the new section's editor, David McCullough, for example, violated the magazine's un-written ban on contemporary or controversial subjects by sympathetically tracing the battles of Harry Caudill, a Kentucky lawyer, against the strip-mining companies of his region. Along the way, it even mildly questioned "the jargon of free enterprise." If this was not enough to start readers wonder-ing what had happened to Nevins' industrial statesmen, the next piece would certainly have had them checking to see whether they had not picked up the wrong magazine by mistake. In a neo-Malthusian article on overpopulation in the United States—*hysterical* would not be too strong a word to describe its tone—Carlton Ogburn, Jr., denounced the "obscurantism" of the Vatican (for opposing birth control and abortion), called for the repeal of all antiabor-tion laws, recommended that couples with more than two children be denied the right to vote, and attacked John Wayne, Jack Anderson, and Nelson Rockefeller for having too many children. Robert Kennedy came in for spe-cial scorn, with Ogburn seriously complaining that if Kennedy's "eleven chil-dren and their descendants reproduced as he had, there would be over 214 million descendants of the Robert Kennedys in the ninth generation."[56]

The air of crisis continued to hover over *American Heritage* for most of the next year, with attacks on industrial polluters and the highway lobby and celebrations of heroic conservationists. Although the magazine's internal pol-itics and its search for a larger audience may have had something to do with the initiation (and later termination) of the new section, it seems more gener-ally to have represented *American Heritage*'s response to an America that was in turmoil. Blacks, students, and women were marching in the streets. But articles on the historical context of racism, imperialism, or sexism were hard-ly calculated to appeal to *Heritage*'s well-heeled, middle-aged, white male readers. Conservation at least *seemed* like a relatively safe contemporary cause, since it was one that affluent Americans had traditionally supported.[57]

At that fractious juncture in time, however, there were no entirely safe contemporary topics, and the experiment had obviously gotten out of hand. Even some articles on topics other than conservation adopted a less upbeat tone and examined formerly taboo subjects. The August 1970 issue, for ex-ample, opened with John Brooks's thoughtful meditation on the collapse of the liberal consensus—the very ideological formation that had shaped and nurtured *American Heritage*. A cartoon drawn for the article showed mini-skirted and bell-bottomed youths tossing "classic" American texts—works by Horatio Alger and Andrew Carnegie, *Reader's Digest, A Message to Gar-cia*—into a trash bin. They might as easily have been disposing of *American Heritage*. "Traditional American ways of looking at things—including the traditional ways of looking at our own past—have suddenly been reversed,"

Brooks told readers. The next issue featured Richard Hofstadter's blast at America's gun culture. Some readers complained that "fanaticism" was creeping into the magazine. And subscription levels, which had begun falling in 1968 (and may have contributed to the decision to try the new section), continued to plummet.[58] By December 1970 the controversial conservation section had been dropped with no explanation.

Yet *American Heritage* did not (or could not) return entirely to its pre-1969 format. The December 1972 issue offers a good example of the magazine's new direction—or perhaps lack of direction. To be sure, we find colorful tales of Burgoyne's army, nostalgic recollections of the Smith Brothers and pocket mirrors (lavishly displayed in color), the curious and engaging tale of a California cattle dealer's epic ride, and a sumptuous portfolio of photographs of 1920s movie stars. Yet the tone is less uniformly upbeat and optimistic than before; a story on the Indian Black Hawk, for example, ends on a decidedly melancholy note with his body stolen from the grave; the social historian David Rothman, discussing poverty in America, finds a "discouraging" legacy; an article on the American Colonization Society acknowledges the existence of racism in America, at least in the nineteenth century. These were hardly radical sentiments in 1972, but they suggest that the magazine was unable to put on the uniformly sunny face that it had displayed throughout the fifties and sixties.

American Heritage—like the history profession—was in transition in the early seventies. The keynote was still the optimism and consensus of the fifties, but there was also a minor chord of disillusion, despair, and conflict. For readers—at least those who read the whole magazine—the result must have been confusing. One example of the mixed messages that the magazine was giving it readers can be found in a 1970 article on the Carlisle Indian School ("The Great White Father's Little Red Indian School"). Written by an army colonel, the article—in classic *American Heritage* fashion—portrays the school's founder, Colonel Richard Henry Pratt in heroic terms. Yet a sidebar by a staff member notes the "appalling aftereffects of the [assimilationist] Carlisle philosophy of Indian education."[59]

These changes accelerated after the middle of the decade when Alvin Josephy, Jr., an expert on Native American history and an activist in Democratic Party politics, replaced the conservative Jensen as editor. The December 1976 issue reflected Josephy's impact. The Marxist historian Eugene Genovese appeared on the magazine's advisory board and even within the magazine's pages, proclaiming that "a spirited defense of our history can no longer minimize the crimes against the Indians, blacks, and white laboring classes, nor can it pretend that imperialism and international hooliganism have played

only a minor role in our development." Lawrence Lader gave a sympathetic
account of the Henry Wallace campaign in an article that would have made
Upton Close blanch. And the same magazine that had long shunned historical
perspectives on current events and serious treatments of women's history provided an account of U.S. involvement with Middle East oil and a reminiscence of a Kansas pioneer woman.[60]

Since the mid-seventies, under Josephy and his successors Geoffrey Ward
(1978–1982) and Byron Dobell (1982–present), the magazine has become
still more liberal and contemporary and less afraid of controversy. In some
ways it has become more like the magazine that Nevins envisioned back in the
1930s. In the past two years, for example, it has treated such controversial
and contemporary topics as Watergate, the draft, immigration, and welfare.
The current editors have even reversed the chronological emphasis of their
predecessors by focusing on the twentieth century almost to the exclusion of
earlier periods. They have also begun to incorporate into the magazine's
pages neglected topics (recent issues have included a full-length treatment of
the General Motors sit-down strike and interviews with women who had been
industrial workers during World War II) and neglected perspectives (such as
the left historian Eric Foner's revisionist views on Reconstruction).[61] These
are significant and praiseworthy changes that testify to the more pluralistic
perspectives of the recent editors, shifts in the historical profession (radical
historians are now part of the historical establishment, after all), new cultural
norms growing out of the civil rights, peace, and women's movements, and—
not unimportantly—the magazine's search for a new audience.

Still, the changes go only so far. The sit-down strike article, for example,
sympathetically and vividly recreates that dramatic moment in recent labor
history. Yet the article slights the role of women and radicals in the strike.
And its conclusion approves of the Supreme Court's outlawing of the sit-
down tactic, sees the UAW's purge of communists as an indication of the
union's reaching "stable maturity," and seems to suggest that labor and management had achieved "parity" by the end of the 1930s. Even more revealing,
perhaps, the article provided the occasion for its editor, then Geoffrey Ward,
to editorialize about "the precious right to organize"—but his reference was
to the "brave workers of Gdansk" not to the air traffic controllers.[62] The story
of the working class has beome a part—albeit a minor part—of the "American Heritage," but the story of class relations and state power has not. Moreover, blacks—not perceived as a major market for the magazine—appear
even less frequently than workers; they have so far won only cameo ap-
pearances in the story that *American Heritage* tells its readers. In general,
most articles in the magazine remain within the boundaries of conventional

liberalism and nationalistic sentiments at the same time that alternative perspectives are making significant inroads within professional history. In the 1950s, oddly, the magazine was probably more liberal (in politics and view of history) than the historical profession; today the positions seem to have been reversed.

American Heritage has not so much abandoned its upbeat view of the American past as added another—and seemingly incompatible—layer to it. Nostalgia and battles are still very much a part of *American Heritage,* but they are no longer the whole story. In the late 1970s, for example, readers encountered articles on Diego Rivera, the 1877 railroad strikes, slave daguerreotypes, urban renewal, Cuba and the CIA, Woody Guthrie, J. Robert Oppenheimer, Marian Anderson, Henry George, Polish Americans, and Vietnam veterans. But these appeared alongside more traditional features on railroad chases, Normandy in 1944, the "last roundup," cowboy heroes, World War I battles, grizzly bears, Lincoln look-alikes, tornadoes, honeymoons, and folk art. The message that the magazine conveys, as a result, is ambiguous and confusing. Racism, sexism, despoliation of the environment, and political corruption have now crept into American history. Yet, at the same time, the story of America is still that of courage, dynamism, excitement, greatness, adventure, and triumph. It is as if a doctor told you that you were suffering from cancer, heart disease, and cirrhosis of the liver, yet assured you at the same time that you were the healthiest person in town. Of course, *American Heritage* is not alone in this muddle. This version of the American past—a combination of fundamental flaws and flawless fundamentals—is increasingly common, whether at Disney World's EPCOT Center or in the latest American history textbooks.[63]

American Heritage's format, changed at least as much as the articles, also combines aspects of the old magazine with some striking departures. In 1980 skyrocketing costs forced the magazine to drop its familiar hard covers; two years later it began to take advertisements.[64] Contemporary photographs and headlines announcing articles are now regularly found on its once staid covers. It looks more and more like *Esquire* or *New York* magazine—not coincidentally two publications that the current editor, Byron Dobell, previously ran. Yet the magazine still retains an air of elegance and refinement, sandwiching its lavish color pictures between equally lavish advertisements for diamonds, cruises, and cognac.

Subscribers have not universally endorsed the changes in the magazine's form and content. One thousand readers wrote in to protest against the switch to soft covers.[65] And readers have voted against the changes with their checkbooks. Between 1968 and 1980 the magazine lost two-thirds of its readers.

The only thing that has sustained the magazine has been the loyalty of a large number of subscribers (the 74 percent renewal rate is still among the highest in the business) who have saved every single issue of the magazine. The current editors blame McGraw-Hill—which bought the company in 1969 from the original owners and then devoted most of its attention to the book operation—for the nosedive in subscriptions. Yet the subscription drop began before McGraw-Hill took over and continued after it sold the company in 1976 to Engelhard Hanovia, a minerals conglomerate. At least some subscribers probably dropped away because the magazine changed and no longer provided the same reassuring, comforting, cheerful version of the past that they remembered. Or, more precisely, its version of the past seemed inconsistent and discordant—simultaneously cheerful and pessimistic, fixed in the past and linked to the present.[66]

The more serious problem is demographic. The current profile of *American Heritage* subscribers mirrors that of 1958 in occupation and economic standing but not in age. Half of the subscribers are over forty-five; a quarter are over sixty-five. Although a quarter of the over-twenty population in the United States is between the ages of twenty-five and thirty-four, less than 10 percent of *American Heritage*'s over-twenty subscribers fall into this age range. The magazine's loyal subscribers are literally dying off and not being replaced by younger readers.[67] So far, the editors have not developed a publishing formula that has captured the historical imagination of the 1980s urban gentry—today's prime market—as their predecessors did for the 1950s suburban middle class. Not only is the magazine marketplace much more crowded than it was in 1954 (with *Smithsonian, Connoisseur, Blair & Ketchum's Country Journal*, and many others vying for the upscale consumer), but the "historical marketplace" is also more competitive and specialized. Such other history magazines as *American History Illustrated* (one of a group of historical publications from Historical Times, Inc.) and *American West* now compete directly with *American Heritage*. Moreover, the glitter of "living history" at Harbor Place and South Street Seaport or the chic of restoring your own brownstone apparently seems more alluring to "yuppies" (many of whom probably grew up in households that subscribed to *American Heritage*) than the glossy pages of any history magazine. At the same time, the "baby bust" has eliminated another traditional market for the magazine.

But *American Heritage* continues to search for new ways to build its audience, which did in fact grow modestly in 1983 and 1984. In the spring of 1985 it introduced a column on American business as well as a different logo and new typography. "The new look will be more pleasing and will lend itself better to more interesting headlines," Dobell told the *New York Times*.

"But," he added in an apparent effort to reassure the magazine's veteran readers, "the changes will be subtle rather than revolutionary."[68] It remains to be seen whether these further changes will enable *American Heritage* to regain the lost glory of the fifties and sixties.

W e are the nation's memory," Oliver Jensen has said of *American Heritage*.[69] If there is a grain of truth in this hyperbole, it is a depressing commentary on the state of historical consciousness in post–World War II America. Particularly in its first fifteen years, the magazine's penchant for the trivial over the significant, its exclusion of vast areas of the American experience from its pages, its reluctance to connect the past and the present, and its inclination to reinforce a false confidence about America's place in the world made it a rather poor substitute for a popular historical memory. Even in its recent, more pluralistic and contemporary incarnation, *American Heritage* has generally failed to address fundamental historical questions about the nature of political and economic power in America. And throughout the last three decades, its smooth packaging has reinforced the perception that the past is fixed, closed, seamless, and beyond the intervention of ordinary people.

Yet such a verdict is perhaps too harsh. After all, in the same years that *American Heritage* flourished, most academic historians abdicated the terrain of popular history. Implicitly, they have often taken the position—as Nevins charged more than forty years ago—that history "should be the possession of a Germanic-minded few, a little knot of *Gelehrten* squeezing out monographs and counting footnotes."[70] Meanwhile, much of the popular history of recent decades—in films, television, novels, museums, historic site restorations—has committed greater sins against the past than *American Heritage*. And it hardly seems likely that the most recent forms of popular historical "activity"—restoring old houses, for example—will spark any more critical reflection on the nature of American society than did *American Heritage*. Finally, any claims about the magazine's negative impact must be acknowledged as speculative in the absence of systematic investigations of popular historical consciousness.

Still, *American Heritage* stands as perhaps the most influential and successful model for presenting history to a broad public audience. What can we learn from its example? First, the magazine reminds us of the importance of the audience. Public historians have sometimes acted as if a popular audience is good simply because it is popular, because it reaches beyond the academy to the "public." Yet, as the story of *American Heritage* indicates, there are many different publics for popular history, and the form, content, and price of what you produce determine which audience you reach. Academic historians would do well to speak to a wide variety of publics rather than their credentialed colleagues alone. They might even try to get their perspectives included in popular magazines like *American Heritage*. Still, there are obvious limits to the value of addressing even the most progressive message to a uniformly upper-middle-class audience. And there are constraints as well as benefits in writing for avowedly commercial media.

Second, we must face the question of how to write and present history to a popular audience. *American Heritage*'s commitment to the visual dimension of the past is worthy of emulation by text-oriented historians. Yet such emulation should be tempered by a recognition of the subjectivity of these visual sources. *American Heritage* also highlights the appeal of storytelling, of human interest tales and adventure yarns set in the past. Such literary techniques offer enormous possibilities for presenting alternative visions of the past. But we need to think about the tendency of much popular narrative history—certainly most of what has appeared in *Heritage*—to look for a happy ending. As the docudrama producer David Wolper has said, he always looks for an "up-ending" in historical properties that he buys for television. This same tendency has also afflicted some efforts at community history that draw uncritically on popular forms. More often than not we get stories of heroic struggle and resistance; less frequently stories of defeat and failure. But history has not always had "happy endings," particularly for the poor, the non-white, and the working person.[71]

More generally, we need to consider whether narrative history—with its focus on the individual ("characters," for example)—can adequately convey a systemic critique of American society. Moreover, narrative history often conceals the political bias of its author, presenting only the "smoothed-over end result," as Martin Duberman has written. Finally, to talk uncritically of narrative history is to ignore fundamental questions about the ideological assumptions embedded in narrative conventions. Even if we put aside such analytical and political concerns, the recent history of *American Heritage* raises some serious questions about whether "narrative history" is really the panacea for the declining interest in history that it is sometimes depicted as. After all, if the masters of narrative history at *American Heritage* were losing their popular audience at the same time that an ostensibly over-analytic and social scientific academic history profession was also losing *its* audience, then "the decline of narrative" may not be the central explanation for the problems facing history in the United States.[72]

Finally, there is the matter of format. The polished professionalism of a magazine like *American Heritage*—compared, for example, to the more amateurish AASLH production or, more relevantly, to the low-budget pamphlet produced by a community group—has an undeniable appeal. But while we search for "professionalism" in what we do, we should also keep in mind the message that form can express. Like *American Heritage* we can easily wind up with a publication (or a film) that implicitly says that history is a neat and tidy package and that history is only done by certified professionals—whether historians or magazine editors and writers— and not by ordinary people. History must seek a popular, nonelite audience in ways that make people critically question the past and connect the past actively to the present and to their own lives.

History in the Fast Lane:

Howard Fast and the Historical Novel

Howard Fast is a popular historical novelist whose career spans more than forty years. He has won fans by dramatizing the underside of American history: the contributions of dissidents and the struggle of ordinary people, stories that rarely appear in textbooks. But Fast's career shows that novels focusing on the underside do not necessarily pose a fundamental challenge to standard textbooks or introduce readers to new and more critical ways of looking at the past. He demonstrates—by both positive and negative example—that a real departure from conventional textbook history requires an examination of the social power relations that have given rise to dissent, shaped the struggles of ordinary people, and determined whose stories will be neglected and whose celebrated.

In the late 1970s, when historical family sagas became an American publishing sensation, Fast seemed to rise from the dead. Decades after his first successes as a dramatizer of the national past had faded from public memory, millions of readers snapped up his four-volume tale of the Lavette clan—*The Immigrants* (1977), *Second Generation* (1978), *The Establishment* (1979), and *The Legacy* (1981). During World War II, Fast had frequently hit the bestseller charts with works in another popular genre: novels of famous chapters in U.S. history. Radically revising conventional images of well-known people and events, he portrayed Native Americans' resistance to colonization (*The Last Frontier,* 1941); George Washington's role as an inspiration to the common people who fought the war for national independence (*The Unvanguished,* 1942); the political activities of America's first professional revolutionary (*Citizen Tom Paine,* 1943); and former slaves' struggle for full citizenship in the Reconstruction South (*Freedom Road,* 1944). These books

BY PRISCILLA MUROLO

made him the country's most widely read radical novelist. But after World War II, the campaign East had once described as his "one-man reformation of the historical novel in America" began to peter out.[1]

Fasts's reformation owed much of its initial momentum to the American Communist Party's Popular Front Against Fascism. Adopting the Popular Front in the mid-1930s, the Party had ended its former isolation from liberals and non-Communist radicals and focused its energies on the construction of left-center coalitions in support of the New Deal, industrial unionism, racial equality, the rights of free speech and assembly, and the international fight against fascism. Downplaying the struggle for socialism, U.S. Communists increased their influence within grassroots movements by embracing a more populist brand of radicalism. They called on government and employers to practice what American democracy preached regarding equality, freedom, and justice. Fast's commitment to Popular Front politics during World War II—when staunch antifascism nudged him toward and finally into the Communist Party—inspired his novels' re-visions of U.S. history. By introducing readers to a national legacy of revolt against oppression, he lent historical legitimacy to the radical Americanism then celebrated by Communists. His reverence for democratic traditions, his talent for fast-paced narrative and vivid characterization, and a political climate relatively friendly to Communists and their sympathizers guaranteed Fast's books a warm reception. Their popularity, in turn, helped to fuel his enthusiasm as a reformer of the historical novel.

When World War II ended and antifascism gave way to anti-Communism in the American political mainstream, the Communist Party abandoned the Popular Front's radical patriotism for an expressly internationalist opposition to the cold war. Fast, guided by the party's new politics, began to focus his novels on the shortcomings of the democratic heritage he had once commemorated without reservation. The project seemed to overwhelm his ability to make radical interpretations of national history come alive. His next novel, *The American* (1946), inserted a left critique of populism and an argument for revolutionary proletarian politics into a portrait of Illinois governor John P. Altgeld. The book suffered from an often sluggish pace, preachy narrative voice, and wooden supporting characters: a Eugene Debs who talks like the Communist Party's William Z. Foster, and a Samuel Gompers whose politics in the 1880s are indistinguishable from those of AFL president William Green in 1945. Fast had begun to use his fiction as a new kind of political vehicle, one that would demonstrate the historical inevitability of socialism. Thoroughly committed to this project, he urged other writers to take it up as well, lest they wind up on the "cultural dung heap of reaction."[2] Fast, however, found it increasingly difficult to follow his own advice with any measure of artistic or commercial success.

Beginning with *The American,* his U.S. history novels grew more explicit, dogmatic, and contrived in drawing parallels between the nation's past and its present, which Fast believed was ripe for Soviet-style socialism. Unidimensional characters, representing modern political tendencies, spoke and thought anachronistically. Fast's narrative voice had an increasingly didactic ring; his plots were less historically accurate and plausible. The Popular Front's disintegration, while undermining his capacity to animate radical history, also took its toll on Fast's access to a popular audience once McCarthyism left him in publishing limbo. *The Proud and the Free* (1950), which appeared shortly after he completed a three-month prison term for refusing to name names before the House Un-American Activities Committee, and *The Passion of Sacco and Vanzetti* (1953), published by the blacklisted Fast's own Blue Herron Press, were his parting shots as a reformer of the American historical novel. Liberal critics ignored these books; more virulently anti-Communist reviewers attacked them; and many dealers boycotted them. Robbed of its original political foundations and sympathetic readership, Fast's "one-man reformation" ended.

In 1957, after Soviet leaders denounced Joseph Stalin as a tyrant, Fast joined many others in quitting the Communist Party. Explaining his defection in the Party's literary journal, *Mainstream,* he declared his intention to "continue . . . solidarity with all the people of good will in America, communist and non-communist, who fight injustice and treasure the precious, the infinitely precious, traditions of Jefferson, Franklin, Lincoln and Douglass—to mention only four of the many great who built the foundations of that most splendid thing, American democracy."[3] This reembrace of Popular Front politics did not, however, inspire renewed attempts to reform the historical novel. His anti-Party memoir, *The Naked God* (1957), received rave reviews and signaled his reacceptance by the cultural establishment. Fast then went to Hollywood and became a prolific and handsomely rewarded author of screenplays, detective stories, children's books, and other lightweight material—including a few short novels about the moral ambiguities individuals faced during the American Revolution. Fast the writer of national historical epics dropped out of sight. A generation passed before he published the Lavette novels, a family saga dramatizing both personal and epoch-making struggles against white supremacy, war, fascism, anti-Semitism, industrial exploitation, McCarthyism, and the subjugation of women.

In *The Immigrants,* the first volume of the saga, the drama revolves around conflicts between Dan Lavette, a self-made millionaire, and his aristocratic wife. Born in a boxcar that was carrying his Italian-French parents from New York to San Francisco, Dan begins adult life as a fisherman but soon starts a shipping business that grows into an empire during World War I. On his way up the social ladder, Dan marries Jean Seldon, an heiress whose contempt for his Jewish business partner, Mark Levy, and Chinese bookkeeper, Feng Wo, represents the bigotry of rich WASPs, portrayed by Fast as the natural enemies of democracy. As the shipping company grows and his marriage falters, Dan fathers three children: Tom and Barbara, born to his wife, and Joe, born to May Ling, the bookkeeper's daughter. Torn between the two women, Dan must choose between opposing definitions of the pursuit of happiness in America. Jean symbolizes ascendancy into the big bourgeoisie; May Ling stands for immersion in the democratic melting pot. The crisis is resolved during the Great Depression, when Dan faces financial ruin, refuses the aid of his wealthy in-laws, divorces his wife, marries his mistress, finds work as a fisherman, and learns to appreciate life among the masses.

In the rest of the Lavette novels, daughter Barbara—who has her mother's money and her father's egalitarian impulses—takes us on a whirlwind tour of popular movements against oppression. *The Immigrants*'s conflict, between greed and power-lust on the one side and democracy and personal integrity on the other, expands to include a supporting cast of millions. *Second Generation* opens in the summer of 1934, when Barbara is an active supporter of the San Francisco longshoremen's strike. The experience changes her life by making her recognize and hate the social injustice and economic exploitation that are invisible to her wealthy relatives. Barbara rejects her mother's elitist lifestyle and, when the strike is over, moves to Paris, where she supports herself by writing for a magazine and falls in love with a French journalist later killed on assignment with the Spanish Republicans. Her lover's death ignites her hatred for war. This sentiment grows deeper during World War II, when May Ling is killed in the Japanese attack on Pearl Harbor and Barbara becomes a war correspondent witnessing the carnage in Europe and North Africa. The war does, however, have its benefits. It not only defeats fascism in Europe but also—and more memorably within the terms of this novel— enables Dan to build a second shipping empire and propels Barbara into the arms of Bernie Cohen, a Zionist who has devoted his youth to killing Nazis and will commit the remainder of his life to the fight for Israel. As *Second Generation* closes, he and Barbara marry.

One hundred and sixty pages into *The Establishment*, Bernie, who was running guns to the Middle East, lies dead in Palestine; and Barbara, the widowed mother of a two-year-old son, is about to receive another blow. In an incident closely resembling Fast's own experience with the House Un-

American Activities Committee (HUAC), she is called to testify and declines to name the friends who contributed to her fund drive for a Spanish Civil War veteran's hospital. She pays for her integrity with six months in prison. Her family's mixed reactions divide the Lavette clan into warring factions, one embodying devotion to democratic principles and the other greedy self-- interest. Dan and a reformed Jean, cozily remarried, are enraged by their daughter's persecution. But son Tom and his wife, Lucy, the child of one of California's biggest banking dynasties and Jean's replacement as the prime emblem of WASPish elitism, are furious over Barbara's refusal to give names. They fear that her notoriety will diminish their standing within a group of west coast financiers who plan to use HUAC as a launching pad for the careers of Republican politicians on the take.

Fast's drama of the early 1950s centers on these divisions between "good" and "bad" Lavettes. But as the decade wears on, the status of women suddenly appears as a historical issue and dramtic device. Joe Lavette and his wife—he is a doctor, she is a movie star—struggle to resolve the conflicting demands of jobs and family. Similarly, Jean tries to combine a happy second marriage to Dan with her new career as an art dealer. And Barbara, at the novel's end, is finally learning to live contentedly without a man.

In *The Legacy,* women carry on the intrafamily battle between democracy and greed, a battle that now centers on the U.S. war in Vietnam. While Dan's grandchildren become participants in the American civil rights movement and the defense of Israel, Barbara writes a bestseller about the difficulties faced by a president's wife, wins a national reputation as a feminist, and founds Mothers for Peace, which quickly becomes one of the country's most influential antiwar groups. Linking pacifism and feminism, Mothers for Peace attracts broad support by arguing that war is simply *machismo* taken to its logical extreme and that women must unite to end this deadly assertion of male ego. All the Lavette women join the struggle—except, of course, Lucy. She and Tom, who has taken over the family business following Dan's recent death, stand to make millions shipping oil and ammunition to Southeast Asia. Their contact in Washington has warned that if Tom cannot control his sister, other companies will get the lucrative government contracts. As the ineffectual Tom stews, Lucy acts. She hires an arsonist to torch Barbara's house, the national headquarters of Mothers for Peace. The organization nevertheless survives. Though the war is still raging as the Lavette saga draws to a close, readers know that Barbara and her allies will eventually succeed in their efforts to bring the American troops home.

If one compares them with the historical fiction Fast produced during World War II, it is difficult not to dismiss the Lavette novels as a purely commercial venture. In both cases Fast sought the widest possible audience and adopted a popular literary form that would help him attract masses of readers. But whereas books like *The Last Frontier* and *Freedom Road* have become radical classics, frequently reprinted to win new fans, it is impossible to imagine a similar revival of the Lavette saga. The years in Hollywood seem to have transformed Fast's longstanding desire to reach many readers into an eagerness to meet the momentary specifications of the mass market. (If that was his aim, he succeeded; *The Immigrants*' paperback rights alone brought in more than $800,000.)[4] The Lavettes made their debut when the huge successes of Alex Haley's *Roots* and the first installments of John Jakes's Kent Family Chronicles guaranteed that *The Immigrants* and its sequels would be widely promoted. Fast's battered but still considerable gift for creating page-turners whose political dimensions add dramatic weight to the proceedings ensured that his new work would be enthusiastically greeted by readers of popular historical fiction. Yet, as if to maximize his chances of producing a blockbuster, Fast rejected Haley's model in *Roots*—a focus on ordinary people whose family history provides an arena for the thorough treatment of a single social-historical theme—for a Jakes-like adherence to the dominant conventions of bestsellerdom. In the annals of the Lavettes and the Kents alike, the central characters are possessed of money, power, and superior talents; and a big, flashy family drama offers many colorful but superficial sidetrips into the realm of social history. As the *New York Times* review of *The Immigrants* happily reported, "you can enjoy this book without a thought in your head."[5] The same holds true for its sequels.

Still, Fast has worked rather hard in these novels to introduce a wide range of radical political themes. The Lavette saga seems to have been shaped by something more than its author's eagerness for a commercial success. In an essay warning persuasively against dismissing the reincarnated Fast as a hack, Alan Wald offers a different explanation for the saga's shortcomings. Popular Front ideology, he argues, "inculcated Fast with the notion that radical politics could be transmitted to a large audience in the garb of liberal sentiments and idealized patriotism, all aimed at a reader imagined to represent 'the common man.' "[6] Fast, in Wald's analysis, has not simply gone for the money but has deteriorated as a radical artist because of his loyalty to Popular Front prescriptions for wrapping revolutionary politics in packages readily acceptable to the mass of Americans.

Wald's argument may well explain Fast's failure to experiment with a noncommercial literary genre that might have limited his audience but provided better opportunities for examining the political themes raised in the Lavette saga. Fast, like the architects of the Popular Front, has sought to influence as many people as possible. This desire might be blamed for his embrace of a family-saga formula that is politically inadequate but whose appeal to the public is well established. But the superiority of Fast's work in the early 1940s—when he was no less interested in writing bestsellers—suggests a more positive evaluation of the Popular Front's effect on his career. Though the wish to reach a wide audience may have discouraged him, then and later, from taking artistic risks, Popular Front politics also enhanced his ability in the 1940s to breathe new life into established literary forms. While guided by these politics, American Communists radicalized widely accepted democratic ideals by using them to illuminate the broken promises of liberalism, which pays lip service to the primacy of human rights and social justice while subordinating them to the so-called rights of property and the maintenance of inequitable systems of "law and order." The novels Fast produced during World War II applied the Popular Front strategy to historical fiction. These books stand far above the Lavette saga because they do not merely treat political themes but also politicize readers' conceptions of history by shedding light on the power structures that have acted against the realization of democratic ideals.

Essential to any novel's historical vision is its implicit or explicit portrayal of politics: the shape and dynamics of power relations among social groups or socially representative individuals whose interests conflict. *The Immigrants* provides an explanation for Fast's current attitude toward the question of power when it ends with lines from Lao Tzu: "And he who does not desire to be ahead of the world becomes the leader of the world." This epigram is meant to lend universal significance to the preceding drama of Dan's choice between Jean and May Ling and his discovery that happiness lies in abandoning bourgeois life and joining the oppressed. But when the same philosophy is applied to the rest of the saga, where much of the action revolves around central characters' connections to popular revolts against oppression, moral drama gives way to historical melodrama. Fast's failure to provide more than a cursory examination of the power relations engendering these revolts prevents him from developing characters whose political stands represent anything more historically significant than personal predispositions toward egalitarianism or elitism, humanitarianism or greed. This perspective locks him into a liberal revisionism that cannot pose a fundamental challenge to conventional textbook treatments of the history he portrays.

Fast relies mainly on two revisionist techniques. The first is an inversion of "great man" history: the exposure of crimes committed in high places. Investigating the discrepancy between public statements and decisions made in smoke-filled rooms, it promises to disclose the secret truth behind well-known events. Recent popular examples of this approach to revising American history are *The Price of Power* by Seymour Hersh and *The Rosenberg File* by Ronald Radosh and Joyce Milton. As Radosh and Milton's "discovery" of Julius Rosenberg's guilt demonstrates, exposé does not necesssarily dispute official history but can also embellish it. Fast uses the technique primarily to indict the greedy Lavettes and, through them the unseen architects of HUAC and the U.S. war in Vietnam. While exposing the corruption of the powerful, however, he joins the textbooks in dodging the issue of power. HUAC did advance the careers of several crooked politicians, most notably Richard Nixon; but its *raison d'être* was disempowering the working-class left, which does not have even a walk-on part in the drama of Barbara's brush with the Committee. Similarly, Fast's exposé of government collusion with war profiteers does not give readers a clue as to why U.S. troops were in Southeast Asia. The question of state power in Vietnam and the reasons for the U.S. government's fear of national liberation movements on the other side of the world remain mysterious. We learn only that big business makes money off war.

Fast's second technique for revising American history is pluralism. While exposé is used by writers of all political persuasions, pluralism has been associated with liberalism and the left. It brings to the fore people whom historians have traditionally neglected and insists that the "national experience" be examined from many divergent points of view. Its most influential practitioners have been the authors of the "enlightened" American history textbooks of the 1970s. Pluralism is not necessarily incompatible with "great man" history. In *The Immigrants* Fast uses pluralism not only to depict the oppression and bigotry faced by newly arrived Italians, Chinese, and Russian Jews but also to show how bold and hard-working individuals from these groups rise above their origins to enter a pantheon of bourgeois heroes.

Pluralism can, however, contradict the claims of consensus history; and this is apparently what Fast has in mind in the saga's later novels, when the struggles of workers, Afro-Americans, women, antiwar activists, and other "minorities" affect the Lavettes' lives. But saddled with a drama of life at the top, he cannot avoid trivializing these struggles. Their main historical function within the terms of the novels is to reveal the mettle of the democratic-minded bourgeoisie and their greedy, elitist foils. The women's movement, especially its critique of the patriarchal family, offered Fast an opportunity to examine power relations; he is, after all, writing about domestic life as well as national history. But he seems reluctant to pay any serious attention to a movement whose adherents are clearly motivated by political and economic self-interest as well as personal needs and an abstract desire for social justice.

The Lavette women never really challenge patriarchy; they simply ask for male respect and understanding. Feminism—represented by one of Fast's "historical" characters, Netty Leedan, author of *The Feminine Enigma*—appears just long enough to shape the politics of Mothers for Peace, which does not seek power but the reeducation of people whose obsession with power is purportedly the root of all war. Here and throughout the later novels, pluralism enables Fast to show that American history is freighted with conflict. But by placing Lavettes who do not "desire to be ahead of the world" at the forefront of insurgence, he also misrepresents the social bases and goals of the historic movements he depicts. For Fast's ruling-class heroes, the struggle for social justice is always diametrically opposed to the struggle for power.

The weaknesses of Fast's current approach to revising conventional history are obvious. As he himself has shown, however, popular historical novels capable of entertaining a very broad audience can blend exposé and pluralism with the dramatization of power relations. In the process, they can raise fundamental questions about the veracity and political purpose of history that views the past from the standpoint of the ruling class. All four of his bestselling World War II–era novels draw attention to the prejudices, lies, and omissions that distort official memory. But two—*The Last Frontier* and *Freedom Road*—go a step further by depicting how and in whose interests the distortions are propagated.

The Last Frontier, set in the winter of 1878–79, is an account of the Northern Cheyenne's successful flight from the Indian Territory (now Oklahoma) to their ancestral home in Montana. As the U.S. Army pursues the Cheyenne and kills nearly one-third of them, Fast shows his readers how the West was won: with military force, colonization, and genocide. But he does not stop at debunking popular myths about cowboys and Indians. Readers also see the creation of the incident's official history—or, more accurately, nonhistory—when the military and the Department of the Interior construct a veil of lies to cover up the Cheyenne's final victory. In an afterword, Fast sharpens the image of purposeful distortions of the historical record by describing the "maze of falsification" he discovered while researching the novel. Although Fast has finally set the record straight, one does not come away from *The Last Frontier* feeling that all is well. Uncovering only one buried story, the novel implies that there are countless others yet to be disclosed.

Freedom Road makes a similar argument by viewing the drama of Reconstruction in South Carolina from the traditionally neglected vantage point of freedmen. The novel centers on a group of former slaves who join with white tenant farmers to purchase and work an old planatation on a family-farm basis. The main architect of this project is Gideon Jackson, an ex-fieldhand elected to the state legislature and eventually to the U.S. House of Representatives. In the state house, in Washington, and at home, Jackson and his allies work to shape a partnership between black and white farmers. Their unity, which does not erase but supersedes white chauvinism, is based on common interests and a belief that together they will be strong enough to wipe out the vestiges of planter power. The experiment comes to a bloody end in 1877, when the disarming of the interracial state militia and the withdrawal of federal troops open the floodgate for a tide of white terror that washes across South Carolina. At the plantation, black and white families move into the deserted manor house to meet an attack by the Ku Klux Klan, which burns the mansion to the ground. None of its inhabitants survives. As Fast explains in his afterword, this and similar episodes cleared the way for powerful men—who had reason to fear black freedom, interracial unity, and agrarian democracy—to concoct myths about the "tragedy" of Reconstruction, myths that became the stuff of conventional history.

In both novels a Popular Front impulse to identify and celebrate indigenous traditions of democratic revolt underlies Fast's challenge not only to the content of conventional history but also to its claim of political neutrality. Placing the Cheyenne and freedmen at the center of historical action and in irreconcilable conflict with their enemies, he explains why Native Americans and Afro-Americans are usually relegated to history's fringes. His narratives show that behind the U.S. Army and the Klan were men whose economic and political power depended on colonization in the West and, in the South, on the control of land and agricultural labor and the disenfranchisement of blacks. This power was publicly legitimized—depicted, that is, as natural—when the Cheyenne's reclamation of their land was covered up and when Reconstruction was crushed and its main participants silenced. Later, as Fast's afterwords point out, the legitimization gained force when it became the basis for conventional history's apology for or denial of racial and national oppression and neglect of revolts against it. Employing his revisionist techniques within this analytical framework, Fast exposes the hidden processes that distort history and uses the exposé to transcend the formality of liberal pluralism, which promises only to give divergent viewpoints equal time. Historical interpretation, he implicitly argues, is always partisan; to ignore the power relations that have shaped the past and our knowledge of it is to misrepresent them as immutable features of a natural social order. *The Last Frontier* and *Freedom Road* do not simply revise conventional history. By examining its sources and the political logic underlying its falsehoods and omissions, they refute it. Moreover, they invite readers to consider official history's role in maintaining an oppressive power structure, which, as the Cheyenne and freedmen have shown, is not unalterable.

The Lavette novels, divorcing exposé and pluralism from an examination of power, cannot begin to raise these issues. Fast cannot help but bolster the "great man" and consensus history he apparently seeks to revise. As in his early work, American history is the story of struggle. On the one side stands a corrupt oligarchy of wealth; on the other side stand "the people," including wealthy and powerful individuals whose hearts are in the right place. One hears a faint echo of the Popular Front program for uniting progressives from all social sectors. But within the Lavette novels, the only consistent champions of democracy are a few humanitarians from the bourgeoisie. Fast's new cross-class alliance, unlike the Communist Party's Popular Front, is not simply joined but also led by ruling-class liberals who forfeit power and privilege to join with those less fortunate. The Lavettes show us that whereas the "bad" bourgeoisie is a source of oppression, the "good" bourgeoisie is the wellspring of a broad, multifaceted opposition to this same oppression. Both groups are part of a class of natural leaders, great men and women whose battles represent the march of history. Even the Lavettes, however, do not *make* history; they merely respond to the moral choices it places before them. The historical processes that bring particular choices to the fore at particular times are beyond comprehension. History, it seems, happens *to* people; it is out of their control.

Discussing *The Immigrants* in a 1977 interview, Fast described himself as a radical but insisted that his politics do not motivate his fiction. "I am always accused of messages," he said. "I don't intend them."[7] The messages are there nonetheless. All novels, whatever the aims of their writers, suggest answers to questions concerning human agency: How can people affect the world around them? What can they expect to achieve? Why do they succeed or fail? The Lavette saga treats these as essentially personal and moral questions, but the answers suggested have political meaning. The world Fast creates defies his characters' efforts to remake it; the balance of power between the forces of democracy and greed is static. Real movement occurs only in the personal-moral realm, as the "good" Lavettes learn to reject the pursuit of power. Their achievements are measured in ethical terms. A corrupt world, Fast implies, is to be transcended rather than changed. The best we can do is take righteous stands on the issues confronting us and try to survive with our virtue intact. This is the formula that redeems ruling-class moralists like Barbara. For the rest of us, who are not only offended but also oppressed by social injustice, it is a program for self-satisfied defeat.

Though he did not intend to politicize them, Fast did try to make the Lavette novels, in his own words, "reasonably good history."[8] Unfortunately, he chose a genre which made this a very difficult task, one apparently beyond his reach. Family sagas in the potboiler tradition are, under the best of circumstances, seriously flawed vehicles for the dramatization of history. Placing individuals within a world too complex and turbulent for any believable character to fully understand, they leave it to the narrator to explain the historical processes that have created and will transform that world. And demanding constant action and a great deal of dialogue, potboilers do not give the narrator much room to explore history.[9] Fast's narrative voice manages to impart many bits of historical information, but it does not integrate these data into an overarching vision of a society in flux. The Lavettes are touched by a number of epoch-making social movements, both progressive and reactionary, but Fast never leaves the personal-moral realm long enough to show how these movements made history as well as affecting individual lives. The outcome is an often stirring melodrama. The drama of history, however, is largely missing.

In the early 1940s Fast was far more successful in linking personal and historical drama. His political ambitions during that era were the bedrock of his achievements. He wanted to legitimate modern democratic movements by identifying a radical American heritage of popular revolt. This led him to create fiction that shows people making history, altering social structures and the balance of social power. The novels thus depict a world subject to change, and this kind of vision is at the core of all "reasonably good history." The superiority of these books also suggests that literary genres that place history itself at center stage and portray real-life people and events can do much more than melodramatic potboilers to make the past immediately meaningful. Novels like *The Last Frontier* and *Freedom Road,* which expose distortions within conventional versions of the past, demonstrate that the history that bored most people when they were in school is not only dull but also full of lies, half-truths, and gaping holes. These books, more than forty years old, have lasting value because they animate the question of power—a question generally ignored even by today's supposedly enlightened pluralist textbooks, which celebrate diversity but will not admit the existence of irreconcilable conflict. Describing how and in whose interests the historical record and historical consciousness are twisted to legitimate an unjust present, such novels can help to politicize our sense of what is at stake when we examine the past. They encourage a critical approach to conventional representations of the way things used to be and a healthy skepticism regarding official pronouncements about the way they are.

Into the Minds of Babes:

Children's Books and the Past

When I was a child, I read children's books. But when I became a man, as they say, I put away childish things. And I did not pick up those books again until I had children of my own. When I returned to them, at first as a self-consciously responsible reader-aloud, I chose for my young listener the novels that had once fascinated and transfixed me. And, in my other role as a struggling history graduate student, I was delighted to find how much these "classics" dealt with the past, being either old, enduring works themselves or set in some bygone time. The rosy glow of my own bygone days returned as I read aloud, but it was uncomfortably tinged now with the ugly hues of racism and sexism. Reading Hugh Lofting's Doctor Dolittle books to my son—fantasies with a readily apparent historical context: England in the 1830s and 1840s—was much like maneuvering about an intellectual minefield as I constantly came upon imperial descriptions of African "savages" and such tales as that of the comical black prince, Bumpo, tricked by the good doctor's promise to make him white.

The physical and mental toll of such reading sessions aside, the stereotypes in the classics—problems, to be sure, specific to the historical conditions of their writing—indicate the need to examine more recent children's history books, both fiction and nonfiction. My point is not to supplant the classics with new works, shunning Hugh Lofting or Robert Louis Stevenson in favor of "correct," if less artful, modern books. Rather, the older works must be complemented, their best qualities expanded and their shortcomings illuminated by the addition of new children's books that provide alternative interpretations and presentations of the past.[1] Young people increasingly display a dismal lack of knowledge about either the distant or the recent past.

BY JOSHUA BROWN

Even so public and protracted a crisis as the war in Indochina is now dimly understood or seen as irrelevant by teenagers just ten years after the fall of Saigon. Historical insensibility only grows worse as we march further back in time.[2] Young Americans' reading skills continue to spiral downward, and there is a related increase in the use of superficial docudramas on television and in motion pictures as the source of historical information.[3] All these factors emphasize the urgent need for engaging juvenile history books.

As I began to read children's history books, I was immediately overwhelmed by the quantity of titles published, including the number of juvenile periodicals devoted to history.[4] That quantity—not always the quality—indicated an enthusiastic commitment to teaching the past of which I had been ignorant, like, I soon discovered, many other historians based in the academy. Children's history books constitute a peculiar pedagogical ghetto: they address a large audience that academic historians never reach, and yet such books are largely unrecognized and rarely discussed in professional historical circles.

Despite this trend, or because of it, we must consider the ways children's books connect or fail to connect their young audience with the past. Many of the books merely repeat old bromides or use the past as a convenient and attractive vehicle for promoting modish trends in style and subject, but they also provide insights into how the past is expressed in print to a broad popular audience. More important, the best children's histories suggest new ways to present information and ideas that remain, for the most part, encased in turgid academic treatises. Defying the expectations of the cynic, a number of recent works do not dilute or reduce historical scholarship in the name of accessibility but rather creatively mold content and form to produce rigorous and accessible studies. The following journey through children's history books makes no claims for comprehensiveness, let alone scientific precision. Consider this a brief, impressionistic view of a vast terrain, previously unknown to this explorer and many other people concerned with the manner and means of presenting history to the public.

T he children's historical picture book is a good place to begin. The illustration of adult fiction and nonfiction has declined throughout the twentieth century, the victim of rising printing costs and, perhaps, more streamlined aesthetics. The wedding of graphics and text in the children's picture book would seem to afford an opportunity to survey a creative departure from such adult fare. Ironically, in the last two decades the children's picture book has filled that gap in publishing. The vagaries of the market have increasingly molded these books in a manner that appeals to an adult and upper-middle-class audience.

Title II of the Elementary and Secondary Education Act of 1964 provided $100 million a year to school libraries for the purchase of books and educational materials. With expanded budgets school libraries made an unprecedented amount of reading material available to students, in the process transforming the children's book industry. In the 1960s, 85 percent of children's books published were sold to school and community libraries. But publishers and readers were not long blessed with federally and state-funded educational largesse: the Indochina War, inflation and recession, and—beginning with the Nixon presidency and culminating in the Reagan administration—the ideological and political attack on such federal and local programs ended the sponsored flow of educational materials into school and community libraries. Library acquisitions declined drastically. The impact on egalitarian access to reading materials for young readers of different classes and races is obvious, if difficult to quantify. For book publishers the impact was clear: for some houses the library market has now dwindled to approximately 25 percent of total sales.[5]

Faced with the contraction of their institutional market, children's book publishers increasingly turned to the bookstore as the focus for sales. And since very few children frequent bookstores (in sharp contrast to their habits in school and local libraries), publishers are now packaging children's books for adults. The adults publishers have targeted tend to be white and upper middle class, with the disposable income to supplement their children's education and fulfill the status requirements of a culture of ostentatious consumption.

What most effectively catches the eye of the affluent, conscientious, and status-conscious book buyer? Publishers have ascertained that swathing well-known and enduring titles in new and elegant packaging satisfies the educational and social aspirations of that adult consumer. In the last few years, the children's book trade has been flooded by newly illustrated deluxe editions of works in the public domain, like those of the Brothers Grimm and Lewis Carroll, which require only an expenditure for a "name" artist or illustrator to adorn them. "The mania for publishing modern classics of children's literature in lush, expensive, newly illustrated editions," the editor of the *Horn Book Magazine,* the leading children's book periodical, has noted, seems to augur the revival of the " 'gift book'—a great commercial success in the early part of the century—which proclaimed the cultivation and taste of its owner."[6]

The quality of these books aside—and many of them display merely updated and shallow versions of the original artwork—the impact on children's picture books, especially those on a historical theme, has been profound. Subject matter is too often dictated by prevailing pop cultural trends and tastes. Successful history-oriented commercial ventures soon wend their way into the children's market. The popular television series *Upstairs, Downstairs* spawned a series of picture books about upper-class Edwardian England; the spectacular, gold-laden Tutankhamun traveling exhibition of 1979 was followed by a line of children's books chronicling ancient Egyptian dynastic life.[7] Now, with the popularity of David Lean's mawkish version of *A Passage to India* and the Public Broadcasting System's dramatization of Paul Scott's *The Jewel in the Crown,* it is fairly safe to predict that the British Raj will be a ubiquitous theme in forthcoming children's histories.

The nostalgia and romance of these productions pervade children's picture books. One of the most prevalent themes is the agrarian past. Donald Hall's *Ox-Cart Man* (Viking, 1979) presents the yearly cycle of a farm family in what looks like early nineteenth-century New England. In simple, unadorned prose Hall relates the varied tasks that supported the household economy. The tale revolves around the farmer's journey to an unnamed town where he sells his produce and buys provisions, returning home to begin the cycle of production and distribution all over again. *Ox-Cart Man* is a calm, quaint, and, in the end, vacuous account of rural life: benign, clean, conflict-free, and untrammeled by any messy social relations that might interfere with the isolated, good-humored constellation of Ma, Pa, and the kids. It is a Reaganesque nineteenth-century paradise, the farm family performing its work and receiving its just rewards, unmediated by any larger, interdependent rural community, let alone governmental structure.

Lest I appear to be making undue demands on a book written for young children or calling for an unpleasant interpretation of the past, consider Martin Waddell's *Going West* (Harper & Row, 1983). Its minimal text, purportedly the journal kept by a young girl chronicling her family's trek westward some time in the mid-nineteenth century, features death and hardship, but in a way that bolsters the agrarian myth. There is a gesture toward understanding Indian-settler conflict (something akin to a tragic failure to communicate); however, all the characters are stock types from Hollywood westerns, from the trusty, crusty scout to both "good" and "bad" Indians.

The texts of these books convey only part of the message. It is in the relationship of words to graphics that they have the potential to create a fuller version of the past, one rich in visual detail and nuance, expanding the limited meaning of their texts.[8] As part of a commercial package, however, the images in these books are geared to support the message of nostalgia and romance. Barbara Cooney's illustrations in *Ox-Cart Man* are rendered in the primitive style of early American wood paintings. The great skill and grace of her artwork won her the prestigious 1980 Randolph Caldecott Medal for "the most distinguished illustrator of children's books." They are pretty, uncomplicated, and as bland as the text they illustrate. Philippe Dupasquier's illustrations for *Going West* are guaranteed to catch the adult eye, but in a different manner from Cooney's. Beautiful, at times majestic, western landscapes are cleverly juxtaposed with the rather cartoony style used for drawing the characters peopling the scenes. The pictures tend toward the whimsical or brutal, making this a kind of lavish comic book. They are often detailed and finely drawn, yet—as in a complicated, two-page overview of the town from which the settler family departs—nothing is really shown beyond a lot of wooden structures, unruly animals, and meandering figures. The cartoon quality of the characters is, I suppose, meant to be endearing, but the careful viewer will note that, in this book at least, all Indians still look alike.[9]

The overall message, which appeals to adults who buy these books for their children, is that life in the rural past was simple and wholesome, if fraught with an elemental kind of danger and excitement. The child reading or being read these books is confronted by a false totality, words and pictures reinforcing one another to create a closed, complete universe devoid of true detail, contradictions, questions, or unsettling ideas. Substance has been tamped down and trendy aesthetics promoted: glitz, pure and simple.

Not all historical picture books rely on color, glitter, and whimsy to attract the adult consumer's attention. Children and grownups are curious about how things worked and how they were built, and a large number of juvenile picture books court that interest. Many can be categorized as illustrated histories of technology, and they tend to be written in more complex prose than the rural idylls, perhaps in an effort to entice and entertain parents as they read aloud to their children. But here one also senses that nostalgia is part of the books' appeal: in an era of megabytes and microchips, they are celebrations of the good old machine, a homage to moving parts.

There is nothing inherently troublesome about the wide assortment of children's picture books about machines and objects. However, the machines and objects are almost always divorced from the social, cultural, and economic conditions within which they were devised, not to mention detached from the people who built and operated them. The fetish of the technological artifact characterizes a book like John L. Loeper's *Galloping Gertrude: By Motorcar in 1908* (Atheneum, 1980), an unrelieved paean to the jalopy expressed through a middle-class family's anecdotal thirty-mile trip, interrupted by occasional facts about the commercial development of the automobile. The use of period advertisements for illustrations only emphasizes the glories of the showroom, a salesman's interpretation of the car's role in early twentieth-century America. [10]

More varied in time and style, the pictures in Norman Anderson and Walter Brown's *Ferris Wheels* (Pantheon, 1983) also fail to relate any qualitative information beyond the impression that an endless number of circular contraptions were constructed. *Ferris Wheels* may be an antiquarian's delight, but anyone who wonders why machines became popular playthings at the turn of the century or about the relationship between the mechanization of production and that of amusement will find it boring and predictable after only a few pages. Certainly, to those who share my bewilderment at the characterization of technological torture chambers as "amusement parks," this collection of pictures and fun-facts on Ferris wheels is neither enlightening nor of compelling interest.

Picture books can do much better. In four books—*Cathedral* (Houghton Mifflin, 1973), *City* (1974), *Pyramid* (1975), and *Castle* (1977)—David Macaulay demonstrates in a lively, detailed, and creative manner that perceptions of the past do not have to be reduced to disembodied structures and objects. In *Cathedral*, for example, Macaulay relates the extended construction, beginning in the thirteenth century, of the imaginary Gothic cathedral of Chutreaux. Although he presents the particulars of Gothic architecture, Macaulay never limits his concerns to stones and flying buttresses, but ties the construction of the cathedral to the social relations of the town, the town's relationship to wider feudal society, and the direct activity of the people who work on the structure. The drawings, an interesting mix of primitive technique and complex perspective, allow the reader to understand the construction in both theory and practice through bird's-eye angles that heighten appreciation for the work of the past. The book is demanding, and adult translation may be helpful for young children. But Macaulay has succeeded in bridging adult concerns for aesthetics and information and children's requirements for compelling reading.

Yet when Macaulay ventures into the industrial era, he becomes engrossed by the kind of fetishism his other books so successfully avoid. *Mill* (1983) is about the structural and technological evolution of the nineteenth-century New England textile factory. But for all his loving detail and careful illustrations—somewhat muddled and muddied by the use of washes instead of the line drawings in the other books—Macaulay overlooks the nature of textile production itself as well as the people who made the cloth on the machines he describes. He is not unaware of this lapse: each chronological section ends with a brief, synoptical selection of letters and journal accounts concerning national events, life in the town, and work in the factories. But their brevity and parenthetical presentation merely inform the reader that these tidbits are of peripheral importance.[11]

Finally, if the rural idyll or past technological wonders do not capture the adult consumer's fancy, a familiar face or name might. Biographies of men and, to a lesser extent, women constitute another major category of picture book, although—since these books so assiduously court adult trends—they rarely depict lives that are not "recognized" or "revered." More women and minorities are now represented than were a generation ago, but because recognition tends to dignify those who were previously beyond the pale, too many picture book biographies excise or ignore the controversial aspects of these lives.[12]

Jean Fritz's celebrated and extremely popular series of Bicentennial picture books about leaders of the American Revolution—*And Then What Happened, Paul Revere?* (Coward, McCann & Geoghegan, 1973), *Why Don't You Get a Horse, Sam Adams?* (1974), *Where Was Patrick Henry on the 29th of May?* (1975), *What's the Big Idea, Ben Franklin?* (1976), and *Will You Sign Here, John Hancock?* (1976)—is characteristic of the recent picture book biography. Pure hagiography has given way to the human-interest angle. Fritz's books are refreshing in their irreverent portrayal of the Founding Fathers, alluding to Hancock's egotism, for example, or Sam Adams' slovenliness.[13] Transforming the hallowed into the picaresque—aided, in particular, by caricaturelike illustrations—certainly "mortalizes" these men, but Fritz's exhibition of their personal foibles ultimately has little impact on the Founding Fathers myth. Their social and political world remains confidently white, male, consensual, and uncontroversial; women are of negligible concern, and blacks were not slaves, you understand, but "field workers."[14]

Picture book publishers appear all too willing to sacrifice intellectual rigor, a textured sense of the past, and complexity in their rush after the adult market. Among picture book biographies, there are rare examples in which the dialectic of art and text is creatively exploited, permitting the tension between the two to enhance complex information, critical perspectives, and a sense of the larger historical context. David Lasker's *The Boy Who Loved Music* (Viking, 1979), illustrated by Joe Lasker, is a model book in the biographical category. Using a deceptively simple format, the book presents the relationship of an individual to his society. Seen through the eyes of Karl, a young horn player in the service of Prince Nicolaus Esterhazy, it is the story of the composition of Joseph Haydn's "Farewell Symphony." We learn about court life in the eighteenth-century Hungarian empire, not through a wide-eyed, glamorous portrait of life in the Esterhazy castle, but as part of a finely detailed social panorama. In text and illustration, with the pictures often adding commentary and information, the Laskers present a charming but extremely caustic picture of the production of "high" culture during feudalism, and of the aristocracy's treatment of the musicians under its rule, as well as a sense of how musicians and other servants responded within the limited confines of the court. *The Boy Who Loved Music* shows that a complicated, sensitive, and critical image of the past can succeed without surrendering to crassly commercial packaging and simplification.[15]

C hildren's fiction in general is the proud progeny of publishing. It is printed with the fanfare of "artistic commitment," receiving lavish attention from book dealers, teachers, librarians, reviewers, and young readers themselves. Jonathan Cott, for example, waxes rhapsodic about fiction's potential to influence children's later beliefs and lifestyles; for those adults who return to the books of their youth, fiction also can restore imagination and recover forgotten experience.[16] In this approving view, there is a certain pretension that only fiction merits consideration as children's "literature," to the detriment of juvenile nonfiction, which we will address later.

Whatever one's feelings about the metaphysical, restorative properties of children's fiction, this attitude is central to our discussion of children's books on historical subjects because, in contrast to picture books, young readers of junior and senior high school age select their own fiction books. Historical fiction is probably the major literary form through which most children are exposed to history outside the classroom.[17] For many educators, fiction is attractive because it lures children toward history, coating "awkward" facts in a patina of entertaining plot and prose.[18] However, children's historical literature can do more than sneak in dreaded facts and figures; it can transform the dead and dry past into tangible experience. It can give young readers an emphatic "feel" for another time and way of life. As Anna Davin writes, historical stories have the power to unsettle and challenge readers if "they engage the emotions [and] they excite the imagination."[19]

The possibilities of that challenge are highly problematic, since these books are affected by history as much as they represent it. Let us consider a classic of juvenile historical fiction, Esther Forbes's *Johnny Tremain* (Houghton Mifflin, 1943), the story of an apprentice silversmith who is caught up in the Boston patriotic cause of the 1770s. Forbes, whose 1942 *Paul Revere and the World He Lived In* won the Pulitzer Prize, based her tale on extensive research and knowledge of colonial Boston; for me and many young readers of the

1950s, her book (along with the Walt Disney movie based on it) shaped early perceptions and understanding of the American Revolution. Returning to *Johnny Tremain* after all these years, I am struck by its detailed and careful social and geographical survey of colonial Boston life, its sensitive portrayal of artisanal work (albeit one that includes only masters and apprentices, no troublesome journeymen), its canny presentation of deference and equality, and its exciting descriptions of popular protests such as the Tea Party. *Johnny Tremain* is compelling historical fiction, but it is also enmeshed in the politics and historiography of its author's time, an amalgam composed of vestigial Popular Front politics and World War II patriotism, which subsumed class divisions and radical politics under a broad coalition defending "traditional" American values, and conservative Whig interpretations of the revolutionary cause as amorphous and broad, with rifts and differences based on personality and not conflicting aims rooted in class position and ideology. Even more to the point, however, is the underlying complacence of the book, an upbeat picture of the Revolution that is dismissive of the "evil" Boston mob and blind to blacks and women, who merely populate the fringes of the plot in benign, but nevertheless racist and sexist, portrayals.[20]

One need only compare *Johnny Tremain* with James Lincoln Collier and Christopher Collier's more recent *My Brother Sam Is Dead* (Four Winds Press, 1974) to get a sense of the limitations of the classics and the postive transformation of children's historical fiction in the present generation. This story of a western Connecticut farm family's division over the revolutionary cause confronts, among other issues, New England slavery and black participation in the Revolution. By the 1970s children's fiction generally reflected the social and political movements that had arisen a decade earlier. Federal funding of schools and libraries and changing attitudes toward pedagogy that shunned standard texts in favor of innovative and more customized methods of teaching encouraged an unprecedented expansion of the subject matter and style of children's literature. Despite the cutbacks beginning in the 1970s, lily-white and tame themes in fiction continue to be replaced by books that challenge stereotypes, have women and members of minority groups as protagonists, and court areas of controversy, from sexuality to violence, from sexism to racism.[21]

The celebrated moments and men of the past have been largely supplanted by the experiences and actions of women in the nineteenth- and twentieth-century movement for equal rights and blacks in the struggle for civil rights in the North and South, the battle for trade union organization and recognition, the destruction of Native American civilizations in the West, and the clash of cultures resulting from immigration.[22] Yet the critical aspects of these books remain problematic and partial. *Johnny Tremain*'s limitations notwithstanding, for example, Forbes's work presented a cogent, textured sense of life in the past, an aspect that more recent works sadly lack. We are now confronted with a plethora of past experiences, a pluralistic portrait of American history that is varied, controversial, and stirring in its quest for justice and equality in the eye of history. People acted in the past, the new historical fiction tells us, many different types of people. What much recent work fails to provide, however, is a sense of the larger context, of the relationship of specific experiences to the general conditions surrounding them, of the contingencies of action and belief, of the structures that acted on protagonists. The "pastness of the past," to use Natalie Zemon Davis' phrase, is missing.[23]

The new emphasis on the publication of "nonracist, nonsexist" books is admirable, yet writers have lurched toward relevance with little concern for the historical integrity of their fiction. Characters are created that conform to current role models: independent women, hard-working and caring parents, solid and democratic families. They do not express the concerns of their time but of *our* time; their aspirations and actions do not reflect the historical conditions that shaped consciousness and behavior in their era but, rather, the concerns of a late twentieth-century author writing to teach relevant, responsible late twentieth-century ideas.[24] The result is not simply muddled history mixed with laudable lessons; it is an illusory image of the past that supports a delusory concept of the present. These historical protagonists are the exceptions, the special people whose gumption and ambition are justly rewarded; their recalcitrant, atavistic, and visionless compatriots go justly unrewarded.

Several recent juvenile novels, all dealing with immigration to the United States and each featuring a self-possessed female protagonist, illustrate the problem. Marge Blaine's *Dvora's Journey* (Holt, Rinehart & Winston, 1979) relates the flight of a Jewish family from their Russian *shtetl* to America in 1904. Relationships in Dvora's family are egalitarian and enlightened (clearly her parents read Dr. Spock). *Shtetl* life remains murky throughout, except for the impression that the neighbors' households lack the nurturance and compassion of our heroine's. The book ends just when it should be taking off, with Dvora and her brother boarding a ship bound for America, where, by clear implication, the streets *were* paved with gold. Lucinda May's *The Other Shore* (Atheneum, 1979) and Bette Sue Cumming's *Now, Ameriky* (Atheneum, 1979) take their protagonists across the Atlantic to New York—one, Gabriella, a young Italian woman, the other, Brigid, a teenager fleeing the Irish potato famine. May's novel displays diligent research on the early twentieth-century labor movement, the padrone system and contract labor, and the 1911 Triangle Shirtwaist fire, whereas Cumming's book is a bit light on concrete information. Both books are unrelentingly melodramatic, forced, and unconvincing. More to the point, Gabriella and Brigid are exceptional individuals, like no one else in their neighborhoods. The novels are uniformly upbeat and fantastic in their tales of final assimilation and uplift, achieved through diligence, effort, and strong character. The heroines rise above their Italian and Irish peers to the ruby-red sunset of the American middle class. One need not quarrel with the cult of social mobility to be dissatisfied with works that fail to acknowledge the complexity of immigrant communities or the nature of cultures that do not conform to a modern, middle-class ethos. Although ethnicity is an issue in these books, class positions are amazingly transitory and have no weight on the characters' ideas, behavior, or relationships. In direct contrast to these books, Sondra Gordon Langford's *Red Bird of Ireland* (Atheneum, 1983), also set in the potato famine era, testifies that an author of children's historical fiction can construct a full and uncompromising portrait of a community, in this case Catholic tenant farmers, against the larger background of class relations in colonized nineteenth-century Ireland. Bravery as well as duplicity and fatalism are shown as a collective experience, even if seen through the eyes of one protagonist.

The issues of relevance and role-modeling cannot be divorced from the didactic structure of many of these novels. There is a sameness to their presentation, a literalness; their characters live their lives within the confines of a traditional narrative with the notecards of the author's research protruding from every other paragraph. The novels come across as thinly disguised lectures. After reading so many juvenile historical novels recently, I found myself asking what kind of impact these lessons had on a young reader. Admittedly, they are accessible, but they are also predictable, unsurprising, and not much fun. The reader is the student, the author is the teacher: the relationship is encased in the form of these novels. Are young readers, let alone authors, limited to one form of presentation in historical literature? Must historical fiction for young readers remain a diluted version of the longer, blustery social melodramas that populate bestseller lists?[25]

Several recent juvenile novels depicting early industrial life and labor indicate that some authors have found different and compelling ways to present the past while maintaining the integrity of the historical moment and interpreting the past through a modern consciousness. An unsuccessful work, Athena Lord's *A Spirit to Ride the Whirlwind* (Macmillan, 1981), will help illuminate the contributions of the alternatives. She treats the side of textile millwork in the Lowell, Massachusetts, of the 1830s that was neglected by David Macaulay. However, the novel is mired in a traditional narrative that confuses the past and present; the youthful protagonists are class-conscious proletarians way before their time. Two other novels, Jean Marzollo's *Halfway Down Paddy Lane* (Dial Press, 1981) and Jill Paton Walsh's *A Chance Child* (Farrar, Straus & Giroux, 1978), use the science fiction convention of time travel to break the bonds of didactic narrative. In *Halfway Down Paddy Lane,* we first meet eleven-year-old Kate within the familiar confines of her gentrified twentieth-century New England town, replete with an old factory converted to a nostalgia-ridden shopping mall. One morning she awakens in the same house over one hundred years earlier. She is a member of an immigrant Irish working-class family employed in the factory she has so often shopped in. The author employs the usual teenage romance and melodrama, but her clever juxtaposing of modern sensibilities and historical setting elicits startling insights about time, consciousness, and conditions that the traditional narrative cannot relate.

A Chance Child begins in contemporary England, where a brutalized boy, knowing only the epithet assigned to him, "Creep," journeys down one of the abandoned industrial canals that laced the country before the era of the railroad. He is transported back to the early nineteenth century, where he witnesses child labor under early industrial capitalism. Accompanied by two children of that time, Creep flees from one oppressive, almost surreal, work environment after another. While Creep is lost in the past, his half-brother desperately searches for him in the present, finally coming across his name in Parliamentary Papers found in the local library. *A Chance Child* is a truly stunning book that combines evocative writing and a subtle understanding of history, exercising imagination in ways that give history greater resonance and meaning than traditional narrative can attain. I can think of no better introduction to the impact of industrial capitalism—or critique of how history is taught—than these two novels, for either children or adults.[26]

C hildren's historical nonfiction might well be called the "junior varsity" of what "real" historians do, unmediated by the frills of picture books and the gloss of fiction. Its familiarity, however, seems to have engendered more of the proverbial contempt than camaraderie. Except for the bread-and-butter product—the textbook—historians barely deign to discuss, let alone read, children's historical nonfiction, disparaging such works as mere dilutions and oversimplifications of their craftwork.[27] And among many of those who judge and promote children's books, historical nonfiction is treated with lofty disdain.

The negative response from children's book evaluators and reviewers derives in part from their defensive and pretentious attitude toward literary merit. In their view, nonfiction cheapens the very name of juvenile literature; the conventional wisdom has given nonfiction the damning label "information book," a volume filled with facts but showing little concern for style or creativity. Nonfiction books are said to lack the hallmarks of craft and art that picture books and stories exemplify. When a nonfiction work is reviewed, critics focus on content; they assume, says Milton Meltzer, a leading author of children's historical nonfiction, "that in children's books nothing is explored in any depth or with sensitivity and, therefore, that writers of nonfiction for children need only find the facts and type them up." Similar treatment of these books in the world of mainstream criticism has only exacerbated this prejudice. The *New York Times Book Review* has for many years virtually ignored children's nonfiction, devoting its already limited space to picture books and novels. Nonfiction is the ugly stepchild of children's books.[28]

To be sure, much of the children's nonfiction published each year seems mass-produced and in one critical author's view "perfunctory, tasteless, and unreadable, although as a feeble defense it is said they fill an educational need." It could be argued that the few "quality" nonfiction books receive the attention they deserve. But while hack novels and hack picture books do get reviewed, the mass of nonfiction—both works meritorious and *manqué*, if you will—does not. This double standard is mirrored in the literary prizes awarded to writers of children's books. Since its inception in 1922, the annual Newbery Medal for "the most distinguished contribution to American literature for children" has been awarded to only six works of nonfiction.[29]

What of historical nonfiction in particular? On rereading, the historical nonfiction classics of my childhood bear out the prevailing negative connotation. The popular Bobbs-Merrill Childhood of Famous Americans series, Grosset & Dunlop Signature Biographies, and Random House Landmark books are severely limited in scope and style. The Landmark titles, some of which are currently being reprinted in paperback editions, tend toward military histories more preoccupied with heroics and bodycounts than context and the laudatory biographies of great white men, with occasional bows to a Clara Barton or a George Washington Carver. In many cases they merely dilute adult bestsellers to broaden the market for an already successful commodity.[30]

The dismal tradition set by such series has been carried forward in many recent works. Publishers' booklists are still infested with apparently authorized biographies and uncritical institutional histories, such as Lawrence Fellows' booster piece, *A Gentle War: The Story of the Salvation Army* (Macmillan, 1979), devoid of any critical or contextual content. And such fact-laden, complacent, and inept packages as Wyatt Blassingame's *The Look-It-Up-Book of Presidents* (Random House, 1968, 1984) continue to fill up somebody's bookshelf (although, I *did* learn that James Monroe's face adorns the five-thousand-dollar bill and that William Howard Taft kept cows on the White House lawn).

Yet, as in the case of fiction, the social and political movements and the new historiography of the 1960s and 1970s had a long-term effect on history written for young readers. The publishing industry lagged behind events, but by the mid-1970s the subjects of juvenile histories had ceased to be white, male, and upbeat. Along with the ever-present hackwork, the current market includes many books that strive for controversy and chronicle the lives of people who were sorely neglected in the consensus fifties.[31] Many of the books that address "correct" topics nevertheless ignore the issue of presentational form and thus limit the impact of their content. Their pedantic, informational quality often dooms them to remain on library shelves, except when called to duty for forced-march homework assignments. Few are likely to be picked up by a youngster and read with enthusaism, let along edification. As the best of the nonfiction writers lament, the general critical derogation of children's "information" books represents a kind of self-fulfilling prophecy: the books are derided for their lack of creativity, but reviewers and educational evaluators find merit in the plenitude of their contents, in the quantity of up-to-date facts they contain. To put it another way, the educational value of nonfiction books is based on a criterion of utility, not one of qualitative writing or pedagogy. The accuracy of information and not the ideas presented or the questions raised are evaluated. On the other hand, many writers have called for a reconsideration of the relationship of content, form, and style; traditional nonfiction should be replaced with a "literary nonfiction" characterized by "storytelling skill, descriptive power, vivid prose, graphic excellence, and sharply defined focus."[32]

Such a call to arms may sound familiar to historians, who have recently heard much talk regarding the decline of literary excellence in the face of pedantic, social scientific cant. Historians have been woefully uncaring about how their history is transmitted and its general inability to reach a wider audience. The decline of historiographic accessibility is one aspect of the larger argument for a return to "narrative" history. And here one must more cautiously evaluate what seems to be a similar call on the part of children's nonfiction authors, historians among them, for a "literary nonfiction." Imbedded in the scholarly debate is a conservative attack on the findings and methods of the last generation, particularly the retrieval and analysis of the new social history, which places the lives of ordinary people alongside those of the great men and traditions previously chronicled. Many historians call for a return to the "wider," more traditional vision of the past. It is the new history's potential to create an alternative vision of the past that is really at issue: the debate represents a struggle over what constitutes "real" history. Therefore, we cannot be content to merely chronicle the past, no matter how attractive that chronicle might be.[33]

With the above debate bumping about the historical profession, one would expect children's historical nonfiction to come out boldly for narrative, but the issue of pedagogy adds another consideration, one that requires that history not simply relate "the what and when of events, but also . . . the why and how." It is not enough to tell a good tale; the young reader must be challenged to think, to question the information at hand. Milton Meltzer speaks for other committed popular historians when he asks:

> Can such books written for young people flower into thought? Yes, if you bore into the subject with an eye sharpened by the need to see beyond fact to value and meaning. If you look for particulars that universalize experience and make it memorable. If you are concerned not with "covering a subject" as the curriculum-constructor thinks of it, but with discovering something meaningful in it and finding the language to bring the reader to the same moment of recognition.[34]

Meltzer's prescriptions for a committed history acknowledge that history is affected as much by the way it is told as by what it tells.

A number of sophisticated and accessible works have boldly offered alternative visions of the past to young readers, works that are surprising both for their complex ideas and theses and for the recent, critical scholarship they reflect. One particularly effective form of children's history is the "social problem" book. Covering a wide range of topics, these books are distinctive for their ability to intervene with a historical consciousness into present-day controversies. The past these books relate is not the detritus left us by our forebears, but events and actions that illuminate the present and, to a certain extent, inform what one may do about contemporary problems. Meltzer himself is a master of this form, and his recent *Ain't Gonna Study War No More* (Harper & Row, 1985) is a skillful survey of moral and political resistance to military service throughout history. Meltzer never succumbs to the vulgarities of relevance—this is not a simple tale of morality—but is always cognizant of the differing historical contexts of the actions he relates and the dilemmas they represent (witness his nuanced discussion of draft resistance during the Civil War as compared with resistance to the Vietnam War). Other "problem" books tackle issues in a different manner, using seemingly mundane or frivolous topics to reveal complex and troublesome historical roots. Georgette McHague's *Meet the Witches* (Lippincott, 1984) is written with great whimsy and enthusiasm, the author practically rubbing her hands with glee over her theme of witchcraft and sorcery. And, indeed, the work is a lot of fun to read. It is also a wide-ranging study of the history of witchcraft with insights into mythology, literature, popular culture, misogyny, feminism, and biology.[35]

Not only do these works display ingenious and insightful methods of relating the past; they are based on original primary scholarship as well. Perhaps most indicative of the impact of primary research are the biographies of individuals sorely neglected in both popular and academic histories. Beatrice Siegel's *Lillian Wald of Henry Street* (Macmillan, 1983) is an impressive, full-scale biography of the Progressive reformer written for a high-school-age audience. A critical and comprehensive portrait of an individual and an era, it addresses issues such as the complications of creating a cross-class alliance of women and the limitations of reform ideology in the Progressive Era. As in the above works, it crosses the line between "adult" and "children's" history, combining narrative skill with conceptual sophistication.[36]

Perhaps the best example of wide-ranging and compelling children's history is John Anthony Scott's Living History Library, published by Knopf in the late 1960s and 1970s. This series of books by popular and academic historians was an ambitious effort to transform the larger conception of American history for young readers through accounts, based on original research and the most recent secondary scholarship, that explained how particular issues or developments appeared to "the anonymous people who were just as much makers of that history as the kings and queens and presidents and generals." Scott and his editor at Knopf, Fabio Coen, wanted to "go beyond the typical narrative history to convey the *quality* of the experience as it was lived and felt by the people who were part of it."[37]

The series is no pure-and-simple populist version of American history; ranging from studies of colonial settlement to the New Deal, its books offer a lucid synthesis of American social, political, economic, and cultural history by pulling together the "great" and "small" to present a broad, transformative perspective on little-known as well as famous events, in both cases challenging traditional conceptions and simplistic notions of the progress of the American past. It is the method of this history, however—telling the story through the eyes of participants and contemporary observers—that is its hallmark. A wide variety of documentary source materials—letters, diaries, memoirs, legislative reports, press accounts—are used, drawing larger context and everyday experience together in a manner that parallels the best academic histories (which are rarely so well-written). Rather than merely asserting the importance of seeing "ordinary people" as the makers of history, the books tell that history through their eyes; this narrative method both animates that interpretation and significantly challenges the traditional narrative of the American past. Furthermore, the books give the reader a brief, tantalizing sense of a historiographical debate, relating the important concept that, even for historians, the past is open to conflicting interpretations. All together, the volumes in the Living History Library present a unique alternative picture of America.[38]

Despite the excellence of the Living History Library series, its use of graphics reflects a general problem in children's historical nonfiction. Each book in the series is heavily illustrated with archival visual material. Thoroughly integrated with the text, the pictures add another dimension to the history being told. Although this is a welcome change from the parsimonious use of graphics in most academic and popular histories, even here one would have wished for a more interventionist approach to the use of illustration. The captions, with rare exceptions, are brief, and the pictures are never used as lessons themselves, to be evaluated as historical evidence, whether for the accuracy of their depiction of events or the ideas and perceptions they portray. Much in the manner of recent textbooks that display colorful and artistic graphics, the illustrations serve to transform the learning of history into a "sensuous experience," but the young reader's critical visual faculties remain unexercised.[39]

The impact of books such as those in the Living History Library should not be underestimated. Even in the short time many of these books have been available, they have become alternative classics, replacing the old, complacent histories of the 1950s and 1960s. Their readership is much wider than the term "children's book" would imply; in fact, many adults read these works. Their accessibility and comprehensiveness, their special form and content, make them ideal for teaching purposes. As just one example, many history instructors use Milton Meltzer's *Bread—and Roses: The Struggle of American Labor, 1865–1915* (Knopf, 1967) for courses in labor education centers as well as college classrooms. It is still the best popular history available, pulling together organizational struggles and the conditions of life and labor in the period, all through the testimony of the men and women who lived that history. Other books have not fared so well.

Excellence and utility in children's historical nonfiction are not sufficient to keep books in print. The Living History Library was discontinued in the late 1970s, and only a handful of the titles have appeared in paperback editions. As economic crisis and the decline in government funding have diminished all-important institutional sales, the innovative quality of such works, paradoxically, makes them a commercial risk. Books that are not about famous people or by famous authors might receive favorable reviews, but librarians are unlikely to expend limited funds on names and writers they do not recognize. In an educational book market dominated by textbooks, alternative children's histories are not as devotedly hawked by publishers' sales staff as the tried-and-true, and less threatening, pedagogical tract. It is a wonder, in the era of Reagan, that these alternative series continue to appear at all. But their fate seems to be dismally assured.[40]

The best children's histories offer a concerned and interventionist approach to popular pedagogy. The authors and their works are actively engaged in discovering how children—and, apparently, many adults—learn history, experimenting in creative and compelling ways with the presentation of the past to a wide public. They effectively bridge the gap between academic knowledge and popular perception of the past. Their efforts are all the more important because professional historians seem unconcerned over whether their findings reach a large audience or not.

But, as we have seen, the problem hardly lies at the door of the academy. The publishing fate of many of the best children's books is alarming. These books offer exciting alternatives to the deadened and predictable textbook, but while the number of text titles multiplies, comprehensive and comprehensible history books for children go out of print. The attack on social funding and the economic crisis threaten to doom the children's history project, if only by forcing writers and editors constantly to start over again. The books themselves cannot create a readership or a solid base of support. Their production requires conditions under which they may thrive and grow and find greater use in both the classroom and the home. The practical accessibility of children's history books will continue to suffer until we discover ways to create institutions that wholeheartedly and uncompromisingly value education and knowledge.[41] But things would be very different, then, wouldn't they?

★5★

John Ford's
Drums Along the Mohawk:

*The Making
of an American Myth*

As chronicles of American history, of white American society's conquest of its continent and the meaning of that conquest, western movies are a powerful ideological vehicle. The genre has done more than any academic history to shape Americans' sense of who they are, how they became that way, and whether they should be pleased with themselves. "I knowed the Indians for what they was, and I knowed General George Armstrong Custer for what he was," says Jack Crabb (Dustin Hoffman) in Arthur Penn's *Little Big Man* (1970). "Listen to my tale, it's a true one, and I ain't gonna tell it like no history man," proclaims the title song in Ralph Nelson's *Soldier Blue* (1970). Both films present accounts of Indian life from the Indians' point of view, in strong contrast to such earlier films as Raoul Walsh's *They Died with Their Boots On* (1941), a romanticized biography of Custer, and King Vidor's *Northwest Passage* (1939), which presents Native Americans as drunken, cowardly, bloodthirsty brutes. A public whose historical imagination has been shaped by the work of Penn and Nelson will have a different view of the clash between Indians and whites from one that saw the work of Walsh and Vidor.

Like academic historiography, historical fiction is more than a simple encounter with the past. Whether academic or fictional, filmed or written, any reconstruction of the past is a cultural artifact, reflecting its own time and intervening in the world in which it is produced. The ideological and social functions of any reconstruction of the past should interest the historian who accepts that the past, the present, and the reconstruction of the past are all part of the world in which she or he lives. The issue is by no means an academic one, for even filmmakers have worried about it. John Ford posed it directly in *The Man Who Shot Liberty Valance* (1962), which uses flashback to render

BY EDWARD COUNTRYMAN

ironic the legends that a community has woven for itself. In so doing, it also makes an irony of the American triumphalism that much of Ford's earlier work had celebrated. Jean-Luc Godard explored the issue from a different perspective in *The Wind from the East* (1969), a film that demonstrates the intensely political character of the conventions that the western uses. *The Wind from the East* is a difficult, even tedious, film. Nonetheless, study of it forces a confrontation with the problem of the terms on which any historical text recreates the past. It demands that its viewer ask what assumptions governed the text's composition. These assumptions establish what the text will treat as important and what it will ignore; what it will accept as "given" and what it will treat as problematic; which questions it will discuss and which ones it will resolve by silence. They form the conceptual framework that the text will articulate.

But unlike academic historiography, westerns have a double framework, for they are fiction as well as history. A historical fiction might be at once deeply unfaithful to the past that it ostensibly presents and highly satisfying as a work of art, as Shakespeare's history plays show. But Hollywood cinema is above all produced for a mass audience in a highly technological and highly bureaucratized society. A Hollywood film *can* be a work of art; it certainly *is* the result of a complex, expensive industrial process. As several analysts have suggested, a fiction made in these circumstances can work to undermine rather than strengthen historical consciousness. It can substitute for an awareness of the *social* character of historical development a general ahistorical sense that whatever exists is natural and unchallengeable.[1] The effect will be all the more powerful when the film's text deals explicitly with the past, as in the classic western *Drums Along the Mohawk,* directed by John Ford and released by Twentieth Century–Fox in 1939.

Drums Along the Mohawk traces the experiences of a young married couple, Gil and Lana Martin (Henry Fonda and Claudette Colbert), on the New York frontier during the Revolutionary War. They endure two major Indian raids, the first causing the destruction of their home and the second the death of their benefactor, Mrs. McKlennar (Edna May Oliver). Before each war sequence a pastoral passage establishes the peaceful quality of pioneer life. At the end the Indians are vanquished and the pioneers return to their task of building civilization. The film is usually treated as simply a lesser Ford western, of interest primarily for its place in the director's artistic development.[2]

But *Drums* deals specifically with the American Revolution, offering its viewers an interpretation of the struggle for independence in one isolated community.[3] Moreover, the film was co-scripted by Lamar Trotti, who in the same year collaborated with Ford on *Young Mr. Lincoln,* the director's most immediate confrontation with the verifiable past. The editors of *Cahiers du Cinéma* have argued that *Young Mr. Lincoln* turned a historical man, living in uncertain, contingent time, into a mythic figure whose future and world-historical meaning were determined by his nature alone.[4] In *Drums,* Ford and Trotti similarly transformed the social history of the Revolution. The film belongs to a cultural stream that has helped convince Americans that their Revolution has nothing in common with those of other peoples. By de-revolutionizing the Revolution even as it reconstructs it, the film has helped rob Americans of an appreciation of their past. Its social meaning cannot be grasped without reference to this other, pseudo-revolutionary, de-politicizing part of its content.

The film took shape as a result of choices made by Ford, Trotti, and their co-workers. By the standards of the "authorship policy" that has played a major role in film criticism over the past two decades, this itself is a sign of Ford's standing, marking him as an original cinematic artist, as opposed to a mere filmer of stories, or *metteur en scéne.*[5] But the literary and historical sources of the film suggest that to read it purely in terms of Ford's authorship is to miss most of the cultural problem that it poses. *Drums* derives from Walter D. Edmonds' novel of the same title (1936), which went through three hardback editions, one of forty-nine printings. A Book-of-the-Month Club selection, it was serialized for a mass middle-class readershp in the *Saturday Evening Post.* Its paperback edition, still readily available in American bookstores, has had at least eighteen printings of its own, and the book is still in print.[6]

The novel's wide circulation ensured that in filming it Ford would confront problems akin to the ones he met in making *Young Mr. Lincoln.* Just as any treatment of Abraham Lincoln had to respect popular hagiography, so a film of *Drums* had to take account of the reading public's familiarity with Edmonds' characters. The film thus directly incorporates whole chunks of dialogue almost word for word. But despite its massive borrowing, the film reworks the meaning of the novel. Edmonds' book was not a "western," concerned in the manner of James Fenimore Cooper's "Leatherstocking" novels with the problems of a society in rapid expansion. Rather, following Cooper's *Satanstoe* and *The Chainbearer,* it was a historical romance concerned with the problems of a society turning upon itself. Edmonds explicitly sought to write a thinly fictionalized popular history of the Revolution. By his own account, only a bare handful of his characters were invented; everyone else he named "played actual parts."[7] Thus, Edmonds recognized that "history from the bottom up" requires an understanding of how public events have been intertwined with private lives, even at the level of eating, feeling, sleeping, and making love.[8]

Edmonds' book explores the human dimension of violent and rapid social transformation. Writing in the depths of the Great Depression, Edmonds showed that the crisis of his characters' lives stemmed not just from questions of political loyalty but also from questions of class, race, ethnicity, and sex. Neither social structure nor personality can withstand this revolutionary world. Spouses grow painfully in different directions; people go mad; pioneers and tribesmen alike divide into royalists and revolutionaries. Edmonds organized his Mohawk Valley not just around the simple categories of red and white, loyalist and patriot, but also around the complex ones of aristocrat and plebian, German and Scot, Seneca and Oneida, tenant and freeholder, and merchant and farmer. Although far from great literature, the novel suggests that the Revolution was a tangled, complex affair whose causes and consequences lay as much in American society as in that dispute about British taxation.

Edmonds' achievement can best be appreciated against the contours of the real Mohawk Valley on the eve of independence. Not newly settled—some white families had been there since before 1700—it was the social, political, and economic preserve of Sir William Johnson, who administered relations between Britain and the northern Indians until his death in 1774. Sir William served the crown well, and his rewards were great: a baronetcy, vast tracts of land, and a fortune well in excess of £100,000. For decades, Sir William had struggled to stabilize relations between whites and Indians, and in the valley he had tried to establish an ordered neofeudal world that would minimize the inevitable frictions of an expanding frontier society. As that world's *seigneur*, he treated his great estates as a domain to be filled with tenants, not as a speculation to be sold off when the price became right. He enjoyed personal ownership both of the local courthouse and jail and of the powers that they symbolized, making and unmaking sheriffs, judges, and assemblymen.[9]

In Johnson's world gentlemen worthy of Henry Fielding exchanged bawdy letters about their drinking sprees and their pursuit of women. Those same gentlemen freely horsewhipped "impertinent" folk who dared to call public meetings on the crisis with Britain. But by 1775 this world lay on the verge of dissolution, not only because of Sir William's death the year before, but also because angry men were challenging the Johnson family's power. Recognizing what their movement implied, Sir John Johnson, the baronet's heir, fortified Johnson Hall, warning that he would have his field pieces fired in the event of an attack and mobilizing both Indians and the many whites who remained loyal to him for civil war.[10] It is into this world that Edmonds introduces the newly married Gil and Lana at the novel's opening, and it is this world whose painful revolutionary transformation the book presents.

Edmonds' book confronted Ford with a text that combined popular fictional form with sophisticated historical content. The language of the text is political, in the fundamental sense of describing struggles over power at every level of human action. But in Ford's film this language disappears, even when the words remain the same. Struggle and dispute within every social grouping give way to a simple conflict between good men and their irrational enemies. Save for a few token whites with the besiegers of the settlers' fort and a token Indian with the defenders, the two sides are defined simply by race, and their conflict is one between natural forces. The film presents the roots of the conflict in psychosexual terms, not in social and political ones. As the French cultural analyst Roland Barthes might have put it, the two versions of *Drums* are constructed in different languages. The novel is couched in a language of historical development, a language that allows for contradiction, social complexity, and human choice in time. But the film is couched in a language of apolitical mythic certainty, in which an unchanging "human nature" is substituted for developing human contingency. Though both versions of *Drums* present a story of conflict, they attribute that conflict to very different causes.[11]

Historian John O'Connor has shown that this change was deliberate. His research in the Twentieth Century–Fox archives and other sources demonstrates the importance that the studio and its head, Darryl F. Zanuck, attached to the film. Zanuck decided to make it and supplied lavish production support, including the use of Technicolor and the funding of expensive location work by an enormous company. From the beginning of the project Zanuck was determined "not to make a picture portraying the revolution in the Mohawk Valley" but rather "to tell a story about a pioneer boy who took a city girl to the Mohawk Valley to live." He wanted to "retain the *spirit* of the book," but most of all he wanted "to *Give A Show*." In addition to Ford, the director, and Trotti, the principal author of the script, Zanuck brought to the film the talents of a sizable group of writers, William Faulkner among them, at various points during production. To speak of *Drums* as a "John Ford film" is thus to use the director's name as a shorthand for a sizable group of men and women.[12]

What representation of eighteenth-century American history did this Hollywood collaboration produce? A parallel reading of the novel and the film establishes the changes that occurred and reveals the devices that were used to get the story from the page to the screen. These devices transform the way in which the events and the characters are conceptualized and expressed. The film is no simple visual rendition of the book, despite Zanuck's pieties about retaining its "spirit." It carries a wholly different meaning. That difference stems from the presence in the two texts of different modes of thought, different forms of speech, different ways of confronting and reconstructing the past.

Making a long novel into a feature film required that Zanuck, Ford, and the others who worked with them not only borrow but also telescope, omit, and transform the novel's material. Borrowing occurs throughout the film. Mrs. McKlennar's character and even most of her lines come directly from the novel. So, in abbreviated form, does the sermon by Parson Rosenkranz (Arthur Shields), with its prayer for an errant young woman, its advertisement for a storekeeper's new stock of goods, and its sudden announcement of impending battle. Ford and the scriptwriters had to omit material for two separate reasons. One was simple lack of space, which forced the filmmakers, for example, to minimize the tragic love story of John Weaver and Mary Reall. The other was the Hays Code, which governed Hollywood filmmaking in the late 1930s and severely restricted the handling of sexual themes. Thus, the issues of seduction, bastardy, lesbian sadism, and interracial union, all raised in the novel through the story of a beautiful mentally impaired servant, receive no mention in the film. The production team telescoped material from separate sections and separate characterizations. The film's Lana, for instance, is a composite of several of the novel's female characters. Similarly, Gil takes over the heroic run for reinforcements made in the novel by his friend Adam (Ward Bond), a shift that is essential to the film's deep structure. And, finally, some things are transformed. Often the transformations reflect the differences between 1936, when the novel was published and domestic tensions ran high, and 1939, when the film was shot and Americans were sympathizing with the Allies' war against the Axis. The red cockades that the militiamen wear in the novel, politically symbolic in the class-conscious atmosphere of 1936, become green ones in the film. The link between the Tories and the British, made explicit in the novel, is weakened almost to nonexistence in the film. Germanic surnames ("Helmer") are replaced by indeterminate ones ("Hartman").

The divergent treatment of loyalists, Indians, and women demonstrates how these devices combine to make the film a different text from the book. In the film the three groups are thoroughly intertwined, the first two presenting threats to the third. This intermixing is demonstrated in the earliest sequences, from the opening shot of Lana's wedding bouquet to the introduction of the loyalist Caldwell (John Carradine) and the friendly Indian Blue Back (Chief Big Tree). These sequences establish the perfect harmony between Lana and her bridegroom, which stands for the perfect harmony of white American society. Their union transcends class and geographic barriers, for the film's Lana is an eastern girl from a wealthy family and Gil is an obscure young man from somewhere to the west. Alone among the men at the ceremony he wears neither powder in his hair nor a wig. He looks ill at ease even in his plain suit. But as the couple leaves, the minister tells Lana's parents that the differences between their daughter and their new son-in-law are unimportant: "It's always been like this since Bible days—every generation must make its own way, in one place or another."

Caldwell meets the couple in a country inn that evening, and his interrogation of Gil confirms that the couple's harmony stands for that of America. His odd black costume, his eyepatch, and his faintly British accent distinguish him from the three Americans, Gil, Lana, and the innkeeper, as does the contrast between the innkeeper's enthusiasm over the honeymooners and Caldwell's cool politeness. Caldwell's prying questions and Gil's firm responses establish that there is no division among the Americans and that the Indians are likely to join the British. A threat has been introduced, but the danger will come from outside the couple and the American community.

Shortly afterward that threat seems to be realized when Blue Back appears. He comes to Gil and Lana's isolated cabin during a rainstorm, just as they have themselves arrived, and a loud thunderclap heralds the first shot of him, taken at a low angle as he stands in the doorway. He comes upon Lana, who is wet, cold, distressed by the meanness of the cabin, and (for the moment) alone. He is so luridly lit that his makeup seems to glow; he is armed; he is an Indian. The first-time viewer can sympathize completely with Lana's instant vision of her rape and death and with her hysterical reaction, for here is the perfect projection of the red enemy of whom Caldwell has spoken. But her terror is misplaced. When Gil answers her screams, he slaps her out of her hysteria and tells her that Blue Back is a "good friend." The Indian himself adds that he is a "good Christian" and that he has brought the newlyweds half a deer. Lana's error is underscored when the first shot of him is repeated as he enters the cabin again. Now we know that despite his iconography he poses no danger. Instead, he offers Gil a stick and instructs him to use it to "beat her good" so that she will be a "good woman." The gift and the instructions are preposterous, and with them Blue Back settles into the comic role that he fills for the rest of the film. But he has foreshadowed other Indians who will not be "good Christians," and even Lana's terror at the sight of him has emphasized her harmony with Gil. We have understood her fear. We have seen her accept the slap with which Gil brings her out of it and his insistence that from then on she will do as he says. Never again in the film will she question, doubt, or resist him.

Lana's encounter with Blue Back establishes several things. Blue Back is acceptable to the whites precisely because he is comic, but his offer of the stick and advice to "beat her good" underlines the fact that Gil has already hit her forcefully. She will, as he commands, do as he says. On another level, Gil's violence both expresses and neutralizes antagonisms between them as representatives of different classes. She has been brought up gently, but now she needs the roughness of which he is capable if she is to survive. He is tougher, but he will not use his toughness against what she stands for. Instead, a symbiosis is established in which her feminine aristocratic gentleness and his masculine plebian strength form a coherent whole. "I need you, Lana," he tells her after he has struck her, but the film is saying that she needs him just as much, that without his plain-folks common sense her eastern upper-class ways will bring her to disaster.

In the novel Caldwell and Blue Back are introduced very differently. Caldwell is one-eyed and sinister, but his goal is to set the Americans quarreling among themselves, not to stir up the Indians against them. Lana dislikes Blue Back, but it is the dislike of a frontierswoman for whom Indian-hating is an old habit and of a house-proud wife who does not like seeing muddy moccasins on her kitchen floor. Ford thus made a number of significant changes when he generated his sequences out of the equivalent passages in the novel. He telescoped an entire community of royalists into the figure of Caldwell, making him *the* white Tory, *the* outside agitator always separate from the community of settlers. Caldwell stands alone in the shadows, watching the militia drill. He leads the first Indian irruption, breaking up the community's gathering to clear Gil and Lana's farm. Realizing his earlier vague threat to them, he is the first enemy to enter their cabin, and he orders its destruction in an Indian tongue. Later he commands the major raid that besieges the fort. He is the malevolent source of all evil, a satanic figure disposing of the powers of the night. But in the book this man is a minor character, figuring strongly only once. The novel depicts other Tories as an integral part of the prerevolutionary community: honest storekeepers who cannot betray their oath to the king, aristocrats allied to the Johnson family, Scots immigrants who do not get on with their German and English neighbors, the people who live in the village over the next hill. One even bears the rare but authentically Mohawk Valley name of Countryman.

Unlike the film's Caldwell, the book's loyalists receive no credit for some vaguely magical ability to manipulate the Indians. Instead, the novel respects the intricate politics of the Iroquois confederacy and the role and astuteness of Joseph Brant, historical war chief of the Mohawk tribe and leader of those Iroquois who did join the British. Edmonds was, in fact, saying nothing new.

His depiction of the Iroquois falls into a long artistic tradition of respect for the Indians, a tradition whose origins reach back to the very beginnings of the white presence in America. That tradition has always emphasized that Indians are members of particular societies and must be represented in their specific contexts, not as featureless horrors. An example that bears directly on *Drums* is the portrait that Gilbert Stuart painted of Brant in 1786. Though the artist was a patriot and Brant an old revolutionary enemy, the portrait treats its subject with respect. There is nothing exaggerated, shadowy, grotesque, or malevolent in its depiction of him. He is a warrior, a Mohawk, and a man who deserves honor.

But the film's handling of both the Indians and the loyalists is part of a different cultural stream. Much of its iconography for Caldwell and the Indians can be seen in Benjamin West's portrait of Colonel Guy Johnson, a genuine loyalist and one of the architects of the region's bloody civil war. Painted a few years before Stuart's Brant, the portrait shows Johnson in a haughty pose, wearing military gear and in full control of the mysterious Indian whom West has placed behind him. Johnson's power, like that of the film's Caldwell, lies precisely in his control over that Indian's terrible ill-will and strength. Other artists of the time showed in explicitly sexual terms what would happen should that strength be released. A good example, again directly foreshadowing *Drums,* is John Vanderlyn's "The Death of Jane Mc-Crea" (1804). It portrays the murder of a frontierswoman by Indians during the Revolutionary War, showing both her and her assailants in terms that are little short of pornographic.

The erotic content of such depictions, whether written, painted, or filmed, has served a major social and ideological function. It began to appear in American art in the aftermath of the Revolution, and it flourished through the nineteenth century. This was the time of white America's rapid expansion across the continent; it was the time of the final destruction of Indian autonomy. It was also the age of genteel sexual repression in middle-class culture, centered on the idealized image of white womanhood. By depicting frontier warfare in strongly sexual terms, with aggressive Indians seeking above all to defile innocent white women, it turns a war for the conquest of land into one for the defense of purity. The real victims, who are the Indians, become not only responsible for their own misfortunes but the authors of all evil.

This tradition, repeatedly stressing that the Indians, not the whites, are the aggressors and that their aggression is above all sexual, became a commonplace theme in western films, and Ford's *Drums* gives it full expression. The Indian threat to Gil and Lana's marriage is only seemingly eliminated when the glowering Blue Back is reduced to the level of a comic sidekick. It reappears powerfully in the second great conflict of the film, following an interlude in which perfect understanding between Gil and Lana has brought them a new home, the best crop in the valley, and a son. It is first stated when two drunken braves invade Mrs. McKlennar's bedroom. In a way, the scene is a comic reversal of Lana's introduction to Blue Back. Whereas a terrified Lana, young and inexperienced, throws herself down on a bed, an insulted Mrs. McKlennar, old and knowledgeable, stubbornly refuses to get up. Lana could do nothing but scream, but Mrs. McKlennar shames the Indian who tries to stroke her leg and orders the invaders to carry her out of the house, bed and all.

This encounter leads directly to the major Indian assault, which the film describes in starkly sexual terms. The settlers flee to their fort, and as the last stragglers come in, Parson Rosenkranz prays, saying, "We all know only too well what will happen to us if they get through that gate." As he says it, the film cuts to the faces of frightened women. After an overnight siege, the Indians finally enter the citadel where the women are hidden. When they force the door, the women meet them with an explosive torrent of boiling water, and as a rescue party of soldiers charges to save them, the Indians are throwing the women down, one by one. The image of rape is sudden and fierce. It is the image the audience has been waiting for since Caldwell's first mention of Indians in the tavern, and since the first terrifying shot of Blue Back.

The Indians of the film version of *Drums* are a natural force. They burn, kill, loot, and rape because that is what Indians do. They have no intelligence, no ability to calculate their own way; instead, any agitator can manipulate them. Even Gil, who makes the most favorable judgment of them, assumes that they will necessarily accept a land-hungry white man's standard of fairness—that there is no other standard of fairness. He denies that they might want to defend their own way of life. The point is made more clearly by Caldwell's role in launching both Indian attacks. The loyalist himself mixes his mastery with total contempt. "Call the filthy beggars back," he snaps during the siege, "we'll wait until the moon has set," as if Indians had never grasped the principles of night combat.

The filmmakers used the same device to create their version of the theme of womanhood. Both the film and the novel are structured around the problem of women's relationship to men on the frontier. But whereas the novel explores the problem in relation to class and makes the family an arena for conflict and strife, the film negates the class dimension and posits an ideal of family life based on consensus and agreement. In both texts the problem is considered through three characters: Mrs. DeMooth, Mrs. McKlennar, and Lana. The film's Mrs. DeMooth, like its Lana, is an eastern lady who has followed her husband into the wilderness. She fails to accept her new situation and becomes the local snob, drawing the meaning of her life from her husband's rank as captain of the militia and from her family's wealth. But though she bursts with pride as her husband leads the militia around the parade ground, she faints when the Indians appear.

Edmonds' Mrs. DeMooth is much more complicated, much more tragic, and much more fully in revolt against the situation in which she finds herself. She cannot abide either the unashamed sexuality of her servant girl or the loss of the social position she had once enjoyed. Ultimately, her madness kills her, but not before she has kicked the pregnant servant in the belly and driven her out to give birth in the snow. She is a victim of circumstances that she cannot control and of a loneliness that she cannot remedy, an upper-class woman who has lost her privileges. Her inability to bear the loss is Edmonds' affirmation that good will alone is not enough to cement a marriage across class lines.

Both the film and the novel are more sympathetic toward Mrs. McKlennar. In the film, she knows that she must be a political outsider, and she finds independence and strength in the sphere she does control. A widow, she loved and served her man while he lived and misses him now that he is dead, but she also revels in her freedom to do exactly as she pleases. She brushes off Gil's prying into her politics by snapping, "I'm a woman, Martin, a woman hasn't got any political opinions." The point is that she has no time for any pretense that women are equal in her society, not that she accepts her subordination. Within the constraints that she has accepted, she is the freest character in the film, free to reject spurious political involvement, free to order her daily life as she will, even free, in 1939 terms, to express her sexuality. She flirts happily with Gil's friend Adam, calling him "good looking" and kissing him with relish during the harvest celebration. But her death during the second Indian attack tells us that there will be no room for her proud individualism in the world of families that the settlers will build. And by giving her house and farm to Gil and Lana, she confirms that they have become the children whom she never bore. Her independence is undermined and reduced to the bravado of an "unfulfilled" woman who has never given birth.

The film's central statement on womanhood turns, of course, on the characterization of Lana. It is her development that holds the deep structure of the film together. Any development in a female character is unusual in a western, and the complex, politically significant set of changes that Lana undergoes can have few parallels in the genre. Beginning as an Albany society girl, at home with chamber musicians, bewigged gentlemen, and living rooms decorated with Ionic pilasters, she adjusts to being a farm wife and to impromptu service as a soldier. Finally she emerges as a living symbol of the United States.

The earliest sequences present Lana as a lady but destroy the idea that her social station defines her. By asserting that she, unlike Mrs. DeMooth, can make the move to the frontier psychologically as well as physically, the film asserts that good will can bridge the gulf of class. As the minister performing the marriage mentions "the wilderness," the film cuts to her mother's anxious face. When she and Gil depart, they pass immediately from her world to his, from her parents' mansion to his covered wagon. The cow tethered behind the wagon bears flowers like the bridal bouquet she has just thrown, and her elegant traveling dress is suddenly incongruous. By the time she and Gil arrive at their cabin, the dress is wet and disheveled, an outward sign of her sagging spirits. The elegance of Albany is on her mind, and she can only cope with the cabin's bleakness by stammering that "starting this way, we'll like our things even more when we get them." The "things" in question must be the life she has left behind, and the only improvement she can envisage is to regain it.

But the dishevelment of her dress and her personality stands for the stripping off of what she must abandon. After the shock of her meeting with Blue Back, she moves easily into a middle period. She stops dreaming of Albany and learns to identify with the world she has entered. The sequence immediately following her hysterical reaction to Blue Back takes place outdoors, in warm sunshine. Now Lana is dressed in checked gingham, bright and cheerful but also sensible and symbolic, for classical Hollywood, of honest domesticity. She and Gil move from making hay together to making love in the hay. By the time Gil goes to muster with the militia, she is pregnant, and though she once more (and for the last time) dons an elegant gown, her behavior toward the plain people she meets at the fort is charming. When the neighbors gather to help the Martins clear the farm, she is wearing the rough blue costume of any frontierswoman and is as enthusiastic as Gil about what is happening. She dismisses her background by telling Mrs. DeMooth that her teapot is "just plain china," not the Wedgwood by which her inquisitor lays great stock.

Still, her identification with the frontier is only partial, as she shows when Mrs. McKlennar's house becomes a hospital for wounded soldiers. Gil has just had his first taste of fighting, and after all hope of his return is gone, Lana finds him in a rain-soaked forest. She brings him home, anxiously nurses him, and listens to his tale of horrors, but keeps telling him not to talk about it. When he closes his narrative by triumphantly saying, "But we won, we showed 'em they couldn't take this valley," she responds, "Yes, darling, *you* won." The action has been his, and as a woman she must be an outsider to it.

From this stage she moves toward a total identification with Gil, his war, and his republic. The couple's unity finds enduring strength through two separate counterpoints, each of them reversing the positions that Gil and Lana initially held. The first reversal cancels the effects of Lana's introduction to Gil's lonely cabin, when she finishes her terrifying encounter with Blue Back by sobbing that her mother was right and that she should never have come west. She and Gil return to the charred ruin of the cabin in the dead of winter and find her prized possessions, her "things," lying in the ashes. Lana fingers the pieces of her teapot, and this time Gil whines, telling her that she had been right "that first night" and that the frontier is "no place for any woman." But she counters his self-pity with the practical suggestion that he take the vacancy at Mrs. McKlennar's. Her eastern ways are gone; born a lady, she will now be the wife of a hired man and herself do menial work. True love has overcome all the differences between them.

The second reversal grows from Gil's run for help when the settlers' fort is besieged. Another man has tried to go, has been caught by the Indians, and has suffered an excruciating death. But Lana, already in a soldier's uniform, tells Gil that she is not afraid and that she wants him to try. While he is gone, she takes part in the fort's defense, making the war hers as well as his. She joins the other women in boiling water to pour on the attackers; she shoots the first Indian to enter the room where the women are hiding; she is grabbed and thrown down to suffer the rape that she once had feared from Blue Back. When Gil returns with the rescue party, he seeks her out in the ravaged fort, just as she sought him out after the battle in the woods. He asks bystanders if they have seen her and receives the same tidings of despair that she heard about him. When he finds her and begins to nurse her, the circle is closed. She has done more than forget her past, come west, and bear his child. She has given him help and received it from him. She has fought their common enemy. He, in turn, has understood her pain at her first arrival, has rocked their child while she watched and prayed that it "might go on like this forever," and has known the despair of thinking that she has fallen in battle. Now each is the other and their fusion is complete.

These massive role exchanges and this complete transformation of Lana's identity make possible the last sequence. Lana emerges from a half-rebuilt church, wearing a blue dress with a white collar and a red bonnet. As she does, the film cuts to triumphant Continental soldiers who carry, for the first time, the Stars and Stripes. "So that's our new flag, the thing we've been fighting for," comments a bystander, and the film cuts to Lana, wearing its colors. Her vapid line, "It's a pretty flag," almost checks the momentum of the sequence, but quick cuts to the flag, to a blacksmith at his forge, to the black servant Daisy, to Blue Back, and back to her to reestablish it. Meanwhile "America" swells on the soundtrack. Somehow, despite all historical evidence, the republic has achieved instant freedom, not just for white males, but also for blacks, women, and Indians. Within the film's world the assertion becomes believable because of the way that Lana, as surrogate for all of these groups, has earned the right to cover her body with its flag. In the strongest terms, her development has confirmed the unity and the harmony of all Americans, qualities that the film has been asserting since the first shot.

The novel likewise turns on Lana's development, but in a very different way. Because she is simply a farmgirl, not the lady that the film makes of her, her growth does not symbolize any obliteration of class differences by national unity. She faces problems quite independent of Gil's, and for a time she becomes totally alienated from him, losing all sexual interest in him and enduring marital rape. He, in turn, comes very close to adultery with Nancy, the promiscuous, mentally deficient servant. The couple eventually reach a tenuous truce, but the novel closes with her solitary musings on the end of two wars, between herself and Gil and between Britain and America. She has lost and she has gained, but there is no suggestion that she and he have fused or that she has come to stand for the Republic.

Her experience thus endorses Mrs. McKlennar's position that in their world "a woman hasn't got any politics." The political involvement of the film's Lana is spurious. She never takes an independent position, never acts as a representative of the interests of her class or her sex. Her political life in the film has required the obliteration of all that made her distinct from Gil. Although in the novel she has no *public* political existence, it is replaced by an intense "politics of the family," and from that she develops a separate perspective and a separate self. The film's position is typical of the sort of historiography that proclaims that women (or blacks or Indians or workers or . . .) too have had their part in the American success story. The novel asserts that the past of any subordinate group must be interpreted in terms of an experience that in many ways is different from that of its rulers, and that if their two pasts are bound up, it is by struggle rather than by fusion.

The film version of *Drums* could not have included all the detail, all the subplots, all the lesser characters, of so long and complicated a novel. Had Ford, Zanuck, and their associates tried to do so, they would have produced a mere précis, for *Drums* was no *Gone With the Wind,* able to command a gargantuan budget and twice the normal screen time. Many of the film's best moments, including the birth of Gil and Lana's son and the community's harvest dance, are characteristically Fordian in their celebration of a folksy, populist community and of happy domesticity. Many of the characters and situations pose problems to which Ford would return again and again. Adam, the unmarried wanderer, prefigures three major Ford protagonists: Wyatt Earp (Henry Fonda) in *My Darling Clementine* (1946), Ethan Edwards (John Wayne) in *The Searchers* (1956), and Tom Doniphon (John Wayne) in *The Man Who Shot Liberty Valance* (1962). The half-rebuilt church at the end of the film points toward one of the most powerful images in *My Darling Clementine* and toward the sterile latter-day town depicted at the beginning and end of *Liberty Valance*. Even Blue Back foreshadows Ford's attempt to do justice to the Indians in *Cheyenne Autumn* (1964).

From the perspective of Ford's personal film authorship, such points are independent both of this film's original source and of the particular conditions of its making. But from the perspective of the film's ideological message, the differences between the two texts take on considerable weight. Edmonds wrote a novel that combined hard research into the dynamics of a historic social crisis with a form that opened that research to a mass public. Ford, Zanuck, Trotti, Faulkner, and the rest made of that novel a film which pictures two forces that must conflict because their nature demands it and which argues that the triumph of the American cause obliterates all divisions, whether of race, class, or sex.

Many factors contributed to that change. The contrasts between the novel and the film reflect the difference between an American consciousnesss dominated by depression and one oriented toward imminent war. They reflect the power that Darryl Zanuck enjoyed at Twentieth Century–Fox and his sense of what was necessary to turn a popular novel into a first-run success. They reflect the direct influence of Ford, as well, for *Drums* is the purest and sunniest statement of his understanding of the meaning of American settlement. They reflect the constraints imposed by the form of a late-1930s Hollywood feature. One cannot, of course, say that the film obliterated the novel. Both texts are important cultural artifacts; both reached wide audiences at first release. Each continues even now to have some effect, the novel through continuing sales and the film through screenings on television and for film students. But precisely because it *is* a film, the 1939 version is an instance of the primary popular art form of technological society. And precisely because it contains in pure form a series of pseudo-historical statements about the past of that society, the origins and the ideological content of those statements deserve our consideration. Here in *Drums,* as in a parade of films that stretches from D. W. Griffith's *The Birth of a Nation* (1916) to John Wayne's *The Green Berets* (1967), is the mainstream Hollywood account of American history. That an informed historian would not recognize it is more than a matter of "inaccuracy"; the gap between historical events and pseudo-history is related to the purpose of history in the Republic's cultural life.

In terms of Ford's larger body of work, the change from the historic conceptualization that underlies the novel to the mythic conceptualization that underlies the film is ironic. Ford may properly be regarded as the cinematic poet of American history, and his work as a whole forms an extended commentary on the Republic's past. His late films explored the problems that he ignored in *Drums* and made a bitter mockery of American triumphalism. But in *Drums* itself he was already in contact with direct, reliable evidence about the complexity of the relationship between great public events and the lives of ordinary people. In his later work he was much more fully in control of the production process himself and did not have to deal with anyone like Zanuck. Here, however, he and his collaborators ignored the complexities that Edmonds presented and made a statement in terms of facts that are so because they are so. A mode of speech that was mythic and natural replaced one that was historical and political. A serious and sophisticated attempt at a people's history was transformed into a myth.

The Painted Mirror:

Historical Re-creation from the Panorama to the Docudrama

On August 13, 1883, Kaiser Wilhelm, emperor of Germany, stepped out onto a Berlin stage. In front of him, a vast battlefield stretched off toward the distant hills. It was an imposing spectacle. Sabers glistened in the afternoon sunlight as the French Seventh Corps Cavalry prepared for a last, desperate attempt to break through the Prussian lines outside the village of Sedan. Near the Kaiser's position, the leaves appeared to flutter in the heavy, still air, but it was an eerie, hushed scene. Officers in full battle dress, platoons of cavalry, and endless rows of footsoldiers—all were as immovable as the slate tile roofs in the village. Ever so slowly, the stage revolved, giving the emperor a panoramic view across the battlefield.

What the Kaiser and his entourage were looking at was not the actual Battle of Sedan, which had taken place thirteen years earlier, but a Panorama—an enormous, incredibly detailed painting. Housed in a circular theater several stories high, the Panorama of the Battle of Sedan impressed a steady flow of visitors who felt as though they were not just spectators in front of a massive work of art, but almost participants, thrust inside the scene by painterly illusions and a carefully worked-out sense of perspective.

As an illusion, the Panorama was an unqualified success. The chief architect, Anton von Werner, and his staff of journalists, historians, painters, and scenic designers had chosen a precise moment in history and recreated it with such fidelity that visitors felt as if they had been transported back in time.[1]

But von Werner's Panorama failed to achieve its main goal—to make money. The Battle of Sedan was financed by investors in a stock company who had hoped that the attraction would run for years. To protect their investment,

BY ERIC BREITBART

the Panorama's builders included a restaurant, an amusement arcade, and souvenir shops, making it a self-contained and somewhat primitive theme park. Unfortunately, business declined rapidly as the novelty wore off. After six months the Panorama closed its doors, one of the last examples of a form of popular entertainment that had existed in England and on the European continent for over a hundred years.

Today, of course, recreating history as a potentially profitable commodity is a sophisticated business, and the means of producing historical illusions are not limited to the painter's canvas or the motion picture screen. Satellites can transmit images instantaneously into millions of homes, without even the need to strike multiple prints from the original negative. Historical recreation is not an experience for a few dozen spectators—which was all the Panorama could accommodate at one time—but a form of entertainment watched by millions of people on an almost daily basis. Convincing as Panoramas were, they never became a mass medium. The cost of making a second or third copy would have been prohibitive, and history itself was still firmly entrenched in the province of the written word. People learned about the past and the present from books.

By the middle of the nineteenth century, however, historical images began to usurp the power of words through the increasingly popular art of photography. Stereo cards showing travel scenes and recreations of historical events found their way into middle-class homes, as well as those of the rich. It was no longer necessary to travel far from home to see the sights of the world. To see them larger than life was another matter, and the nineteenth-century Panoramas and Dioramas attracted audiences by virtue of imposing physical size. Still, large as they were, the Panoramas lacked movement. Innovators like Daguerre added light effects, smoke, and mist to convey the feeling of movement, and it worked—for a time.

With its ability to record motion, the movie camera opened up an entirely new world for entrepreneurs and the public. In 1895, less than a dozen years after the opening of the Battle of Sedan Panorama, the Lumiere Brothers held the first motion picture shows before a captivated audience in a Parisian cafe. People were awestruck by simple images taken from everyday life—streetcars, workers leaving a factory, a train entering a station—because they *moved.*

The dim, flickering images appeared to be leaping out from the screen, causing spectators to duck under tables or run out into the street. Early films often borrowed from the Panorama. A camera would be attached to the front of a train or a trolley as it moved across the countryside or through a city landscape; no longer was the spectator's position frozen in paint and canvas.

Movies gave audiences a changing perspective from which to view the world. The giant Panoramas were like dinosaurs, curious artifacts frozen in time. Soon, they were buried under a flood of moving images.

The intimate, cafe theaters of the 1890s gave way to majestic palaces, seating thousands of spectators at a time, with images projected on enormous screens whose dimensions surpassed those of even the largest Panoramas. From simple records of daily life and postcard-like travelogues, motion pictures developed quickly into what was called "the seventh art," and the world's screens were filled with elaborately-produced tales of foreign adventure and historical fantasy. Hollywood became the center of movie-making. Like Detroit, it was an industrial city—only its product was not automobiles, but dreams.

Editing for dramatic effect—using shots out of sequence, and intercutting close-ups and long shots—broke the traditional unities of time and space, but audiences were still able to identify with the action taking place on the screen. Just how this process of identification took place was a question that intrigued psychologists and physiologists, as well as film directors and theater owners. The illusion of movement was of particular interest—not simply the phenomenon of retinal image persistence, whereby an image remains "imprinted" on the retina and is absorbed into the succeeding image, creating the illusion of movement—but the *psychological* process: how the illusion affects the mind.

One of the scientists intrigued by this question was the industrial psychologist Hugo Munsterberg. His book, *The Photoplay,* published in 1913, was one of the first theoretical studies of the movies. "Depth and movement alike come to us in the moving picture world," Munsterberg wrote, "not as hard facts, but as a mixture of fact and symbol. They are present and yet they are not in things. We invest the impressions with them."[2] Often, the moving image's power of suggestion was so strong that audiences suspended belief and accepted as true scenes that could not possibly have been recorded by the camera.

Jay Leyda recounts the story of a French film producer who manufactured a "newsreel" of the Dreyfus case from other films he happened to have in his suitcase in order to take advantage of popular interest in a contemporary event—even though the famous trial took place prior to invention of the motion picture camera. The audience's craving for information overcame the rational knowledge that the images could not be real. It was as if the images already existed in people's minds, waiting for a medium to bring them to life.[3] The hybrid did not acquire a name until sixty years later, but the docudrama had begun to take shape.

The ability of movies to blend the real and the recreated was not lost on early producers. Cameramen working for Thomas Edison's studio around the turn of the century had no qualms about restaging naval battles of the Spanish-American War with toy models and using stand-ins for historical personalities—a practice that continued through the 1940s. Newsreels like the "March of Time" employed on-screen actors as well as narrators to impersonate world leaders who were unavailable to meet press deadlines. They also substituted stock footage for events that could not be filmed.

Once recorded in the "March of Time" archives, such scenes became fact and were soon reproduced in other films and newsreels. In the 1920s and 1930s, every motion picture program featured newsreels, and, slowly, images began to replace words as the means of conveying what was going on in the world. For the first time in history, a vast body of images preserved—or purported to—actual events. What was considered important was recorded on film. Everything else, in a way, ceased to exist.

Although cameras recorded a few isolated incidents during the Spanish-American War, World War I was the first war in history to be given extensive motion picture coverage. It was also the first war in history in which public perceptions of the conflict were influenced by visual propaganda and public relations on a mass scale. In the early years of the conflict, particularly on the Allied side, access to the front was restricted to "official" photographers and cameramen; violators were threatened with being shot as spies. The French and the British did not want any random scenes of death and destruction undermining civilian support for the war. As soldiers fought in the trenches, squads of military film producers fired propaganda salvos at their own publics and toward the still-neutral United States.

What was called "the Great War" demonstrated the effectiveness of film propaganda as well as the destructive power of modern weaponry. Cameras had recorded history, but how people *perceived* it depended on how films were edited and the context in which they were seen. With only slight changes in narration, titles, and music, the same images were often used for vastly different purposes. When America entered the war in 1917, the Allies prepared a newsreel, *Under Four Flags,* emphasizing the cooperative effort. Each country used the same footage in its own newsreels, but minimized the others' contributions. The camera could record actuality, but the "truth" it presented was manufactured in the studio.

After World War I, newsreel archives were often used to recreate history, but nowhere was the practice so fully developed as in the Soviet Union. Lenin was one of the first twentieth-century political leaders to recognize and encourage the power of the man and woman with the movie camera. In the hands of skillful filmmakers like Esther Schub, innocuous home movies of the czar and his family sunning themselves outside the Winter Palace became central elements in a stirring indictment of a decadent society. Schub's *Fall of the Romanov Dynasty* (1926) assembled clips from many sources to construct a picture of the revolutionary transformation of Russian society.

How these images affected an audience interested Russian filmmakers like Eisenstein, Pudovkin, and Vertov as much as the process had intrigued Hugo Munsterberg a decade earlier. For Eisenstein, the secret lay in montage, or editing, a dialectical process of juxtaposing shots to create a new meaning or synthesis. But limiting oneself to documentary footage was like working with only one hand, and the efforts of Schub and her co-workers were soon eclipsed by the fiction film's ability to borrow documentary tehniques to enhance its power.

Writing of Eisenstein's *Potemkin,* released in New York City in 1926, the American critic Wilton Barrett remarked that the film was supposed to be an exact recreation of actual events, based on official government sources and archives. "Whether or not the above is entirely correct," Barrett wrote, "[*Potemkin*] bears the stamp of something that is actually occurring before our eyes, as if the screen on which it is projected were a square hole through which we looked at events in the making . . . . [W]e not only understand what the spirit of the revolution is, but see it being set in motion and that motion explained through a visual impact of all the facts as they happened as well as of the passions at the roots of the facts before happening."[4] The art of the motion picture, Barrett suggested, was to see for the audience things beyond its power of sight.

Even in its early, primitive form movies changed the way people viewed the world. "The nickelodeon," one movie critic wrote, "is tapping an entirely new stratum of people. It is developing a section of the population into theatergoers that formerly knew and cared little about the drama as a fact in life."[5] For a few hours, an audience could relive the perils and pleasures of another time and another place. What movies had to offer the popular imagination was, of course, motion and drama. In the United States, many film epics of the 1920s glorified American patriotism and the nineteenth-century expansion cross the continent. Such movies as John Ford's *The Iron Horse* (1924) and James Cruze's *The Covered Wagon* (1925) showed an America whose spirit was strong and unbroken by the ravages of war. History was not only something to be studied in school, or learned through books, but a form of popular entertainment as well.

Historical drama remained one of the staples of Hollywood's dream factory for the next fifty years. Armies of designers, costumers, and technicians could spend enormous sums of money to recreate images of past times. Even when television began to chip away at the movies' popularity, six-inch wide images in black and white could not compete with the glories of wide-screen Technicolor. Television's few historical shows of the late 1940s were limited by tiny studios, and even smaller budgets, but television had one quality, though, that the movies lacked—immediacy. Events could be broadcast as they happened, something that the newsreels could never do. Television producers capitalized on the medium's ability to transmit real events in dramatic shows like "You Are There", broadcast by CBS from 1953 to 1957, and again in 1971. Marked by the sonorous voice of Walter Cronkite, and the famous opening lines: "The time . . .; the place. . . . All things are as they were then, except YOU ARE THERE!," the show re-created historical events in the form of television newscasts.

"Armstrong Circle Theater," broadcast from 1953 to 1963, was another of the first television series to use the docudrama format on a regular basis. Shows such as "Assignment: Junkie's Alley," about Philadelphia's narcotics squad, and "John Doe Number 154," the story of an amnesiac's search for his memory, were adapted from timely news stories in order to "arouse interest, even controversy, on important and topical subjects." According to the producer, Robert Costello, the series was looking for "understandable problems . . . the themes of success over obstacles, long-awaited and long-deserved . . . hopes fulfilled, or a crisis met and mastered." Production guidelines distributed to potential writers and producers further suggested that "basic human characteristics must be behind each triumph—courage, honor, love, righteousness, and honesty."[6] Network documentaries of the time often covered exactly the same stories as "Armstrong Circle Theater," but real life sometimes refused to conform to production guidelines.

One of the most prolific docudrama producers has been David Wolper, whose productions, including "Roots" and "The Rise and Fall of the Third Reich," have consistently attracted more viewers than those of any other producer in the history of television—a reputation that Wolper's orchestration of the opening ceremonies for the 1984 Olympics in Los Angeles further enhanced. In a trade publication interview, Wolper explained that a docudrama should give a sense and a feeling of how things were, not necessarily offer a factual record. "[A docudrama] isn't a book," he continued. "You don't go back and refer to it for information. You see it once and whatever you remember of it stays with you. If what stays with you is the truth, how you got there, to me, is not overly relevant."[7] When asked what he looks for in a script, Wolper answered, not entirely tongue-in-cheek, "Perfect drama with great dialogue and easily definable characters . . . a beginning, a middle, and an end—a climax and an up-ending. I like an up-ending in some way."[8] Unfortunately, history does not always yield subjects that fit this dramatic format. Yet over the past ten years, television has become a veritable history machine, spewing out a constant stream of historical, semihistorical, and pseudo-historical re-creations.

During a recent year, for example, an American audience could have watched docudramas on the trials of General Yamashita, Lee Harvey Oswald, Lieutenant Calley, and Julius and Ethel Rosenberg; the Cuban missile crisis, the Israeli raid on Entebbe, and the Jonestown massacre; three different versions of Watergate; and portraits of Senator Joseph McCarthy, Martin Luther King, Jr., Margaret Sanger, Douglas MacArthur, Franklin D. Roosevelt, and John and Robert Kennedy.

Television has drastically altered the way people perceive the world. Particularly in the United States and Western Europe, where average viewing time exceeds four hours a day, television, for many people, is the main source of information about the past as well as the present. "It is clearly one of the unique characteristics of advanced industrial societies," writes Raymond Williams, "that drama as an experience is now an intrinsic part of everyday life. . . . Watching dramatic simulation of a wide range of experiences is now an essential part of our modern cultural pattern."[9] Williams might have added that watching the dramatic simulation of *history* has become an essential part of our cultural pattern.

Influential producers and directors, like Wolper, Alan Landsburg ("The World at War," "Washington Behind Closed Doors"), and Marvin Chomsky ("Roots") are, in effect, mass educators, redefining the nature and perception of history for a large audience. "More people probably learned more about slavery from my series," Wolper has said, "than they ever learned from books. I could reach 5 million people with a high-class program. With *Roots* we reached 125 million. Television is powerful, and you should set out to reach as many people as you can."[10]

Producers and network executives are not unaware of the "educational" value of historical docudramas, particularly if the distribution of study guides and promotional material aimed at teachers will increase a series' visibility. The production of these guides has become a big business. For a mini-series on John F. Kennedy that NBC produced in 1983, the network corporate information service sent out nearly a hundred thousand guides to junior and senior high school teachers and twenty thousand more to libraries and universities. Almost without exception, however, such study guides deliver only mainstream messages about their subjects, often in a superficial manner. For the 1980 mini-series, "Shogun," based on the adventures of a seventeenth-century English ship captain who arrives in Japan and experiences culture shock, the study guide featured quotations from Confucius, the poet Leonard Cohen, and, naturally, Alvin Toffler of *Future Shock* fame.

The ascendancy of the docudrama as a vehicle for teaching history has not gone unnoticed. A recent symposium on the docudrama, bringing together television producers and historians, revealed the tensions between the demands of drama and the constraints imposed by historical accuracy. One participant, the producer Alan Landsburg, had made documentaries before switching to docudramas. He had been unhappy with the documentary's limitations. "I found it a frustrating form, finally, and I was delighted to find docudrama occurring as an avenue of being able to communicate more than the existing or shootable film allowed. I could film the bloody White House for so long and I couldn't get into the damn Oval Office where the action was, so I was forced to guess. . . . Now, in the docudrama at least, I can mount that guess."[11] Many of us, no doubt, have guesses as to what goes on in the Oval Office, but few have the resources to beam those guesses into eight million homes.

Another symposium participant, the historian Eric Foner, observed that his students came to him with a conception of history already conditioned primarily by television, and secondarily by movies. Foner argued that producers are, in effect, mass educators, not simply filmmakers, and that they should take that responsibility seriously, showing a greater respect for the complexities of historical events and a recognition of the power of television to create its own reality.

The criticisms of Foner and the other historians drove most of the television professionals into two defensive camps. Some, like Landsburg, hid behind the banner of neo-Aristotelianism, saying that they were dealing in dramatic illusions, not reality, and that viewers could understand the difference. The others were led by veteran producer and talk-show host David Susskind, who reacted as if he had been accused of perjury. "We are foresworn to tell the truth," Susskind shouted, "and we do."[12] No one would openly admit to sacrificing historical accuracy for dramatic effect, and the only point of agreement seemed to be that the docudrama as a television genre was here to stay.

The proliferation of docudramas raises an important issue—the blurring of distinctions between fact and fiction. Motion pictures too can be "real" and convincing, but they exist for a finite period of time in a clearly delineated space—the movie screen. Docudramas are part of a continuous flow of images, some real, some imagined—commercials, station breaks, news flashes, previews of up-coming shows—that wash over viewers as they connect to points in the outside world. On New Year's Eve, 1981, for example, ABC presented a docudrama on the 1968 invasion of Czechslovakia, produced by Granada TV in England. What was unusual about the broadcast was its presentation under the auspices of ABC's *news* division. When questioned about this, ABC executive Pamela Hill, like Alan Landsburg, argued that facts can only take you so far. "Given the sharp restrictions those countries place on the flow of information," she said, "it may be the only way to give the American public a greater understanding of historical events that take place in the Communist bloc."[13] Based on the memoirs of Zdenek Mlynar, secretary of the Czech Presidium, "Invasion" had an extreme anti-Soviet bias and drew not-so-subtle parallels to the then-recent declaration of martial law in Poland. The problem here is not the dramatization of events—a worthy artistic endeavor—but the *substitution* of the dramatic recreation for the real thing.

Since the broadcast of "Invasion," distinctions between fact and fiction have blurred further. Because of the desire for higher audience ratings, producers are more interested in subjects that are still "hot" (or at least warm). As historical mini-series have proliferated during the 1980s, the range of subjects has broadened. History remains important, but it has come to mean news events of the last few years or well-known figures from history or the arts— George Washington, Christopher Columbus, Mussolini, Hitler, Napoleon, and Picasso, to name the subjects of a few recent or future adaptations.

Dramatization of crime cases, such as "Fatal Vision" (the trial of Green Beret doctor Jeffrey McDonald, who was accused of killing his wife and children) and the "Atlanta Child Murders" (a film that argued the innocence of a convicted murderer)—cases that are still under consideration in the courts—has drastically increased television's power to influence public opinion and revived the smoldering controversy over mingling fact and fiction. In an editorial criticizing "The Atlanta Child Murders" and its producer, Abby Mann, the *New York Times* argued that the license to fictionalize requires giving up the license to claim reality. "All storytelling involves some distortion," the editorial stated. "But the difference between news and fiction is the difference between a mirror and a painting. Let the artist boast keener vision, but don't let him palm off oil on canvas as a reflection in glass."[14]

Apologists for the docudrama are fond of citing Homer and Shakespeare as "docudramatists before their time"—writers who distorted historical events for dramatic purposes—as if today's television writers were descendants of a long and noble line. The epic poets of the small screen, however, are using history in the way Anton von Werner used real rocks and trees in the foreground of his Panorama—as window dressing to further an illusion. The ancients had Thucydides, Herodotus, and Virgil. We have Susskind, Wolper, and Abby Mann.

Whatever criticisms it may receive, the blending of fact and fiction has achieved a permanent place on television and not in the movies. The sequel to *Patton,* a popular movie in 1970, will appear on television, not in theaters. Movies seem to be catering to a younger audience—one that has, presumably, only a minimal interest in history—while older people are staying at home in front of the television set.

The changing American political and cultural climate in the 1980s has led to a resurgence of shows promoting American patriotism. As the television producer David Gerber, who did the eight-hour mini-series "George Washington" in the spring of 1984, told an interviewer, "we're a pendulum society. We went so far the other way with the self-flagellation of the 60s and 70s that we had to spring back."[15] Because of the enormous costs involved in producing a mini-series—the eighteen-hour broadcast of Herman Wouk's "The Winds of War" in 1983 cost $38 million, for example, and the sequel, "War and Remembrance," planned for the 1986–87 season, is budgeted at over $60 million—only subjects already implanted in the public's consciousness can be considered for network broadcast. And for many Americans, the story of World War II will be the story of Pug Henry, Wouk's hero, and his family.

The 1960s have not fared as well as World War II. ABC had high hopes for "Call to Glory," a series that the network hyped unmercifully during the broadcast of the 1984 Olympics and that seemed to benefit initially from the flag-waving atmosphere in Los Angeles. "Call to Glory" focused on the family life of Colonel Raynor Sarnac, a fictional Air Force officer stationed on a Texas base during the 1960s, and intercut historical news footage of events like Kennedy's speech during the Cuban missile crisis and Martin Luther King's March on Washington with dramatic scenes. The theme was unabashed, old-fashioned American patriotism. In one scene, Col. Sarnac calms his fearful son by saying: "My country needs me and I'll never turn my back on this country. . . . If you believe in something, you have to make sacrifices." For a few weeks "Call To Glory" flew high in the ratings; then it seemed to run out of gas and took a nose dive to oblivion.

The very existence of historical dramatization as a popular television genre is, in part, a response to people's desire to understand what is happening in the world. While a series like "Call to Glory" can be seen as a respite from most television historical dramas that focus on the deeds of great men, it does so by reducing history to the level of the soap opera. Real news footage is used only as window dressing. In a larger sense, the perceived need of television drama to personalize events—at least on the part of those who control the medium—means that history will continue to be redefined within the limits of

American commercial television. As the head of CBS's mini-series division said in an interview, "We have to get to the people rather than to the events. We have to show what the wife said to the husband on the way to signing the treaty rather than just showing him sign the treaty."[16] Real events, in other words, can only be seen through the eyes of the fictional characters.

In *The Culture of Narcissism,* Christopher Lasch argues that the history of theatrical innovation thrives on the conventions of formalized illusions. "Our sense of reality appears to rest," he wrote, "on our willingness to be taken in by the staged illusions of reality."[17] Television, however, seems to have dispensed with the artistic conventions and concentrated on the illusions.

None of this is inherent in the medium. European docudramas such as Peter Watkin's "Edvard Munch" and the "Battle of Culloden," Rosselini's "Blaise Pascal" and "The Rise of Louis XIV"–all originally produced for television—demonstrate the possibilities of using its intimacy and accessibility to reach a mass audience with programs that attempt to convey something of the texture of a historical period in terms of the contradictory, nonlinear, non-Freudian motivations of real historical characters. Each of these programs breaks with the conventions of television language and advances the somewhat radical idea that historical characters lived in a world different from ours.

The demands of American commercial television—half a dozen advertising breaks per hour—make it unlikely that shows like these will ever appear in this country. In spite of the popular success of shows like "Roots" and "Holocaust," American television seems to be singularly ill-equipped to deal with the task of presenting history to a mass audience in other than the commonly accepted forms of the commercial docudrama.

Once in a while, though, American television *is* willing to try something unconventional. When it happens, the result is a shock. In the spring of 1983, NBC broadcast *Special Bulletin,* a made-for-television movie about a group of antinuclear terrorists who take hostages and threaten to blow up the city of Charleston unless they are given television coverage. The show was produced on videotape, using television news techniques, which gave it an immediacy and believability reminiscent of Orson Welles's famous radio broadcast of "The War of the Worlds," which sent audiences racing to their cars in order to escape a Martian invasion. Although "Special Bulletin" was peppered with regular warnings that said, "The following is a realistic depiction of fictional events. None of what you are about to see is actually happening," the show was eerily reminiscent of Norman Mayer's real-life threat to blow up the Washington Monument, which kept television audiences captive for over eighteen hours—a continuous mini-series. A casual viewer might well have believed that terrorists were threatening the Charleston harbor—except when the program broke for commercials. "Special Bulletin" may not have been great art, but it was a convincing demonstration of the power of television to shape our perception of events—not simply *what* we perceive, but *how*.

As new advances in computer-generated imagery promise even greater control over the combination of "real" and "created" events, the power of mass media illusionists will increase tenfold. One response is the funny, cynical humor of Woody Allen's movie *Zelig,* in which Allen and his cinematographer Gordon Willis skillfully inserted a fictional character—Leonard Zelig—into real newsreel footage of the 1920s and 1930s. The movie is, in one sense, a send-up of the documentary format. Filmed interviews with real-life intellectuals like Saul Bellow and Susan Sontag, discussing the fictional character Zelig—much like the historical "witnesses" Warren Beatty used in *Reds*—give the film what can only be called a fake authenticity. In spite of the humor, Allen is making a serious point: you can make people believe anything they really want to believe. By using "real" intellectuals, whose opinion carry the heavy weight of legitimacy, to bolster the existence of a fictional character, he is reminding us that experts too can be fooled. History, "Zelig" tells us, is a matter of perception, not evidence.

The original model for the Panorama was Philip de Loutherborough's Eidophysikon, a mechanical device much like a modern special effects stage. Lights, sound, and studio miniatures, enabled painters to observe "the sublimities of nature captured in the studio." Once, according to a contemporary account, a real thunderstorm occurred during a presentation of the mini-spectacle, "A Storm at Sea." Many in the audience considered it a warning against the blasphemous recreation taking place on the stage, but de Loutherborough was delighted to have the opportunity to test his illusion against the real thing. Clutching the famed painter by the arm, he is said to have exclaimed, "By God, Gainsborough, our thunder's best!"[18]

No modern audience would be fooled into thinking that a model stage with tiny ships and mechanical waves was anything but a pale imitation of a real storm, but projected on a screen, or transmitted through a television set, the illusion takes on a life of its own. As a promotional trailer for one of the Kennedy-related mini-series, ABC broadcast a clip showing a recreation of Jack Ruby's killing of Lee Harvey Oswald—an event that was first recorded on television. As the fictional clip was rebroadcast over and over again, the memories of the *real* event faded away. A clone had taken its place.

We have reached a point in history where the terms "fiction" and "documentary" have, to all intents and purposes, lost their meaning. What counts is whether an audience believes that what they are seeing is the truth. As computerized studios allow the recreation of historical scenes from photographs, without resorting to actors or live locations, producers may soon be able to dispense with historical images entirely.

In the twenty-first century, the past may unfold before us in three-dimensional holograms, and today's television will seem no more real than von Werner's Panorama or the primitive newsreels of 1900 do now. Production systems may be simplified and made more accessible to diverse viewpoints and interpretations of history, enriching our understanding of the present, as well as the past, but only if producers and historians take their social responsibilities seriously.

The dark side of the vision, though, is the nightmare of media technology at the service of commerce and ideology, and the possibility that audiences will turn away from the light, rejecting written history and the events of the real world, and turn instead toward the shadows of Plato's cave. Faintly illuminated by the glow of giant television screens, people will watch an endless flow of well-crafted images of past, present, and future that will be more dramatic, more persuasive—more real even—than life.

Anatomy of a Disinterment:

The Unmaking of Afro-American History

In the summer of 1984, workers clearing a stockpiling site for a proposed quarry find a number of abandoned graves. As dictated by Virginia statues, the location of the rural Piedmont gravesite is duly noted, and clearing operations cease. The stone-mining company asks the court's permission to relocate the gravesite. It is eager to resume activities, since its development plans have already been delayed by local residents who have challenged the company's bid to rezone the site, have opposed its request for tax-free, low-interest, revenue bonds, and now challenge its request to remove the graves. What can these graves and the ensuing court hearing disclose about the nature of public history and in particular Afro-American public history?

This conflict exposes the manner in which history can be used to serve different interests, and it illustrates the significance of recognizing underlying cultural assumptions when we discuss the "historical consciousness" of social groupings. Most important, the issues raised during this conflict point to the centrality of power in determining which facets of the past are remembered and celebrated.

The discovery of the graveyard transforms the quarry issue into a complex conflict between the company and local county residents, between different factions in the county, and eventually between opposed views of history. The mining company consults a historian, a burial vault company, and an undertaker. The historian finds that the gravesite is most likely a nineteenth-century Afro-American one and suggests that the removal of the graves to a new site would present no historical problem, while the other two experts confirm the

BY GERTRUDE FRASER AND
REGINALD BUTLER

company's argument that removal of the graves is technically feasible. Armed with this testimony, the stone-mining company institutes legal proceedings in the local circuit court.

County residents who oppose the company's request fall into two distinct factions. The most vocal group, white homeowners who live near the proposed mining site, argue that it would destroy the rural character of the county and devalue their nearby homes. Other opponents, also white, believe that the gravesite may contain the remains of their ancestors rather than those of blacks. The legal recognition and preservation of the graves as an ancestral site would both legitimize their claims to deep roots in the county and enhance the county's status as an important historical area.

County residents who favor the stone-mining operation and the transfer of the graves also place a high value on kin and are proud of the county's historical heritage. They are more concerned, however, with broadening the tax base, fostering industrial growth, and increasing local employment. Representing the whole spectrum of the county's white population, these individuals believe that "progress" should be encouraged. For some, progress means increased business possibilities; for others, increased employment. But they agree that historical preservation and rural aesthetics are secondary issues.

Despite the gravesite's identification as Afro-American, black county residents do not involve themselves publicly in the disinterment controversy. Although 20 percent of the county's 11,000 residents are Afro-Americans and the black presence in the area can be documented as far back as the early eighteenth century, most Afro-Americans seem to support the quarry. We will explore the reasons for this "support" and for the Afro-American community's apparent indifference to the gravesite's relocation.

But first the testimony. The spoken and unspoken discourse between the lawyers and witnesses reveals the lines of conflict, the hidden assumptions, and the relative weight given to selected aspects of the past. Thus, we closely follow the original phrasing and ordering of the testimony as it was presented.

The mining company's vice-president testifies first. He answers his lawyer's questions about the cemetery. Yes, he has seen the "abandoned" graveyard, which is hard to reach by conventional transportation. Marked by a few sunken holes, without headstones, no fence demarcates its boundaries. It has not been maintained; only patches of periwinkle and the sunken holes indicate that the area was once cleared and used. It is in every sense—both legal and practical—an abandoned graveyard.

But the vice-president tells of a second cemetery, also discovered during his company's timber-felling operations. It presents a sharp contrast. It is the "right" kind of cemetery—a historically significant one. According to the vice-president's testimony, the second graveyard, discovered on the northern part of the acreage slated for mining, is "white." Set back in the woods, some miles away from the abandoned graves, and situated near land that was once the home of a plantation family and their descendants, it is encircled by an old iron gate. Inside the gate among the weeds are cultivated boxwood trees and a large cedar. Marked headstones identify the graves of at least five individuals with the same family name—one with deep roots in the county. These graves belong to the plantation's former owners. The ruins of the old plantation house still stand nearby.

On this cemetery's perimeter, but outside the fence, are several unmarked graves. These, according to the vice-president, are the graves of family slaves and servants. Here, at the second cemetery's southeast corner, his company wishes to relocate the graves from the abandoned gravesite. This will be "better suited" for everyone concerned.

The historian, in proper hierarchical order, takes the witness stand next. He is obviously well versed in the county's history, having written an extensive volume for its bicentennial. He has read, he testifies, 25,000 manuscript pages, xeroxed almost 4,000 documents, and seen at least 200 graveyards in the course of his research. Yet only 28 of the 579 pages of his book are devoted to the two hundred years of Afro-American history in that county. Nonetheless, at the court hearing, the historian's language—the language of historical authority—gives credibility to the company's relocation plans. A paid expert witness, he lists his qualifications—nineteen years at a local college teaching Virginia and British history, a master's degree in history acquired in less than a year, publication of the bicentennial volume (his first book), articles in state historical publications, and membership in various local and national professional associations—and then proceeds to testify.

He basically repeats the vice-president's testimony. The graveyard sits on a small hillock that is indeed covered with periwinkle. It was planted, he argues, because the plant is a sturdy form of groundcover, not—as the opponents to the graves' relocation claim—because it was a traditional funeral plant of the Virginia landed gentry. About thirteen indentations suggest graves facing east and north. Although there are no headstones, he believes that the three or four stone blocks sitting at the head of the site were used to set off the graveyard. But these stones are unmarked and of undressed, unchiseled granite. The unmarked stones, the absence of a fence, and the gravesite's location away from the main plantation house are strong evidence, the historian testifies, that the abandoned cemetery is a black cemetery. Having seen at least fifteen similar graves, he roughly dates it to the post-Reconstruction period.

How is the cemetery's presence on former plantation land to be explained? And why are these black individuals buried at such a distance from their counterparts? It is likely, the historian argues, that former slaves or free black plantation workers were given a separate plot to bury their dead. That they are not buried close to the plantation house on the periphery of the white cemetery suggests that they were not close family servants or slaves. He believes that freed blacks may have returned to bury their dead on land that held the remains of family members. He further testifies that the appropriateness of the removal of these graves to the perimeter of the white cemetery is indicated by the presence there of undressed granite blocks of the same type as those found on the abandoned gravesite. These indicate, he testifies, that black people were buried both on the perimeter of the second cemetery and in the abandoned graveyard.

Despite his detailed testimony, or perhaps because of it, the historian answers in the negative when the company lawyer asks if the abandoned graveyard has any "historical significance." None whatsoever, he answers, reciting from memory the Virginia Landmark Commission's criteria for historical significance. He points out that the abandoned black graveyard has no unique or special design and has no important person buried there. Furthermore, it is neither on the site of the home of a famous individual nor the birthplace of a noteworthy individual. Finally, he finds no evidence that a Civil War battle or skirmish occurred on the site.

All historically significant landmarks, he declares, must be culturally, architecturally, politically, or socially valuable to the community, Virginia, or the nation, and clearly the abandoned black graveyard does not meet this standard. The historian testifies that he can see no moral or historical problem with the company's plans to relocate the graves. Besides, he adds tangentially, even Napoleon was moved. The local paper later quoted the historian, who "felt bad about testifying against residents [the county's white residents who opposed the quarry] with whom he felt a certain kinship, but [he] had to be true to historical matters as he saw them".

The burial vault representative's testimony follows that of the historian. He has moved at least two hundred graveyards and foresees no special problems with this one. He admits that he is not a historical expert (though he wishes he were). Still, he estimates that the graveyard and graves are at least a hundred years old, and no burial has taken place during that time. Although he is hesitant to say for sure, he is also of the opinion that blacks are buried on the site. It is his understanding that most blacks did not have the money to buy dressed and etched headstones. This witness states most emphatically what has previously been assumed but left unsaid. The abandoned graveyard is unimportant not just because it is abandoned, but because it holds the remains of nameless blacks—perhaps destitute and unable to afford much more than a few granite blocks and a borrowed plot of land.

In response to questions by the company lawyer, the burial vault representative confirms that enough space is available to inter thirteen or more bodies on the second cemetery's periphery. This move is especially suitable, he agrees, since some "form" of black people are already buried there. He responds negatively when asked if in his examination of the abandoned graveyard he had come across any gun or "any other thing that is historic" and stresses that the disinterred remains will be buried "honorably." They will be scooped up separately, interred in individual stone containers, and reburied one at a time at the new site under the supervision of an undertaker.

But the cross-examination reveals that neither the burial vault representative nor the funeral director has any experience in historical archaeology. The witness admits, for example, that he would be unable to tell if a particular casket had any historical significance; nor, since the graves are to be unearthed with a backhoe, will their contents be closely examined. He doubts, however, that this will present a problem, as he feels that most people with historical significance were well-off. In his candor, the witness articulates the point of view of the majority of those present in the court on both sides of the issue. To be historical in the present is to have been affluent in the past. And if affluence cannot be proven, then it is better to be white than black, if you want to be officially remembered and recognized.

As the lawyer for those opposed to the quarry calls his witnesses, we are again reminded of the hearing's focus on the relative importance of the abandoned cemetery to whites. He directs his defense solely toward the possibility that the abandoned cemetery may contain the remains of his clients' ancestors: no testimony that would establish the historical value of a free black graveyard is ever presented.

His first witness is a member of the Daughters of the American Revolution (DAR) as well as the local historical society. Having done genealogical research for fifteen years, she suspects that the graves are on property that belonged to her great-great-great-grandparents. Her grandfather's DAR-certified status as a southern patriot gives, in her opinion, support to the view that the graves and the land have historical significance and should not be disturbed. Furthermore, she argues, her ancestors did not believe in slavery and freed their slaves. Thus, she is almost positive that the graveyard could not be a black one. The presence of periwinkle indicates to her that the graves are those of affluent landholders, as she thinks that the plant was used as a funeral decoration exclusively by Virginia gentry. But if the graves do not contain the remains of her white forebears, she has no objection to their reinterment on the second cemetery's periphery.

Other descendants of former property owners take the stand. One witness is able to trace ownership of land near the site to the late eighteenth century through his mother's line. Another feels that her great-great-great-grandfather may be buried in or near the abandoned gravesite. But neither, in the presiding judge's view, presents plausible evidence to support these claims. Finally, a direct descendant of the former plantation's last owner speaks. Her ancestors are buried in the second cemetery. Once assured that this cemetery will not be disturbed by the mining company, she has no objection to the disinterring of the abandoned graves and their relocation on the periphery of the second cemetery—her family cemetery. She insists, however, that they are not to be buried within the fence. If these are the graves of blacks, the witness presumably wants to maintain the distance accepted by her slave-owning forebears; whites with headstones on the inside of the fence, blacks in unmarked graves on the outside.

The company lawyer, in his summation to the court, rejects the possibility that the abandoned black graveyard may have historical significance outside of its relationship to the white cemetery. Relying on his historian's testimony, he argues that the graveyard falls far short of any criterion for historical significance. He maintains that opposition to relocating the grave is based on the false assumption that because the ancestors of certain witnesses once owned the land, they are buried there. It is, he asserts, appropriate that the remains of nineteenth-century blacks be reburied on the second cemetery's outer edge, since other blacks are already buried there. Expressing a belated concern for the graves' welfare, he points out that the move will make them more accessible and easier to maintain. But he does not explain why hitherto abandoned graves will suddenly be cared for in a new location.

Having heard all the evidence and both summations, the judge rejects the opponents' call for further study and consultation with archaeologists. Their lawyer has presented no expert testimony and has failed to show just cause for delaying the company's development plans. Finding no proof that the abandoned graveyard is historically significant, and convinced that disinterment will proceed with honor and dignity, the judge rules in favor of the company.

Although the court hearing is the core of our analysis, the graves are only an endpiece to larger struggles between opposed socio-political and economic interests. As this case study aptly illustrates, history is publicly presented in specific economic and social contexts. In fact, to say that history is "presented" is too passive an expression. Public history is created. Past events and circumstances are actively fashioned and refashioned so that they may more closely accommodate the dominant audience's economic, moral, and political concerns.

The history of the abandoned gravesite became public initially as part of an ongoing public debate about the relative advantages and disadvantages of rural industrialization. But as the trial proceeded, the dispute focused on the gravesite's identity. The company's interests would be best served if the graves were identified as Afro-American, since this would facilitate its plan to relocate the cemetery. By contrast, the opponents wanted to prove that the gravesite contained the remains of their white ancestors. The graves were pawns in a battle between the economic interests of the company and the economic and cultural concerns of the white opponents. Yet the two opposing factions both used elitist notions of history in arguing for or against the disinterment.

The view of history as the story of large events, old buildings, and important white personages dominated the proceedings at the court hearing. And in both the lawyers' arguments and the testimony of witnesses for and against the disinterment and relocation, this view obscured the Afro-Amerian role in county and state history. The setting of the hearing made the same point. The interior of the courthouse featured portraits of Founding Fathers and dead and retired judges (many of whom represented for the county's Afro-Americans a long history of legal and social injustice), and its expansive lawn contained a prominent, well-cared-for monument to the valor of the Confederate soldiers. The many brave Afro-Americans who struggled against their enslavement were nowhere publicly celebrated.

The unstated assumptions of the hearing's participants as well as their stated opinions revealed racist attitudes. These attitudes provided a framework within which the company's lawyer established a rationale for disinterring and relocating the graves. The logic was circular but effective. Since the graveyard had yielded no obviously important artifacts (Civil War weapons, buttons from uniforms) and had none of the accoutrements of the white cemetery, then it must have been Afro-American. In turn, since the gravesite *was* an Afro-American one, there was little reason to preserve it or even to examine it archaeologically before its disruption. Indeed, a cornerstone of the company's testimony was the historian's characterization of the graveyard as Afro-American. By contrast, the local residents attempted to establish that the graveyard was important precisely because it was *not* Afro-American.

An important aspect of these obverse perspectives was the decision to relocate the cemetery around the periphery of the white cemetery. Despite the hearing's focus on honorable reinterment, its participants wanted to ensure that whites not be inadvertently buried with blacks. Racial distinctions were to be preserved during the relocation.

This emphasis on the racial separation of the dead superseded any other issue of historical merit and ignored the distinctions that nineteenth-century blacks may have made among themselves. Perhaps the establishment of a separate burial site was a conscious effort by these free blacks to emphasize that they were no longer chattel. If so, why did they bury their dead on land owned by their former owners? What of the granite blocks and periwinkle? Did the orientation of the graves to the east and north have any significance? The historian had convinced the court that such questions were irrelevant. Yet in his ability to give detailed testimony about the gravesite from the few visible surface artifacts and from his familiarity with similar sites, he contradicted his own contention that little historical information could be gleaned from a closer examination of the gravesite.

The abandoned black cemetery became a pawn in a struggle between interest groups with surprisingly similar views of history; in this rural county the issues remained in the domain of "white folks' business." In the atmosphere of the court hearing, there was little room even to broach the suggestion that the gravesite was important because it might have contributed to an understanding of the development of the Afro-American community. The company's lawyer (with the historian's help) successfully circumscribed the terms of discourse so that this was the only logical conclusion. By the end of the hearing everyone (except those opponents who lived near the quarry) agreed that the decision to relocate the graves was appropriate.

Although Afro-Americans were publicly silent during the controversy, they did have a stake in the proceedings. Among the factors that contributed to the absence of Afro-Americans from the controversy was their de facto exclusion from the decision-making process. This exclusion, however, was not a calculated one. The debate surrounding the discovery of the abandoned graveyard was highly publicized across the state. There were no explicit attempts to bar the participation of Afro-Americans. What then is the reason for this voluntary absence, and what are its implications for an understanding of the relationship of Afro-Americans to facets of their historical heritage?

The threads of memory about a graveyard used by former slaves of the plantation and their families were probably easily frayed and broken in the aftermath of the Civil War. This is characteristic of Afro-American history in rural areas of the South, where few written records of Afro-American life exist. The official criteria of the Virginia Landmark Commission played an important role in the company's argument precisely because of the hearing's focus on tangible, easily documented history. As we have seen, in the event of a choice between black history and "progress," the rare physical markers of an Afro-American past are easily destroyed.

The absence of vital records, combined with political and economic circumstances preventing Afro-Americans from owning the land they occupied, makes it difficult to "prove" the presence of Afro-Americans. White witnesses at the hearing could fairly accurately trace their family trees to the pre–Civil War period, but blacks rarely can. Surnames, for example, are frequently not given for slaves and free blacks in the surviving county records. It would have been almost impossible for black claimants to assert an interest in the abandoned cemetery since the individuals buried on the site did not own the land.

The very terms of the debate and its setting in the county courthouse, with hired lawyers, a professional historian, and a judge, precluded the involvement of a majority of the county's Afro-American residents. What was there to celebrate in reminders of servitude and of an exploitative relationship, the effects of which were still being felt? This, we believe, explains why the county's middle-class Afro-American residents failed to spearhead black opposition to the disinterment. Having distanced themselves from poverty, they had little to gain from throwing their energies into preserving an unidentified graveyard of obviously dependent individuals who were not related to them.

Our discussions with Afro-American residents of the county also revealed that they did not involve themselves in the controversy in part because they did not live in the area of the proposed stone-mining operation—a section that we later learned was initially slated for development as a planned upper-middle-class (white) community. The specific concerns of the quarry's most vocal opponents—that the quarry would affect the water supply, cause undue traffic, and have adverse health effects—had little relevance for Afro-Americans. And there was tacit support in the Afro-American community for the quarry. A member of the county's small black middle class noted that he did not know of any black people who opposed the quarry.

Afro-Americans with whom we spoke all either supported the quarry or expressed no opinion on the issue. One informant suggested that Afro-Americans were far too much concerned with day-to-day problems of finding and maintaining jobs and supporting families or with keeping up with their businesses to pay much attention to the destruction of a gravesite. The possibility that the graves were those of free blacks seemed not to matter. Initially, we connected this tacit Afro-American support for the quarry with the increased job opportunities presented by its opening. Actually, the county has a 2.6 percent unemployment rate—one of the lowest in the state. Local Afro-Americans work in the nearby city, in the local penal institution, and seasonally in the timber and pulpwood industry. As one informant suggested, "Most people who wanted jobs, had them." The quarry would have little economic impact on black residents. Overall, it would provide only twenty to twenty-five new jobs, most of them to be filled by engineers and other skilled personnel (probably white) from outside the county.

These facts suggest that there were other reasons for Afro-Americans' tacit support of the quarry. For black as for white supporters, the march of progress took priority over a few graves. Progress was better even if it was not clearly in the best interests of most of the county's residents and the county itself. According to a long-time black resident of the county: "There is nothing in there but the soil. So if they move it over there, what difference does it make?" The stone-mining corporation had successfully gained the support of a majority of the county's residents, blacks and whites, affluent and poor, by drawing on the powerful symbols of industrial growth and rural progress. But were there other reasons for the public silence of Afro-Americans on an issue that ostensibly concerned their history?

During the court hearing the company's lawyer and historian deliberately juxtaposed the enclosed white cemetery with the abandoned and overgrown Afro-American gravesite. Their emphasis on the material poverty of the Afro-American graveyard implied a parallel poverty of historical importance. The underlying suggestion was that the Afro-Americans' historical impact on the county was also negligible. These assumptions did not coincide with those of Afro-American residents, but neither did the company's description of the disordered condition of the abandoned graveyard mesh with their collective representation of their own past. Thus, blacks chose to distance themselves from the debate because they found it to be unrelated to *their* community history.

The experiences of blacks in the county were dramatically different from those of whites. This accounted for their contrasting view of history. Yet despite these differences, rooted in slavery, segregation, and unequal ownership of resources and access to power in the county, both groups shared a reference point when they evaluated the importance of the past. Social history's current concern with the everyday experiences of ordinary men and women has had little effect on the historical thinking of most people, either black or white. Whites in the county defined history in terms of famous personages and great events. Blacks also used a "great persons" approach to Afro-American history that drew attention to the achievements of the past. Both groups thus tended to see a forgotten Afro-American graveyard as not worth preserving. Yet this same act—the abandonment of the gravesite—marked the power of whites and the lack of power of blacks.

In another respect the Afro-Americans' approach to the question of historical importance differed sharply from that of white supporters and opponents of the quarrry. An Afro-Amerian informant, when told that the gravesite might have importance as a burial ground for free blacks, replied that this hardly mattered, since the graves could not be traced to any particular family. From his perspective, the cemetery would be important not in its abstract relationship to county or Afro-American history, but in its concrete connection to a specific black family. Afro-Americans, in part because of the history of slavery and segregation in Virginia (and in this county), judged historical worth in terms of the achievements of named (not anonymous) black persons or families and on the basis of their membership in the Afro-American community. The graves rested on property that none of our Afro-American informants remembered as ever being owned or lived on by blacks. Thus, they reasoned that little would be lost if the graves were moved, particularly since there was the likelihood that the new quarry would provide a few more jobs.

This view does not point to a *lack* of historical consciousness on the part of these Afro-Americans but reveals instead a particular form of historical consciousness. Its expression is closely related to the manner in which community members relate contemporarily to one another. On first meeting, the most important questions are directed to finding out "who you are" and "where you live." These questions are not idle; the answers place the individual in a firm context of family connections, residence or land ownership in defined sections of the county, and membership in specific churches. Together they help determine the basis of the initial relationship between the questioner and the person being questioned.

Historical merit is judged along the same lines. Is the event, place, or person important to a specific Afro-American family, to an area in which Afro-Americans traditionally lived, or to a generally known story about a person, place, or event? This concern with family and community history runs parallel to a more general knowledge of Afro-Americans on the national scene. People like Martin Luther King and Harriet Tubman are considered important, for example; county history and Afro-American history as a generic category are considered less important.

The thrust of the white quarry opponents' argument was that the abandoned gravesite was important not only to their families but also to the county. For whites, family genealogy had everything to do with county history. The white supporters of the quarry shared this view, and this is why they argued that blacks, not whites, had been buried on the site. Pride in one's family history derived in great measure from pride in the county's past. By contrast, the county's Afro-American residents found little to celebrate in the county's official past—a story that, in their view, detracted from rather than added to the public history of their families and community.

In the final summation, the fate of a few sunken holes and scattered stones in the woods is likely to be irrelevant to the broader history of Afro-Americans in the county. What is of essential importance are the underlying assumptions of the participants in the court hearing and in the Afro-American community—assumptions that shaped their approach to historical problems.

What, then, is the role of the historian in telling the historical tale of the unheralded ancestors of Afro-Americans? It is to insist on the historical centrality of Afro-Americans in the making of America. It is to insist on the complexity of that contribution; to celebrate and to denounce; to acknowledge those who surmounted oppression as well as to give voice to the majority who just survived, and to those who did not survive. It is to rail against the alienation of Afro-Americans from facets of their own history and to insist that they explore the basis of that alienation. Eventually it is to tear at the roots of hidden and explicit ideologies that perpetuate the asymmetry of economic and cultural relationships in the present.

★ II ★
Professionalizing the Past:

Reflections on Applied History

Visiting the Past

History Museums in the United States

On any given summer afternoon, a considerable number of Americans go to visit the past. They drive to Greenfield Village, or Colonial Williamsburg, or Old Sturbridge. They stroll through old houses, admire antique cars, or watch colonial farmers and shoemakers at work. They might also see a movie, read a guidebook, or listen to costumed interpreters explain the way things used to be. Hundreds of these history museums dot the U.S. landscape; millions of people visit them each year; and it seems reasonable to suppose that they help shape popular perspectives on the past.

In this article I intend to discuss the *kinds* of perspectives the museums promote. This can best be done by looking at their history. I will try to demonstrate that from the mid-nineteenth century on, most history museums were constructed by members of dominant classes and embodied interpretations that supported their sponsors' privileged positions. I do not contend that those who established museums were Machiavellian plotters; the museum builders simply embedded in their efforts versions of history that were commonplaces of their class's culture. From the 1930s onward, elite control of these markers of the public memory came under increasing challenge. This survey will examine how the museums responded and conclude with some speculations on their future.

Antebellum Americans were not sentimental about saving old buildings. In the midst of the War of 1812, the state of Pennsylvania tried to tear down Independence Hall and sell the land to commercial developers. Protests saved the building, but not before two wings had been demolished and the woodwork stripped from the room in

BY MICHAEL WALLACE

137

which the Declaration of Independence had been signed. Most other venerable buildings situated on valuable real estate fared less well. This exuberant and cavalier demolition of the remains of the past reflected partly a booming land market and partly the antihistorical bent captured in Thoreau's contemptuous dismissal of England as "an old gentleman who is travelling with a great deal of baggage, trumpery which accumulated from long housekeeping, which he has not had the courage to burn."[1] It was not until the approach of civil war in the 1850s that a small segment of the patriciate, frightened that the Republic seemed to be coming apart and persuaded that a memorialization of the nation's founders might serve as an antidote, began to reconsider this position. In 1850 Governor Hamilton Fish asked the New York State Legislature to save George Washington's revolutionary headquarters in Newburgh from impending demolition. The legislators agreed, noting, "It will be good for our citizens in these days when we hear the sound of disunion reiterated from every part of the country . . . to chasten their minds by reviewing the history of our revolutionary struggle." On July 4, 1850, the flag was raised over the first historic house in the United States—as much a shrine as a museum.[2]

Three years later a group of businessmen tried to buy Mount Vernon and turn it into a hotel. This provoked another and far more significant preservation effort. The governor of Virginia asked John Washington, the current occupant, to sell it to the state. Washington agreed, but asked a stiff $200,000. The price, he noted somewhat defensively, "may appear to be extravagant, yet I have good reason to believe it is not more than could be readily obtained for the property were it in the Public Market." The governor asked the Virginia legislature to appropriate the funds, arguing that although the figure might be "exorbitant," if considered as an "ordinary transaction of business, . . . dollars become as dust when compared with the inestimable patriotism inspired by a visit to the tomb." The outraged legislators balked, and the movement to preserve Mount Vernon shifted to private hands.[3]

Ann Pamela Cunningham, daughter of a wealthy South Carolina planter, announced a crusade to save the homesite. She, too, wanted to create a rallying point for nationalist forces, but was perhaps even more worried by the disintegrating effect of a commercial and capitalist political economy, of which the attempt by "soulless speculators" to disturb "the shades of the dead" was yet another symptom. Because it was thought to be Woman's special role to preserve the frail bonds of social solidarity against threatening Commerce, she turned for help to wealthy, socially prominent women who had family connections to the revolutionary generation. Cunningham and her new colleagues formed the Mount Vernon Ladies' Association (MVLA) and set out to create a "shrine where at least the mothers of the land and their innocent children might make their offering in the cause of the greatness, goodness and prosperity of their country." The MVLA campaign soon attracted members of the middle and upper classes, North and South, who were working to preserve the Union. Edward Everett, a former Massachusetts senator and secretary of state, gave an immensely popular oration on the life of Washington to 139 gatherings across the country and contributed the proceeds to the MVLA. He hoped that Mount Vernon would offer "a common heritage for the estranged children of a common father, the spell of whose memory will yet have the power to reunite them around his hallowed sepulchre."[4]

Mount Vernon was saved in 1859, but the Washington cult failed to spark a pro-Union revival. Nor did it inaugurate a widespread change in attitude to the past. John Hancock's house was demolished during the Civil War: he had been an exemplary revolutionary hero, but when the market value of the land reached $120,000, his birthplace was turned over to the wreckers. In the postwar Gilded Age, it was definitely business as usual, and even the Centennial celebrations of 1876 looked more to the dynamos of the future than the inheritance of the past.[5] Still, the crusaders of the 1850s had blazed a trail to the past. Their legacy included an insistence that private gain be subordinated to larger concerns, a demonstration that it was possible to appropriate the aura that Washington's presence had invested in particular buildings and put it to work, and a certification that it was proper for upper-class women to preserve and present history to the public.

In the 1880s the dominant classes' attitude toward history began to change. By the 1890s it had undergone a remarkable transformation. Upper and middle-class men and women established ancestral societies and historical associations in great numbers. They also set about rescuing old buildings and displaying them to the public, preserving battlefield sites, and erecting shrines and monuments. By 1895 there were twenty house museums; by 1910 there were one hundred.[6] How are we to account for this?

These were, of course, years of triumph and consolidation for corporate capitalism in the United States. But the masters of the new order—the industrial magnates, the financiers, the old patrician families, and the powerful middle class of managers and professionals—found their position contested by social classes who had also been summoned into being by the new order of things. The battles with immigrant workers, discontented artisans, and disgruntled small farmers were often brutal and direct trials of military, political, and economic strength. But the combat had cultural dimensions as well, and it was in this area that new attitudes toward history were generated.

The Haymarket affair and the great strikes of the 1880s appear to have been the events that galvanized the bourgeoisie into reconsidering its disregard for tradition. Convinced that immigrant aliens with subversive ideologies were destroying the Republic, elites fashioned a new collective identity for themselves that had at its core the belief that there was such a thing as the American inheritance, and that they were its legitimate custodians. Class struggle was transmuted into defense of "American values" against outside agitators.[7]

The progenitors of this class culture were chiefly the older patrician elite—those who had inherited landed, mercantile, or early industrial wealth. They found longstanding cultural and political authority suddenly being challenged: the Adams family's turn to the past accelerated markedly after the Knights of Labor captured the Quincy town meeting in 1887. Nor were they pleased with the rawboned plutocrats whose command of immense concentrations of capital had catapulted them to political prominence. Patricians discovered in their historical pedigrees a source of cultural and psychic self-confidence and took the lead in forming a host of new institutions. Some were exclusive ancestral societies like the Sons of the American Revolution (1889), the Daughters of the American Revolution (1890), and the Mayflower Descendants (1897). They also took part in establishing historical societies and preservation groups, like the Association for the Preservation of Virginia Antiquities (1888), the Native Sons of the Golden West (1888), the American Scenic and Historic Preservation Society (1895), and the Society for the Preservation of New England Antiquities (1910).[8]

Patricians formed the vanguard of these groups, but the rank and file often included middle-class professionals, small business men, and civic and political leaders. Some big capitalists followed their lead, either as members (John D. Rockefeller joined the SAR) or as fiscal underwriters (Jay Gould supported the still-flourishing MVLA and C. F. Crocker, California's first millionaire, aided the Golden Sons), but the center of gravity of the movement lay in the ranks of the old monied.[9]

A central and enthusiastically pursued activity of these groups was the construction of shrines and memorials, including finding and marking the graves of old soldiers.[10] The MVLA was the model; many of the leaders of the new organizations were daughters of MVLA members. They sought out, bought up, restored, and displayed the houses in which famous men had lived. These projects enabled the elite to associate themselves and their class with the virtuous and glorious dead. In the process they also constructed and cultivated a class aesthetic: seventeenth- and eighteenth-century architecture became something of a cultural emblem. Some groups (like the Society for the Preservation of New England Antiquities, founded by William Sumner Appleton, the grandson of Nathan Appleton, one of the first textile magnates) were consequently willing to preserve buildings hallowed by association with the entire pre-immigrant social order, even if not connected with any particularly distinguished patriot. This class aesthetic tastefully demarcated them from both immigrants and vulgar *nouveaux riches*—the railroad barons, mine owners, and streetcar magnates then transporting dismantled European castles to the United States in order to live in "simulated feudal grandeur."[11]

The house museums also served a didactic function in the patricians' cultural offensive. Along with campaigns for patriotic and military education and drives to foster a cult of flag and Constitution, the museums sought to Americanize the immigrant working class. The shrines were thought magically to transform aliens brought within their walls. Mrs. J. V. R. Townsend, Colonial Dame, vice-regent of the MVLA, and chairwoman of the Van Cortlandt House Committee in New York City, explained in 1900 that the "Americanizing of the children—by enlisting their interest in historical sites and characters has a great significance to any thinking mind—the making of good citizens of these many foreign youths." Good citizenship meant accepting bourgeois rules of political action and abandoning radicalism. The working classes, one speaker told the Sons of the American Revolution, must be educated "out of all these crass and crazy notions of popular rights . . . into a true understanding of American liberty as handed down by our Fathers." The past, including the revolutionary tradition, had been transformed into an abstract symbol of Order.[12]

It is difficult to assess the impact of this Americanizing campaign. A rich literature shows that working-class communities fought to preserve their various national customs, traditions, and communal cultures. Sometimes their efforts took defensive, conservative, and ethnocentric forms; at other times they offered a base for revolutionary fervor. But always the community provided a self-identity that aided resistance.[13]

It seems likely that the Americanization campaigns had the greatest impact on those who organized them. The bourgeoisie buckled History around themselves like moral armor. The more they felt threatened, the more they grew convinced of their inherent, because inherited, legitimacy. Finally, what had been a relatively benevolent, if patronizing and provincial, mentality turned nasty and belligerent. Groups like the Immigration Restriction League (IRL)—bankers and professors driven to the point of hysteria by strikers and socialists—began to argue, with ever-greater racism and religious bigotry, that, in the words of IRL member John Fiske (the ancestral societies' favorite historian), "the antidote to the bane of foreign immigration" was "the enforcement of those American ideas inherited from the Revolution."[14] This tendency reached its peak in 1917–19 when the U.S. bourgeoisie, terrified first by the Bolshevik victory and then by the postwar strike wave, transmuted Americanization into a xenophobic and antileft demand for 100 percent Americanism. The viciousness of the time—the crushing of strikes, the raids on radical parties, the incarceration or deportation of critics, the support for lynch mobs and vigilantism—was fueled in large measure by the bourgeoisie's self-righteous conviction that it was defending not simply class privilege but a historic legacy.

After the war corporate capital moved to the forefront of the return to the past.[15] With labor and the left set back severely, business leaders began to exude a smug assurance that they were the sole and legitimate heirs of the American tradition. The president of the National Association of Manufacturers was sure that the citizens were "tired of chasing the will-o-wisps of radicalism in government, in religion, in art, and in social life, and are about ready to return to the god, the Bible, and the fundamental principles of their forefathers."[16]

Increasingly in the 1920s, businessmen became involved in bringing history to the masses. Some of these interventions into public history followed the patterns developed earlier. In 1923, for example, a group of New York lawyers and financiers directed a drive to save Thomas Jefferson's Monticello. But though Wall Streeters, not patrician women, were in charge, the outcome was the same: another traditional shrine.[17] The really decisive transformations in the history museum genre came at the hands of Henry Ford and John D. Rockefeller, Jr.

Before the war Henry Ford had been the very model of the ebullient, go-ahead capitalist; the mood of the 1880s and 1890s barely touched him. He had dabbled in Americanism, albeit of a forward-looking sort. At the Ford Company's English School (compulsory for all non-English-speaking employees), students acted out a pantomime in which some, dressed in national costume and carrying signs denoting their country of origin, entered a giant "Melting Pot"; simultaneously, prosperous-looking students streamed out of the pot dressed in business suits and waving little U.S. flags. In 1916, convinced that he and his class were revolutionizing the world, Ford made his most famous pronouncement: "History is more or less bunk. It's tradition. We don't want tradition. We want to live in the present and the only history that is worth a tinker's dam is the history we make today." Lampooned as an ignoramus, he stuck to his guns. "I don't want to live in the past," he told John Reed. "I want to live in the Now."[18]

The war years badly shook Ford, a committed pacifist, and the postwar labor upheavals unsettled his conviction that American capitalism could transcend class struggle via such devices as the five-dollar day. By 1919 he had discovered a new respect for the past.[19] In that year Ford began excavating and restoring his own history. He fixed up the old family farm, a schoolhouse he had attended, an inn he had once danced in. He and his friends dressed up in old costumes and held nostalgic parties.[20]

In 1923 he intervened in a more traditional preservation effort. A drive was on to save the Wayside Inn, a Sudbury, Massachusetts, hostelry built in 1702 and celebrated in a Longfellow poem. Ford bought the place outright and single-handedly restored it, added on a new wing and a ballroom, purchased 2,667 surrounding acres, built a special highway to detour auto traffic away from it, and transported there a gristmill, a sawmill, a blacksmith's shop, and a little red schoolhouse allegedly once attended by the Mary of "Mary Had a Little Lamb." When he had finished, he had created one of the first museum villages in the United States at a cost of somewhere between three and five million dollars. "I'm trying," he said, "in a small way to help America take a step, even if it is a little one, toward the saner and sweeter idea of life that prevailed in prewar days."[21]

Little steps soon grew to giant strides. Ford reformulated his position on history: only history as traditionally taught in schools was bunk. It concentrated too much on wars, politics, and great men (perhaps he had the ancestral societies in mind) and not enough on the material reality of everyday life for common folk. It also relied too heavily on book learning. "The only way," he thought, "to show how our forefathers lived and to bring to mind what kind of people they were is to reconstruct, as nearly as possible, the exact conditions under which they lived." This required assembling "the things that people used." "Get everything you can find!" he ordered the 35,000 Ford dealers across the United States. He wanted "a complete series of every article ever used or made in America from the days of the first settlers down to the present time." As Ford was the richest man in the world, offers to sell poured in, and in short order he had become the world's greatest collector of Americana. Carloads of relics were dumped into the tractor plant warehouse in Dearborn. In 1927 Ford announced that he would open an Industrial Museum to display his now immense horde of objects. By 1929 he had constructed a fourteen-acre building (with a replica of Independence Hall for an entrance façade) that housed exhibits recording the mechanization of agriculture and industry, the evolution of lighting, communications, and transportation, and the development of objects used in domestic life.[22]

In 1928 Ford announced that he would construct an Early American Village next to the museum and had trucked in a windmill from Cape Cod, the courthouse where Lincoln practiced law, two slave cabins, which went behind the Lincoln courthouse, a country store, an old inn, a New Hampshire firehouse, a Massachusetts shoeshop, several assorted buildings associated with his own youth, and the entire Menlo Park "invention factory" in which his good friend Thomas Edison had invented the light bulb.[23]

Ford's museum village—popularly known as Greenfield Village—was inaugurated in 1929 in the grandest possible manner. The Ford Motor Company teamed up with General Electric to reenact Edison's discovery of the electric light bulb in a ceremony presided over by President Hoover and attended by such titans as Charles M. Schwab, Gerard Swope, Otto H. Kahn, Owen D. Young, Henry Morgenthau, and John D. Rockefeller, Jr. History had arrived. Greenfield Village also became a popular success, with attendance figures dwarfing those compiled at the shrines. In 1934, the first year records were kept, 243,000 visited; in 1940, 633,000 stopped by.[24]

Most historians of the Ford phenomenon believe that Greenfield Village lacks any "clear central idea." Keith Sward finds it a "hodge-podge, despite its core of excellent restorations. It has the appearance of an Old Curiosity Shop, magnified 10,000 fold." But there are, I believe, some clear messages embedded in Ford's construction.[25]

The first is that life was better in the "saner and sweeter" Good Old Days of the rural republic. The vehicle to prove this assertion was the Early American Village. Perhaps unwittingly, the Village drew upon a well-established European genre—the open-air museum. A brief sketch of that earlier movement will help illuminate Ford's vision.

Back in 1891 Dr. Artur Hazelius had opened Skänsen, a seventy-five-acre outdoor museum on a site overlooking Stockholm harbor. There he assembled farm buildings from various parts of Sweden and soon added an iron-master's house, a manor house, a log church, windmills, stocks and whipping posts, and a series of craft shops. He staffed the museum with guides dressed in folk costumes, stocked it with farm animals, and threw in strolling musicians and folk dancers. It became quite popular. Similar enterprises soon opened in Norway, Finland, Russia, Germany, Belgium, Wales, and the Netherlands. The Skänsen movement blended romantic nostalgia with dismay at the emergence of capitalist social relations. As the new order had introduced mechanized mass production, a burgeoning working class, and class conflict, these museums, often organized by aristocrats and professionals, set out to preserve and celebrate fast-disappearing craft and rural traditions. What they commemorated, and in some degree fabricated, was the life of "the folk," visualized as a harmonious population of peasants and craft workers.[26]

Ford's Greenfield Village can best be understood as an Americanized Skänsen. Ford celebrated not "the folk" but the Common Man. He rejected the DAR's approach of exalting famous patriots and patrician elites. Indeed, he banished rich men's homes, lawyers' offices, and banks from his village. This museum-hamlet paid homage to blacksmiths, machinists, and frontier farmers, celebrated craft skills and domestic labor, recalled old social customs like square dancing and folk fiddling, and praised the "timeless and dateless" pioneer virtues of hard work, discipline, frugality, and self-reliance. It was a precapitalist Eden immune to modern ills, peopled with men and women of character. As Ford's friend and collaborator William Symonds wrote during the Depression, a "significant lesson of the Village" was that in the old days, when Americans "looked to themselves for a means of livelihood rather than to an employer," there had been "no destitution such as is seen today in large industrial centers during slack periods."[27]

Ford's village was a static utopia. There was no conflict, no trouble within its grounds. Ford had banished war and politics. He had also—by excluding banks, lawyers, and the upper classes—precluded discussions of foreclosures, depressions, and unemployment. That, in turn, obviated the need to refer to farmers' movements, strikes, and radical political parties. Ford's thrifty and self-reliant common folk (if only his assembly-line workers had been half so virtuous!) acted as individuals; square dancing was about as close as they got to collective action. There was no hint that nineteenth-century shoemakers and blacksmiths had possessed a vibrant alternative, and often anticapitalist, culture.

Ford did not leave Greenfield Village trapped in an idyllic past. In the Industrial Museum he supplied the motor force of history. The serried ranks of machines, arranged in developmental order, and the tributes to inventors and entrepreneurs like Edison (and himself) conveyed the other unmistakable message of Greenfield Village: life had been getting better and better since the good old days. Progress—as evidenced by ever-improved machines and commodities—had been made not by the farmers and craft workers, but by the mental labor of men of genius and rare vision.

The two messages together—life had been better in the old days and it had been getting better ever since—added up to a corporate employer's vision of history. From the vantage point of the village a gentle criticism of the current order was permitted; the declension in virtue from the times when men were men (and women were women) could be bemoaned. Still, one would not really want to turn the clock back to those primitive times, so it was best to get on with life, perhaps inspired to emulate not George Washington but the sturdy pioneers. Greenfield Village distorted the past, mystified the way the present had emerged, and thus helped to inhibit effective political action in the future.

But why would the billionaire master of mass production indulge in a vision that contained even a smidgeon of anticapitalist nostaligia? Why would the man who presided, in the 1920s, over a plant regarded as one of the worst sweatshops in Detroit, laud even a fictionalized and gutted old order of farmers and craftsmen? Part of the answer is that by the 1920s Ford had become a most atypical capitalist. Ford Motor, though gigantic, was still a family firm. He hated the newer forms of organization and the initiation of competition through models and colors, instituted by Alfred P. Sloan over at General Motors. He also despised financiers and considered Chrysler a plot by Wall Street bankers to do him in. It was precisely when Ford began to lose out to these new forces, as his biographer, James Brough, notes, that he sought to underline the closer connections of his own business approaches to traditional ways. Greenfield Village took shape at just the time that the Model T was forced into retirement. More broadly, Ford was something of a utopian and really believed that mass production/mass consumption capitalism could be made to work. The upheavals of 1919 had disturbed him, and so he spent the 1920s oscillating between past and future. When it all collapsed in 1929, he turned sour and ugly, bitter toward the bankers he held responsible, and vicious toward his protesting employees. In the 1930s he spent more and more time at Greenfield Village. It became for him a retreat from which he could criticize contemporary society without having to examine too closely the part he had played in creating it.[28]

G reenfield Village departed dramatically from the DAR formula. The other great enterprise of the twenties, John D. Rockefeller, Jr.'s Colonial Williamsburg, was more rooted in the traditional house museum mode but in the end proved equally revolutionary. Unlike Ford, Rockefeller, Jr. was quite comfortable with the new world of corporate capitalism; he had, after all, been born into it. But what really engaged his mid and spirit was not business, but buildings.[29] In 1923 he embarked on his long career in historic restoration. Attending a June fête at Versailles, he was disturbed to find the walls crumbling and water coming

[handwritten: Rockefeller restored buildings]

through the roof. He discovered to his dismay that Fontainebleu and Rheims were in a similarly deplorable condition. He immediately sent off a check for a million dollars to the French government to help repair the structures; he added another $1.85 million in 1927. His donations enabled the French to replace acres of roof. Rockefeller was particularly pleased that workers had also been able to revive the thatched houses and hedged lawns of Marie Antoinette's play peasant village, and to restore her marble-walled dairy to working order. It was, he thought, a "perfect dream of beauty and delight."[30]

From fixing up the abodes of French monarchs, Rockefeller turned next to the planter elite of eighteenth-century colonial Virginia. The original idea of resurrecting Williamsburg belonged to W. A. R. Goodwin, a local minister. He had first written to Henry Ford, heatedly insisting that the Motor King underwrite the cost of restoring the town the automobile culture was destroying, the town where Washington, Jefferson, and Patrick Henry had once walked. Ford never answered. But Rockefeller, to whom Goodwin next broached the idea, was hooked. He authorized Goodwin to buy up property in the town anonymously, sending him money under the name of "David's Father." When, in 1928, Goodwin disclosed who was behind the massive purchases, some old southern families were outraged at this intrusion of Yankee gold (as of 1980 a Mrs. Armistead was still refusing to sell). But the majority waved such reservations aside, and restoration began. *[handwritten: Goodwin + Rockefeller]*

Rockefeller and a host of supporting experts selected the 1790s as a cut-off decade and proceeded to demolish all 720 buildings constructed after that and to remove as many traces of modernity as possible, even rerouting the Chesapeake and Ohio railroad. Then they restored 82 surviving eighteenth-century buildings and, after meticulous research, reconstructed 341 buildings of which only the foundations remained. Rockefeller took to spending two months each year in Williamsburg. Ruler in hand, he was all over the site, insisting on scrupulous accuracy, regardless of cost. When architects discovered that they had reconstructed a house six feet from where new research showed it had actually stood, he immediately provided the money to move it. "No scholar," he said, "must ever be able to come to us and say we have made a mistake."[31]

When the bulk of the work had been completed, in the mid-1930s, Rockefeller, at a cost of $79 million, had built an exquisite little eighteenth-century town, clean, tidy, and tasteful. He was delighted. So was Virginia. In 1942 the commonwealth made him an honorary citizen, the first person so honored since the Marquis de Lafayette in 1785.[32]

Williamsburg, however, was far more than simply a personal indulgence à la Antoinette. Nor was it a Greenfield Village. Perhaps Ford's project had whetted Rockefeller's competitive appetite a little. But though there would be craft shops and costumed guides at Colonial Williamsburg, Rockefeller was not the least bit interested in recapturing the culture of "the folk." There were precious few "folk" in evidence, and there was absolutely no reference to the fact that half of eighteenth-century Williamsburg's population had been black slaves. This town commemorated the planter elite, presented as the progenitors of timeless ideals and values, the cradle of that Americanism of which Rockefeller and the corporate elite were the inheritors and custodians. Rockefeller had suggested such a connection as early as 1914. A member of a congressional committee investigating the Ludlow Massacre, perpetrated by the Rockefeller family's Colorado Fuel and Iron Company, asked whether he would continue to fight unionization "if that costs all your property and kills all your employees?" Rockefeller responded that he would do whatever was necessary to defend the "great principle" of the open shop: "It was upon a similar principle that the War of the Revolution was carried on."[33]

But Colonial Williamsburg was more than simply the DAR approach writ large. The ancestral societies had saved isolated houses. In a 1937 statement about his motives in building Williamsburg, Rockefeller wrote that "to undertake to preserve a single building when its environment has changed and is no longer in keeping, has always seemed to me unsatisfactory—much less worth-while." What had attracted him about Williamsburg was that it "offered an opportunity to restore a complete area and free it entirely from alien or inharmonious surroundings." A similar concern for an all-encompassing approach characterized his other projects in the 1920s and 1930s. While he was staking his claim to the past at Williamsburg, he was building Rockefeller Center, his notion of the future, in midtown Manhattan. Tearing down 228 brownstones and stores, he raised in their stead a mammoth entertainment-business complex in which, for the first time, skyscrapers became constituent parts of an integral order. He applied a similar logic and practice to land conservation. Touring western national parks in the mid-twenties, he was appalled to find that Jackson Hole, a valley in the Grand Tetons, was being developed in a hodge-podge, piecemeal fashion. His response was to buy out every single private owner in a 33,000-acre area—ranchers, farmers, lumbering industries, everybody—and deed the land to the U.S. government as a park. Like his father, who had made his fortune by overcoming the anarchy of production by a multitude of individual entrepreneurs in the Pennsylvania coal fields, Rockefeller, Jr. was interested in totalities.[34]

Colonial Williamsburg flows from this perspective. It does not simply borrow and display a historical aura; it embodies a vision of a total social order. Unlike Greenfield Village, Williamsburg's order flows from the top down. It is a corporate world: planned, orderly, tidy, with no dirt, no smell, no visible signs of exploitation. Intelligent and genteel patrician elites preside over it; respectable craftsmen run production paternalistically and harmoniously; ladies run well-ordered households with well-ordered families in homes filled with tasteful precious objects. The rest of the population—the 90 percent who create the wealth—are nowhere to be seen. The only whiff of conflict appears in recollections of the stirring anti-British speeches in which the Founders enunciated the timeless principles since passed down, like heirlooms, to the Rockefellers and their kind. Colonial Williamsburg was the appropriate past for the desired future; in this sense, Williamsburg and Rockefeller Center formed a matching set. Ford, at least, had grappled with history in the course of mystifying it; Rockefeller denied that history had ever happened.

The crash, Depression, and revivial of working-class movements brought the decade of complacent capitalist supremacy to a sudden end. The great corporate and genealogical museum projects would grind on through the thirties, but as the balance of class forces shifted, so did the nature of public history.

Franklin Roosevelt's administration supported new approaches to the past. Partly this was a matter of symbolic politics. He attacked—by mocking—the DAR, reminding them that they were descendants of immigrants and revolutionaries; when they denied Marian Anderson access to Constitution Hall, he supported Eleanor's arranging the famous concert in the Lincoln Memorial.[35] Apart from such cultural signals that elite claims to exclusvie possession of the past were now open to question, Roosevelt and his advisors embedded within the federal government an approach to public history that expanded the definition of the historic. Several bureaucratic agencies demonstrated that the state could compete with private capital as guardian of the public memory.

In 1933 a National Park Service architect proposed to Secretary of the Interior Harold Ickes that unemployed architects be set to work surveying and recording all "historic" buildings in the United States. Within two weeks 1,200 were employed by the Historic American Building Survey (HABS); by 1938, they had produced 24,000 measured drawings and 26,000 photographs of 6,389 historical structures. This campaign was remarkable in that many of the buildings surveyed had no connection whatever to famous men; their historical importance was rooted in local memories and traditions. Similarly, the Works Progress Administration (WPA) set writers and historians to work in the Federal Writers' Project. The WPA state guidebooks and collections of local lore reflected a populist shift away from the approach fostered by traditional and corporate elites, uncovering legacies of struggle and redefining

American history as something that included common people as historical actors.

In 1933 the Civilian Conservation Corps began actual restoration projects, and in 1935 the Historical Records Survey hired thousands to inventory public records in every U.S. county.[36] In the same year the Historic Sites Act authorized the Department of the Interior, acting through the National Park Service, to undertake an extraordinary range of preservation activities, including the actual acquisition of property, the preservation and operation of privately owned historic sites, the construction of museums, the development of educational programs, the placement of commemorative tablets, and the perpetuation of survey programs similar to HABS. Almost overnight, a massive federal presence had been authorized. It was not, however, exercised. In a few years the forces of reaction and the onset of war put an end to the New Deal and its public history initiatives.[37]

I n the postwar period labor gains were rolled back, left movements were suppressed, and multinationals and the military moved internationally to establish what they hoped would be the American Century. The cultural concomitant of capital's renewed supremacy was the thorough suffusion of cold war ideology, with stultifying effects on public presentations of history. The appropriators of past labor reappropriated labor's past. The populist openings of the thirties were checked and reversed, and the meaning of "historical" was narrowed once again, as the bourgeoisie set out to uproot "un-Americanism" and celebrate, with renewed complacency, "the American Way of Life." This revanchist movement took a variety of forms.

First there was what might be called the Corporate Roots movement. Boeing invested heavily in a new Museum of History and Industry in Seattle in 1952. The American Iron and Steel Institute spent $2,350,000 in 1954 to restore the seventeenth-century ironworks at Saugus, Massachusetts. R. J. Reynolds, Inc., donated substantial funds to restore the Miksch Tobacco Shop in Old Salem in 1957 and went on to pour large amounts into the restoration and "interpretation" of the old Moravian Community. The Stevens family and others in the textile industry sponsored the construction of the Merrimack Valley Textile Museum in the late fifties and early sixties. Most of these enterprises promoted a fetishized history, focusing on technological developments and ignoring social relations of production, to say nothing of class struggle. Visitors to Boeing's museum were not introduced to the Wobblies or the 1919 Seattle General Strike.[38]

postwar 2

Second, several Skänsen-type villages were established. The Farmers' Museum at Cooperstown, New York, composed of buildings transported from nearby sites, was dedicated to chronicling the everyday life of pioneer farmers and craftsmen. The museum focused relentlessly on objects and work processes rather than social relations or politics (visitors learning nothing, for example, about the antirent wars in New York State). In the Ford manner, the Farmers' Museum projected a sentimentalized portrait of the past and celebrated the transcendence of primitive living conditions. It romanticized the drudgery of women's domestic labor— "here was a sense of contentment, and satisfaction with a long day's work well done, which we might well envy"— yet also praised the new textile mills as labor-saving devices without asking who worked in those mills or what crises in the countryside had forced women into them.[39]

Another example of this genre was Old Sturbridge Village, which opened in 1946 after a long oscillation between the Ford and Rockefeller approaches. Albert B. Wells, a wealthy businessman, had begun collecting à la Ford in 1926. In 1936 Wells decided to build a museum village and called in the Williamsburg architectural firm of Perry, Shaw, and Hepburn. He soon fired them, believing that they had no feel for the locality and were too much influenced by their collaboration with Rockefeller in a project where they "had all the money in the world." After a visit to the Scandinavian open-air museums in 1938, Wells settled on a plan of bringing together a few local buildings and adding local craftsmen plying the old trades. He wanted to demonstrate both the early New Englanders' "ingenuity and thrift" and the way that "modern industry assures a life far more abundant than what existed under a handicraft system."[40]

3   The third kind of postwar enterprise was the traditional patriotic shrine, now converted to cold war purposes. One million people visited Mount Vernon in 1948, and in the 1950s new shrines, like the Independence National Historical Park, were opened. But the flagship of the fifties fleet remained Colonial Williamsburg.[41]

In 1939 John D. Rockefeller III became the chairman of the board of Colonial Williamsburg and called for an aggressive educational and public relations campaign. During the war he arranged a liaison program with the armed forces, and troops were brought to Williamsburg for inspirational purposes.[42] The wartime effort proved to be the prelude to a massive cold war enterprise. Rockefeller III, Williamsburg's president, Kenneth Chorley, and the educational director, Edward P. Alexander, set out to make Colonial Williamsburg "a shrine of the American faith," a source of "spiritual strength and understanding" at a "historic time of trial, questioning, and danger." Thomas J.

Wertenbaker, a Princeton historian who retired from teaching to work at Williamsburg, stressed in 1949 the political importance of the museum's mission:

> It would be difficult to exaggerate the educational value of historical restorations. At a time when the foundations of our country are under attack, when foreign nations are assailing our free institutions with all the misrepresentations which malice can suggest, when they are seconded by a powerful Fifth Column within our borders, when it has become a frequent practice to attribute selfish motives to Washington and Jefferson and Hancock and Samuel and John Adams . . . it is of prime importance that we live over again the glorious days which gave us our liberty.[43]

Chorley hoped that millions would come to Williamsburg and be reminded of the ancient heritage of contemporary ideals. John Edwin Pomfret, president of neighboring William and Mary College, suggested that such visits would help Americans "overlook those real or illusory differences of political or economic interest which ordinarily divide us. The flame of the patriots' passion welds us as nothing else can into a spiritual whole."[44]

Alexander, in his capacity as Williamsburg educational director, drew on the latest techniques to "create a historic mood through sensory perception." He wanted to generate a "moving inspiration of the American heritage" for visitors, and to inform them, through guidebooks, precisely what that heritage was. He taught that "eighteenth-century Williamsburg embodied concepts of lasting importance to all men everywhere." There were five such concepts: "opportunity," "individual liberties," "self government," "the integrity of the individual," and "responsible leadership." There was no mention of the concept—much less the reality—of slavery, nor of equally plausible revolutionary legacies like "equality" or "the right of revolution" or "anticolonialism." Williamsburg's concepts, though certainly capable of being invested with democratic meaning, were more often drafted into the service of the status quo. In the 1950s Chorley counseled the nation to follow its leaders as the young nation had harkened to the counsel of the Founding Fathers ("responsible leadership"), arguing that contemporary Americans should recognize that this "is becoming such a world as the Common Man cannot operate."[45]

Alexander's "concepts" could be bent to almost any purpose because they had been detached from the realities of eighteenth-century life. In the 1950s, as in the 1930s, Williamsburg was profoundly ahistorical. Fittingly, it received an accolade from the scholar most committed to the consensus history of the period, Daniel Boorstin. He applauded, as democratic and un-European, Williamsburg's attempt "to reconstruct the way of life of a whole past community." "Williamsburg," Boorstin said, was "an American kind of sacred document." It asserted a "continuity of past and present" and reminded us that "the past," rather than any "political ideology," was the living wellspring of contemporary ideals.[46]

Williamsburg launched aggressive programs to attract visitors. The Williamsburg staff initiated the Student Burgesses program, which brought together student leaders to discuss the nature of Freedom; International Assemblies for foreign students, at which they could learn about American ideals; and Democracy Workshops (co-sponsored by the U.S. Junior Chamber of Commerce and the Radio-Electronic-Television Manufacturers Association) on freedom of expression. At the 1955 Democracy Workshop—co-moderated by the president of the American Committee for Liberation from Bolshevism—Vannevar Bush explained that preservation of the Bill of Rights would depend on a "natural aristocracy."[47]

With the arrival of the Eisenhower administration in 1953, Williamsburg became a semiofficial auxiliary of the state, a site of great bourgeois rituals and political ceremonies. Williamsburg served as the customary arrival point for heads of state on their way to Washington. Winthrop Rockefeller would greet the arriving dignitaries and ride them down Duke of Gloucester Street in an eighteenth-century carriage; the guests would make brief remarks; they might attend an evening's ball at the Governor's Palace; and the next day they would proceed to Washington. Over a hundred heads of state went through this Rockefeller rite. Nor were lesser luminaries ignored. Together with the Department of State and the United States Information Agency, Williamsburg worked out a foreign visit program for political and professional leaders, and hundreds came to town each year. (The trustees also made foreign visits themselves, as when they presented the Williamsburg Award to Winston Churchill at a glittering gathering at Drapers' Hall, London, in 1955. Churchill fondly recalled, in mellow after-dinner remarks, that his 1946 Williamsburg visit had helped him recapture "the grace and the ease, and the charm of by-gone colonial days.") By the late 1950s, Williamsburg required a staff of over 1,900 people to manage its booming affairs.[48]

I n the 1960s there occurred another transformation in the museum field. Again it was closely connected to larger social and political developments. Since the late 1940s the highway and housing industries had been tearing up the material, cultural, and historical fabric of the country. State-backed developers rammed roads through cities, demolishing whole areas; urban renewal then devastated much of the remaining urban landscape.

By 1966 fully one half of the properties recorded by HABS in the thirties had been torn down.[49]

By the early sixties the people most threatened with urban dislocation and disruption had begun to protest. Amid this ferment, a small band of social scientists, architectural critics, psychologists, and journalists began to fashion a compelling critique of the social and psychological consequences of the urban renewal and highway programs. People like Jane Jacobs, Herbert Gans, Edward Hall, and Ada Louise Huxtable argued that the demolition shattered social networks and healthy urban communities, replacing them with bleak new high-rise projects and sterile suburbs. The new housing forms, they argued, denied human needs for historical connectedness: suburbs and projects alike undermined individual and social identities by ripping people out of history.[50]

These social critics and others long involved with the historic preservation movement noted that the history museums exhibited a similar temporal one-dimensionality and historical disconnectedness. And so, in the course of criticizing the American present, they leveled their guns on the American past. Colonial Williamsburg, Huxtable thought, "pickled the past." It lacked "any sense of reality, vitality or historic continuity." David Lowenthal found this to be true of most of the museums: "The American past is not permitted to coexist with the present. It is always in quotation marks and fancy dress . . . an isolated object of reverence and pleasure . . . detached, remote, and essentially lifeless." The sterility of the museums now came under scrutiny. "Williamsburg," Walter Muir Whitehill thought, is a "fantasy in which the more pleasing aspects of colonial life are meticulously evoked, with the omission of smells, flies, pigs, dirt and slave quarters." It was "history homogenized, cleaned up, and expurgated . . . an entirely artificial recreation of an imaginary past."[51]

"Williamsburg," another critic noted, "has the flavor of a well-kept contemporary suburb." Others pointed out that the reverse was also true: postwar suburbs looked like Colonial Williamsburg. This was not mere coincidence. Banks and insurance companies had accepted "false colonial" as a sound style on which to base their lending programs, and so vast areas of the East and Midwest modeled themselves on the restoration. During the fifties the United States was "Williamsburgered": there were Williamsburg drive-ins, Williamsburg hotels, Williamsburg gas stations, Williamsburg A&Ps. Small wonder that Daniel Boorstin saw past and present as continous: past and present looked remarkably alike.[52]

To this set of criticisms, rooted in resistance to wholesale devastation of historic properties and urban neighborhoods, was added another critique that came out of the political upheavals of the decade. Black, feminist, Native American, and antiwar (hence anti-national-chauvinist) activists began producing history in order to grasp the deep-rooted nature of the processes they were protesting against and to dismantle those readings of the past that provided powerful justifications for the status quo. In this climate of increasingly widespread awareness of the selective and distorted character of official history, the history museums' celebratory certainties became harder to sustain.

These various streams of thought and action produced a great ferment in the history museum field in the 1960s and 1970s. Grassroots museums sprang up around the country to preserve and commemorate local heritages. Many were amateur enterprises with an anticommercial ethic. "We are not out for the almighty buck," wrote one of the citizens of Russell Springs, Kansas, who saved their old courthouse and used it to display antiques, diaries, manuscripts, and memorabilia contributed by town residents. "We simply want to show people our past, of which we are rightly proud." Black residents in Bedford-Stuyvesant, New York, rallied in 1969 to block the demolition of four farmhouses that had been the nucleus of a nineteenth-century free black community and converted them into a black history museum. "One does not have to be a member of the Daughters of the American Revolution to be interested and concerned about their roots," insisted a black Kansas City preservationist: "It was good that we saved, and now maintain, Williamsburg, Virginia. And for the same reasons, we must save and maintain the slave cabins and some of the shotgun houses, little frame churches, jails and one-room school houses around the country that tell the story of black people in America."[53]

There were also instances of fruitful collaboration between community groups and younger historians whose work reflected a critical approach to the past. At Lowell, Massachusetts, community and university people produced a museum—housed in a still-working textile mill—that examined the history of the town from a perspective sensitive to working-class history and diverse ethnic cultures, and attuned as well to the nature of capitalist development in the nineteenth century.[54]

Many of the professional history museums changed with the times as well.[55] Some abandoned the filiopietistic approach (in some cases only after considerable internal conflict), insisted on rigorous standards of historical accuracy, and adopted the premises of the social historians then practicing in the academy. Many developed imaginative strategies for creating a more comprehensive portrait of past communities.

In the middle and late 1960s museologists unhappy with static reconstructions launched the Living Historical Farm movement. They sought to create a dynamic picture of farm life by organizing working farms that employed old agricultural processes. At some of these, like Plymouth, Massachusetts, interpreters lived in the old houses to accustom themselves to the furnishings and work practices. Structures developed a lived-in look; chickens and sheep wandered in and out of the buildings, which consequently became (as they once had been) fly-ridden and smelly. Abandoning Howard Johnson standards of cleanliness allowed a marked gain in historical accuracy. Even where simulations were not taken so far, as at Old Sturbridge Village, the museums reflected the influence of a new generation of historians and educators concerned with exploring work and family life with ever-higher standards of accuracy and, in some cases, with an eye to modern parallels.[56]

The waves of change even beat against the walls of Williamsburg. Winthrop Rockefeller stayed at the helm until his death in 1973, when Supreme Court Justice Lewis Powell took over, and Rockefeller money continued to flow; so did the stream of domestic and foreign dignitaries (the Shah of Iran stopped by three times). Still, the pressures were intense. A series of blistering critiques lambasted Williamsburg's focus on elites, its pinched definition of the revolutionary legacy, its stopped-time quality, its genteel banishment of dirt, disarray, and disorder.[57] One of the few people who had anything good to say about Williamsburg during this period was Alvin Toffler, and he liked it precisely because it was so unreal. A future-shocked society, he argued, will "need enclaves of the past—communities in which turnover, novelty and choice are deliberately limited. These may be communities in which history is partially frozen. . . . Unlike Williamsburg, . . . however, . . . tomorrow's enclaves of the past must be places where people faced with future shock can escape the pressures of overstimulation for weeks, months, even years, if they choose."[58]

Finally, in the 1970s, slavery was discovered at Williamsburg. The 1972 edition of the guidebook maintained Alexander's interpretive framework of the five concepts (he retired that year), but noted that, for example, the concept of individual integrity had been conspicuously limited in reality for slaves, women, debtors, and others. This trend was continued during that decade as a new, "modernizing" management team brought in a staff of young social historians who felt ill at ease with the traditional approach and who worked to transform the interpretive program. They consulted local black community groups and black historians on how to include the slave experience at Williamsburg and employed some imaginative street-theater techniques as a beginning. Alexander himself came to agree that the museums had been "too neat and clean, and [did] not pay enough attention to the darker side of human existence—to poverty, disease, ignorance and slavery," and he called for interpretations that would appeal "not only to the affluent and the elite, but also to the underprivileged and the discontented."[59]

But if the limits of the acceptable had been pushed back, limits remained nonetheless. Many museums abandoned "the American heritage" notion for a more pluralistic conception of the U.S. past: Williamsburg was now willing to set the story of the black slaves alongside the story of the planters. What they were less willing to tackle were the relations between those classes. Much in the manner of some of the "new social history," they shied away from politics and struggle: slave culture was one thing; slave revolts were another. Nor did the museums often explore how the present evolved out of the past. Williamsburg did not, for example, explain the economic connections between eighteenth-century slavery and twentieth-century sharecropping and debt peonage, or slavery's cultural legacies of racism and black nationalism. Admitting that the reality of exploitation contradicted the ideal of liberty was only a first step.

These limits were interconnected and reinforced each other. The refusal to confront internal conflict lent a static and falsely harmonious quality to the projects, which in turn diminished their capacity to explain historical movement and bring their stories down to the present. Many of the farm museums concentrated on sowing and reaping; they balked at examining tenantry, foreclosures, world markets, commodity exchanges—the processes of capitalist development at work in the countryside—and the agrarian movements that responded to these processes. They were therefore unlikely to help visitors understand how the old family farms (whose values many of the Living Museums enshrined) had succumbed to the corporate agri-businesses that today dominate American agriculture. Some industrial museums could now explore, often quite critically, the unfortunate living conditions of textile workers in the 1850s; the most advanced could even admit to historical memory the legacy of strikes. But it proved more difficult to locate the source of these problems in the dynamics of a capitalist political economy, dynamics that are still at work.

Alexander pointed to one crucial reason for the museums' reluctance to press beyond these limits when he noted, in his 1979 retrospective, that the museums were not interested in "securing social change." The disconnection of past from present and the separation of culture from politics was itself a political act. History was to be confined to providing entertainment, nostalgia, or interesting insights into vanished ways of life. It was not to be freed to become a powerful agent for understanding—and changing—the present.[60]

J. H. Plumb has noted that the "acquisition of the past by ruling and possessing classes and the exclusion of the mass of the peasantry and laboring class is a widespread phenomenon through recorded time."[61] I have argued that history museums were one way the dominant classes in the United States—wittingly or unwittingly—appropriated the past.

They did so, first, by presenting particular interpretations. Of course the museums cannot be faulted for having read the past selectively. There is, after all, no such thing as "the past." All history is a production—a deliberate selection, ordering, and evaluation of past events, experiences, and processes. The objection is rather that the museums incorporated selections and silences on such an order that they falsified reality and became instruments of class hegemony.[62] The museums generated conventional ways of seeing history that justified the historic mission of capitalists and lent a naturalism and inevitability to their authority. Perhaps more important, they generated ways of not seeing. By obscuring the origins and development of capitalist society, by eradicating exploitation, racism, sexism, and class struggle from the historical record, by covering up the existence of broad-based oppositional traditions and popular cultures, and by rendering the majority of the population invisible as shapers of history, the museums inhibited the capacity of visitors to imagine alternative social orders—past or future.

The museums served established power in a more indirect way as well. Quite apart from any particular message a museum suggested, its very structure promulgated a deeper one: history was irrelevant to present-day concerns. Recall here that the museums emerged in an inhospitable culture, one marked by a profound contempt for encrusted tradition. Businessmen had few qualms about demolishing the past in the interest of profit, and ruling groups took much longer to become attentive to the uses of the past than did their European counterparts. When patrician women and mugwumps turned to the past to legitimate their social order, their interventions necessarily took the form of rescuing isolated bits of the old order from the juggernaut of progress. The museums became preserves where the past, an endangered species, might be kept alive for visitors to see. The museums and other "genuine historical places" thus conveyed, by their very form, the idea that the past was something sharply separated from the present. History became antiquarianism—pleasant but irrelevant to present concerns. The museums did nothing to help visitors understand that a critical awareness of history, although not a sufficient guide to effective action in the present, was an indispensable precondition for it, and a potentially powerful tool for liberation.

If we now know a little about the museums' messages, we know a great deal less about how they are (and have been) received. Reception, in part, depends on who is listening, and we do not know who visits the museums. It is clear that there has been a steady increase in their popularity.[63] There is some evidence that current museum-goers are better-off and better educated than the average American; almost certainly they are overwhelmingly white, although schoolchildren are bussed in from inner-city ghettos in large numbers.[64]

Nor do we know why people go. One hypothesis often advanced is that increased attendance is simply a function of the spread of automobile culture and the increase in leisure time. There is clearly some truth to this, but vacationers could motor elsewhere. The museums have some obvious appeal: many are charming places that demonstrate interesting old craft techniques and exhibit quaint old objects; there are, after all, real pleasures in antiquarianism. The museums are also safe, well promoted, and one of the few available "family" experiences. Probing a bit deeper, some analysts suggest that the sterility of suburban life generates an attraction to places embodying a sense of authenticity and human scale.[65]

Perhaps advanced capitalism itself has fostered a desire to visit these mythic precapitalist enclaves. If there is indeed a human need for temporal connectedness, then capitalism's ruthless destruction of the old—its severing of people from one another across time as well as in space—may have created a desire to reestablish linkages to the past. The postwar years, after all, witnessed the breakup of tight local, ethnic, and regional communities, the fragmentation of families, the increasing segregation of the population into age ghettos, the devitalization of folk traditions, and the rise of corporate-dominated mass communications. It is conceivable that these concomitants of capitalist development made it more difficult for people to hand down their own history to the next generation and that citizens have been, in this as in other areas, partially transformed into consumers. Were tradition alive and vibrant, people might not be so willing to pay to visit these embalmed remnants of the past: zoos did not become popular until everyday familiarity with animals had become a thing of the past.[66]

Nor do we know what visitors come away with. Perhaps the well-off find their world ratified. Perhaps those not so well served by the status quo nevertheless prove susceptible to the museums' messages. But maybe they invest the messages with different meanings. There are, after all, truly radical di-

mensions to the U.S. tradition, and the shrines may serve to celebrate democratic as well as capitalist values.

Scholars have only just begun to investigate popular attitudes toward the
past, so we are in no position to render definitive judgments. There are some
heartening signs that popular memories of radical traditions are still intact,
and we would do well to explore that possibility. Most Americans, however,
know relatively little about their past and have an underdeveloped sense of
how history happens. This is not a reflection on popular intelligence, but an
estimate of the strength of our historicidal culture. People are clearly interested in the past, but when they seek understanding they are confronted
with institutions (of which the museums are only one) that tend to diminish
their capacity to situate themselves in time. The political consequences of this
impoverished historical consciousness are profound, and it is a critical task for
historians to contest those institutions which promote it.

I f we are to take part in the history museum movement, it is important
to assess what lies ahead for it. The burden of my argument has been
that this question cannot be answered without considering the social
and political state of the nation. The eighties are a period of right-wing
offensives. Those who seek to repeal working-class, women's, and black
gains in the present are also working to reverse their gains in the field of
history. It is necessary to resist these moves to reappropriate the past.[67]

One avenue is to work with the local museums created in recent years,
many of which might survive because they are community-supported and not
critically dependent on state funds. We should also support the more established museums in what I think will be their spirited resistance to any attempts
to reimpose right-wing nostalgia. The social history movement, despite its
limitations, was a decided advance, and should be defended. Critics have
been too quick to dismiss the Williamsburgs out of hand. Despite their origins, there are splendid possibilities inherent in them for popularizing a meaningful and critical history.

More generally, as participants in the work, or as supportive critics, we
should urge the museums to press ahead beyond social history to become
places that deal with politics as well as culture; that reconstruct processes as
well as events; that explain the social relations as well as the forces of production at work in the societies whose stories they seek to tell. The museums
should give credit to historical actors where due, but stop short of inculcating
an incapacitating awe. If their subjects were critics of their society, the mu-

seums should refuse to blunt the jagged edges of the original message. The museums should work to break down the distinctions between amateur and professional that stultify both. They should walk that difficult line between, on the one hand, fostering a definition of the present solely in terms of the past, and, on the other, disconnecting the past so thoroughly from the present that we forget that people in the past produced the matrix of constraints and possibilities within which we act in the present. Above all, the museums should consider it their fundamental mission to assist people to become historically informed makers of history.

If you own major historic property anywhere in the USA, we can help you profit from the past.

The real estate marketplace has a new and important product line: *historic and nonhistoric properties built prior to 1944 and in need of renovation.*

If you own a hotel, resort, commercial or multiple-unit residential structure that meets the above description, we'd like to talk to you about acquiring, syndicating, securing debt financing or joint-venturing it with you.

They make excellent vehicles for rehabilitation, syndication and profits. And as a broad-based development-investment company, we've got the capital, capability and track record to make it work. Explore the profit possibilities. Call Mitchell Davis or Arthur Fefferman at (212) 354-5756 or write to the address below.

Sybedon
We'll help you profit from the past.

SYBEDON CORPORATION. INVESTMENT BANKER TO THE REAL ESTATE INDUSTRY.
1211 Avenue of the Americas / Rockefeller Center, New York 10036 / Telex: 125651

Reflections on the History of Historic Preservation

Immediately on moving into the White House, Ronald Reagan replaced the Thomas Jefferson portrait hanging in the Cabinet Room with one of Calvin Coolidge. Then he set out to restore Silent Cal's 1920s, rather as if the last sixty years of history were a movie that could be run in reverse. That Reagan intends to dismantle civil rights, environmentalism, the welfare state, and the entire panoply of New Deal and Great Society reforms is a commonplace. But he and his team also want to scour away a host of secondary programs that are no less pernicious, in neoconservative eyes, for being less well known. One of these is historic preservation, which the right accuses of constraining the "free market" from demolishing the nation's built inheritance whenever it is profitable to do so.

The charge is accurate. Indeed, the historic preservation movement was born, over a century ago, in opposition to a free-wheeling, free market era, when profit-seeking Americans—as disrespectful of the past as of the environment —routinely demolished what prior generations had constructed. Historicide, like ecocide, had become embedded in the culture.

Slowly, some groups began to resist these attitudes and activities. Boston Brahmin anthropologists sought to rescue the remnants of Indian cultures. Old New England families preserved their homesteads. Descendants of southern planters fashioned legislation to prevent the marketplace from demolishing their homes. By the 1920s these genteel classes had carved out some historic enclaves and preserved them from the onrush of development.

The great boom of the late 1940s and 1950s threatened to reverse, even erase, these small victories, as a remorseless juggernaut of development crunched its way through the nation's heritage. The patricians broadened their

BY MICHAEL WALLACE

165

movement, rallying a coalition of disparate social groups to contest this historicidal onslaught. Launching a brilliant counteroffensive against the bulldozers, this preservation coalition achieved passage of the Historic Preservation Act in 1966, a law that began to curb the rampage. In the next decade the
movement allied itself with a broad spectrum of anticorporate forces ranging
from populist neighborhood conservationists to environmentalists and
achieved a further series of legislative and judicial triumphs.

For a time, in the 1970s, it seemed as if the entire culture had done an
about-face. Community groups and corporations, banks and courts, state governments and private developers—all supported "historic preservation."
Thousands of organizations set about saving whole swaths of city and countryside from demolition, rehabilitating old houses, setting up historic districts,
reusing old factories, conserving and preserving the past.

In the 1980s, however, this movement has come under attack. To the Reagan right, protecting the past is as objectionable as imposing health and safety
rules on corporations. And the historic preservation movement has found its
considerable victories quite vulnerable to reversal. In no small part, I will
argue, the movement's current fragility stems from its recent tactics—an
abandonment of militant allies, an alliance with traditional enemies. This essay will sort out the tangled history of the historic preservation movement in
order to assess its critical contemporary situation and suggest an alternative
strategy for the future.

I n the colonial period and the seventy years of explosive growth following the Revolution, Americans evinced little interest in saving the built
environment. Given the country's history to that point, this is not
surprising.

The European colonists had inherited little in the way of historical artifacts
to preserve. The truly old remains were not theirs. Indian ruins were either
obliterated (like the Indians themselves) or set aside (again like their creators)
on reservations, as trophies of conquest or reminders of a barbarism now
happily overcome. Each advance into the continent set transcendence of history more firmly at the heart of the national culture.

The European migrants were ambivalent about their own past. Although
they honored Old World roots, they emphasized New World beginnings (a
tension nicely caught in the place names they chose: New Amsterdam, New
York, New Hampshire, New Orleans, New Haven, New Sweden). The
American Revolution enhanced this ambivalence. On the one hand, the re-

bels, staunch republicans and good Protestants, took a historical view of their position; they considered themselves inheritors of a millennia-long struggle against aristocratic, monarchical, and priestly rule. But when the new Republic had been established, most statesmen, businessmen, and men of letters exuberantly dismissed the past. Their youthful society would shed outworn European customs and perhaps break free of the burdens of history altogether.[1]

Certainly the new nation's ruling classes felt little need to base their legitimacy on an appeal to antiquity, as European monarchs and aristocrats did. Quite the reverse—northern merchants and industrialists proclaimed their self-made status and promoted the idea that all Americans were free to escape the past: if ordinary people believed that they were *not* shackled to an inherited place and could, in time, rise economically and socially, they would have no need to challenge those currently in authority. Even the southern slave planters, who adopted Walter Scott flourishes, claimed that they were "natural" aristocrats rather than descendants of a distinguished lineage—an intelligent strategy, as few of their pedigrees would have withstood close scrutiny.

As a corollary, American elites had little class interest in preserving history's residue. When remains of the past hindered the present accumulation of profit, they were routinely dispatched to the dustbin of history. Such tributes as were due republican forerunners could be made conveniently compatible with the imperatives of progress. New buildings could evoke old forms— Grecian banks and Roman railroad stations allowed a future-oriented culture to pay its respects to an honored tradition.[2]

The *majority* of the population may have had different attitudes toward preserving the past. Most seventeenth- and eighteenth-century European immigrants were displaced peasants and artisans who envisaged America as a Great Commons where they might reconstruct social relations demolished by the rise of European capitalism. They resisted the emerging market culture and considered land less a commodity than a homesite. Urban artisans— staunch upholders of a revolutionary republican tradition—similarly held out against dehistoricizing tendencies. Slowly, during the nineteenth century, this would change as the communal restraints and legal safeguards that had braked the emergence of American capitalism crumbled. Some small farmers would be displaced through the workings of the speculative and mortgage markets, driven west, and disconnected from traditional roots. Others, seduced into the new order by rising land values, would plunge with gusto into real estate speculation, imbibing its attendant disregard for tradition. And artisanal workplaces and communities would be repeatedly torn apart or relocated to suit the demands of capitalist development. Defeat, opportunity, and the continuing arrival of immigrant newcomers with minimal historical connections to their new locations eventually would produce a working-class variant of upper-class ahistoricism.

But for those who presided over the country's economy during most of its early history, "progress" took precedence over preservation. As a New Yorker remarked in 1825, "We delight in the promised sunshine of the future, and leave to those who are conscious that they have passed their grand climacteric to console themselves with the splendors of the past."[3]

B etween the 1880s and the 1940s four groups began to protest against the casual demolition of the past. The first was composed of descendants of the merchants and textile magnates of ante-bellum New England. By the end of the nineteenth century, these patricians found their inherited political and cultural authority ebbing away to plutocrats above and immigrants below. To restore their position the Brahmins assumed custodianship of the "American" inheritance. Banding together in genealogical and historical societies, they underlined their pedigree by preserving its tangible remains, saving threatened properties by passing the hat among members of their class. These crusades helped to crystallize a genteel sensibility that condemned the unrestrained working of the market—a sensibility all the easier to sustain because, like the European aristocrats with whom they identified, the Brahmins were living off an earlier generation's accumulation.[4]

Brahmins also engaged in preservation activities in the West. After the Civil War, pacification drives broke the back of armed Native American resistance, and the Plains Indians, like so many before them, were put on reservations. Hard on the army's heels came America's first anthropologists and archaeologists, many from the northeastern patriciate, intent on exploring the artifacts of Indian cultures. They found, to their dismay, that stockmen and prospectors had preceded them and were busily looting ruins and gravesites to meet the demands of a booming market in Indian antiquities. Using methods preservationists had worked out back East, the anthropologists bought up historical relics and transferred them to public ownership, thus fencing them off from the market. Frederick Putnam of the Harvard's Peabody Museum, for example, raised funds from preservation-oriented Bostonians, purchased the Great Serpent Mound, and deeded it to the state of Ohio.[5]

But the threatened areas were so vast that the preservationists soon concluded that only Congress could protect the past from the present. In 1906 they obtained passage of the Antiquities Act. The law gave the president authority to set aside public lands as national monuments, to levy criminal fines for excavating or destroying ruins, and to grant permits for field work to scientific and educational institutions. In 1916 management of federally owned "historic properties" was centralized in the National Park Service, within the Department of the Interior.[6]

T he second group of 1880–1940 preservationists were descendants of the antebellum planter class living in the backwater river and seaport towns of the Old South, some still wealthy, others reduced to genteel poverty. Like the New England Brahmins, they were preoccupied with the past, the golden days when their ancestors had been undisputed masters of the region.[7]

In the 1920s the aristocracy woke abruptly to find itself under assault. The grillwork and paneling of the homes of the Old South had become fashionable. (This demand, like the earlier craze for Indian relics, may have been fueled by Hollywood's national circulation of local images, first of the Wild West, then of the Old South.) Northern connoisseurs and avaricious museum directors flocked south to cannibalize the estates of the gentry. Oil companies wanted to set up gas pumps in the middle of southern towns to meet the needs of the new automobile era. Southerners organized to beat back these new Yankee invasions.[8]

Charleston led the way. In the 1920s the Society for the Preservation of Old Dwelling Houses, composed of "society" women from the old battery district, fought to ward off Standard Oil filling stations, but steadily lost ground. Then, as the Brahmin anthropologists had done in the case of western lands, they turned to the state for support. In 1931 the ladies, supported by alarmed civic leaders, got a city ordinance passed establishing the Old and Historic Charleston District. A Board of Architectural Review was given authority to approve all changes in historic buildings in the area.[9]

Thus was born the first "historic district" through an innovative use of zoning, itself a newly popular exercise of governmental authority. Zoning had emerged in the period between 1900 and 1920 as a way of confronting the obstacles private ownership of property presented to profitable urban investment. City zoning began by blocking uses of the land that could "ruin" a neighborhood; in New York, Fifth Avenue stores got industrial sweatshops zoned out. Initially frowned upon because it restricted property rights, zoning was accepted once it became clear that by promoting stability it enhanced property values. In the decade after 1910, zoning underwrote the creation of exclusive upper-class residential suburbs and villa districts as insurance companies and banks flocked to invest in planned and safeguarded communities. Charleston's law essentially zoned by building age, rather than by building type.[10]

The historic district device was soon copied, particularly in the South. In New Orleans, for instance, local business groups, architects, civic leaders, and property owners set out to save the Vieux Carre—the historic French Quarter. A constitutional amendment passed by the voters in 1936 empowered the city to create the Vieux Carre Commission, which it did the next year. In 1939 a court ruling established the commission's authority to place restraints on private property holders' rights to demolish historic buildings.[11]

The third preservation-minded group comprised a handful of multi-millionaire industrialists, including Henry Ford and John D. Rockefeller, Jr. Though their products were helping to dismantle the old society, they turned to saving parts of it from devastation. Restorations such as Rockefeller's Williamsburg and Ford's Greenfield Village became popular enterprises among the corporate rich in the 1920s.

The superwealthy, I have argued elsewhere, sought partly to celebrate their newly won preeminence and partly to construct a retrospective lineage for themselves by buying their way into the American past. Preservation also afforded a way of carving out a distinctive cultural position within the larger capitalist class. Monopolists had little love for the competitive scramble of the marketplace. Some of these millionaires were still involved in direct capitalist accumulation; others, like Rockefeller Jr., were second generation; but all could afford to turn up their noses at imperatives that still ruled regular businessmen. The grand restorations simultaneously demonstrated their disdain for the market and their ability to transcend it.[12]

A fourth body of nouveaux preservationists came from the professional and managerial strata, a group that assumed a critical role in American life in the 1880–1920 period. Summoned into being by corporations and governmental bureaucracies, professionals developed an independent culture of efficiency with a distaste for the market at its core. Appalled by chaos, congestion, contagion, and class strife, some repudiated capitalism. Most, however, worked within the system to overcome antiquated and irrational practices that blocked the efficient accumulation of capital. This concern led some of them, by a variety of indirect routes, to historic preservation.[13]

In the 1890s some architects, landscape architects, and engineers tried to rationalize and discipline U.S. cities by beautifying them—reorganizing them around a matrix of broad avenues and monumental neoclassical buildings. The White City at the Columbian Exposition of 1893 embodied their hope that the authority of antiquity could restrain the anarchy of modern America. They soon learned that pseudo-historical architecture alone could not generate a desirable social order.[14]

Increasingly, many of the new professionals sought state intervention to halt or regulate various anarchic business practices. After the turn of the century, ministers, engineers, doctors, lawyers, and architects set out to ameliorate the worst offenses. Land use was a key concern. On the national level, they worked to put western land and water management into professional and "scientific" hands. This dovetailed nicely with Brahmin archaeologists' wishes to regulate access to Indian relics and contributed to the passage of the 1906 Antiquities Act. At the municipal level, the planning fraternity was instrumental in fashioning zoning legislation, which the southern gentry adapted to preservation ends.

Slowly, alongside the corps of ladies (and some gentlemen) who had been the backbone of preservation efforts, a body of (almost invariably) male historic preservation professionals grew up. Restorationists (Rockefeller, in particular) hired architects and engineers to renovate or reconstruct old buildings. Southern gentry worked with businessmen and lawyers to forge preservation law.

It was not until the 1930s, however, when the federal government began to involve itself in preservation, that these professionals developed a semi-independent operating base. In the early thirties, the National Park Service took on professionally trained historians to do public interpretations at historic parks and battlefield sites and hired 1,200 unemployed architects to survey and record all "historic" buildings in the United States for the Historic American Building Survey (HABS). The Works Progress Administration (WPA) hired archaeologists to excavate and record sites about to be flooded by such massive river-damming programs as the Tennessee Valley Authority and set historians to work on Federal Writers' Project Programs. And between 1934 and 1941, the Civilian Conservation Corps undertook restoration projects that employed hundreds of historians and historical technicians.[15]

In 1935 came the most dramatic New Deal entry into the preservation field. The Historic Sites Act authorized the Department of the Interior, acting through the National Park Service, to acquire property, preserve and operate privately owned historic or archaeological sites, construct museums, develop educational programs, and place commemorative tablets. Almost overnight a massive federal presence had been authorized, and the National Park Service swiftly established a Branch of Historic Sites and Buildings to carry out the mandate. This Branch of History, as it was informally known, hired a cohort of historians who began planning a massive educational program linking a chain of historic sites to illustrate major themes in U.S. history.[16]

The National Park Service was never able to institute a general plan for heritage preservation. It was limited by the Historic Sites Act, which reflected the approach of the traditional preservation community, particularly those responsible for Colonial Williamsburg. (A Rockefeller lawyer drafted the bill eventually adopted by Congress.) The Park Service historians did not have the power to acquire endangered property through the exercise of eminent domain. Nor could they halt the extensive demolition work undertaken by the New Deal itself through its slum clearance and roadway construction programs. Indeed, in St. Louis the National Park Service was forced to serve as a sponsor for the Jefferson National Expansion Memorial, an urban renewal project cum real estate scam that destroyed a historic riverside area in the name of honoring the frontier past.[17]

Still, the publicly funded programs expanded the preservation movement and broadened the meaning of "historic" from its upper-class definition. The HABS project, for instance, recorded buildings with no connection to famous white men but with important meanings for local communities, and the WPA state guidebooks, commemorative markers, and collections of local lore reflected a populist conception of public history. The tendency of the rapidly growing body of state professionals, once freed from dependence on private sector employers, to move leftward was arrested by the termination of the New Deal and the outbreak of war. Federal historical programs were slashed and converted to caretaker operations or purveyors of patriotic agitprop. But the experience left its mark on the veterans of the 1930s, people who would form the cadre of postwar preservation programs.

To summarize: between the 1880s and the 1940s—in many ways the heyday of American industrial capitalism—a constituency emerged that questioned the prevailing dismissal of the past. Northern old money, southern patricians, the crème of the monopoly capitalist stratum, and new professionals in and out of government—all developed a distaste for unrestrained capitalism. Historic preservation became an emblem of that distaste: historic artifacts were not to be subjected to market considerations, partly because they were more valuable to these groups as symbols of legitmacy.[18]

But if preservationists rejected conventional cultural codes, they did not succeed in overturning them. Quite the opposite: "modernist" sensibilities emerged in architecture, fashion, and the fine arts. Twenties intellectuals reveled in the accelerated tempo of time, the rupture of traditions, the liberating break with conservative constraints, and the exhilaration of commodity abundance. Functionalists stripped away and cast off nineteenth-century Victorian cultter, but with the gewgaws went much of that culture's historical concreteness. And the new culture of consumption, spurred by the advertising industry, substituted novelty for memory as a cultural imperative.[19] In such a culture, the best preservationists could do was declare a few sites to be historic "reservations"—off limits to developers. The larger culture tolerated these parenthesized places—New England homes, antebellum planter residences, historic battlefields, colonial reconstructions, and Indian "homelands"— partly because there were so few of them, and partly because they were so utterly irrelevant to the onrushing flow of events.

N evertheless, by the mid 1940s preservationists were pleased with their limited gains. Moreover, the war had diminished the threat to the built environment by curtailing building programs. Still, preservationists looked to the postwar period with foreboding. They were right to worry.[20]

After victory, a flood of federal money poured into urban renewal, suburban development, and highway construction. A government-fostered "growth coalition" of real estate developers and urban planners, city Democrats and suburban Republicans, bankers and construction workers, quasi-public "authorities" and corporate-dominated planning bodies, ripped up slums and "blighted" areas, replacing them with the corporate command and control centers that the new multinational economy required. The middle class left happily (or was squeezed out) and motored to the new suburbs on the new highways.[21]

The impact on the historic environment was devastating. Roads were rammed through city centers, urban renewal demolished vast downtown tracts, and by 1966 fully one half of the 12,000 properties recorded by HABS thirty years earlier had been torn down. The growth coalition seemed to revel in leveling the past. It was the Age of Robert Moses, and theorists of capitalist civilization cheered, applauding the system's willingness to destroy the old in the interest of innovation and productivity.[22]

The growth coalition's activities between 1945 and 1966 galvanized the various preservation constituencies. It drew them together, forced them to pool resources and expertise, and eventually led them to broaden their social base in order to resist the onslaught on the past. In a sense the bulldozer battalions *created* the modern preservation movement.

In 1947, responding to the quickening pace of development, preservationists organized the National Council for Historic Sites and Buildings to plot strategy. The meetings included leaders of genealogical societies, amateur and professional historians, architects, archaeologists, engineers, and civic planners, but were dominated by the National Park Service professionals and the Williamsburg people. Financing was provided by the Mellon family. The council drew up plans for a National Trust that would propagandize for historical preservation. Like the English National Trust, the new body would also assume title to historic properties whose owners could no longer keep them up, and operate them as museums.[23] Congress obligingly created the National Trust in 1949. The Lilly Foundation and the DuPonts chipped in to support the new organization, but the Mellons remained the real underwriters: in 1957 they gave the Trust a $2.5 million endowment.[24]

The Trust acquired and managed some historic properties; got the HABS revived in 1957; and, with Colonial Williamsburg, worked to "professionalize" historic site interpretation. The period thus saw the strengthening of one of the major constituency groups of the movement, the professional public historians created in the 1920s and 1930s by private organizations and the federal government.[25]

What the National Trust did not do was make much headway against the 1950s' juggernaut of progress. It succeeded only in supporting the creation of more reservations and establishing itself as the organizational voice—albeit a weak one—of historic preservation. Facing overwhelming odds, the Trust was further hampered by its narrow base in a thin sliver of the upper classes.[26]

In the 1960s wider support for historic preservation began to emerge, rooted largely in the growing resistance to urban renewal. Some opposition came from working-class neighborhoods resisting demolition, though in this period their efforts were usually in vain. A much stronger counterforce was generated by inner-city middle-class constituencies. In 1961, for example, Jane Jacobs, an editor of *Architectural Forum,* organized successful opposition to an urban renewal project in the West Village.[27]

Jacobs, along with Herbert Gans, Edward Hall, and Ada Louise Huxtable, argued that destroying old buildings destroyed the fabric of healthy urban communities. The bleak postwar high-rise structures were inhuman: their spatial arrangements shattered social networks, and their bland environmental and temporal homogeneity denied the need for spatial diversity and historical connectedness. Both the suburbs and the projects undermined people's personal and social *identities* (this was the period of greatest popularity for Eriksonian theories about identity crises). One supporter argued that the continuing demolition of traditional historical neighborhoods and landmarks constituted a "national emergency" because "individuals feel both more secure and more purposeful when they recognize that they exist as part of an historical continuum."[28]

These concerns dovetailed nicely with the cold war fears of the Kennedy and Johnson administrations that destruction of the past might engender a *national* identity crisis that the nation could ill afford. National Trust leaders played to this concern. They warned of "a future in which America found itself without roots, without a sense of identity, with nothing to lose."[29] The marriage of these concerns over personal and national identity was reflected in Jack Kennedy's discourses on national purpose and Jackie Kennedy's restoration of the White House and celebration of its historicity in television tours.

Black urban rioting soon gave power and force to these arguments. The 1964 Harlem eruption, soon dwarfed by those in Watts (1965) and Detroit (1967), had many roots, but prominent among them was the assault of urban renewal and highway construction programs on the already tattered fabric of inner-city life.[30] To critiques of social scientists and protests in the streets were added the concerns of some big-city mayors who, much as they liked downtown construction, began to fear the consequences of steady population loss and the consequent erosion of the middle-class urban tax base.

While these diverse opponents eroded the prestige of the growth coalition—planners rethought their theories about urban renewal, Robert Moses began his slide from power, historic districts spread—the developers were being undercut from quite a different direction. The development of mass tourism in the 1950s and 1960s, buoyed by the new roadways and the general prosperity, made it apparent that there was money to be made by preserving the past. There had been hints of this possibility before. The conversion of historic houses into shrines often had promotional overtones. Preservationists, understandably enough, had appealed to entrepreneurial self-interest when soliciting donations. And Ford and Rockefeller had opened hotels to house the growing number of visitors to their restorations. But these harbingers were as nothing compared with the postwar tourist boom.[31]

In 1964, 94.5 million people drove their 34 million automobiles over 130 billion miles on their vacations and spent more than 20 billion dollars as they went. Many of those millions motored to historic sites. Colonial Williamsburg's paid attendance went from 166,000 in 1947 to nearly 710,000 in 1967, and the increase was not unusual. Old Sturbridge went from less than 12,000 to over 520,000 in the same period, and Greenfield Village passed the 1,000,000 mark in 1960. Between 1960 and 1962 attendance at all historic sites in Massachusetts went up 50 percent.[32]

The phenomenon transcended the big-name sites. In 1960 New York State's Joint Legislative Committee on Preservation and Restoration of Historic Sites reported: "Tourism has become big business. . . . And historic sites more and more are luring the tourist." In 1964 twenty-nine states listed tourism as one of their three largest industries. As Jonathan Daniels proclaimed, "History has become a cash crop as eagerly tended as the hope for industrial plants."[33]

Even the historic districts—originally conceived of as residential enclaves—proved to be wildly profitable draws. A 1964 study done for the New Orleans Chamber of Commerce found that the French Quarter brought in more money than anything except the Port itself. Tourism had made New Orleans one of the top four convention cities, influenced the decision of national and regional corporations to locate there, and accounted for much of the extraordinary strength of the city's retail, hotel, and office market. The study set a dollar value of $150 million on the city's historic architecture.[34]

As the evidence mounted, historic preservation began to appeal to enterprising local boosters, and small businessmen began to rethink the demolition/development approach. Beginning in 1959, for example, a young investment banker, Leopold Adler II, presided over a sharp change of direction in Savannah's preservation community. Working with a successful suburban developer, Historic Savannah employed a revolving fund (basically a line of credit from now-sympathetic banks) to purchase, restore, and resell old buildings with restrictive covenants attached. They worked out public relations themes, designed highway signs, and developed historic house museums, tour routes, brochures, visitors' centers, and restaurants and motels that carried through historic themes. It worked. Construction, real estate activity (with attendant commissions and profits), land values, tourist revenues, bank deposits, the restaurant business, and retail sales all soared. *Fortune* magazine was impressed: "Anachronism can be made to pay off in urban civilization."[35]

B y the mid-1960s, then, the original core of genteel preservationists had been joined by potentially powerful allies: middle-class professionals resisting wholesale destruction of old but viable communities and local businessmen sniffing profit in the past. But these groups held quite different perspectives. Traditionalists wanted to save old buildings for their use-value as homes, communities, symbols. Entrepreneurs were less interested in meaning than marketability. How were these traditional enemies to coalesce?

A path to cooperation emerged from contemporary objections to historic museums. The proper way to preserve the past, critics were suggesting, was to integrate it with the present. "Preservation," Ada Louise Huxtable argued, "is the job of finding ways to keep those original buildings that provide the city's character and continuity and of incorporating them into its living mainstream," not placing them in "sterile isolation."[36]

Thus was born the doctrine of "adaptive reuse." Historic buildings should not be mummified, but recycled. The exterior shell should be kept and the interior devoted to some profitable use. To these preservationists, unlike the DAR types, the original "aura," the building's connection to specific people and events, was unimportant. They shifted their emphasis from meaning to ambience.

"Adaptive reuse" declared an end to the antagonism between preservation and development. Traditionalists could save and reuse instead of isolate and venerate; (re)developers could incorporate the old into the new; together they could take on the bulldozer developers and their allies in the federal bureaucracy. "Adaptive reuse" was thus a progressive philosophy in its original context, but, as we will see, by justifying "a new building in the old shell" a "modern" solution that still manages to evoke the past," Huxtable and her colleagues were on the road to legitimating the developers she had been battling so long.[37]

The immediate question, however, was how to forge an effective political program, a problem addressed, in 1965, by a blue-ribbon commission assembled by the National Trust and Colonial Williamsburg. The group issued a manifesto, *With Heritage So Rich,* condemning unrestrained growth as a danger to national identity: "A nation can be a victim of amnesia. It can lose the memories of what it was, and thereby lose the sense of what it is or wants to be." Adaptive reuse was proclaimed the solution: "let us save what we have around us that is good, not for exhibition, not for 'education,' but for practical use as places to live in and to work in." The federal government was declared the proper agency to accomplish these ends.[38]

A whirlwind legislative campaign followed, orchestrated by National Trust Chairman Gordon Gray, a powerful man with entree into the highest congressional circles through his connections with the R. J. Reynolds family and high-level service under Truman, Kennedy, and Johnson.[39] In response Congress passed the National Historic Preservation Act, which wrote virtually every one of the Trust's recommendations into law, a wholesale victory for the "adaptive reuse" approach. The law established a National Register of Historic Places, which was to list all sites, buildings, structures, and objects found by professionals to have been "significant" in American history, architecture, archaeology, or culture. It also authorized matching grants to states to further local preservation projects; required each state to develop coherent plans to preserve its historical legacy and to appoint a State Historic Preservation Officer to coordinate the program; and put the National Trust on the federal payroll. Finally, and crucially, the act created the Advisory Council on Historic Preservation, which all federal agencies were required to consult before demolishing properties listed on the National Register. The Advisory Council did not have authority to halt other federal bureaucracies, but the prior review process did slow the hitherto smooth workings of the highway and urban renewal macines.[40]

Two other 1966 acts rounded out the victory. The Department of Transportation Act blocked destruction of historic properties by five major agencies unless they could prove that there was "no feasible and prudent alternative," and even then they were required to "minimize harm." The Demonstration Cities Act—a major reaction against urban renewal—enjoined the Department of Housing and Urban Development (HUD) to "preserve and restore areas, sites and structures of historic or architectural value" and authorized grants of two-thirds of the cost of surveys of such sites.[41]

T he growth coalition did not roll over and play dead with the passage of the Historic Preservation Act of 1966. For a time (1966–72) Secretary Weaver at HUD slowed the pace of bulldozing and increased that of rehabilitation (by 1972 it was three times as high as the 1955–65 rate). But soon the Model Cities program, under fierce pressure, backed away from social and environmental planning, aid to the poor, and citizen involvement. Selling out to the growth interests, the program became a public works bonanza for medium-sized cities.[42]

Nixon and Ford scrapped or consolidated many of the 1950s and 1960s programs (Urban Renewal, Model Cities) through the 1974 Housing and Community Development Act. The act was supposed to eliminate urban slums, and it requred that low- and moderate-income populations be included in the planning process and benefit from the programs. But under the "New Federalism," local governments were given Community Development Block Grants to subsidize private development projects and allowed to do as they pleased with the money, so local power elites sent the money flowing to convention centers, office buildings, shopping malls, and the like. This process accelerated with the 1977 institution of the Urban Development Action Grant (UDAG) program, which provided, as urban renewal had, federal money for land acquisition, site clearance, and infrastructure improvements. Responsibility for complying with federal environmental legislation was transferred to local governments[1] hands and once again hotels and convention centers began to replace historic structures. Despite the preservationists' victories, it was still open season on the cities.[43]

Faced with these ongoing challenges and responding to the climate of the late 1960s and early 1970s, the preservation movement expanded to include a burgeoning new urban gentry and militantly populist neighborhood conservationists, who drew energy from the black, women's, ecology, anticorporate, and antiwar movements. By the mid-1970s the strengthened preservation coalition had scored a succession of legislative and judicial triumphs against their bulldozer enemies.

I n the late 1960s and early 1970s, as corporate and financial headquarters flourished in city centers, demand for white-collar professional, managerial, and technical workers rose significantly (25 percent between 1960 and 1970). Most commuted to the central business districts from the suburbs, but many others—especially those who had come to the city as youths to study or work—sought housing near their work. This stay-in-the-city trend was fed by the demographic and cultural upheavals of the times: smaller and more numerous households (widows living alone, children leaving home earlier, couples marrying later and divorcing more often, wives working outside the home). The baby-boom singles and working couples either did not care for the child-centered suburbs or found that housing and commuting costs priced them out of the suburban market. These young professionals and managers formed the core of a new urban gentry.[44]

What attracted them to a section of the city, apart from location and price, was the neighborhood's "historic character." Perhaps their sensibilities had been shaped by rebellion against the rootless suburbs in which they grew up and a desire to live in a community with an authentic and aged heritage. The "urban homesteaders" researched their homesite's past, got caught up in the excitement of restoration work, and lovingly defended the built environment against developers.[45] But in their attentiveness to their neighborhood's past, some gentry ignored its *recent* history—and, most crucially, how they themselves had displaced the former residents.

Realtors and developers insulated many from such realities, buying up houses, evicting tenants, rehabbing, and reselling at fat markups to wealthier buyers. Surviving old residents were flushed out at the next stage as tax assessments went up, fancy shops arrived, the old infrastructure crumbled, and it became too expensive or too alienating to hang on. And if they stubbornly did remain, local governments would enforce long-unused codes and condemn old housing for investors waiting in the wings. If need be, thugs and arsonists would finish the job. The end result might be an exquisite "golden ghetto," restored to a pristine moment in time, stripped (as Williamsburg had been) of all traces of those who had been its inhabitants in the intervening years.[46]

If some gentry were blind to displacement, others knew perfectly well what they were doing. They wanted temporally scarce commodities because they knew their value would rise. The existing community was a hindrance: it undermined the "historic" ambience that would make the investment pay off.[47]

Still other gentry responded with neither naiveté nor calculating ruthlessness but with moral righteousness: they were not destroying impoverished communities with long-established folkways and deep roots, but wiping out "blight" and crime. The head of the Spring Garden Civic Association, noting that Hispanics were being driven out of that gentrifying Philadelphia neighborhood, was pleased: "When all else fails, try capitalism. It works. . . . The private market is changing the neighborhood, and it's changing it in an appropriate way." Others cultivated an imperial attitude; seeing themselves as beleaguered islands of civility, the new gentry sought to expand their territory. One New Orleans proponent of transforming the multiethnic Irish Channel community admitted: "Renters are being displaced. It's sad, but the only hope for the neighborhood."[48]

Living in a historic area became a badge of class distinction. Such areas were expensive and, given their scarcity, exclusive in a way that even the fanciest suburb could not be. In an echo of the DAR era, proprietorship of the past once again became a vehicle of legitimation (though now it did not require ancestral connections) *and* it afforded a source of accumulation at the same time.

The ultimate gentry objective was to have their neighborhood designated as a historic district. District status roped off an area and forbade demolition or unapproved alterations within it. Like suburban zoning, the districts attempted to freeze time and the accumulation process at a moment favorable to the gentry. "Historic" status would protect them from both the slovenly poor and crude developers, yet would not unduly restrict their right of private property: individual historic buildings remained salable commodities.

In 1955 only twenty cities had historic district commissions. By 1966 there were 100, and by 1976, 492, in all fifty states; by 1982 there would be 900.[49] At first—in keeping with the precedent set by Williamsburg and the Brahmins—only the eighteenth century would do. But the increase in demand meant that soon there were not enough eighteenth-century remains to go around. The historical charm and values of the nineteenth century were accordingly discovered. After the Victorian craze had run its course, the Art Deco style of the 1920s—previously scorned—was reevaluated and found desirable. The expanding definition of "historic" opened new terrain to speculative assaults and ensuing displacement.[50]

Ironically, those who refused to rein in the market fell victim to it themselves. In New Orleans' French Quarter, for example, rents and prices did not stop climbing after the poor were gone. Upper-middle-class whites soon found themselves priced out of the historic district as "unassuming little houses were converted into spiffy pads for the very rich." In New York, those squeezed out of Manhattan were forced willy-nilly to become the agents of gentrification in new areas in Brooklyn. The spread of the "brownstoners" often had a negative impact on preexisting communities, but at the same time it widened the territory controlled by those with the resources and the commitment to fight the wrecking crews.[51]

The second set of 1960s recruits to the preservation movement were working- and lower-middle-class people, largely white ethics, who set out to save their neighborhoods from demolition. Their goal (similar to that of the original Charlestonians) was to preserve not simply historic *buildings,* but historic *communities.* Adopting the tactics of the civil rights and antiwar movements, grassroots organizations sat in, picketed, petitioned, and began to slow the bulldozers. The Chicano community of Tucson, Arizona, for example, learned in 1971 that a planned freeway would destroy their barrio. They were particularly incensed that the projected route ran right through El Tiradito (the Wishing Shrine), the symbolic, spiritual, and historical center of the neighborhood. They marched on the State Highway Department, circulated petitions, worked with local architects, historians, journalists, and churches, turned the freeway into a major political issue, and won. Even when local groups were not able to stop projects, community fury made developers increasingly wary and raised the cost of doing business.[52]

These neighborhood groups linked up to form support networks such as National People's Action and the National Association of Neighborhoods. These umbrella groups in turn demanded and got reforms such as the antiredlining laws—the Home Mortgage Disclosure Act (1975) and the Community Reinvestment Act (1977). In 1977 the Carter administration responded to their growing political muscle by creating the National Commission on Neighborhoods. The commission recommended establishing neighborhood cooperatives; attacked growth-industry-related banks, state legislatures, and municipal unions; asked for an end to federal support for suburbs; and called for federal development money, winning, in 1978, a $10 billion community investment fund to finance, purchase, and rehabilitate 300,000 housing units.[53]

The neighborhood conservationists were a complex lot. At times they were classic populists, beating off the attempts of speculators, developers, bankers, and state bureaucrats to commodify their neighborhoods. They had a strong commitment to the traditional. They contested the homogenization of their culture and stood for particularity, originality, and irreplaceability against the monolithic uniformity of corporate architecture, which had blotted out neighborhood distinctiveness. They often supported micro-history movements and underwrote local museums, oral history programs, community pageants, grassroots Bicentennial celebrations, and ethnic revivals. The local historians reminded many neighborhoods that they had once been independent municipalities. This fostered local pride and sometimes, though not inevitably, led the community to seek historic district status; some actually refused a historic designation.

On the other hand, many of the neighborhood conservationist groups were fearful, defensive, parochial, and racist. Many—especially those created in the aftermath of the 1960s black riots—sought to keep "traditional" (white) values intact by beating back black inroads, including public housing and school busing. Ethnic roots could be celebrated in a chauvinist and exclusive way.[54]

In the seventies, the established preservation movement reached out to this new constituency by broadening their definition of "historic." In 1974 the American Institute of Planners called on the movement to "preserve the unique pasts of all groups." By 1976, the Advisory Council reported,

> No longer does the term "historic district" necessarily mean cobblestones, arching oaks, and serene federal-period houses. It may now also designate a working class area of rehabilitated houses and corner bars that reflect both an epoch of local history and an ethnic or cultural strain that has figured prominently in community development.

Broadening the definition of "historic" to cover entire working-class areas expanded communities' available defenses against developers by extending to them existing legislative protections.[55]

A third, quite special set of conservationists were those, chiefly blacks, who set out to preserve their neighborhoods from historic preservationists. In 1970 the president of the Capitol East Community Organization denounced restorationists as "scavengers [who have] come in and squeezed out our people." His group placed red placards in storefronts and home windows stating "Capitol East Is Our Community and We Will Fight to Stay." CECO also passed out leaflets that read:

> Niggers, wake up! Do you realize that blacks used to live in Georgetown and were pushed out? They were asleep! Do you see blacks being removed daily from Capitol Hill? Brothers, you are sleeping! They are starting to push blacks out again! Everytime you see an expensively restored house it means another black man is out. Wake up![56]

In Kansas City, Joe Louis Mattox, founder of the Birdland Historic Preservation Society, agreed: "It is not the time for blacks, the faithful, to turn over the keys to the cities to those who ran off and left their heritage." Carl Holman, president of the National Urban Coalition, asserted in 1978: "You're going to start seeing some very rough clashes when these same blacks and browns who could not live in other folk's neighborhoods find they cannot stay in their own."[57]

In the 1970s blacks occasionally blocked foundation or government support for gentrification or engaged in rehabilitation programs of their own. But there was seldom overwhelming support for preservation in black communities. Many were ill-disposed to preserving places indelibly connected with white supremacy or poverty. It was one thing to restore a historic site, like Weeksville in Brooklyn, that black people had constructed and controlled; quite another to be reminded about the bad old days. Blacks preferred, where feasible, to move into new and modern buildings in the cities or suburbs.[58]

Traditional preservationists had a lot of trouble establishing an alliance with black constituencies, even apart from black reluctance. Partly this was because they felt, in their bones, that "historic" meant beautiful, and many sites of poor people's housing or worship were not pretty. Another problem was that such strategies as preservationists had developed for dealing with the problem did not work well in black communities. Protecting a black area by making it into a historic district might destroy it. Jackson Ward, in Richmond, Virginia, was a nineteenth-century free black community. In 1976 it was placed on the National Register to protect it from land developers and highway builders. This set off a boom among real estate speculators and affluent young whites attracted to its certified "historic" character. In other situations it proved difficult to get National Register designations for securely black neighborhoods, such as Houston's Fourth Ward and Austin's Robertson Hill, if local developers wanted the land for urban renewal projects.[59]

Even the best-intentioned preservationists could not grapple fundamentally with displacement, because they accepted the framework of a marketplace of privately owned property. Their response to the threatened destruction of buildings or communities boiled down to preemptive buying. But when the potential buyers were poor or lacked the political power to command state funds, failure was guaranteed: the communities would pass to those who commanded stronger purchasing power.

Back in 1964 Arthur Ziegler noted that Pittsburgh preservation was devastating the poor. He founded the Pittsburgh History and Landmarks Foundation "to involve them in the restoration activity rather than dislocating them." But Ziegler's minimal successes depended on spillover Mellon money ("in Pittsburgh we were blessed with private foundations that invested in our proposals") and worked only in areas where liberal gentry wanted to retain a neighborhood's multiracial character. Foundations and the government refused to support antidisplacement programs in all-black areas.[60]

Similarly, Lee Adler left the Historic Savannah Foundation in 1967 because it was displacing the poor. He set up the Savannah Landmark Rehabilitation Project with the laudable goal of buying half the houses in a gentrifying black area, restoring them (using minority contractors, neighborhood workers employed under the Comprehensive Employment and Training Act [CETA], local capital, and federal money), and then subsidizing the original tenants with federal funds. After two years of work, SLRP had saved just two dozen units; later, the supporting federal programs were eliminated. Their mistake was believing that they could achieve real power through the marketplace. "The one consistent method that does not fail and produces tangible results," Adler said, "is that of buying and selling properties. So, the name of the game is real estate." Thinking themselves hard-nosed, they were in fact naive victims of the utopian capitalist fantasy that profit motives can be harnessed for the public good.[61]

Still, the established preservation movement did acknowledge the situation of preservation-displacees and tried to respond to the problem. Its members sponsored conferences, wrote books, and launched programs, like the Inner City Venture Fund, aimed at preserving the historical resources of minorities, Native Americans, and ethnic populations.[62]

I n the sixties and seventies, then, the movement reached out to and gathered strength from new constituencies. In 1966 there were 2,500 preservation groups; in 1976 there were 6,000. Moreover, the cultural and political tide seemed to be running in the preservationists' direction. Everywhere a new sensibility rejected unrestrained "progress," "growth," "newness." Urban renewal was intellectually and culturally discredited in the planning community. In 1974 Robert Caro wrote a biography excoriating Robert Moses and got a Pulitzer Prize for it the next year. Management of scarce resources was the order of the day during the energy crisis. Conservationists, environmentalists, and historic preservationists (considered a species of temporal ecologists) fashioned an emerging alliance under the banner of "heritage preservation."[63]

The new allies were crucial because despite the temper of the times and the 1966 laws, the growth coalition's offensive continued. HUD, for instance, routinely ignored Advisory Council comments and tore down historic areas at the behest of local developers. So the National Trust returned to the cloakrooms and corridors of official Washington seeking an expanded federal role.

First, the Trust sent many of its best people *into* the bureaucracy to battle for administrative adherence to established legislation. Preservationists in the Park Service's Office of Archeology and Historic Preservation struggled, in the late sixties, to save immediately endangered sites. They were hampered by minimal funding and checked by experienced fighters in other agencies. Blocked in the bureaucracy, they went back to Congress and helped win the Environmental Protection Act of 1969, which strengthened their hand. In 1971 they got President Nixon to issue Executive Order 11593, which required recalcitrant agencies to conduct inventories of historic properties in their domains and to "exercise caution" about demolishing them.[64]

These efforts slowed, but failed to halt, the momentum of destruction. A visit by Trust and Advisory Council experts to Western Europe, Japan, and the Soviet Union, where preservation efforts were far more advanced, convinced them that they needed stronger legal authority. In 1974 they set up a lobbying group—Preservation Action—and launched a new legislative drive. They redeployed old legitimation arguments, given new edge by a decade of protest and upheaval. They also tested new arguments, praising the greater energy efficiency of old housing stock and the employment possibilities of labor-intensive rehabilitation projects. Finally, they drew upon their allies in the neighborhood conservation movement, a source of considerable political strength. In the history-conscious Bicentennial year, Congress gave them two crucial pieces of legislation.[65]

One, the National Historic Preservation Fund Act, expanded their power within the bureaucracy to hinder or prevent other federal agencies from demolishing "historic properties." The Advisory Council on Historic Preservation was given rule-making authority, upgrading its recommendations from guidelines to laws. The act also declared that properties the Council deemed "eligible" for the National Register were entitled to the same legal protections as those already on it, and it added financial muscle by authorizing a 700 percent increase in funding and 70–30 matching grant funds to states for preservation planning.[66]

The second law, the Historic Structures Tax Act, opened up a new front on one of the key terrains of the federal government—the tax code. It mandated tax disincentives for the demolition of historic buildings and tax benefits (quick write-offs) for those who rehabilitated historic properties and used them for income-producing purposes. This law went a long way toward eliminating the biases against preservation embedded in the tax code.[67]

W hile the National Trust had been engineering a massive expansion of preservationist power in the federal government, states and cities had been energetic in passing historic district legislation. The resultant body of law and regulation, although not as powerful as similar state provisions in the Soviet Union and Western Europe, nevertheless constituted a remarkable assertion of government control over the private land market. It was inevitable that such constraints would come under legal counterattack.[68]

The constitutional basis for preservation law was the state's so-called police power—the right to enforce regulations that constrained private property owners without having to pay them compensation because such regulation was for the "public good." This was a shaky position. Since 1909 the Supreme Court had deemed only health and safety sufficient justification for police power intervention. Mere "aesthetic" considerations were not. Preservationists had been unwilling to deploy the far more powerful constitutional basis of "eminent domain"—the unquestioned right of the state to *take* private property in return for just compensation—because they knew full well that U.S. landed capital would vigorously fight such state impairment of its prerogatives. Besides, having the state buy each and every endangered building would be murderously expensive and require a gigantic bureaucracy.[69]

In the 1960s and 1970s, pro-preservation lawyers fought for a breakthrough in police power jurisprudence. The National Trust sponsored the first National Conference on Historic Preservation Law in May 1971. In legal briefs and scholarly articles, delegates sought a formula that would reconcile a heightened concern with aesthetics (historic continuity was placed under this rubric) and traditional owners' rights. But this was difficult to do. Consequently, in the course of confronting the contradiction between private and public desires, some preservationists went so far as to argue that a completely new view of property rights was needed, one that recognized social needs as paramount and curtailed centuries-old rights of private ownership. And the statutes, ordinances, court decisions, and administrative procedures effected in the seventies inched their way toward that position.[70]

A critical step forward came in 1978. Ten years earlier the Penn Central Railroad had announced plans to build a two-million-square-foot office building on top of a historic landmark it owned—New York City's Grand Central Station. The city sued to block the project. Penn Central argued that the historic district law, because it prevented it from exploiting the developmental possibilities of its property to the fullest, constituted a "taking" of property that, under the Fourteenth Amendment, required it be paid "just compensation." The Supreme Court ruled, six to three, that Penn Central's position was "simply untenable." The court majority noted that the corporation was already getting a "reasonable return" on its property and that the law allowed it to transfer the unused development rights on its airspace to another property, and found a law "providing services, standards, controls, and incentives that will encourage preservation by private owners and users" to be clearly constitutional. To find otherwise, Justice Brennan noted, "would of course invalidate not just New York City's law, but all comparable landmark legislation in the nation." While hardly adopting the proto-socialist arguments advanced by some preservation lawyers, the decision, when measured against the legal situation fifty or one hundred years earlier, was a startling restriction on the rights of private property and the freedom of the marketplace.[71]

T he preservationist alliance's triumph coincided with the collapse— and conversion—of its traditional enemy. In the mid-seventies, a worldwide recession knocked the wind out of the growth movement and brought development to a halt. As boosters and builders suddenly confronted an "age of limits," their attitudes toward historic preservation changed.[72]

The recession bit immediately into housing construction. Rising mortgage rates lowered demand, high interest rates made new construction more costly, and the federal government imposed a public housing moratorium. Housing starts plummeted. In 1976, for the first time, more Americans repurchased old houses than bought new ones. By 1982, 85 percent of American families had been priced out of the housing market, just at the time the baby boomers were trying to enter it.[73]

This set off a preservation surge. People who could not afford to move began to fix up what they had. At the same time, it became more profitable than ever to rehabilitate old buildings and gentrify them. A 1980 study confirmed soaring real estate values in historic districts. Prices in Savannah's had risen 276 percent in the previous ten years, compared with an average rise of 184 percent for the rest of the city. Banks that had once redlined inner-city areas now leaped to finance them. By 1977 residential property rehabilitation costs were estimated at $32 billion—38 percent of all construction spending for the year.[74] Rehabilitation money also began flowing to the casualties of the previous generation. Main Streets attracted funding in their attempt to combat the malls, undertook façade renovations, and traded on their old-time ambience.[75]

Even more capital flowed into providing services to the residents, office workers, tourists, and regional middle-class shoppers who had been drawn to the central business districts. One particularly lucrative enterprise was the historic market movement. Developers like James Rouse, finding the suburbs saturated with malls, now parlayed historic designations into funding magnets, attracting investment from federal, state, city, and private sources. San Francisco's Ghirardelli Square had pioneered in 1964; it was followed by Denver's Larimer Square, Seattle's Pioneer Square, Atlanta's Underground, St. Louis' Laclede's Landing, and equivalents in Annapolis, Louisville, Boston, and Pittsburgh. They paid off handsomely; one businessman enthused that the markets "demonstrated conclusively that preservation and business are compatible." "We have seen the past," he said, "and we see that it works."[76]

More dramatically still, whole towns whose economies had been demolished by long-term capital flight or the recession decided to exploit the tourist potential inherent in their history. Relics of former stages of economic development were recycled by private developers blocked from growth projects. They turned industrial plant to service sector uses: factories became boutiques, breweries became museums, warehouses became restaurants and condos, iron furnaces became offices, mining towns became ski resorts. Lowell, Massachusetts, capitalizing on its nineteenth-century industrial "character," attracted $350,000 from banks, $2 million from a bond issue, and $26 million in local, state, and federal commitments.[77]

The financial rewards engendered a wonderfully expedient development of historical interest. Seneca Falls, N.Y., a declining manufacturing community, had paid virtually no attention to its local women's rights legacy. Following its rediscovery by feminists and historians, and congressional establishment of a Women's Rights Historic National Park, local businessmen poured money into remodeling the downtown district, even designing statues of feminist heroines. As a Village Trustee noted, the enthusiastic merchants "don't give a hoot" about feminism, but "they see the money opportunity. I mean, if you've got Old Faithful in your town, you are in favor of geysers."[78]

The preservation boom stimulated a demand for more professionals. Williamsburg and Cooperstown had long been running training seminars; now the universities entered the field. James Marston Fitch had started the first graduate course in the preservation of historic architecture at Columbia in 1964. By 1975, ninety architecture schools in the United States and Canada offered either degrees in preservation or preservation-related programs and courses. Some of these graduates joined the cadre of preservation professionals called into being by the new federal legislation. Some worked directly for the Department of the Interior, the Advisory Council, or the many agencies who developed "on-staff" to cope with new regulations, and others labored throughout the country as State Historic Preservation Officers. Others worked, as employees or consultants, for communities and developers, helping them do the bureaucratic paperwork required to qualify for federal funding.[79]

Finally, in the altered conditions of the 1970s, even the behemoths of business moved toward a preservation stance. From the 1920s until the mid--1960s, U.S. corporations had routinely torn down old plant and built anew, despite steadily rising construction costs, because costs of capital had declined enough to offset them. By the 1970s, expensive capital had generated rethinking. It became apparent that converting old office or factory space was 30 to 40 percent cheaper than constructing from scratch; that rehabbing took less time because work could continue during the winter; that it was less disruptive of business operations; that it reduced land costs; and that it avoided environmental impact statements, local building code hassles, and battles with preservationists. Given the new culture of retrenchment, preservation even afforded good publicity and advertising outlets.[80]

Banks, oil companies, insurance corporations, and heavy manufacturing firms—often using special development subsidiaries—began recycling their own buildings or buying up old plant for adaptive reuse. Between 1970 and 1977 rehabilitation of nonresidential buildings increased from 3.5 percent to 25.0 percent of the construction market, representing approximately $20 billion worth of construction. By 1982 the estimated value of commercial rehabilitation had reached $51.6 billion.[81]

The 1976 tax laws speeded the process. Developers now *sought* to have buildings or areas designated as historic sites because that entitled them to tax benefits. National Register listings went from 13,538 to 24,347. In four years 2,500 rehabilitation projects, valued at $1.2 billion, qualified for preservation tax benefits. UDAG money began flowing to preservation projects—by 1980, 39 percent of the total allotments. Increasingly, federal dollars would underwrite a historic core (as at Lowell), and developers would benefit from the boost in property values around its periphery.[82]

Diehard developers did an about-face. Businessmen had long viewed preservation as a constraint on their right to maximize returns on their property, and the movement's anticommercial tone had only exacerbated their suspicions of it. Preservation had been grudgingly supported as a prop to legitimacy, but this uncongenial task had been left to genteel elites, patrician women, and super-rich dabblers. And even then most businessmen, believing accumulation itself to be capital's best legitimation, feared that preservation would inhibit the cornucopia of commodities. Now, however, preservation was useful not simply in legitimating capital, but in accumulating it, and business embraced it with enthusiasm. As one mortgage banker explained:

> Historic preservation is in many ways a sophisticated type of real estate development. . . . The stereotype of the local ladies club attempting to save some old building is long out of date. . . . It is possible to identify several *billion* dollars of historic preservation projects in the portfolios of financial institutions in this country.[83]

For their part, the preservationists eagerly welcomed their new allies. A National Trust vice-chairman rejoiced that the movement had "learned to shift from aesthetic appeals to bottom-line shrewdness. . . . After the decades of saving presidents' birthplaces and war heroes' headquarters, the preservation movement has leap-frogged into alliances with environmentalists, developers, and merchandisers."[84]

F or a short period in the depressed late seventies, then, it seemed as if *everybody* liked historic preservation. People flocked to join the National Trust. Individual membership went from 30,000 in 1970 to 160,000 in 1980. Major corporations such as Alcoa, American Iron and Steel, CBS, Chemical Bank, Exxon, Ford, IBM, Time, and Xerox signed on as National Trust Corporate Associates—over a hundred by 1979.[85]

The coffers and political clout of the National Trust swelled accordingly. Its staff went from forty-seven to over two hundred, and it provided services to all the members of its now wildly contradictory constituency—grants to local neighborhood conservationists and poor tenants threatened with displacement, educational programs and conferences for preservation professionals, vocational training for restorationists technicians, legal information to developers, private owners, towns, and corporations. The Trust dealt with its internal contradictions by fudging or ignoring them. And why not? It worked. The barbarians had been beaten.[86]

I n the eighties, the barbarians struck back. Proctor & Gamble landed one of the earliest blows. In 1980 the company was infuriated to learn of the impending involuntary designation of its corporate headquarters as a historic landmark. Aware that, given the Penn Central decision, its hands would be tied once the designation was announced, it muscled its way onto the floor of Congress. Representative Joseph McDade (R-Pa.) attached to pending legislation an amendment requiring an owner's consent before industrial facilities could be put on the National Register. National Trust lobbyists, hitherto so successful, found to their dismay that they were utterly unable to roll back this "ominous" provision. Indeed, Congress went on to institute owner-consent provisions for *all* Register designations and repealed the disincentives provision of the 1976 Tax Act.[87]

At the same time, the judicial victories came under attack. The Supreme Court had stated explicitly in the Penn Central decision that the question of what "historic" *meant* would remain subject to judicial review. In August 1980 a federal judge in Virginia reversed the Interior Department's 1974 designation of 14,000 acres in the state as a rural "national historic district"; the court even barred the government from accepting gifts from Virginia landowners of "scenic easements" by which they bound themselves not to alter the architecture or landscape. The court thus upheld a strip-mine developer (behind whom lay W. R. Grace & Company, the chemical conglomerate) who argued that the "historic" designation was improper. As a local preservationist pointed out, "this decision, if it stands, will bastardize retroactively every historic landmark designation in the country. Not one of them is now safe from challenge."[88]

Another dramatic indication of the shifting temper of the times came on December 4, 1981, when Detroit police removed armed members of the Poletown Neighborhood Council from the Church of the Immaculate Conception, ending four years of resistance by community residents in the courts and the streets to the planned demolition of their homes. General Motors had agreed to build a plant that would provide 6,000 desperately needed jobs within Detroit city limits if the city would seize and raze 450 acres of a mixed Polish and black working-class neighborhood. The residents proposed alternatives that would allow factory and community to coexist. GM was not interested. The unions, city administration, and courts backed the corporation. Demolition proceeded, leveling 1,500 homes, 150 businesses, 16 churches, and a hospital.[89]

GM's heavyfooted intervention signaled a reversal of attitudes. The takeover was motivated as much by a macho desire to reassert corporate prerogatives as by a simple search for profit in hard times. Most of the cleared land was to be used for parking lots; vertical parking could have avoided much demolition. GM's decision not to swerve or compromise recalls Robert Moses' hauteur. Pro-GM spokespeople denounced preservationist attempts to save Poletown. Detroit's director of planning insisted that a "community whose heyday has passed may glory in the past. . . . But a group attempting to better its condition needs to focus on the future." She undoubtedly found significant support in the black community when she argued that Detroit could not afford to "dwell excessively on the memories of its former white community or else it will not give living expression to . . . its present population, which is over 50 percent black."[90]

These straws in the wind accurately forecast the coming of the Reagan administration hurricane.

The right wing considered historic preservation—like rent control, environmental protection, occupational health and safety regulation, and laws against usury—an intolerable constraint on private accumulation. Moreover, preservation, to these throwbacks to the old accumulative order, was a cultural and political danger. No fools, they had sniffed out the antimarket logic in the emerging body of administrative rules and legal decisions. Now creative destruction's time had come round again, and they set out enthusiastically to reverse every gain the movement had made since 1966.

For openers, Interior Secretary James Watt called for *zerobudgeting* the entire historic preservation program: he asked Congress to eliminate *all* funding for the National Trust and the state historic preservation organizations. Other Reaganites fanned out to undermine the preservationists' position in the bureaucracy. Their agenda, as summed up in the January 1984 report of the Grace Commission (headed by the same Peter Grace involved in the strip-mining lawsuit discussed above), was to wipe out the Advisory Council's ability to halt other federal agencies from destroying historic properties; to repeal the section of the Highway Act reining in the Department of Transportation; to remove constraints on the Interior Department's ability to undertake strip mining; to end restrictions on what could be done with funds from Community Development Block Grants. The administration also proposed establishing enterprise zones in U.S. cities (modeled on Hong Kong and Taiwanese practices), which would suspend *all* controls on entrepreneurial freedom of action: condo-men would be free to bulldoze as they pleased.[91]

On the other hand, Reagan's 1981 tax laws actually *enhanced* benefits for preservation. The law provided a 25 percent investment tax credit for approved rehabilitation of certified historic structures: renovators could subtract one of every four dollars spent on preservation work directly from their federal income taxes. Watt explained that the Trust's "historic mission of working with the private sector is logical and appropriate to this administration's philosophy." What he meant was that Reaganism would dismantle any *constraints* on capital, but had no objection to providing handouts to banks, developers, landlords, and construction firms. If economic forces in the eighties favored preservation over bulldozing, that was fine with Watt.[92]

T he response of the preservation movement to the Reagan offensive was to scurry toward its real estate right and away from its populist left. Preservationists largely abandoned attempts to build a mass base, wrote off the displaced, and hitched their wagon to their traditional worst enemies. The National Trust, in particular, cast its lot with capital. It hired as its new president Michael Ainslie, a thirty-six-year-old businessman with experience in management, marketing, and real estate development, who announced his intention to adopt "more financial- and real estate–oriented approaches." The coordinator of Preservation Action, Nellie Longsworth, enthused that "rehabilitation and preservation have finally made it into a larger arena and we can take pride in the results that are produced by private investment." There were side offerings to the displaced—the Inner City Ventures Fund made limited funds available to nonprofit neighborhood self-help groups to acquire housing in historic districts for low-income and minority residents—but concern over displacement and the neighborhoods dwindled dramatically. Environmentalism and ecology were out; entrepreneurship was in. The editor of the National Trust's magazine, *Historic Preservation,* laid it on the bottom line: "Making a profit makes preservation possible. . . . If an entrepreneur doesn't have a fighting chance to end up with a profit, it's going to be good-bye old building."[93]

On the face of things, tacking to the right worked brilliantly. Appeals to Congress for support on the grounds that preservation made money for developers and provided jobs paid off. Here was a constituency that had the clout to withstand the neoconservative offensive. In every year of Reagan's first administration, Congress overrode zerobudgeting and reinstated preservation funding, albeit with serious cuts. The enterprise zone proposal passed the Senate three times, but was thrice beaten back by the House, and was dropped in the 1984 tax proposals. And Congress overruled a direct attempt to slash the authority of the Advisory Council. The preservation position was eroded through countless administrative and budgetary decisions, but far less than Reagan and Watt had intended.

And the strategy saved buildings. Major real estate syndicators who might have torn down old structures now rushed to certify them as "historic," thus qualifying for the tax breaks of the 1981 act. As one certification official noted, "We're seeing a new type of clientele—bankers, lawyers, developers." In 1980, $346 million worth of rehabilitation projects had been approved for tax breaks; by 1983, $2.2 billion worth had passed historic muster. By the end of fiscal 1984, a total of $7.8 billion had gone into 9,000 historic rehab projects, which had generated 310,000 jobs, $5.5 billion in new earnings, and $19.5 billion in increased retail sales. Historic preservation had become big business, and big business could hold Reaganism at bay.[94]

But the preservation community, seemingly triumphant, was in fact in an extremely dangerous position, having grabbed a wolf-in-sheep's-clothing by the tail. Its strategy ignored the fact that capital had no commitment to preservation except as a convenient cover for quick returns in hard times, a device to transfer state benefits to private developers and give the handouts a "conservative" patina. As Paul J. Goldberger noted, "developers now routinely use preservation rhetoric for their own ends without adopting its values, and their ends are often antithetical to the preservationists'."[95]

One of the many consequences of the rightward tilt was a continuing decline in the traditional preservationist concern for authentic symbolic meaning. Seldom, now, did the adaptively reused artifacts illuminate the roots of the present, set in motion mythic reverberations, or expand contemporary historical consciousness. The DAR and the Rockefellers, for all their distortions of the past, at least had been concerned with meanings; the contemporary crowd were into surfaces, styles, the historic as stage setting.

A droll example of this was the emergence of Façadism (also known as Façadectomy and Façadomy). In this form of Potemkin preservation, developers tore down an old building but preserved its streetfront wall. This they affixed, like a historic veneer, to a high-rise condo or hotel. It was, someone said, like preserving polar bears in the form of rugs. The preservation community began to split over this burlesque—interestingly, along the lines of its original formation. In Charleston, where it all started, UDAG money helped a developer plop an office complex (including a 430-room hotel, a 500-car garage, and 64,000 feet of retail space) right in the heart of the 1931 historic district. This was acceptable to the Historic Charleston Foundation (descendants of the business joiners) because the complex was fronted by the preserved façade of the row of old buildings it replaced. But the 2,700-member Preservation Society, with its roots in the preservation movement of the 1920s, denounced this as an outrage, and sued—unsuccessfully—to halt it.[96]

More alarmingly, it soon appeared that although the Reaganites would assist profitable projects, they had no compunction whatever about reverting to old-style bulldozing when *that* was the path to profit. In 1981, for instance, UDAG gave $21.5 million to build a hotel in New York City's Times Square (and the city added another $100 million in tax abatements). Standing in the way were three old Broadway theaters; one was on the National Register, another was eligible. Watt muscled the Advisory Council into approving their demolition.[97]

Worse was to come. In November 1984, to the preservation strategists' shock and dismay, Reagan's Treasury Department issued a tax "simplification" plan that called for the total repeal of tax incentives for historic rehabilitation. The move was not specifically aimed at the preservationists. Rather, Pentagon voraciousness dictated massive cutbacks in domestic spending, and neoconservatives wanted to dismantle a host of tax-code-supported social policies. Some in the administration even regretted the likely impact of the changes on a program that stimulated private investment. But sacrifices were in order, and repeal seemed likely to pass in some form or other. Repeal would send a wrecking ball swinging toward the preservation edifice, made brittle by its excessive dependence on tax policy and fairweather friends.

P reservationists may survive this current assault, but what of the future? In considerable measure that depends on larger trends in the economy.
        If interest rates drop, oil prices come down, and the economy recovers, capitalists will drop their new-found commitment to preservation in a flash. Façadism, Reaganism, and the Poletown putsch are only indicators of a larger truth: preservation's allies in the big-business world have no *principled* concern for preservation. Banks and development corporations have only the thinnest sense of being members of communities whose histories merit recalling. They see their country not as a society, but as an economy—a grid of opportunities—and their actions are dictated by the probabilities of profit. In an economic revival, preservationists, deserted by the right, would find few allies on the left. Indeed, the movement's inability or unwillingness to confront displacement and its lack of ties to the labor movement leave it wide open to attack by a revitalized growth coalition that appeals for black and working-class support in the name of housing and job development against "limousine liberal" preservationists.

It is also possible that the economy will *not* recover, but will continue to lurch in and out of recessions. In the presence of continuing high interest rates, and the absence of reindustrialization or a housing boom, real estate and corporate capital will probably continue to accept historic preservation as the best bargain available. But if the current approach to preservation is maintained, it will simply accelerate the paired processes of gentrification and displacement. In that event, older American cities will proceed down the European road. In the last generation, almost every major city in Europe, as well as hundreds of smaller ones, has had its historic center preserved and its social relations transformed by a new urban enclosure movement. One by one, working-class areas have been invaded by the new gentry and their former inhabitants resettled in high rises on the city outskirts. Now only the wealthy and the corporations can afford to reside in the historic centers of Paris, Rome, or Amsterdam.[98]

Unless something is done, U.S. cities will go to the same route. Displacement is the order of the day all over the country. The process is startlingly clear in New York City, where the eighties may well see the gentry invasion of Harlem. Manhattan may become a preserve for corporate offices, small shoppes, theaters, adaptively reused historic markets (South Street Seaport is a harbinger), hotels, and gentry housing, with blacks, Hispanics, and poor whites packed off to the periphery. In a still grimmer vision, American cities will be heavily patrolled and well-fortified "historic" ghettos, defending themselves against beggars, muggers, and squatters, and the past itself will have become a hated emblem of class domination.[99]

I s there an alternative? Perhaps, but it will require a massive reversal of direction by the organized preservation community. Recall its trajectory to date.

For its first century, preservationism remained an upper-class movement intent on blocking the free market demolition of old buildings through either preemptive purchase or state intervention. The genteel and the wealthy were motivated partly by aesthetic concerns and partly by a desire to enhance their own legitimacy through an association with hallowed symbolic artifacts. Between the 1940s and the early 1960s, to gain additional support in their losing battle with developers, they allied with middle-class professionals and small businessmen who were also threatened by the march of progress. This required a shift in strategy from parenthesizing to adaptive reuse. At the time this seemed a reasonable compromise—indeed, a step forward. Huxtable was convinced that putting "a new building in the old shell" was a "modern solution that still manages to evoke the past." This belief was sustainable for a time, but in retrospect we can see that adaptive reuse, by pulling back from the older antimarket critique, facilitated the process of gentrification. There was nothing inherently wrong with adaptive use except that in practice it meant that only those with market power got to use and enjoy old buildings.[100]

In the late sixties and early seventies, the movement expanded again. It increased its base in middle-class gentry neighborhoods, worked with businessmen attracted by the profitability of the past, and also reached out to working-class neighborhood conservationists and anticorporate environmentalists. The tensions between history as heritage and history as commodity grew sharper, but the overarching imperative of combating the growth coalition kept the contradictory coalition together.

In the early eighties, with growth proponents weakened by recession and a reactionary administration in power, preservationists succumbed to the temptation to rely on the market, now suitably guided by tax policy. Buildings and communities were saved if they had pecuniary possibilities, gentrification's impact on the poor was benignly overlooked, and the movement's already attenuated concern with historic meaning was weakened to the vanishing point. After a century of sensitivity to the menace of an unrestricted marketplace, the preservationist leadership now convinced itself that the pursuit of profit could be harnessed to serve social needs.[101]

This was, I believe, a reversible error. Historic preservation can survive without corporate backing, but only if it rebuilds its shrunken political base. The history of the movement suggests that preservationists' natural (if not always comfortable) allies are environmentalists, tenants' organizations, civil rights groups, neighborhood conservationists, unions, public housing activists, and others working for large-scale social change. For historic preservation, like these others, is a reform movement: it goes against the grain of the dominant culture.

To make such a connection, however, would require preservationists to be more aware of and more committed to overcoming the negative effects of the preservation process. Preservationists might establish their sensitivity to the concerns of potential allies by admitting that historic continuity, while an important human need, must be balanced against other human needs, such as that of the present generation for housing. To gain the support of potential colleagues, preservationists might back policies that guaranteed affordable housing for all citizens, even if such policies alienated bankers, developers, and some of the gentry, such as the irate couple who wrote recently: "Housing of the poor never was and should not be an objective of the preservation movement. If we are not housing the poor adequately, our social programs are to blame, not the preservationist, and definitely not those who have made a personal commitment to rescuing the past from obliteration." This may be true, but if the movement is to garner widespread support, it will have to demonstrate its commitment to *changing* those blameworthy social programs.[102]

It might do this by making historic preservation part of an overall land-use package that included rent subsidies, nonmarket allocation of credit (replacing private mortgages with direct government grants and low-interest loans), support for nonprofit community-based developers and neighborhood organizers, rehabilitation programs that guarantee current tenants controlled rents or relocation in equivalent housing, city investments in vacant or blighted buildings, tax reassessments, and the abolition of tax shelters for speculators. The experience of popular coalitions in Hartford, Cleveland, Berkeley, and Santa Monica during the seventies suggests that local taxing mechanisms and regulations can successfully control developers, bankers, realtors, and speculators in the short run. But ultimately the goal might have to be the abandonment of the current government-subsidized "free market" housing system and its replacement with a system that guarantees decent housing to all citizens as a social right.

Preservationists have argued that we must treat city centers as valuable artifacts. But unless they address the pressures that make it difficult or impossible to do so, their chances of success are not high. I am suggesting that if we enhance popular control over the production and distribution of goods, including housing, provide shelter for those who need it, and make resources available to those who want to fix up their own neighborhoods, people would likely be more than willing to honor collective memories. Only when citizens are not confronted with the choice between a preserved past and a squalid present can preservationism have a secure future.[103]

In a revived coalition, it could be the special role of architects and historians, Park Service professionals and local history amateurs, neighborhood activists and historic house enthusiasts, to forge a preservationism that negates the ahistorical, uncritical, and self-centered sensibility of much contemporary culture; that saves the material remains of the past in a way that illuminates the course of American history; that uses historic artifacts to provide more than just sterile ambience and a sense of cozy continuity; that severs the connection between preservation and class privilege, thus avoiding the looming fate of the American city; and raises for popular consideration the possibility that ultimately the only way to prevent the private appropriation, perversion, and destruction of our common heritage is to overhaul the social system that threatens it.[104]

★ 10 ★

Exhibiting Women's History

The search for women's history in museums turns up a surprising array of representations, a diversity that suggests both the power and the unevenness of a changing social consciousness about women. Designed between 1964 and 1984, the exhibits discussed here show a marked shift, from early portrayals that unselfconsciously depict women in traditional family and social contexts to later exhibits informed by the concerns of the women's movement and recent scholarly work in women's history.

Such exhibits are themselves cultural artifacts. First, they offer an oblique view of popular historical understanding, refracted through the lens of curators' ideas about their audiences. Exhibits necessarily embody assumptions about what audiences already know; like other social texts, they carry on an implicit dialogue with an imagined audience. The terms of that discourse will not be an exact reflection of a single popular understanding, but they can alert us to significant categories and common themes. Second, as highly visible spectacles, exhibits themselves occupy a privileged position in that discussion, influencing and shaping popular consciousness about women's history.

Taken together, these exhibits chart a dramatic but partial transformation in public preservations of women's history. Both American historiography and museum practice have changed considerably over the last twenty years. Diverse in form and scope, the exhibits suggest the range of choices available to historians working in museums and the special possibilities and constraints of their medium. We begin by comparing the oldest and the most recent of our sample of exhibits to demonstrate the original vision and then the revision of

BY BARBARA MELOSH AND
CHRISTINA SIMMONS

women's place in public life as presented at the National Museum of American History (NMAH) of the Smithsonian Institution. The First Ladies' exhibit, which opened in 1964 with the museum itself (then named the National Museum of History and Technology), is political history with a twist, showing the women behind the presidents. Next to it an exhibit that opened in 1984, a sympathetic and searching portrait of Eleanor Roosevelt, implicitly revises the older presentation of First Ladies as famous helpmates. Other exhibits embody the historical revisions of the 1960s and 1970s. The hand of social history is visible in "A Nation of Nations," a 1976 installation at NMAH, and at Conner Prairie, a living museum depicting the lives of rural midwestern men and women. Two very different exhibits reflect an emerging feminist consciousness in their celebrations of women's achievements in public life: in the Sewall-Belmont house, the National Woman's Party tells its own story of activism for women's rights; and "Black Women: Achievements Against the Odds," a portable exhibit first developed by the Anacostia Neighborhood Museum, Washington, D.C., and now sponsored by the Smithsonian Traveling Exhibition Service, reveals a moving history of individual triumph over race, class, and sexual oppression. Finally "25 Years of Barbie Dolls," at the Indiana State Museum, focuses on that well-endowed icon of the sexual-revolution-gone-consumerist, reflecting on the history and cultural significance of a familiar contemporary object.

T he First Ladies' Hall is probably the best-known historical representation of women's lives in the United States, a perennial favorite of visitors to NMAH. Closely allied to a conventional history of "great men," the exhibit nonetheless extends this view by focusing on women's place in the ceremonial life of the presidency.

In the hall, an atmosphere of reverence usually prevails: lighting has been dimmed to present fading of the fabrics, and visitors respond by lowering their voices. The elaborate gowns dominate the hall. The figures appear in chronological order, each accompanied by a small placard identifying the First Lady and the dates of her administration. The text focuses on the fabric and construction of the dresses, in the manner of newspaper marriage announcements. (Two of the dresses actually were wedding gowns.) The mannequins' faces are identical, with the same dark eyes, straight nose, and pale lips set in an expression of repose. An accompanying note explains that the curators chose this form of presentation so as not to distract from the dresses.

The First Ladies' hairstyles are historically accurate, and the mannequins vary in height and girth to fit the dresses, lending some individuality to the figures.

Upper-class women began the collection, and the exhibit implies much about the function and place of these women. In 1912 Rose Gouveneur Hoes, a descendant of President Monroe, contributed several nineteenth-century gowns that she owned and persuaded Helen Herron Taft to donate one of hers. The exhibit grew as the curators obtained a formal dress from each administration. Most were worn by the First Lady for the inaugural ball or another state occasion; gowns typical of the period, though not worn by the First Lady herself, fill gaps in the collection. The richness and formality of the gowns reflect the status of the presidents, and the entire exhibit demonstrates the wearers' roles as hostesses and supervisors of White House furnishings and decoration. The First Ladies' Hall embodies the notion of women as cultural symbols of beauty, graciousness, and service to men.

This unselfconscious presentation of elite women's place provides some information of interest to contemporary women's historians engaged in rediscovering and reinterpreting upper-class women's relationship to dominant ideology. Knowing how each woman chose to exercise her duties and prerogatives would tell us something about elite women as guardians of manners and high culture. The exhibit contains some intriguing hints. One card, for example, notes that Van Buren's daughter-in-law, Angelica, introduced European manners and formality to the White House, offering suggestive evidence about the predilection of the American upper class in 1840. The enforcement of temperance at the White House links other First Ladies to the larger social history of female reform. But although the exhibit provides glimpses of a broader social and cultural history, its guiding intention lies elsewhere.

The actual First Ladies assume second place in an exhibit shaped by conventional political history. Depicting wives of famous men in itself assumes that history is about powerful political and economic figures—those who act in the public sphere. The families or friends of political leaders and the duties, pleasures, or rituals of domestic life take on significance only because of their association with public figures. Not even Eleanor Roosevelt's card suggests that she was more than a hostess. The ordinary duties of the First Ladies hold no interest from a traditional historical perspective, and hence require little suggestion of activity, choice, or individual personality in their depiction.

Although the First Ladies as historical actors have little if any importance in the exhibit, their dresses provide historical information about design, crafts, trade, and manufacture. The Empire waist of Dolly Madison, the cloak worn by Andrew Johnson's daughter with its Arab burnous, and the names of twentieth-century designers illustrate the history of clothing fashion. The kind of fabric and place of manufacture are noted. Many early dresses used Oriental silks, no doubt obtained in the China trade. In 1889 Caroline Lavinia Scott Harrison wore the first dress made entirely of American materials, acknowledging the maturity of domestic manufactures. Other displays indicate the use of indigenous plants and animals in embroidery and tapestry designs, signs of growing national identity. The labels point out the last dress that was entirely hand-sewn (Sarah Polk's, 1849) and the first machine-stitched gown, worn in the next administration by Margaret Mackall Smith Taylor; the text notes the invention of the sewing machine in 1846. The exhibit is strongest and most successful as a history of upper-class costume.

This undeniably engaging exhibit draws hundreds of thousands of visitors each year. Typically, the audience is more female than male by a proportion of about three to one, with many children in the crowd. Visitors marvel at the construction of the dresses and debate about the most beautiful; a placard even notes what seems to be the perennial favorite, Buchanan's niece's dress, a white wedding gown. As seamstresses and embroiders ourselves, we were fascinated by the decoration of the gowns and the enormous amount of time and craft skill involved, especially in the hand-sewn ones. In effect, visitors respond actively to the repetitive format of the exhibit by commenting on, judging, and choosing their favorite costumes. Part of the appeal of the First Ladies' Hall may be that it is one of the few public displays that give attention to women's lives, even though these are unusual lives presented with conventional assumptions about women's roles.

"Eleanor Roosevelt: First Person Singular," organized in 1984 to commemorate the centennial of her birth, signals a new departure in the Smithsonian's presentation of First Ladies. The exhibit's placement clearly ties it to the First Ladies' Hall: one entrance is just to the left of the opening of the Hall, and visitors exiting from the case of recent First Ladies' gowns must walk through the opening of "First Person Singular." The contrast between this exhibit and the older one dramatizes the changing status of women's history. In 1964 the organizers of the First Ladies' Hall made their way alone, without the support of a broader scholarly community committed to serious consideration of women's lives. In 1984 a new scholarship and politics lend vigor and depth to this moving portrait of Eleanor Roosevelt.

The thoroughly contemporary theme of this exhibit is Eleanor Roosevelt's struggle to transcend the traditional female roles of daughter, wife, and mother. The opening label quotes her memories of submergence in marriage and motherhood and her determination to work in a larger sphere: "I began to want to do things on my own, to use my own mind and abilities for my aims." The exhibit recounts her lonely childhood and unrewarding marriage, poignantly evoking Eleanor's dutiful obedience to her overbearing mother-in-law, Sara Delano Roosevelt; her painful shyness in Washington social circles; her feelings of uselessness on the early campaign trail; and the devastating discovery of Franklin's infidelity. A quotation, set in large type, acknowledges the strain of motherhood: "I was always just getting over having a baby or about to have one." In its portrayal of Eleanor Roosevelt's personal life, the exhibit deepens its celebration of her exemplary public life with a feminist consciousness of the constraints of gender.

Like all good biography, the exhibit provides a careful and nuanced understanding of the intimate relationship between private and public life. The narrative presents Eleanor Roosevelt as brave and resourceful in her decision to remain with Franklin but to develop a life of her own. A prominent panel shows visitors the little world of Val-Kill, the cottage in the woods of the Hyde Park estate that provided her with solace and a means of escape. "We three ladies"—Nancy Cook, Marion Dickerman, and Eleanor Roosevelt—appear in an evocative photograph, and the text acknowledges their close relationship: "The three women shared the Val-Kill cottage and grounds. They gave each other affection, family-like support, and encouragement." Illustrating some of Eleanor Roosevelts many activities and accomplishments, the exhibit affirms the personal satisfactions of public life through her words: "More than anything else, [politics] may serve to guard against the emptiness and loneliness that enter some women's lives."

The profusion of Roosevelt memorabilia and documentation offers a rich field for exhibition, and this presentation makes notably good use of these opportunities. For example, Eleanor's relationship with her difficult mother-in-law, described in the text, is underscored in Sara Delano Roosevelt's records of dinner parties; one page shows the seating plan, with Franklin at one end of the table, Sara at the other, and Eleanor relegated to an ignominious middle position. In the Val-Kill section, linen towels embroidered "EMN," for Eleanor, Marion, and Nancy, strikingly convey the intimacy and domesticity of their relationship. Eleanor Roosevelt's encyclopedic Christmas book, methodically listing the hundreds of presents she gave, testifies to her thoughtfulness and Victorian selflessness. Her fox fur, curled up with a pair of sunglasses, conveys her family wealth and position, and a suggestion of wry humor in the arrangement—the fox's shiny eyes peer conspiratorially at the visitor—subtly acknowledges the distance between her historical and class position and the lives of most visitors.

The theme of Eleanor Roosevelt's self-realization provides a coherent interpretive frame, and the exhibit effectively uses quotations and film to give immediacy to its evocation of her. This theme, however, tends to distort one aspect of her politics: her often-distant relationship to feminism. We get no hint of the divisions of the women's movement after suffrage was won, nor of Eleanor Roosevelt's prominence among those who emphasized other social reforms, sometimes at the expense of a broad vision of women's rights. In this regard her own words may be somewhat misleading. The exhibit text does not identify the source or date of these quotations: some are clearly recollections; others may be from diaries or letters. The theme of self-realization may reflect Eleanor Roosevelt's later interpretation of her life, and it certainly touches contemporary feminist sensibilities. But we need at least a suggestion of the strategic differences among feminists, of the conflicts between feminists and other reformers, and of the changing meaning of feminism itself over the twentieth century. Finally, although the exhibit deals frankly with Franklin's infidelity and affirms close female friendship, it avoids the historical controversy about the emotional and sexual content of Eleanor Roosevelt's relationships with women, a critical interpretive issue.[1]

D
eveloped for the Bicentennial, "A Nation of Nations" embodies the social history of the 1960s and 1970s, self-consciously rewriting American history "from the bottom up." Its successes illustrate the contributions of this reimagined history. "Nation" brilliantly defuses the jingoism implied by its title, instead expressing an ebullient pluralism that finds strength in ethnic and racial diversity. At the same time, "Nation" also reveals the limitations of a social history that fails to address conflict or to analyze relationships of power and inequality, a shortcoming that is most pronounced in the presentation of women. Attentive to daily life, the exhibit everywhere includes women. Yet "Nation" never acknowledges gender as a significant historical category: women are visible, but our history is invisible.

The sweeping presentation of American history from early European settlement to the present is integrated through the theme of pluralism and the narrative of the transition from agricultural to industrial life. Objects, displayed in rich profusion, lend eloquent testimony to these arguments. Color-coded labels give the many cultural sources of artifacts, underlining the theme of American ethnic and racial diversity. As the exhibit unfolds, the visual shift from hand-made to mass-produced objects reinforces the text's description of the impact of industrialization. Later sections show the same complementarity of medium and text as videos tell the story of mass culture and a wall of neon advertising signs illustrates twentieth-century consumption.

"A Nation of Nations" moves beyond symbols and prescriptions to depict women's daily lives. Women take their places in the agricultural household economy of the early nineteenth century, as millworkers in early textile manufacture, as entertainers. One section presents the interior of an Italian immigrant family's home in 1925; this exhibit draws much attention as women who remember living and working in similar quarters stop to describe this experience to their children. Displays of work clothes include a nurse's uniform. In addition, the writers quoted in interpretive placards include a number of women—Mercy Otis Warren, Sojourner Truth, Willa Cather, and Bessie Smith.

Although women, implicitly, hold up half the sky in "Nation," no effort is made to render the differences between male and female experience. Despite its central theme of industrialization, the exhibit nowhere comments on the movement of single and then married women into the paid labor force. The 1920s home evokes domestic labor for female visitors, but the text does not recognize this household as a workplace and thus misses an opportunity to explore household technology and consumption as aspects of women's unpaid work. "Nation" depicts family life but does not acknowledge that men and women might have different interests within it, and nowhere does the exhibit show women organizing on their own behalf as women.

In its most vital moments, "Nation" edges past pluralism to acknowledge power and inequality, though the exhibit ultimately pulls its punches. Depiction of slave trading and the dramatic testimony of slave manacles and Jim Crow signs present the oppression of blacks with stark realism. Visitors' responses indicate the novelty of such portrayals in museum exhibits: many people hurry past the Jim Crow section, and we overheard one white man telling his son, "That was before they ran everything." A 1915 schoolroom and its text interpret education as one vehicle for an aggressive Americanization. Accompanying a section on Ellis Island, a prominent chart itemizes the increasing restrictions in immigration law from the earliest European settlement through 1965, a powerful documentation of nativism and racism. But "Nation" fails to pursue the themes suggested by these glimpses of ethnic and racial conflict. Most strikingly, in an exhibit that considers the transformation of American work and leisure through the evidence of hundreds of artifacts of mass production and consumer culture, the question of class never arises. Instead, "Nation" evades these harsher historical truths to affirm a Whitmanesque ideal of democracy, embracing all in a celebration of multiplicity.

Similar to "Nation" in its presentation of social history, Conner Prairie Pioneer Settlement, northeast of Indianapolis, affords an excellent example of the "living museum." This recreation of an Indiana settlement in 1836 was developed during the 1970s by the museum program of Earlham College on the grounds of the William Conner home, bought and restored in the 1930s by the drug magnate Eli Lilly.

Conner, a trader and farmer, negotiated treaties with the local Indians that pushed them farther west and opened the area to white settlement between 1790 and 1820. After his Indian wife and six children moved west with her tribe, Conner married a white woman and built a Georgian mansion for her in 1823. Guides in cordoned-off rooms explain the furnishings and Conner's life without idealizing him as a "great man": they confront Conner's role in evicting native peoples, including his own wife's tribe. This account offers a good example of the key role of Indian women in white-Indian relations.[2]

Far more engaging is the area adjacent to Conner's house— Prairietown, a "living museum" that represents a white farm settlement made possible by Conner's negotiations. Throughout the year interpreters' activities reflect the cycle of seasonal work and holidays as it would have been in 1836. Farm labor, handloom weaving, the operations of country store and inn, and a "blab school" can be observed. Weaver Fenton explains links between the frontier and industrializing New England by noting the availability of spun cotton yarn at the store—for those who can afford it. The portrayal of a single year in the life of one town is broadened by reference to national developments.

The actors' humor and direct interaction with the public enliven the presentation of social conflicts. The town's regular physician explains the theory of humors and disparages the Thomsonian herbal remedies espoused by Weaver Fenton. Special "Candlelight" events in December compare the Fentons' moral opposition to the Christmas holiday with the Virginia doctor's festive Episcopalian celebration of it. The doctor's wealth and social status contrast with the humble position of the herbal practitioner to suggest the social and economic correlatives of their conflicting medical and religious persuasions. To move beyond this evocative but understaged approach to social differences, however, would require more dramatization of direct conflict— perhaps the staging of arguments or street confrontations. Such activities would be possible at a "living museum" but might challenge and disturb audiences, as does the Jim Crow display in "Nation."

At Conner women are shown enmeshed in family and social life, as in "Nation," but gender is marked as a category as well. Women's lives and work are treated thoroughly because the museum focuses on daily existence in a household economy. Women do productive work, child care, and domestic chores. The blacksmith's wife demonstrates spinning, describes the extended household, and explains her hopes that prosperity will free her daughter from tedious household manufacturing. The Conner program has also prepared guides to deal with women's status and their conflict and cooperation with men. One male character evokes laughter by explaining that he acquired his farm by marrying a woman who had inherited one: "Now it's my farm, of course." A discussion at the doctor's house reveals the employment of midwives or doctors at childbirth and refers to the use of sponges as contraceptives. Do women come to the doctor to "be made regular," inquires one visitor, referring to the prevalence of abortion in this period.[3] No, the guide replies, although women "pass such notions around among themselves" and some are known to drink tansy tea, an abortifacient. If this wife did that, he'd beat her. The commentary not only provides information on women's reproductive rituals but also suggests a separate women's culture, its potential subversiveness, and an antagonistic, proprietary response to it by men.

Advertising for Conner cultivates the ideas of adventure and amusement: "At Conner Prairie you will enjoy living history as you have never enjoyed it before. Leave the twentieth century behind and experience life in the 1800s!" History there is not merely passive entertainment, however. In addition to interacting with interpreters, museum visitors can participate in quilting, candlemaking, log splitting, and other work at the Pioneer Adventure Center. The activity may well encourage critical reflection by pushing visitors beyond schoolroom passivity. Both women and men, for example, may attempt tasks that were sex-typed in 1836 and thus blunt the legitimizing effect of the traditional division of labor observed elsewhere.

Audience response reflects the prevalent vision of history as progress. Questions about how long it took to ride to Indianapolis or whether many infants died imply that, "adventure" aside, many feel life is much better today. Yet visitors to the schoolhouse responded with nervous laughter to the strict discipline exhibited there, suggesting anxiety about the freedom of modern youth. When the actor-guides skillfully evoke responses from the audience by raising issues of contemporary concern, from wifebeating to electoral politics, members of the audience are fruitfully engaged and hopefully made more sensitive to the conflicts and choices they face in their own world.

F eminists and achievers, unusual rather than common women, occupy the stage in two exhibits that differ markedly from "Nation" and Conner. The National Woman's Party headquarters and "Black Women: Achievements Against the Odds" begin with the premise of gender and racial conflict rather than ignoring or understating it.

Women have seldom had the economic and social resources or the historical self-consciousness to initiate our own presentations: most exhibits come from institutions controlled by men. A notable exception can be found at the Sewall-Belmont house, headquarters for the National Woman's Party (NWP) since 1929. In this exhibit, form and content are curiously at odds: a staid institutional history commemorates militant feminism.

The house's recent history demonstrates the struggle to reclaim women's history. Overlooking the Supreme Court and the Capitol, the building was threatened with demolition first to make way for a parking lot (1958) and then to accommodate the Senate's expanded quarters (1972). A new Senate building now looms over the house, but through the efforts of the NWP, it has been named a national historic landmark and thus has gained a modicum of security.

The National Woman's Party has yet to claim a place in most conventional histories, despite its significant role in the twentieth-century feminist struggle. Its origins lie in the last years of the suffrage fight. In 1913 Alice Paul, American feminist and reformer, returned from a stay in England where she saw and admired the militant activism of the Pankhursts. She revived the National American Woman's Suffrage Association's (NAWSA) lobbying committee with such vigor that she was soon embroiled in conflict with more cautious and conservative suffragists. By the end of 1913, Paul and the NAWSA had parted ways, and her newly formed Congressional Union had launched itself with a suffrage march of five thousand women that drew crowds away from Wilson's inaugural parade. In 1917 the Congressional Union was renamed the National Woman's Party, with Paul as chair of the executive committee and Mrs. O. H. P. Belmont as president. The party set lobbying in motion in all forty-eight states and continued its campaign of relentless pressure on Congress and on President Wilson. As one early historian wrote, "[W]hile the National Association led, the Woman's Party drove."[4] After suffrage was won, the NWP struggled to keep a broad and uncompromising feminism alive in the uncongenial climate of the next decades.

The NWP's appeal for landmark status called for "an historic shrine which would commemorate the women's movement," a phrase that reveals much about the approach taken there. Under a beautiful stained-glass fan window, the "Hall of Statues" presents portraits and busts of the great women of the suffrage and women's rights movement. The four central figures face one another in pairs across the hall: Susan B. Anthony and Elizabeth Cady Stanton on the left, Lucretia Mott and Alva Belmont on the right. Portraits commemorate militant suffragists who were jailed when they refused to remove their picket from the White House gates. Also dramatic is a portrait of Inez Milholland Boissevain on a white horse. Exhausted from campaigning for suffrage through seven states, she collapsed and "died for the freedom of women." At the end of the hall, a marble and ivory statue of Joan of Arc evokes the hall's themes of female leadership and sacrifice for a cause.

The tour emphasizes the dedication and accomplishments of women involved in the struggle for women's rights, while the genteel elegance of the house reveals the party's upper-class connections. Portraits of NWP members line the walls. The Chairman's Room, for many years Alice Paul's workroom, is furnished with Susan B. Anthony's desk and a chair used by Elizabeth Cady Stanton, embodying the hard work and staunch commitment of feminist foremothers. In the rear, a formal dining room filled with Alva Belmont's china, glass, and furniture indicates the class background of many of the NWP leaders. (Belmont donated the house to the NWP in 1929 and served as the party's president from 1917 until her death in 1933.) Upstairs, only two bedrooms can now be seen. One is for visiting NWP scholars; the other was occupied by Alice Paul for many years. A planned addition downstairs will hold a library of materials related to women's rights.

This museum challenges the canon of historical "great men" but shares the conventional definition of "history" as politics and public life. Its presentation reclaims a significant chapter of women's self-organization, and it affirms feminist struggles by celebrating heroines who resisted the limits of patriarchal society. The NWP also provides a kind of compensatory history by commemorating women who were unusually outspoken or accomplished in traditionally male arenas.

But in the end the exhibit suffers from the common myopia of institutional self-portraits. Its political history is one-dimensional. The tour offers only a vague sense of the divisions in the suffrage movement from which the NWP emerged. The party's subsequent history is reduced to the unchanging struggle for the Equal Rights Amendment, with little explanation of the conflicting strategies and the historical significance of twentieth-century feminism. In the troubled years after suffrage, when many women turned to the reforms of "social feminism," the party looked back to reaffirm the broad demands of the 1848 Seneca Falls convention, rejecting the notion that women's rights were won with suffrage.[5] Their journal, *Equal Rights,* considered the whole range of issues raised at Seneca Falls, from women's rights in the public world of paid work and government to their place in marriage and family. Rightly or wrongly, the Woman's Party saw the ERA as an appropriate vehicle for their broad commitments. The tour largely neglects this history, and in the account of the long battle for ERA, the NWP seems reduced to a simple "interest group" obsessed by a single issue. Oddly, the visitor will find little here to challenge a complacent belief that the women's rights movement is virtually over, its major objectives achieved. When we first visited the Sewall-Belmont house in 1980, with campaigns to ratify the ERA in full force, the issue was relegated to handouts available at the end of the tour. On the recent defeat of the ERA, the museum is silent. Finally, we get only glimpses of the internal life of the NWP, its conflicts and decisions, the relationship between national and local organizations, the texture of daily life in the headquarters itself. The presentation embodies a curious irony: it has frozen the militant history of the NWP in a mythic past, distant from the confusions, struggles, and aspirations of the contemporary women's movement.

"Black Women: Achievements Against the Odds" melds a message of black pride and feminist consciousness. The opening label quotes Margaret Walker to introduce a history "born not only of [black women's] enslavement, long years of servitude, and suffering, but also of their hopes, aspirations, and initiatives." Dozens of biographical sketches honor these women's contributions in literature, art, reform, the "healing arts" (dentistry, pharmacy, medicine, and nursing), law, business and industry, government, entertainment, education, sports.

"Achievements Against the Odds" is compensatory history at its best, proclaiming black women's struggles and accomplishments in vivid biographical sketches. Some honor courageous foremothers who fought for freedom and equality, such as Sojourner Truth, escaped slave, abolitionist, and suffragist; Harriet Tubman, heroine of the underground railroad; Rosa Parks, the civil rights activist who sparked the Montgomery bus boycott. Biographies of the black lives behind the stereotypes of white popular culture make powerful statements about the constrained choices available to blacks seeking success in a white world. Thelma Butterfly McQueen, who played the scatterbrained Prissy in *Gone With the Wind,* aspired to Shakespearean roles but for many years had to make her living in menial jobs. Hattie McDaniel, who won the first Oscar awarded to a black person for her role as Mammy in *Gone With the Wind* and went on to play "Beulah" on television, drew criticism from blacks for perpetuating degrading stereotypes through her acting. Her retort defended individual upward mobility: "It's better to get $700 a week for playing a servant than $7 for being one." By reporting this exchange, the exhibit acknowledges the painful terms of success in a white world and the potentially divisive experience of mobility.

Many of the sketches commemorate black women's firsts: Mary Elizabeth Mahoney, the first black nurse (graduated in 1879) and a founding member of the National Association of Colored Graduate Nurses; Maggie Lena Walker, the first American woman to become a bank president (1903). In documenting these achievements, the exhibit points to the double barriers of sex and race. The biography of Lucy Ellen Moten (1851–1933), educator, explains that one board of education worried about her good looks and made her promise to give up theater, cards, and dancing. Rebecca Lee, the first black woman doctor, graduated from the New England Female Medical School in 1864; Howard University's black medical school did not graduate a woman until 1877. The exhibit goes beyond the NWP's search for a past by including many living women and conveying the message, both explicitly and implicitly, that the struggle for equality continues.

The show fully achieves its goal of presenting examples of black women's successes. Louise Hutchinson, curator of the original Anacostia Neighborhood Museum exhibit, explained that the women were deliberately selected for their accomplishments in traditionally male fields in an effort to balance a history that honored black women mostly as loyal mothers, wives, sisters, and daughters. Like "Nation," "Achievements Against the Odds" recognizes the categories of race and sex, and it goes farther to acknowledge sexism as well as racism.

But these women's lives raise questions that the exhibit evades. The presentation abstracts biography from historical and social conditions, emphasizing the exceptional personal qualities of this pantheon of heroines. Certainly their individual strengths and determination are worth celebrating; but do these women share other characteristics that might also help explain their achievements? How do they compare with white women, with black men, with less successful black women? An effort to generalize from these women's experiences would deepen our understanding of the meaning of race and sex in their lives and over time. It would also demand some attempt to address the divisions of class and color within black communities. The labels provide some intriguing contrasts that call for comment: some of these women were born into slavery; some were children of sharecroppers or tenant farmers; others appear to be from middle-class families. How did these different life situations affect the women's struggle against the odds? Ironically, given the focus on race, the exhibit fails to confront the volatile issue of color: light-skinned blacks have often been the first to gain niches of acceptance in white society, and Afro-Americans themselves have sometimes followed the dominant culture in placing a value on lightness. How did these women experience the white standards of beauty that governed access to many public positions and often influenced black communities as well? The dimension of historical change is also curiously missing from this exhibit. The topical organization overwhelms a needed sense of the shifts and continuities in black lives over three centuries.

Most striking is the complete omission of private life from the biographies. The exhibit offers no sense of how many of these women married, how many became mothers, how they lived out commitments to work and family. In one sense this choice is positive, enforcing a strict historical equality. The exhibit presents black women as public figures; in viewing comparable profiles of famous men, we are not likely to ask whether they were husbands or fathers. At the same time, the omission seems contradictory: the exhibit singles out sex as a significant category and then excises a critical, perhaps determining, element in accounting for achievements against the odds. In the nineteenth and early twentieth centuries, white women who succeeded in public roles were much less likely to marry than others, and those who did marry rarely had children. Is this true for black women? If not, what sustained them in bearing the load of work, family, and community responsibilities? How do the contemporary figures manage the still formidable burden of the double day? Finally, "Achievements Against the Odds" joins the virtually universal conspiracy of silence about women who choose other women for emotional and sexual relationships.

Although "Black Women: Achievements Against the Odds" leaves one wanting more, it is nonetheless innovative both in content and in form. First developed at the Anacostia Neighborhood Museum (ANM) in 1974, the show was picked up by the Smithsonian Institution Traveling Exhibition Service (SITES), touring to enthusiastic audiences at over a hundred locations. It has now returned to ANM, a small, informal museum that is part of the Smithsonian Institution. Removed from the bustling central Mall and the downtown area, ANM is off the beaten track for most out-of-town visitors but very accessible to the mostly black residents of its southeastern Washington neighborhood.

The exhibit has reached a national public through several resourceful techniques of distribution. It traveled on easily mounted placards, and was then redesigned on twenty paper panels available for purchase at $200 a set, including a program handbook that gives tips on public affairs programming and black-and-white glossies for publicity. Its first print run of 1,000 sets is selling briskly. The exhibit is still available for rental, with a new tour tentatively planned for 1986–87. SITES also contracted with GMG PUblishing, a New York house, to produce a three-year calendar incorporating much of the exhibit text and illustrations. This combination of flexible exhibiting methods and imaginative distribution makes "Black Women" unusually accessible—a real triumph over the problems of cost and logistics that restrict the circulation of most exhibits.

A major artifact of recent consumer culture and the sexual revolution stars in the exhibit "25 Years of Barbie Dolls," originated and displayed at the Indiana State Museum (ISM) in downtown Indianapolis. This temporary exhibit (on display in 1984 and 1985), consisting almost wholly of dolls lent by local women, attempts both to acknowledge Barbie's tremendous popularity and to assess critically the doll's relationship to recent American history.

At the entrance to the exhibit room, pink panels, lettering, drapery, and balloons create a stunningly feminine contrast to the formality of the adjoining rotunda. Barbies, Kens, and other friends line the walls of one large room wearing some of the hundreds of costumes available. Barbie appears as a pregnant woman, a Playboy Bunny, an Olympic skier, a candy striper, and an Army recruit. Barbie accessories—houses, swimming pools, coloring books, and sewing patterns—occupy large cases. "The Business of Barbie" calls attention to the $9 million annual sales revenue derived from the dolls and their worldwide marketing. Costumed mannequins illustrate the Mattel Corporation's involvement in the fashion industry: sixty new costumes for Barbie, reflecting trends in women's wear, appear each year.

Throughout the exhibit Barbie is set in historical context. The chronological section, where annual models are mounted along a wall, demonstrates three major shifts in appearance—from the cool, formal fashion model of 1959, to the more youthful, straight-haired doll of 1967, to the wide-eyed, smiling "SuperStar Barbie" of 1977. Her progressively younger look and changing styles parallel ideals of beauty in fashion and society from 1959 to 1977. The text alludes to the controversy over Barbie's busty figure, though it does not explicitly discuss the sexual revolution. The civil rights movement spurred Mattel to produce the unsuccessful "Colored Francie" in 1967 and later a number of better-selling black "friends." Afro-styled hair did not appear until the creation of "Black Barbie" in 1980. McDonald's uniforms for Barbie acknowledge the jobs of many contemporary teenagers. History certainly is not progress, however, since "Crystal Barbie," a 1984 model gowned in metallic fabric and perched in a silver Corvette, is "totally romantic and feminine." (By early 1985 Barbie had also appeared as a pink-suited career woman with briefcase and credit cards. This model is not included in the exhibit.)

The emergence of women's liberation and its criticism of decorative femininity plays an indirect rather than explicit part in the presentation. The exaggeratedly feminine entrance display makes a subtle criticism of the doll's fashion model or starlet image. More straightforward comment appears in the opening text: a dictionary definition of *doll* as both toy and "pretty but empty-headed young woman." Interpretive texts throughout assume without stating that the viewer will see the Barbie image as outdated—an assumption that is unwarranted. Barbie's wardrobe for the wage-earning woman occasions the most explicit feminist criticism: "The medical outfits 'RN' (1961–64), 'Candy Striper Volunteer' (1964), and 'Dr. Ken' (1963–65) linked gender with specific aspects of a profession." Barbie's clothes, cars, pools, and houses, including one with a "wall safe for her valuables," encourage aspiration to a middle-class lifestyle; Barbie books, magazines, and sewing patterns may have educational value (as Mattel suggests), but they also make money for the sellers (as the texts point out).

Whatever the aims of the manufacturer, however, the children who play with the dolls are not passive victims but creative users who respond variously to the messages about femininity and consumption. The exhibit suggests but does not explore fully this important point. The tenacity of traditionally feminine child's play is noted humorously in a cartoon that features a hippie couple discussing their opposition to sex-stereotyped dolls like Barbie; in the last frame their daughter uses a hammer and wrench from her Christmas tool set to represent Barbie and Ken. Yet Barbie's appeal may not indicate simple adherence to media versions of femininity. An adult doll with an abundance of clothes and equipment may allow wider possibilities for imaginative play than the traditional baby doll, who seems most appropriate for mothering. Our informal survey of Barbie users found that Barbies had been dressed in vines and leaves as cave women and had earned glory as adventurers who rescued kidnapped children. The curators also conducted a survey of children and learned, for example, that two-thirds of doll-owners had made at least some clothes for Barbie. The maternity dress shown was hand-made, for example; Mattel marketed nothing for pregnancy.[6] But the results of this survey were not included in the exhibit, where they might have served to demonstrate children's ingenuity and to explore why girls actually like Barbie. Addressing questions about the role of Ken and the significance of the dolls to male children would also have broadened the exhibit's analysis of the uses and the social significance of these dolls.

The visitors at the exhibit, black and white, children and adults, but predominantly female, gained a heightened appreciation of the monetary value of the dolls as collectors' items and enjoyed recognizing dolls they owned. Young girls were sometimes seized with a desire to obtain some of the models on display. These reactions confirm the value of legitimizing the female experience by placing it on public display, as in the First Ladies' exhibit. They also illustrate the continued formidable appeal of a traditionally feminine artifact. The most popular exhibit ever displayed at ISM, "Barbie" attracted over 100,000 visitors in its four-and-a-half month run.[7]

This fascinating exhibit comments on the interplay of production, advertising, and consumption in the lives and socialization of female children in recent America. By drawing attention to the processes of manufacture and marketing and through criticism of feminine roles and images, the exhibit attempts to suggest the negative influence of the doll on American girls. A major question is whether the understated criticism can penetrate the halo of legitimacy bestowed by the choice of Barbie as the object of display and by the evidence of her great popularity. Spelling out more explicitly the objections to Barbie, whether from feminists or moralists, and devoting more space to the uses of Barbie by children might dampen this sanctifying effect.

Historians interested in reaching a larger audience in their teaching, writing, or public history projects can learn much from the successes and shortcomings of exhibits like these. All effectively draw the audience into their presentations. The regalia of the First Ladies and of Barbie dolls charm the visitor with an idealized femininity touched by the aura of politics, high fashion, and entertainment. "Eleanor Roosevelt," the National Woman's Party headquarters, and "Achievements Against the Odds" inspire visitors with the creation of heroines, using conventional standards of "great man" history to show female public figures as the counterparts and equals of men. Through the artful mixture of strange and familiar objects, "Nation" acknowledges and touches the diverse histories of its mass audience. The living theater of Conner Prairie evokes wonder and perhaps nostalgia as it recreates the life of early Indiana.

Once engaged, what sort of women's history does the audience learn? The First Ladies' Hall, set up before the flowering of women's history, unselfconsciously reproduces the nineteenth-century division of women and men into separate spheres, based on a belief in their essential difference. The figures do not even act out traditional ideology; they simply represent "Woman" at the nation's highest social level. The exhibit offers important information about fashion and ideals of womanhood, but the display of gowns cannot convey women's historical agency. Between 1964 and 1984, the opening years of the First Ladies' Hall and "Eleanor Roosevelt," the women's movement and historians of women subjected the ideology of the separate spheres and its twentieth-century modifications to critical scrutiny, both questioning the legitimacy of gender division and inequality and examining the tension between prescription and actual historical behavior. The presentation of Eleanor Roosevelt manifests these changes by depicting a vivid and active personality, a First Lady who chose to forge a public identity that built on but transcended her role in the family and as the president's wife.

The Sewall-Belmont house and "Achievements Against the Odds" both offer compensatory women's history by setting forth little-known examples of women's courage and persistence in struggling against sexual and racial barriers. Both exhibits document resistance to dominant ideology and repression and, among black women, considerable unacknowledged success. The compensatory model limits these displays: in their search for heroines, neither explores or analyzes the roots and context of the women's public accomplishments—social class, sexual and marital life, women's oppression, and internal struggles and conflicts.

Social history animates "A Nation of Nations" and the Conner Prairie museum, challenging traditional notions of women's historical significance. Both accord recognition and esteem to the domestic lives and paid and unpaid labor of ordinary women. "Nation," however, echoes too uncritically the democratic and pluralistic ideology that portrays women as mere citizens, neither special nor separate; the exhibit ignores power and inequality in gender relations. Conner, on the other hand, suggests women's separateness and inequality simultaneously with their integration into family and economy.

Finally, "25 Years of Barbie Dolls" combines cultural and economic history. This novel exhibit shows how mass marketing of the Barbie doll promotes a glamorous femininity and marriage to the detriment of female individuality and nontraditional careers. Exploring the doll's creation and influence usefully illuminates the investment of business and advertising in traditional sex roles and takes seriously an artifact of female life. Without sustained attention to the activities of the doll's users, however, this historical approach may suggest that consumers are mere victims of ideological manipulation.

An ideal public history of women would present women fully as actors in economic, domestic, social, and political life; it would be sensitive to divisions among women by class, race, ethnicity, sexual orientation, and marital status; above all it would treat gender as a significant category and acknowl-edge the relationships of power and inequality that have constrained women's lives. No one presentation can encompass the full range of female experience, but exhibits can sketch the context in which their subjects lived and suggest comparisons with relevant groups. In developing women's history for mu-seums, curators should especially cultivate innovative media and concepts that actively engage the audience. As visitors abandon the passivity of spec-tators to explore the past, they will better appreciate how women have worked, loved, struggled, suffered—and shaped history.

★ 11 ★

A Contemporary Depiction Of An Historic Event In American Industry

"THE BREAKUP OF A. T. & T." . . . . .
AND A BUST OF ALEXANDER GRAHAM BELL

The artist, CAM HARRIS, effectively portrays a span of history in the communications industry by showing a youthful Alexander Graham Bell as a kite-flying enthusiast prior to his becoming interested in human speech and ultimately the telephone.

The fragmented telephone pole and crossarms indicate the seven divested regions, leaving a somewhat frazzled "Long Lines" or A. T. & T. Company suspended in mid-air. The shadow of the displaced pole remains but the hole (whole) is missing. The crows flocking into the scene depict competition entering into the industry.

Conclusively, the artist has, in a subtle manner, revealed the sorrowing bust of an aged Alexander Graham Bell, viewing distressfully the fracturing of his creation — the finest telephone system on earth.

Corporate History, or Giving History the Business

In the past decade the development of new jobs in business for historians has offered an alternative to the grim job prospects in the academy. Corporate history takes many often overlapping forms, but five predominate: records management, public relations, celebrations of corporate anniversaries, problem solving, and labor relations. For this study I interviewed and read the work of corporate historians with diverse historical and political perspectives and work experiences. Two historians whom I interviewed work as consultants; the others work within corporations. Most are generally comfortable with the corporate world view, but three are radicals. Radicals are a smaller minority in the field than this sample would indicate, but in reconciling their corporate assignments with their own personal needs, political values, and commitment to history, they articulate particularly well the tensions and contradictions of the work. Everyone interviewed asked that some remarks remain off the record; most insisted on anonymity.

Ultimately, corporate history is a contradiction in terms. The corporation is the public historian's "client" and boss simultaneously. Those who labor within its confines or consume its products remain less subjects of these historians than audiences for them. However imparital the historian, the partisan character of the corporate work environment sets clear boundaries. One historian who works in a supposedly more progressive setting—the education department of a trade union—articulated the problem that seemed implicit in the concerns of all the corporate historians interviewed: "If there's one criterion for the organization, loyalty is it."[1]

BY DANIEL J. WALKOWITZ

H istorians are not newcomers to business. The Firestone Tire and Rubber Company, for example, hired an archivist and established a record-keeping program back in 1943.[2] But the modern multinational corporation's sudden enthusiasm for corporate history has a more immediate historical context. The intensified rate of plant closings, technological change, robotics, buy-backs, buy-outs, and mergers create one set of government, community, and labor pressures on the contemporary corporation. Another set originates in environmental disasters, runaway mills, and product recalls, readily publicized by public interest groups and consumer advocates like Ralph Nader. Business today is increasingly sensitive to the persistent questioning of corporate decisions by stockholders, community groups, or government. Government contracts, state subsidies, and sales themselves can rise or fall with changes in the corporate image.[3]

Because they are convinced that history can be useful in public relations, policy making, and labor management and are required by state and federal legislation to provide historical evaluations of some projects, corporations have dramatically expanded their use of historians' services. Some, especially construction companies, have employed historians working free lance or in their own consulting firms, but many more jobs have arisen inside the corporation. A 1969 survey of 700 firms reported 133 with some form of archive, though only 13 had a full-time archivist on staff. By 1975, 196 companies listed archives, with 30 archivists, and by 1980, although the number of archives had remained about the same, the number of archivists had doubled. These archives are widespread, if uneven in quality. Corporate institutions with archives include International Harvester, Corning Glass, Anheuser-Busch, Atlantic Richfield, Walt Disney Productions, and almost every major American bank as well as the New York Stock Exchange.[4] Perhaps the largest of these archives, the Wells Fargo Bank History Department, has a staff of nine: two with Ph.D.s in history, one with an M.A., one with an M.L.S. and archival training, one with training in historic preservation, two with museum experience, and two stagecoach drivers.[5] Corporate history also includes numerous legal researchers, archivists, and public relations experts who do historical research without thinking of themselves as historians.

Although most corporate historians probably are involved in little more than records management, the organizing and opening of business archives for historical investigations may be the least intellectually compromised and most successful service of the corporate historian. Typical of these historians is one we shall call Fred Jones, who works as an archivist for a large utility company, processing and cataloguing company records. "I could not have imagined doing this a few years ago," he explained, but "if you want to work as an historian, where's the work today?" Like most other corporate historians, he would need company "clearance" and a check by superiors for "factual accuracy" before he published anything based on the archive. He describes both steps as formalities, although he has not in fact sought such permission yet. A leftist critical of capitalism, Jones resolves the "personal dilemma" of working in "one of the largest companies in the world" by maintaining that he provides "intelligent access" to records of which others can ask good questions. The intellectual standards of such work or the ethics of assisting a company that might be supporting oppressive regimes are not issues for him, since he describes his work as "rather low-level history."[6]

When they move beyond record keeping, other corporate historians function uneasily between the public relations and research departments. Because they actually write corporate history, they are the major focus of this article. Like much academic history, the research and scholarship produced inside the corporation varies widely in quality.

Deborah Gardner's beautifully illustrated twenty-page pamphlet, *Marketplace: A Brief History of the New York Stock Exchange* (1982), is typical of the less self-congratulatory brand of corporate history. The essay is a serious historical effort, yet its high-gloss production and concern with documenting the Exchange's "finest facilities, service and leadership" reflect public relations tendencies. Gardner demystifies the jargon of the marketplace in a lively narrative history of the institution's two hundred years—all in fifty typewritten pages. Members of the Exchange read the manuscript before publication, as did Professors Dorothy Helly of Hunter College and Kenneth Jackson of Columbia University.[7]

Gardner is not an apologist for American capitalism, but her history would have been very different if she had asked questions about investment policy, corruption, labor, and the social impact of vast corporate holdings. Gardner discusses speculation and the 1929 crash in *Marketplace,* but the pamphlet ignores a 1948 Exchange strike, although her archive includes the union records of the Exchange's organized workers. Although she places the Exchange within a broader social context, the study largely remains an institutional history of managers and their decisons.[8] On a $120,000 budget, Gardner and her colleagues produced 60,000 copies of a high-quality pamphlet that won several design prizes. The Exchange management uses the history as a high-class public relations piece. In 1982, accompanied by a note from the chairman, the pamphlet was given out at Christmas to every employee. Free copies are now distributed to college students, schoolchildren, and educational programs.[9]

Wells Fargo, in contrast, seeks a more popular audience. Although the

Wells Fargo Department does local research, much of its work involves preparing promotional material. Most recently, for instance, the historians have been giving workers in the advertising department a twelve-hour course in the bank's history in order to give the company's advertising "a boost".[10]

Wells Fargo literature reflects the conflation of history and public relations. Facsimile newspaper handouts for the Wells Fargo museum in Old Sacramento thoroughly romanticize Wells Fargo's and Sacramento's history, stressing the bank's twin goals of service and progress. Bank agents all exhibit "business acumen" and "community spirit"; nowhere are readers told how these agents defined "community," what policies that maintained, to whom they did and did not loan money. The telegraph, the stagecoach, and the Pony Express mail routes are celebrated as Wells Fargo's contribution to the "winning" of the West, with a discreet silence about government subsidies and campaigns for public ownership of utilities.[11]

Wells Fargo & Company: A Brief History is an unpretentious twenty-four-page photo-offset pamphlet that discusses in detail the corporate amalgamation of the bank but ignores its political and economic power. Like the handouts, the essay would have readers believe that the bank was never involved in investment. The authors' treatment of one of the more delicious episodes in the bank's history—its struggle to capture Black Bart, the hooded highwayman who held up its stagecoaches twenty-eight times between 1875 and 1883—demonstrates how romantic tales fail as history. The bank's historians present a lively saga of greed. Yet on two occasions the bandit left Well Fargo poetic messages suggesting a larger context of social banditry; the authors ask the reader to judge "whether Black Bart's poetry was worse than his banditry":

> I've labored long and hard for bread
> For honor and for riches
> But on my corns too long you've tred
> You fine haired sons of bitches.[12]

From the perspective of the bank and its historians, one was as bad as the other. Black Bart's nineteenth-century supporters, though, may have admired the poetry as well as the banditry; there is room here for a more critical view of the bank's place in the community.

Connected to their public relations function is the public historians' role in the celebration of corporate anniversaries. Any such celebratory history, whether for the national Bicentennial, a village centennial, or a university sesquicentennial, presents serious historical problems: no one wants to look bad at anniversary time. Herbert Parmet, Distinguished Professor of History at the City University of New York, discovered this when officers at the Bank of New York insisted that he omit references to a bank error from *Two Hundred Years of Looking Ahead,* a volume he had been hired to write for the bank.[13]

Even though much corporate historical work consists of generating pulp for the publicist's mill or processing corporate records, some corporate historians aspire to research and policy planning. They lecture trainees on the company's history and assist legal departments on antitrust litigation; a title insurance company waxes enthusiastic about the money it saved by using a historian, rather than a lawyer, to research property deeds. A spokesman for Safeco Title explains the corporate calculation: you can "get more out of them [historians] for less money, and that's the bottom line."[14]

Stephen Kobrin, a professor of management at the New York University Graduate School of Business, which established the model Careers in Business Program for humanists, insists that public historians can provide useful contexts for policy decisions by supplying data "on relationships between the broad range of political contingencies faced by firms and the political environment"—in other words, by assessing investment risk in the context of a region's history of political stability and asking whether social discontent threatens the security of private property. Kobrin argues that firms are politically neutral and that investment is value-free. Companies do not care about "political events and processes *per se,* but the mangerial contingencies that they may generate." They are less interested in macro-risk situations like Cuba—which one suspects are beyond the investment horizon—than in "micro-risk contingency situations."[15] Still, few historians have cracked the corporate planning room; business people, notes a public historian, "still rarely call upon the professional historian for managerial decisions."[16]

Ralph Jeffries (a pseudonym) does the work most corporate historians aspire to do—he evaluates the economic, social, and political development of various countries for the international investment division of a major bank. Jeffries, a radical, places these developments in a historical context but believes that he was hired as someone with economic skills who could deal comfortably with questions of social class, government power, and interest politics. At the time he needed a job, and it seemed worth a try. He does not feel that he has been punished for his politics, although he avoids potentially divisive political discussions on the job.

Jeffries prepares monthly reports on the trade climate of a European of Latin American country. Using his report as a starting point, a bank committee then makes recommendations about long- and short-term investment. He believes that what he learns about bank policy and corporate thinking will be useful for him in the long run as a radical social critic. He also maintains that he can promote progressive bank policies: for example, he notes that banks can be persuaded that dictators who squander money or stimulate revolutions are poor investments. But basic marketplace assumptions about profits and social policy cannot be questioned; the corporate historian must live with the consequences of these assumptions or ignore them. Jeffries acknowledges tha he "feels mixed" about his work, particularly in relation to Central America.[17]

More often, historical assessments of corporate policy appear as company histories, such as *The Bank for All; A History of Citibank, 1812–1970,* published by Harvard University Press in 1985. Harold Van Buren Cleveland, a lawyer who is an economist with the bank's Paris branch, and Thomas Huertas, a University of Chicago Ph.D. in economics who studied economic history with Robert Fogel, co-authored the book. Huertas was a Citibank economist when he was asked to write a history of Citibank managerial strategies, both successes and failures, for a new generation of corporate leaders who were about to take command. A board of five mainstream economic historians (Alfred Chandler, Stanley Engerman, Anna Schwartz, Richard Sylla, and Vincent Carosso) advised the authors and read chapters and two entire drafts of the manuscript. The bank also had its own unofficial reading committee, chaired by its chief economist. The result was what two of the advisors described as "good business history, free of polemics," but including "embarrassing episodes" such as "reasonably detailed descriptions of foreign investments in Russia (1917) and Cuba (in the 1920s and 1930s)."[18]

The Citibank book may prove to be among the best of the new corporate histories, but it still illustrates the general conditions under which corporate history is written. Huertas, the main author, is a confirmed monetarist deeply commited to the bank's policies. By ending their narrative in 1970, he and his coauthor avoid touchy legal matters and the danger of offending the current bank administration. This cutoff date was also used to explain the omission of any sustained discussion of redlining or investment in South Africa, as if both were only current bank policies.[19] Not surprisingly, the histories of other financial institutions, such as Wells Fargo, the Bank of New York, and the New York Stock Exchange, also ignore such matters.

Some historians, most notably the "business consultants" in the Winthrop Group, make thoughtful efforts to get inside corporations with fresh historical analyses of managerial techniques and strategies. Still, they measure corporate success from the capitalist-managerial perspective.[20] This same bias is evident in oral history archives, which rarely interview people outside management ranks.[21] Such history may be competent and interesting, but managerial history alone does not make good corporate history. The less competent corporate histories quickly degenerate into public relations palaver intended to "educate" employees and the public. As a rule; corporate histories romanticize the corporate past, provide little social context, exhibit a limited understanding of capitalism, and express antilabor sentiment.

The antilabor theme is, of course, most evident when corporate historians are mobilized for labor relations efforts. The purpose of corporate history then becomes the boosting of labor morale, with an implicit assumption that labor must learn to share management's "logic." For example, according to the corporate historian of Atlantic Richfield (ARCO), the corporation's official history "will enable ARCO employees better to understand and identify with their company."[22] Similarly, in the *Harvard Business Review*, George Smith and Laurence Steadman describe Hewlett-Packard's corporate history program as "a vehicle for sustaining employee morale."[23] Smith and Steadman then offer an example of corporate history's "liberating effect" on employees in a plant where labor-management relations had broken down because of company consolidation and technological change. The plant's history, they explain, enabled labor "to begin to understand management's problems and to gain a better understanding of the economic and organizational realities of the company." The history lesson cut both ways, however; management came "to see how employees' trust had eroded" and to acknowledge employees' "expectations and rights." The ultimate meaning Smith and Steadman draw from the experience suggests the fairly crude social control objectives of such histories: "As a result, labor–management relations have vastly improved, information flows more easily from the top down, and employees more readily respond to work-related requests." The new technology was implemented, and the plant, we are told, now generates strong profits, a model for other branches of the corporation. Corporate history had effectively prevented a strike, and "a detailed case study of the plant's past has now become required reading for new employees."[24]

H istorians working in business like to contrast their corporate work environment with that of the academy. Only one of the eight people interviewed for this article had faced any censorship, and all celebrated the collegiality and conviviality of the corporate world in contrast to the backbiting, tenure pressures, and money-grubbing of academic life.[25] On the whole historians are treated like middle managers, with the same perquisites and obligations. Salaries vary; a bank policy analyst received a 30 percent increase over his prior academic salary, whereas an archivist received a modest hourly wage, less 20 percent kept by the temporary agency through which the company insisted on employing him. On average, however, salaries seem at least equivalent to academic pay, and some corporate historians also receive substantial Christmas bonuses.[26] The combination of pleasant work conditions with good pay will continue to attract historians to corporate work. Yet only the person working for a union had any job security. The others, like any other managers, faced annual reviews by their superiors and could be fired at a moment's notice. All, however, thought this possibility was remote.

But conviviality does not ensure an independent critical analysis of all the evidence. Corporate historians assume that some of the traditional rules of scholarly inquiry change when one works under contract for a client. Some constraints appear legitimate: the protection of copyright agreements and trade secrets or the repression of data related to on-going litigation. As noted above, an early cutoff date for published corporate history may avoid such delicate matters.[27]

But where legitimate concerns and censorship begins can be hard to judge. Corporate historians' subordination to top management complicates the problem. As one corporate historian writes, they are expected to work for the "senior executives of the company, whose heritage and stewardship historians will be chronicling, analyzing, and, by inference, judging."[28] Corporate leaders naturally want historians to ensure their place in the corporate pantheon, and public relations chiefs hire them in the abiding belief that history can be "worth a lot of public relations dollars."[29] In most companies the historians report to the head of publicity or public relations; the public relations department at one financial institution currently forbids all employees, including the archivist, to speak directly with the media without clearance.[30] But nowhere is the managerial allegiance of the corporate historian more clear than during labor-management conflicts. Corporate historians are hired into management-level positions, and, predictably, one financial instituion recently trained its historian to take the place of workers threatening to strike.[31]

To minimize organizational interference, corporate historians have begun to seek formal contracts ensuring full access to all sources and complete research autonomy. Business, of course, "owns" the product and holds the copyright, but corporate historians urge—to date, with uneven success—that the author receive formal credit on published work. They concede management the right to review the manuscript and correct factual errors.[32] Most corporate history is written by hired hands who work without contracts, but even those companies that contract with their historians have power, money, and influence enough to suppress "offensive" history. For example, one union leader, unhappy with an account of his leadership in a history whose publication the union had subsidized, threatened not to promote the book to the rank and file. The historian's contract with the publisher and the union turned out to be less important than the union head's friendship with the publisher; to ensure distribution, the historian diplomatically amended the text.[33] Such constraints do not bother those corporate historians who believe that history can be separated from its use. "Every consultant must recognize legitimate proprietary rights," asserts George Smith, the president of the Winthrop Group of historical business consultants.[34]

The job structures advanced by the insurance executive quoted earlier illuminate both the ethical aspects of the willful suppression of historical work and a historical vision that may be endemic in corporate history. The company insured property holders along California's Humbolt Bay against efforts by the City of Eureka to reclaim land that the city argued had been acquired fraudulently. In preparing their defense, the company hired a historian to research the acquisition. "Our researchers," the executive noted, "must find out everything and anything about the case." So far so good. "But in this case, the material you're digging up is not only helpful to your employer; it could be helpful to the other side [the city]. So it's not for publication, formally or informally."[35] The ethic advanced may be appropriate for an attorney, but it undermines all the rules of historical inquiry. In addition, this position erroneously assumes that all sides have the funds to gain equal access to the past and in effect makes the historical record a prize for the highest bidder. Historians occasionally apply their skills to nonhistorical ends, but if they willfully suppress pertinent evidence, they do not labor as historians and must not advertise such work as history. History-for-hire is problematic whether labor or capital wins the bidding wars, but in fact, as a survey of the varieties of corporate history shows, most is written in service to management.

The case of Richard Marks (pseudonym), a historian in the education department of a labor union, places the politics of corporate history on center stage while reminding us that constraints on the professional integrity of the historian are not unique to corporate assignments. Marks's research is not constrained; his publication is. The union is particularly sensitive about its radical past, and Marks's editor often deletes references he thinks will tarnish the union's image. "I can usually pretty much say what happened," Marks notes. "I can't always say *why* they happened. . . . Certain kinds of analysis are absent." Marks's dilemma is that of a historian, not a trade unionist. He takes for granted that historians are not independent agents and that they are judged partly by the values of the organizations they serve. He believes in the union's "struggle and that this union carries on that struggle in a democratic and progressive way." Accordingly, Marks believes that he wears two hats— a union partisan's and a historian's.

Marks's situation is similar to that of other corporate historians, but it differs in two ways: he acknowledges the limitations it places on him, and the politics of his "company" are on the other side of the labor-management divide. Marks's complaint that union officials "have a reasonably narrow sense of what history is" applies equally to Citibank and Wells Fargo. Unlike many others, however, Marks seems refreshingly aware of the contradictions in his work situation. He is at home with both the historical limitations and the political context of his work: "What is important for me is to get as much of the history of the union out to the membership as possible and with as much integrity as possible."[36]

R ichard Marks's experience seems to be unique. None of the other corporate historians interviewed have found censorship a problem. The reason may be that corporate historians simply do not ask hard questions that would provoke the blue pencil. Corporations naturally hire historians who fit into the company. In fact, corporate history is self-selective: people who choose it as a career tend to be those who find corporate capitalism a congenial world. Corporate consultant George Smith acknowledges that people in the field are "comfortable with the strivings of people in a capitalist society. I'm not uncomfortable with this society, and I'm quite sure the people who hire me know it." He is quick to add that he is also "quite sure they don't know what I'm going to come up with."[37]

Other corporate historians repeat variations on this theme. For instance, Susan English (pseudonym) believes that she has confronted no censorship in her office, but she admits that this situation could easily change if either she or her boss were a different person or if the questions she asked were markedly different.[38] Similarly, when asked to characterize the political range of historians employed in the Wells Fargo History Department, a spokesman kept repeating, "We're all Americans; we're all Americans." He insisted that they were a "cross-section of the profession" but admitted that none were New Left or Marxist historians.[39]

Many corporate historians have a conservative bias that informs their writing. For example, the historian of Manufacturers Hanover Trust celebrates the role of bankers called upon by the government to resolve "social crises at both the community and international level. . . . To record their singular achievements is sufficient justification for undertaking the writing of the corporate history."[40] Another historian asserts that "the best business history of the last generation has demonstrated that when humane criteria of long-term economic growth are applied, 'big business' often loses the anti-social stigma with which traditional historians have marked it."[41]

In the public history literature, corporate historians are repeatedly advised that they must appreciate, if not absorb, the corporate mentality. Although a disproportionate sample of radicals was interviewed, in fact one is working for a labor union, one does mostly archival work, and the third works more as an economist than a historian. Still, all corporate historians are expected to heed injunctions "to become a company man for a while"; succeed on the company's terms first; participate in management as part of the team.[42] "We're still learning to think like business people," another historian complains ruefully but hopefully.[43] Financial images are liberally sprinkled through the texts, which urge historians to remember what is "most valuable from a dollars-and-cents point of view."[44] Corporations are encouraged not to fear a "warts-on" history, for it can be "worth a lot of public relations dollars. The public can sympathize with a corporation of real people making wise and foolish decisions."[45] With historians who have learned "to think like business people," little wonder that the public relations office finds their historical "products" saleable. Consequently, the writing of in-house business history today hardly seems to need the protection of tenure or an advisory board. Identification with management, a group to which most corporate historians belong, shapes the questions asked and the understanding of business parameters.

Corporate historians are partially to blame for this development, but the narrow character of corporate history merely reflects the parochialism of mainstream business history. William A. Williams' economic history has been around for a long time now, and equally impressive work in economic, social, and labor history by such people as Immanuel Wallerstein, David Noble, David Gordon, and Eugene Genovese and Elizabeth Fox-Genovese, to name but a few, has notably broadened the scope of business history.[46] But mainstream business history, and corporate history in its wake, remains underdeveloped, obscuring or ignoring the politics of corporate development, the social consequences of investment, work inside the plant, and the perspective of both workers and consumers. "Warts and all" corporate history is occasionally urged, but the warts depicted are more like beauty marks or, at worst, cases of acne that can be cleared by a dose of historical sunshine.

The present generation of corporate historians working in records management and cataloguing and opening corporate archives may in fact make it possible to begin the writing of a New Business History. But the usefulness of archives will be limited unless corporate historians change the questions they ask. More effective training would help; few corporate historians specialized in business or economic history while in graduate school. The members of the Winthrop Group, for example, may be among the few to retrain in business history; originally three were colonialists, one was an African historian, and a fifth studied early modern British history.[47] Even if a reconceptualized business history is widely accepted and a battery of new corporate historians trained, however, it is questionable whether it will be possible to attract historians of all persuasions into the work.

Corporations' use of historians reflects in part their flexibility and willingness to respond to new conditions. Historians like George Smith who press executives to examine managerial failures as well as successes are even welcomed. But there is an analytic line that these corporate historians do not cross. Ultimately, businesses do not want a different kind of corporate history. They want historians who can be company men and women, people who can separate what they write from any responsibility for how it is used. In the words of one corporate historian, "You may have opinions about the matter, but your role is over."[48] Business can rest comfortably while such corporate-minded historians are on the job.

The problem with corporate history runs deeper than its tie to public relations, preventing changes both in the nature of corporate history and in the kinds of historians who are hired to write it. The omission of labor and consumers is no accident: they are seen as the problems. Antitrust research is but one example of history's service to the corporation at the expense of the public. As an advocate of corporate history has more innocently observed, the political context is much broader: "an ongoing company history program" can aid a corporation "in accounting for itself to society."[49] The political agenda of the modern corporation is central to its historical mission and to the mission of its history. Company history reflects the growing sophistication of corporate strategies for dealing with consumers and labor in the 1980s; corporate history is the modern multinationals' answer to Ralph Nader. And that's "the bottom line."

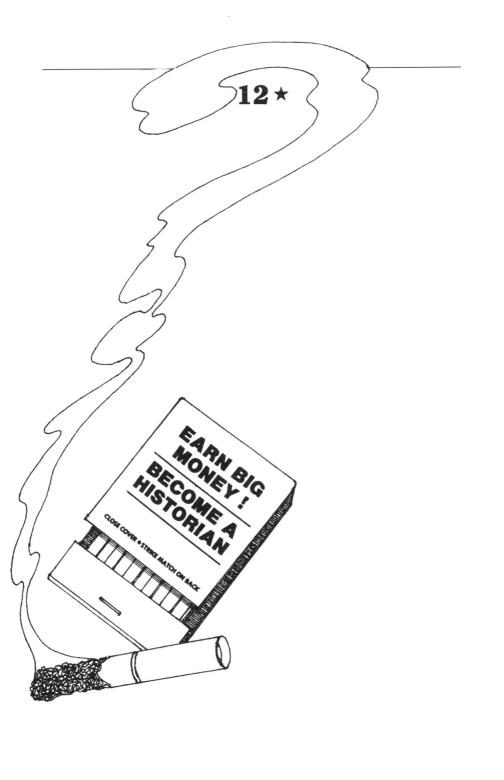

Pitfalls Along the
Path of Public History

The news could not be better. Clio has come out of the closet and now, with the other muses, consorts in the marketplace. History has gone public. One cannot help but wonder how Clio ever got into the closet in the first place. Until the end of the nineteenth century, and in some places for even longer, every educated person was something of a historian, just as he or she was something of a naturalist, a logician, a philosopher. One read one's Taine and Gibbon, one's Lecky and Carlyle, as a matter of course, whether one was a clergyman or a soldier, a merchant, or a squire.

Indeed, as late as 1911, 70 percent of the members of the American Historical Association were what we now rather patronizingly call amateur historians; that is, they were not academics. Following World War II this changed. History retired to the academic closet, that place where, E. M. Forster once said, "men handle so much and experience so little."

There were still, of course, two settings in which history remained public in the United States: American secondary schools and American historical societies. Together they served to keep history common, as it should be, an ordinary part of ordinary life. Unfortunately, academic historians, by and large, did not join in this effort, but rather kept their distance from both the schools and the societies. The result is that all three—academy, school, and society—have been impoverished. All the more reason, then, that we now rejoice at the good news that from the academy itself has come this impetus to combine scholarship and practice. Now all of us will prosper.

Human nature being what it is, however, it is always the case that in the flush of new enthusiasms we tend toward extremes, and that we tend as well to overlook the results of such extremes. That is what I think is happening in

BY TERENCE O'DONNELL

239

public history: in our haste and enthusiasm we are overlooking some of the pitfalls that lie along its path. It seems to me that there are four such pitfalls. I have named them, somewhat facetiously, the pragmatic fallacy, the perfidious boondoggle, the heinous compromise, and endless ennui. I should now like briefly to discuss each of these, beginning with the pragmatic fallacy.

Soon after I began writing this article, I realized that I was somewhat provincial, and so I decided to explore the world beyond. By reading from cover to cover each issue of the journal of public history, the *Public Historian,* published by the University of California at Santa Barbara, I knew I would find a wealth of information on public history from all quarters of the nation. On finishing my reading, I was struck by one theme—though of course there were others—that appeared in every issue and occasionally several times in a single issue: history is usable and must be sold. Darlene Roth claims that "history is a functional thing. We all know that, and we want to go out and prove it."[1] In another issue, Roth repeats the theme: "It is certainly the job of the public historians to sell history to the public."[2] Stephen Mikesell, a public historian at the University of California at Davis, believes that "above all else, the public historian must insist that he or she does not deal with a dead past but with a past that has real meaning for the present."[3] Thad Sitton and Claudette Harrell, in describing an oral history project, state that we must "rectify the lack of a usable past."[4] And Wayne Rasmussen, chief historian of the Department of Agriculture, insists that "we cannot afford research for the sake of research: we must do research that is relevant to today."[5] Public historian Paul Friedman tells us that in his internship he "learned a few lessons . . . that every public historian should be aware of: how to market history. . . . Now, whenever I begin a new historical project I keep an eye open for publicity as well as for new research leads."[6] Maurice Matloff, director of the U.S. Army History Program, says that the object of his work is "to turn out sound, usable history."[7]

These comments place considerable emphasis on "selling oneself," that interesting American idiom. Lawrence de Graaf, oral historian at California State University, Fullerton, is particularly dedicated to this form of merchandising. The historian's ability to see multiple facets may, he says, provide "one way of selling ourselves and the whole idea of public history. . . . [T]he more prepared one is to move from one project to a totally different one, perhaps with no relationship with the first, the better one can sell himself as a public historian."[8] Likewise, Joan Hoff Wilson, formerly professor of history at Arizona State and now executive secretary of the Organization of American Historians, believes that "it is up to us as humanists to sell ourselves in an increasingly technological society."[9]

It is, however, Larry Tise, a prominent public historian employed by the Pennsylvania Historical and Museum Commission, who most explicitly states this theme of the usability and salability of history:

> Neither the historian nor his organizations can survive in the coming world merely as students of the interesting, the unique, the heroic, or the nostalgic. Both the professional historian and his institutions must come to play functional and needed roles in society. Whereas in the past we have been able to collect and preserve papers, objects, and structures associated with people and events which we found interesting, instructive, and significant, such will not be possible as a primary pursuit in the future. . . . We must become greatly more concerned than we are at present with the economies, practicalities, and the usefulness of history. Except in times of flushed economy, history in the U.S. has never been supported except to the extent that its study or practice would serve a useful social, cultural, or governmental purpose. . . . Although few historians would like to admit it, the pursuit and practice of history in the U.S. has always been directly related to the social, cultural, and political needs of American society.[10]

In other words, history must be cost-effective or drop dead.

I confess that I am made uneasy by such claims and urgings. Is history in fact that usable? Must I sell myself? (The very phrase always suggests to me the act of prostitution.) I have no objection at all to the marketplace, so long as one is not obliged to misrepresent one's product, to claim for it efficacies that it does not in fact possess. And I do not agree that history is really usable, at least in the conventional sense. I probably take this position because I learned most of my history abroad: Europeans by and large do not believe that history is useful. Indeed, Europeans in general wish to know in order to know, whereas Americans more often wish to know in order to act.

This is not to say that Europeans consider history unimportant, any more than they consider the Brandenburg Concertos, the tragedies of Shakespeare, the sonnets of Rilke, the glories of Michelangelo, unimportant. All these things are enormously important, but that is not to say that they serve a useful purpose, at least in the narrow sense in which we find that phrase used in the pages of the *Public Historian*. In the larger sense, Europeans would agree that history serves a useful purpose in that it reminds us that we are only passing through, that others have come before us, that others will come after us, that neither our achievements nor our failures are unique, that (to quote from one of the most interesting of history books) "the race is not to the swift, nor the battle to the strong, neither yet bread to the wise, nor yet riches to men of understanding, nor yet favor to men of skill: but time and chance happeneth to them all." The usefulness of history lies in reminding us of the human condition and its dimensions.

But, the *Public Historian* is talking about another kind of usefulness, and its claims are more specific. For example, Robert Pomeroy tells us that "the successful conduct of business requires the use of skills well known to historians."[11] Yes, but the successful conduct of business also requires certain other skills less well known to historians. Although businesses should not look with disfavor on an applicant with a degree in history, one would not blame them for looking with somewhat more favor on an applicant with a degree in business.

Another area in which it is claimed that public history has much to offer is urban planning. Yes, here it has something to offer, but can it, as Stephen Grable tells us, "predict the direction, density, and physical characteristics of future urban growth"?[12] In another article on the same subject, Roy Lopata implies that by virtue of being a public historian he was better qualified as an urban planner than the planners themselves, whose ignorance of and indifference to urban history he cites.[13] But surely the lesson here is not that planning bureaus should hire public historians, but rather that there should be more history in a planner's training. The solution is not, as Tise describes it, that only historians will do history work, but rather to ensure that everyone is a historian, at least to some degree.[14]

In policy analysis, too, history is claimed to be usable and public historians essential. Edward Berkowitz, for example, describes his work as a policy analyst with the Department of Health, Education and Welfare. His analysis concludes that public programs take on the attributes of the era in which they are created and that warnings of potential problems within programs tend to be ignored by those who disagree with the warnings.[15] Again, do we really need a historian to tell us this?

Such statements provide examples of the second pitfall along the path of public history: the perfidious boondoggle. By claiming too much for history, we inevitably create these boondoggles, long studies whose results are unnecessary or at best obvious. Was it really necessary for Paul Israel to inventory 3,000 highway bridges in California, a state where public libraries were closing down or curtailing their hours? And what of Paul Friedman's history of the noise problem at the Los Angeles airport and his principal conclusion that public complaints arose with the advent of regularly scheduled jet traffic. With all due respect, could this not have been surmised or, if not surmised, derived from brief talks with any of the airport's older employees? Did it require a large-scale study? I think not. Projects like this one suggest makework—cultural welfarism.

One must, I think, be very careful about how much we claim for history. Often it is neither relevant nor usable, at least in the narrow sense. However, having condemned the extremes to which some have gone, I ought not go to other extremes myself. History does have a place in business, in urban planning, in public works, in policy analysis. Indeed, history has a place in everything. We must be careful, however, not to create for it a place larger than it deserves just because we want a job.

Next we come to our third pitfall, the heinous compromise. The pressures for ethical compromise are greater in the marketplace than in the academy, though of course they exist there as well. Our principal ethical obligation is very simple: to tell the truth, insofar as we are able.

Again, I go to the *Public Historian* to check the direction of the wind. The book reviews are interesting. Norm Cohen, in reviewing five books on the history of the National Aeronautics and Space Administration by in-house public historians, notes that though they are not "official" histories, in their lack of criticism of the agency they are not far from it.[16] Similarly, Jeffrey Stine's review of four histories produced by the Army Corps of Engineers finds that only one of the books is fairly objective, whereas the other three have "the characteristics of a panegyric."[17]

Then we have Darlene Roth at a public history seminar at Santa Barbara discussing the disposition of a damaging file in a hypothetical corporate archive. The public historians present concluded that they would not destroy the file but would agree to keep the file separate from the other archives and under lock and key.[18] Doesn't this mean, in effect, the suppression of the file? And then we have Lawrence de Graaf, speaking of some of the differences between academic history and public history: "It [public history] has to be a client-oriented research, and in some respects may have to bend the findings to the whims or the project design that the client has in mind.[19] Is this the way to practice history, public or otherwise?

Finally, we come to endless ennui. People going into public history must be careful if they are not to find themselves becalmed in the sloughs of boredom. Let us take local history, a subject that has received a great deal of attention from public historians. That, I think, is all to the good. Local histories are important: they give people a sense of their own place, they often provide a bridge to the larger historical scene, and they have done much to bring to our attention the neglected roles of women and ethnic minorities. I am all for local histories; the more of them the better. On the other hand, one must not forget that the history of many places, like the history of many people, is not really all that interesting.

Other areas, too, can be soporific. I mentioned earlier Paul Israel's report on his inventory of 3,000 state highway bridges in California. Israel concluded by saying that California is now considering a three-year inventory of all county bridges in the state. "This may provide work," he writes, "for many historians with a background in the history of technology."[20] If this inventory were to take place in certain cantons of Switzerland famous for the beauty and technical excellence of their bridges, it could be interesting. But to inventory thousands and thousands of California county bridges, most of them built to the same specifications, could be a colossal bore. And since we are speaking of matters technological, I must say that a history of noise at the Los Angeles airport or of waste disposal (i.e., sewage) in Kansas City, Missouri, doesn't exactly grab me either.

Another sign of endless ennui appears in the *Public Historian* in an article by James Laichas. Discussing the use of public historians in the insurance business, he says, "I am looking forward to the time when my staff has more nonlawyers [that is, public historians] than lawyers because I'll get more out of them for less money and that is the bottom line."[21] There you have it. The old ratio: the duller the work, the less money you earn for doing it.

These are, then, the major pitfalls along the path of public history. The pragmatic fallacy claims a usefulness for history that it often does not have and insists that we sell ourselves, even if it means a little stretching of the truth. And this of course leads inevitably to the perfidious boondoggle. I have said it is wonderful to have Clio out of the closet and into the marketplace, but we must not turn her into a tart working the depths of heinous compromise and, finally, the endless ennui.

In conclusion, I believe that avoiding these pitfalls is important for two reasons. One is that public history should be a clean and interesting field. If this means fewer jobs in the field, and I think it does, so be it. The other reason is that only by avoiding these pitfalls can public historians develop respect for their work and gain true satisfaction from it. In each of these endeavors I wish them the best of luck.

★ III ★
Politicizing the Past:

Toward a People's History

★13★

Oral History and Community Involvement:

The Baltimore Neighborhood Heritage Project

During the past several years, community history projects have sprung up throughout the United States. Although these projects differ widely, most share certain broadly humanistic purposes: the encouragement of cooperation between professional historians and lay people, the presentation of community history to the public, the use of history to build community identity and pride, and the encouragement of appreciation and rspect for the participation of nonelite groups in the community's history. Some projects also adopt progressive social goals and give a historical perspective on current local issues in the hope of encouraging activism and change.

These are all laudable goals. Yet my own experience with the Baltimore Neighborhood Heritage Project persuades me that unless such local history efforts are firmly rooted in the communities being studied and have well-developed links with local institutions and organizations, these goals will be translated into a series of awkward public meetings, a collection of oral history tapes, or a photograph exhibit. Such efforts may for a time stir up some enthusiasm for the community's history, but they ultimately go nowhere. The project becomes a series of discrete events and products, not a process of enhancing the historical consciousness of the community's residents. This outcome is particularly likely when class differences separate the project organizers and the members of the community.

Developing links between a community history project and its community is difficult. Any such project that seeks to involve local people in producing their own history and to have meaning for the community itself must confront complex social relationships and problems of interpretation. I will address

BY LINDA SHOPES

some of these difficulties by discussing my own and others' experiences
working on the Baltimore Neighborhood Heritage Project (BNHP), a community history project that has tried to recover and present the history of six
working-class and ethnic neighborhoods in Baltimore.

T he BNHP began in 1977. Local activists and academics with an
interest in local social history got together with city agency personnel to design and seek funding for a community history project that
would focus on one of Baltimore's older working-class ethnic
neighborhoods. The group wanted to democratize the historical record, both
by documenting the daily life experiences of ordinary people and by working
from "the inside," from the perspective of the people themselves; to nurture
the self-respect of senior citizens, whose life experiences are all too often
devalued by our culture; and to communicate to younger generations, especially schoolchildren, a sense of their own family, neighborhood, and city
identities. Some of us also believed that if community residents began to
connect their personal histories with broader social processes, they not only
would be personally enriched but might feel that their communities were
"worth something" and so be moved to take a more activist, critical stance
with respect to their social and economic circumstances.

   Although unsure about how to achieve these goals, we had some ideas. We
did not want to limit our research methods to oral history interviews alone, but
we felt that the process and products of interviewing could be a powerful tool
for achieving some of our ends. We also knew that we wanted our research to
have tangible products that could in some way be returned to the community
we were researching. Lastly, we sought to involve neighborhood residents in
every step of our project.

   In early 1978 we received a grant from the National Center for Urban Ethnic Affairs to develop a project that would put some of these ideas to a practical test. The NCUEA, a national, nonprofit research, educational, and technical assistance organization, has been involved since the 1970s in efforts to
catalyze neighborhood power. Recognizing that the majority of the country's
urban working class is of ethnic origin and aware also of the potential value of
bringing neighborhood activists together with university personnel, it has frequently supported town-gown collaborative projects that celebrate ethnic diversity. We began, then, by outlining a plan to develop an oral history program at a senior citizens' center in Highlandtown, a stable and rather prosperous white working-class neighborhood with strong Polish, German, Italian,

and Greek roots. We chose this area because it had a clear geographic and social identity and had developed, through a series of bitter battles with City Hall over the siting of a road, a certain self-consciousness as well as a public presence. In addition, a number of its leaders, who had a citywide reputation, were on our board and could, therefore, introduce us to the community. We hoped that this oral history program would catalyze a general enthusiasm for local history, train senior citizens in oral history methods, develop historically oriented public programs, help locate (often hidden) written primary source material, and encourage the publication of a popularly written local history. Initial staff was to include two Highlandtown residents who would be trained in the methods of oral history and then interview people at the senior citizens' center. These local oral historians would, we believed, be particularly sensitive to the details and nuances of the local culture and would encourage a community identification with the project from the outset. A history graduate student, who was to supplement the interviews with research into the written record; myself, who was to train the community oral historians and senior citizens in the methods of oral history; and the project director composed the rest of the staff.

A serious problem arose immediately. Despite our board members' network of contacts, we could not find two community oral historians. Our inability to do so suggests that historians' enthusiasm for community history is not widely shared as a formal aspect of our culture—that people's sense of their own history is private, personal, and grounded in the family and therefore is not congenial to institutional frameworks. Repeatedly it took longer than we had foreseen to explain to people what we were trying to do and why, and to engage their support and participation.

In the first of many readjustments, we shuffled our staff so that the graduate student and I began doing interviews. Because little background information was available to inform our interviews, because we wanted to remain as open as possible to our interviewees' ways of structuring and interpreting their own experiences, and because we could not agree about how to focus the interviews, we did not develop a tight interview outline. Instead we followed a life-history format, eliciting chronological accounts of our interviewees' lives and then focusing on topics they seemed most willing to talk about. We used this general format throughout the project, though interviews emphasized more specific topics as we learned more about a neighborhood's history.

In fact, our entire interview collection suffers from a lack of focus that stemmed from a fundamental confusion about the kind of information we wanted. As historians, we clearly went after specific historical information—data—about family, work, and community life. Yet as any thoughtful interviewer soon realizes, interviews are equally valuable as sources of insight into consciousness, and we—more intuitively than consciously—also approached interviewing from this perspective. So, on the one hand, many of our interviews contain valuable, but maddeningly spotty, information on standard topics of interest to historians. On the other hand, they have richly detailed ethnographic data suggestive of the beliefs, values, and perceptions of interviewees, but this kind of material is not explored as fully as it could have been.

My colleague and I began to visit a Highlandtown senior citizens' center, trying to build interest in the project and do some interviews. Though people were cordial to us, we found that they were not at all anxious to share what we thought were very rich life stories. They thought we were prying. But gradually, as we created a certain amount of trust, a few people agreed to be interviewed. These were uniformly warm encounters. But they were not consciousness-raising, at least for the interviewees; the interview process did not lead them to put those individual stories into any social context. People told me personal stories about hard times during the Depression, exploitative working conditions, and family difficulties. The meaning or interpretation they gave to the experiences of their lives was personal—generally a feeling of sturdiness, of pride in having survived difficult circumstances. If anyone's consciousness was raised, it was mine, for try as I would to get at feelings of outrage or exploitation, or some perception of broader social forces shaping their lives, I would always end up hearing some version of: "Times were rough, but we survived," or "Life has been a long string of experiences, but I've made it through for sixty or seventy or eighty years." In fact, people agreed to be interviewed in part because they wanted to communicate this sense of survival to me and others who would listen to the tapes. Ironically, this "insider's view" ran counter to some of our original ideas about community history's potential.

Why did this theme of survival figure so deeply in the two hundred interviews that the BNHP collected? The popular ideologies of independence, individual achievement, and respect for the "self-made man" have obviously stamped this perception on many Americans. In addition, the social position, closeness to the immigration experience, and age of our particular set of interviewees gave this notion of survival particular force. Though we were sensitive to class, sex, racial, and ethnic differences in choosing interviewees, they were an essentially self-selected group: sociable and open people with the time and energy to talk with relative strangers in a fairly intimate way; self-assured enough to feel that they had something worth saying; visible, available members of the community. Indeed, all were, within the context of the neighborhood, survivors, We did not seek out those who had done less well. As first- and second-generation urban Americans, who still had strong memories of extremcly hard times in the old country or the rural South and during their early years in Baltimore, they are proud of having coped with all of that, of having done well enough on their terms, of working steadily, of raising a family, of buying a home. Finally, our interviewees were all elderly, primarily in their sixties and seventies. Most people, but especially older people, seek to understand their past as meaningful and worthwhile. Memory tends to shape experience in this light, and our interviewees thus emphasized survival, defining it in the very terms that described their own experience: achieving enough security to be self-reliant in their old age; raising children who now felt a responsibility to help care for their elderly parents; maintaining the will and the vitality to "get around."

In the fall of 1978 I began teaching oral history to a small group of Highlandtown residents in the hope of recruiting local interviewers. This class included several of our initial interviewees, some of their friends, and a few younger people from the community committed to recording its history. Again, several problems arose. People apparently came to the workshops as much to talk among themselves about old times as to learn how to interview. My efforts to discuss good interview topics often led to long strings of reminiscences. Frustrated with their lack of focus and seeking to ensure some consistency in the interviews, I gave them an interview outline, an adaptation of the chronological and topical outline the project had developed earlier. As a result, I, not they, determined the historically "appropriate" interviewing questions. I did not let people do their own history.

Not that it mattered. The community interviewers usually ignored my outline and questioned people about what they thought was important. And so, in addition to the stories of struggles during hard times that seem so important to Highlandtown residents, these intervicws are filled with descriptions of the area in years gone by as well as sentimental stories of family life. Topics of importance to historians —the workings of local institutions or the local political machine, the conditions and social relations of work, immigration and the process of assimilation or nonassimilation into American life—receive little coverage. Although most historians would find these community-produced tapes of limited value, the interviews do offer some clues into how Highlandtown residents view their own history.

The tension between professional and community historians' approaches appears here at two levels. The first is the difference in the information the two groups think is historically important. What do we mean when we say that we want people to do their own history? Whose version and definition of the past are we seeking? A related methodological tension arises when community residents record their own history. These community historians have a stake in maintaining good relations with their interviewees, and since they share the same social world and world view, are unlikely to challenge them in any case. As a result, their interviews are uniformly polite and unchallenging, shaped by a reluctance or an inability to be critical of the collective neighborhood experience. These unresolved tensions in the case of the BNHP produced difficult historiographic and social problems, which were further complicated by the nature of the evidence that oral history interviews provide.

E arly in 1979 we received Comprehensive Employment and Training Act (CETA) funds from a city agency to expand the project into five additional Baltimore neighborhoods. In order to select our neighborhoods judiciously, we had to be more precise about what we meant by a "neighborhood." Defining it in terms of bounded geographic and social space as well as a set of shared experiences, we decided to work in neighborhoods that were spatially self-contained and had a definite class, racial, or ethnic identity. We also sought to reflect the city's racial and ethnic diversity and to work in areas where previous community activism or scholarly research would give us some base upon which to build. Our selections included South Baltimore, a multiethnic community not unlike Highlandtown; Hampden, a community built around the textile industry; Old West Baltimore, the largest self-contained black community in the city; the local "Little Italy"; and Lower Park Heights, a lower-middle-class, primarily elderly Jewish community.

The choice of these neighborhoods led indirectly to a thematic bias in our subsequent work. The underlying question of our inquiry became: why have these neighborhoods remained stable in the midst of significant urban flux? We were savvy enough not to romanticize the neighborhood as a category, but we perhaps overemphasized the value of rootedness and stability. We did not, for example, interview many people who left a neighborhood, having for one reason or another found life there unsatisfying. And we did not pay enough attention to the centrifugal forces threatening and even destroying neighborhood life.

An even more fundamental problem, however, was the relevance of our notion of neighborhood to the local residents. On one level our definition was a reasonably accurate reflection of community perceptions: most people, when asked what made their neighborhood "theirs," talked first about certain physical landmarks and then about the special "friendliness" of the people there. Yet "neighborhood," as a category of social experience, may not have been as significant to local residents as the overlapping communities shaped by family, church, work, and ethnic group. Indeed, the oral testimony shows the close integration among these realms of experience in people's lives. "Neighborhood" as the overall organizing concept for the BNHP may have been an artificial or at least an oversimplified construct.

With CETA funds we hired twelve oral historians, two per neighborhood; their job was akin to that of anthropological field workers. Using a local senior citizens' center as a base of operation, they were to get the "feel" of the neighborhood, conduct interviews with long-time residents, locate primary source materials, develop historically oriented local programs, and generally catalyze a formal, public interest in the area's history.

We now decided that our interest in using local people as interviewers was a false issue. It was not necessary that interviewers live in the neighborhood they were studying, so long as they had self-conscious social and political commitments to it. We tried to hire people with both a sensitivity to neighborhood values and some analytical distance from the neighborhood experience. Our best interviewers were generally younger people who had been born in the neighborhood they were working in or one similar to it, but who had left for schooling or a less circumscribed way of life. Unemployed community organizers, such as the former VISTA volunteers who seem to abound in Baltimore, proved to be particularly good interviewers.

Shortly after we hired our community oral historians, we received a grant from the National Endowment for the Humanities (NEH) to hire professional historians and graduate researchers who would use written and oral sources to write six popular neighborhood histories, which could be made widely available to the city schools and the public. These histories were one way we hoped to return the history to the community. The project formed a research team for each neighborhood, consisting of the two oral historians, the professional historian, and the graduate researcher.

After a summer of work by the research teams, the entire staff reviewed the results and raised questions about the use of the oral history materials similar to those raised previously about the Highlandtown tapes. The professional historians felt that the interviewers lacked the historical background and analytical framework to pursue certain subjects in sufficient depth. In addition, they would at times let the interviewees ramble on about topics that were of little historical or ethnographic interest. These problems probably could have been remedied in time. If the professional historians had taken a hand in selecting the interviewers, and if research teams had met for more than just a summer, perhaps the oral historians would have been more fully inducted into the craft of historical inquiry.

At the same time, the professional historians failed to appreciate the tapes' value. They used the oral testimony simply as a source of specific information, illustrative quotations, or interesting anecdotes that fit their own analytical framework. They were unable to penetrate beneath the surface of the informants' words. One project historian, for example, noted the lack of education among the residents of the mill community he was researching and concluded that education and, by implication, upward mobility were unimportant to them. But if he had listened more carefully to the stories of mill workers going to work at the age of fourteen or twelve or even ten, had heard their pride in their way of life, and had perceived the way the factory owners' paternalism had both satisfied and restrained them, his interpretation of their lack of formal education would have been more subtle. He would have understood that although upward mobility was part of *his* value system, it was neither possible nor particularly desirable for these millworkers.

I had a similar experience in my own interviewing, an instance in which the cognitive structure my interviewee used to interpret her experience simply did not correspond to mine. I asked her if she had ever worked outside her home for pay. She said no, and we went on to another line of questioning. Then, in another context, she mentioned that she had occasionally worked as a waitress in a local restaurant. Wasn't this a job, I asked? "No," she said. Although she did earn money at it, it wasn't really a job; she was simply "helping out" Helen, the restaurant owner and a friend of hers. I then asked her if she had ever "helped out" anyone else and found that she had had a number of such jobs. What she clued me into, of course, was an entirely different perception of work outside the home than I had expected, one in which work itself was primarily an extension of her role as a good neighbor and friend.

Oral history material must be used in much the same way as intellectual historians use their documents—as clues into the mind of a person or a group. Such information can then be coordinated with the data gathered from more traditional social history sources to provide not just an "insider's view" but a more powerful social analysis. Yet the problems involved in doing this are as much social as intellectual, for the historians on our project, like most historians, operated in the halls of academe, not in the streets. Their graduate training, professional identity, and relatively privileged social position created an intellectual framework that shaped their historical analysis. But the talk of ordinary people often fails to penetrate the professionals' world view in any meaningful way. Professional historians thus find it hard to give such interviews the sensitive interpretation they demand.

Our field worker–oral historians, though naive in history, were skilled social observers whose sensitivity and observations have significantly enriched the insight of the professionals. Their historical naiveté made them especially sensitive to interviewees' ways of structuring their own experiences. Although interviews should be a dialectic between interviewer and interviewee, they can be highly manipulative encounters. Interviewers often "lead the witness" to support their theses. Our oral historians, unlike the professional historians they worked with, had no such theses. They had to figure out how to get into the mind of each interviewee and were open to fresh insights and perspectives. Moreover, precisely because the oral historians lacked an in-depth knowledge of conventional categories of historical inquiry, which generally focus on the more formal, public aspects of experience, their interviews are especially rich in details about the more private dimensions of daily life, such as family dynamics or coping with limited resources. Admittedly, these details are often embedded in a meandering, anecdotal style of recollection, and it takes real effort to hear them amid all the words.

I n line with our goals of developing the community residents' sense of ownership in the project and returning the history to the neighborhoods, each research team submitted a draft of its history for community review. Several residents read each draft; others heard informal oral presentations. These review sessions corrected certain factual inaccuracies, yielded some further information about each neighborhood, opened up additional lines of inquiry, and helped sustain community interest. But they also raised new problems. Many community reviewers disliked the essays' academic style. Historians writing for a popular audience obviously must adopt a clearer and more vivid prose style than they typically employ. More troublesome was the booster spirit many residents seemed to favor. Some noted the scant mention of locally prominent people in the histories, a deliberate omission intended to avoid the "hit parade" approach to local history. Others did not want the histories to include anything that might be construed as even mildly critical of the neighborhood. One woman, for example, objected to the mention of the local nuns' strict teaching methods. Handling such criticisms was a delicate matter. This defensive neighborhood pride has roots in the neglect many residents of Baltimore's older urban neighborhoods have experienced at the hands of the city. At the same time, we need to challenge the parochialism and ethnocentrism that runs through this assertion of identity, since it encourages a defensive withdrawal from broader urban participation. Our popular histories ought to convey an understanding of neighborhood not as an isolated collective experience but as a collective experience that is part of, that has been shaped by, a larger urban process.

The publications resulting from the project have been partially successful in addressing these issues. The three neighborhood histories that were ultimately completed appeared in *Maryland Historical Magazine* in the spring of 1982. Lack of funds made it impossible to issue them as separate pamphlets. All three essays have an engaging narrative style: information culled from an impressive array of sources is organized around a loose chronological framework and presented in clear prose enhanced by details, anecdotes, and quotations. The subjects of the essays are the ones social historians typically address: work, family, community institutions, and neighborhood politics. The essays are predictably weakest in interpretation; themes of survival and stability, intra-community solidarity and extra-community conflict, are present but unfocused. Although the authors render the community histories with respect and sympathy, they fail to subject them to a clear social analysis. The essays are not exercises in antiquarianism, but neither are they particularly illuminating. The most serious problem is *where* the essays appeared—the *Maryland Historical Magazine,* the publication of the frankly elitist state historical society. Though the receptivity of the magazine's editors to these articles was commendable, their publication in this journal made the essays essentially irrelevant as popular history. The general public does not read the *Maryland Historical Magazine:* it does not even know it exists.

Much more accessible has been the project's widely distributed "picture book," *Baltimore People: Baltimore Places: A Neighborhood Album,* published by the University of Baltimore (1980), which contains photographs accompanied by brief quotations from the oral history interviews, organized around the same subjects as the narrative histories that appeared in the *Maryland Historical Magazine.* The book is self-consciously celebratory. It validates aspects of working-class culture, but since it makes no effort to examine that culture critically, it is an exercise in populist nostalgia.

Our major effort to return the history we gathered to the neighborhood was a theater production, *Baltimore Voices,* a series of neighborhood sketches produced and acted by a troupe of professional actors associated with Baltimore's Theatre Project under contract to the BNHP. *Baltimore Voices* was pieced together almost entirely from the actual words of our interviewees. During the winter and spring of 1980, it was presented at approximately thirty-five local neighborhood centers, churches, and schools, drawing audiences ranging from ten to two hundred people, from a variety of social groups— young and old, working- and middle-class, black and white. An informal discussion between audience and actors followed each production. An analysis of this play suggests clearly why community history projects need well-developed links with community organizations and institutions if they are to be effective.

Baltimore Voices was potentially the best tool for political consciousness-raising that our project produced. An interview is essentially a private act, as is reading a local history. The play, however, brought people together to share a collective experience and reflect upon it afterward. It could have catalyzed or been part of a broader community dialogue about both the value of the neighborhood and the larger social forces to which it has been subjected. For a dramatic production is an especially powerful means of arousing community consciousness, putting before people's eyes the literal drama of their own and their neighbors' experiences and rendering those experiences publicly meaningful.

I am not certain that *Baltimore Voices* worked this way. Admittedly the people in the neighborhoods loved the well-written and well-acted production. People were touched and moved by it and made to feel important. Reminded of their own experiences, or those of their parents and grandparents, they left the play with a sense of well-being and expansiveness. Furthermore, as people in one neighborhood caught a glimpse of how people in other neighborhoods lived, the play may have helped break down neighborhood isolation and broaden people's consciousness of the city as a whole.

But like the interviews on which it was based, *Baltimore Voices* largely emphasized the theme of personal survival. This theme was conveyed not only through personal vignettes about the Depression and World War II but also through the vitality and wit of the people as portrayed by the actors. Certain political themes were touched upon—union organizing, racial tension, and housing displacement—yet always in personal terms. No links were made between individual experiences and broader historical processes. Despite the play's tone of "the neighborhood" versus "the powers that be," the resolution of this conflict was always presented in terms of self-help and not social change. Finally, the form of the play, focusing for about twelve minutes on each of the six neighborhoods we worked in, made any sustained exploration of issues impossible. Thus, although *Baltimore Voices* celebrated the city's working-class culture and the people with whom we worked, it did little to move people beyond themselves. And the half-formed feelings and ideas that might have been roused by the play were left half-formed. There was no mechanism for following up on them or shaping them into some new form.

There were other problems too. *Baltimore Voices* was a fairly informal play with little distance between actors and audience and a very simple set, but it was still a big production that toured the entire city. Though neighborhood representatives previewed the play and offered comments and criticisms (in much the same way as they were invited to review our popular histories), people still viewed the play as entertainment staged by the BNHP. Some residents felt that they were able to "help out"—as numerous interviewees put it—but they continued to lack a feeling of ownership in the play or the project. Though the cast of *Baltimore Voices* and the entire project staff were quite down-to-earth in dealing with all kinds of people, considerable social distance remained between the professional staff and the people whose history we were producing. Moreover, because the play was such a big production, it required technical assistance as well as substantial planning, coordination, and publicity. A good bit of this work fell to our oral historians, and it effectively kept them from developing small neighborhood-based programs within the communities. Their efforts, too, ultimately turned on *Baltimore Voices*.

L ike most critics, I am surer of the problems than the ways to solve them. But it does seem that the development of links between community history projects and community organizations can help resolve many of the problems *Baltimore Voices* and the BNHP have faced. Such links can help give a political edge to the historian's work and some perspective to the community organization's concerns. By working with activist community organizations, historians might learn how to integrate the "we survived" theme in working-class culture with an analysis of the social and economic structures that have surrounded and shaped that culture. I am not suggesting that history projects necessarily embroil themselves in community politics nor that they only pursue themes and issues of immediate local relevance, though they certainly may do these things. What I am suggesting is that a neighborhood's history is a broadly political story—a story of power relationships, between, for example, neighborhood and city, or employee and employer. To ignore these relationships and focus only on survival continues to support a very privatized, individualistic sense of one's place in history. The purpose of community organizations, however, is to move people to take seriously their dissatisfaction wtih existing conditions and to bring them together in public action against the status quo. This perspective can be expecially instructive, indeed challenging, to historians unfamiliar with working-class life who, anxious not to patronize, tend to celebrate the humanity of working-class people at the expense of social and political analysis.

These links can also bring historians and community residents into a more sustained and broad-based interaction than oral history interviews provide.

And these contacts can lead to a mutual appreciation of how each group—historians and community residents—thinks. The BNHP's oral historians tried to gain insight into the local social world and world view by talking informally with people at the senior citizens' centers and by hanging out, as much as time allowed, with others. This approach was practically inefficient and intellectually limited; it took a great deal of time and was extremely random. Broad-based community organizations, however, can provide a convenient means of introducing historians to diverse local groups. Community organizers, moreover, though certainly not without their own blinders, are frequently able to provide a succinct description of local social groups and processes, again facilitating historians' work both practically and intellectually. Finally, because these organizations are oriented more toward social change and less toward social service than senior citizens' centers, they seem to connect with people who are especially aware, thoughtful, and enthusiastic about the community's history, people who will, in fact, encourage historians to make a social and political analysis.

For a community history project to link up with a community organization—to share office space with it, for example—can also lead to a greater local identification with the project, a greater investment in it, and more long-term interest and participation. The history group's products and programs would likely be on a smaller scale than *Baltimore Voices,* but they would have a more lasting connection to the community. Furthermore, though senior citizens are certainly the best sources for a neighborhood's history, they are often the least interested in community history projects, for they already know the history. Community organizations can provide a wider audience for a project than the senior citizens' centers where the BNHP based much of its work.

Finally, links between history projects and community organizations can provide the practical mechanisms by which feelings of identity and pride stirred up by projects can be channeled into the ongoing lives of communities. Community history projects could be part of a much broader local organizing effort or of modest community improvements. Our oral historians, for example, found numerous wonderful storytellers but lacked a way to arrange for some of these storytellers to visit local schools and talk with young children about life years ago. An established organization could easily have set up such a project.

My experience with the BNHP has tempered my rather naive initial enthusiasm for community history projects. It has also made me aware that if such projects are to be intellectually and socially responsible, they require time, commitment, and substantial grounding in the community itself. The fate of the project since the conclusion of *Baltimore Voices'* 1980 neighborhood tour both confirms this perspective and further suggests the serious obstacles to the long-term collaborative efforts I am advocating. By the fall of 1980 most of the project's work had been completed. Both NEH and CETA funds were running out. The project staff was sharply cut. The survivors spent most of their time processing the oral history tapes and photographs according to proper archival procedures. Some efforts were made to do more public programming with material already developed, and an additional grant was received from the Maryland Humanities Commission to develop a slide show on the history of local waterfront laborers. *Memories,* a film documenting the work of the project in the neighborhood of Hampden, was completed after two years of production. With the end of our NEH grant, the *Voices* company ceased its affiliation with the BNHP. The company revised the play for broadcast on local public television in the fall of 1982 and over the next two years secured its own grants to develop theater pieces based on local social history in cooperation with neighborhood groups and labor unions. Most of these activities felt like steps toward shutting down shop, the closure of what had obviously *not* become a permanent local history project. By 1982 the BNHP had effectively closed up.

The onset of Reaganomics in early 1981 was central to the project's collapse. CETA's termination and NEH's reorientation toward more traditional forms of inquiry cut our major sources of funds. Moreover, the project had not established enough of a community presence to make local support possible. In fact, the production-oriented activities that NEH and similar funding agencies required had undercut efforts at developing that long-term community presence. We had been funded to develop an oral history collection, a photographic archive, a theatrical production, and traveling museum, not to work with people to develop new forms of historical consciousness.

But the deepest impediment to sustained collaboration between the project and the community was profoundly social. Few historians, including those who were affiliated with the project, think of themselves as community members with specific skills and insights to share. Rather, our primary affiliation is with a nationally organized profession. This social disjuncture between professional historian and local resident erodes long-term community-based historical work. Historians are not likely to feel much social commitment to a specific locale. Colleges and universities give little support or recognition to faculty members who operate in the public arena. We are under constant pressure to engage in other, more rewarded professional activities. Given our level of training, historians are also apt to be impatient and discouraged with popular historical ideas and attitudes.

The BNHP was instrumental in developing a climate of respect for popular community history, both locally and nationally. It also helped develop a loose network of people with an interest in neighborhood history these interests in the city, and several of us associated with the project have continued our involvement with public history. Yet in retrospect I am struck by the ephemeral quality of much of our work.

★14★

A Report on Doing History from Below:

The Brass Workers History Project

From the start of the nineteenth century through the first half of the twentieth, the Naugatuck Valley in western Connecticut was the center of the American brass industry. In 1979 a video producer, a community organizer, a union education director, and I, a labor historian—all of whom had connections in the Valley—developed the Brass Workers History Project in order to record the history of Naugatuck Valley brass workers and to present it in popular book and video formats for a nonspecialist audience. We hoped that such a project would present to the public some of the themes developed by labor historians over the past two decades and would also be a unique experiment in the participation of working people in uncovering and presenting their own history.[1] The project received major funding from the National Endowment for the Humanities (NEH) and began work in 1980.

The forms of worker/community participation we proposed were frankly experimental. We proposed to organize history committees in local unions, senior centers, and other organizations, and to help them preserve their own history while involving them in our project. We also planned reunions of former brass workers and a Community-Labor Advisory Panel.

First we made the rounds of local organizations that might in one way or another be affected by our activity: union locals and retirees' chapters, senior centers, and local historical societies. These courtesy visits acknowledged the importance of each group and allowed us to explain what we were doing before they heard about it—quite possibly in distorted form—from somebody else. At the same time, we laid the groundwork for future requests for help. In the case of the unions, our ticket of admission was the official support of the regional office of the principal brass workers' union, although we approached

BY JEREMY BRECHER

267

locals independently if they were not on good terms with the regional office. Visits to historical societies and other cultural institutions allowed us to solicit their help, to acknowledge their "turf," and to make it clear that we were not planning to invade it. They were pleased with our plan to turn over the material we collected to a local historical museum, a policy that also indicated our desire to contribute to rather than exploit the community.

We made some of our best initial contacts at community events sponsored by local groups. For example, at a cultural exhibit at the Lithuanian Club of Waterbury, we met many people who would be extremely helpful over the course of the project, including a man who had for years been collecting old photographs of the Lithuanian community and became one of our star interviewees.

On the whole, Brass Valley residents met us with a combination of interest and reserve. We developed the philosophy that they were right to be cautious in dealing with us. After all, they had very little reason to think we were there for any reason except to rip them off, turning their lives, sufferings, and triumphs into the stuff of our own academic or media careers. We had seen all too many cases in which scholars and media people had exploited individuals and communities, taken their stories, and given nothing in return. Our belief that people were entitled to be wary of exploitation helped us to respond positively to people who were cautious in dealing with us, and it helped us control our anxiety at the lack of immediate acceptance.

Our attitudes in face-to-face situations influenced the responses we received. When we communicated interest and respect for the people we dealt with, they were likely to give us a fair hearing; when we communicated lack of respect, they were not. Once we set up a photographic session for a group of previously interviewed workers. They had dressed up in their best clothes and were looking forward to the occasion. The photographer was unable to make the session or even to call. We were told later that the workers had interpreted this as a sign that they were not important enough for us to make sure that the photographer showed up. Fortunately, this incident was unique; too many of this kind would have seriously undermined people's faith in our respect for them.

It took time and effort to gain people's trust. Repeated phone calls or visits were often necessary to gather photographs, track down interviewees, or check facts, but these efforts had the secondary benefit of reminding people that we were still there and still interested in their participation. Maintaining contact on a one-to-one basis was a time-consuming job. But after three years we had developed a range of contacts and a depth of trust that supported an infinitely greater degree of participation than would have been possible in the early months of the project.

The personal demands of this work were considerable. We tried to deal in a human way with the two hundred or so people who became involved in one manner or another with the project. We tried not to rush when we were with people, not to act like reporters running to file stories, not to schedule so many meetings and interviews that we could not be "there" for those we talked with—despite the pressure to produce materials and meet tight deadlines. We had to learn to deal diplomatically with a very wide range of people and to get rid of the prejudices that we constantly discovered in ourselves.

Even after several years we were not accepted as insiders. Even those who liked and trusted us no doubt concealed some dirty linen. Yet we were able to deal with many different groups in the community in a way that would have been difficult for anyone identified with one particular faction. The status we achieved with many people might be described as that of "pet outsiders."

Conceivably, the project could have been attacked as an incomprehensible waste of the taxpayers' money, a pinko plot, or simply weird. To some extent we were protected against such charges by the auspices under which we functioned. We were, after all, sponsored by a government agency; we had official support from the regional office of the United Auto Workers; we maintained good relations with all sections of the state labor movement. We worked closely with people who had been active in the anticommunist section of the local labor movement as well as with some who had been on the other side.

What protected us most, however, was that scores of people met us, talked to us, and could see who we were and what we were doing. Our making the rounds of community organizations and institutions meant that we were not some mysterious invading force but people whose actions and character had been observed. I suspect that the grapevine spread information about us pretty far, especially in labor circles, if only for our novelty value. This meant that if anybody was suspicious of us, they had ways to check us out other than asking the local paper to call the FBI.

We worried a lot initially about how to explain the project. We knew how to describe and justify what we wanted to do to radical historians and academically educated social activists, for whom "people's history" done with and for those whom it was about was understood as a potential contribution to movements for social change. We had learned how to present it in the unique conjunction of academic and populistic worlds that was the NEH at that time. But this presentation would have been almost totally alien and alienating to the people of the Valley.

We eventually developed a press release, a brochure explaining the project and soliciting participation, and a pretty good idea of what we should say when we spoke to meetings. Although I am sure that the brochure was excellent, it strikes me that I no longer recall what it said. We distributed it quite widely and gave copies to everyone we dealt with in the early stages of the project, but most people responded to talks, calls, and other forms of personal contact far more than flyers or even letters.

After a few score efforts to explain the project to various people, I realized that, whatever we said, people would form their own ideas of what we were up to. People would evaluate our behavior and decide who we were and what we were doing on the basis of their own knowledge and experience, not what we said about ourselves. More important, I came to the conclusion that it was fine for people to form an understanding of the project that differed from our own. Whether their idea of what we were up to coincided with ours mattered less than whether they felt that they had good reasons to cooperate with or avoid us. Some people thought that what we were doing was silly, others that the products we talked about were fantasies that would never be realized, but they still gave time and assistance to the project. In some cases they may have done so because we were nice, idealistic young people whom they wanted to help, in others because we listened with interest and respect to reminiscences they enjoyed sharing.

Over time I came to think of introducing the project less as explaining what we were doing than as negotiating a basis for a mutually rewarding relationship. I described the project as briefly as possible, often saying little more than that we were telling the story of the brass workers and their families, that we were making a movie and writing a book, and that we wanted to talk to people about their experiences. If people asked questions, we answered them frankly. But we did not give detailed explanations unless people wanted them. This allowed people to focus on what interested them about the project, and it came to be many things to many people—something we learned to accept.

The Valley was notorious for its social factionalism. Some of the past lines of cleavage we knew. Battles between left and right, which at times had brought people who worked side by side to fisticuffs, had fractured the local labor movement in the 1930s and 1940s. Ethnic rivalry marked local politics, and racial tensions had been high in several of the communities.

Other tensions we discovered later. For example, there was considerable rivalry among the various union locals, and there were divisions within the district between pro- and anti-administration forces. One of the locals itself was polarized into two factions, one of which had held a sit-in at the union office a few years before. All in all, it was like entering a minefield.

We tried to avoid becoming identified with any one group by taking the position that "we're here to learn, not to take sides." We tried to be genuinely sympathetic to different positions, even to those with which we personally disagreed, on the grounds that people had reasons for their feelings and beliefs that it was our responsibility to understand, regardless of our own opinions.

Initially we had intended to organize reunions and group interviews. We were worried, naturally, that these might lead to sterile confrontations in which the old battles would simply be relived and rehashed—and which might embroil us in conflicts that would undermine our future community relations. In the end we decided that we would meet with people only individually or in their own groups. We also avoided telling people what others had been saying to us. At the time this seemed rather the coward's way out, but in retrospect I think it is really a form of respect for community divisions: if people have chosen to be antagonistic, it is not really appropriate for us to try to force them to change.

In a broader sense it was part of our job to help people see their immediate experience in a larger context and thereby see what they had in common with people they might otherwise consider antagonists. But reconciliation could only be a result of our work, not a premise. A particularly dramatic example was the case of two men who had been rank-and-file leaders on opposite sides of the left/right union struggle in the 1940s. After working closely, but separately, with each of them for nearly two years, we finally decided to risk inviting them both to a party along with several dozen other participants in the project. They initially greeted each other with wariness, but after the hours had passed and the liquor had flowed, we found them together in a back room helping each other explain to a circle of younger activists why people like them had never sold out. As each of them spoke, he tapped the other on the knee and said, "As Mike will tell you . . ." or "As Bill will tell you . . . "

During our initial courtesy visits, many people had expressed some degree of interest in the project, but nobody was ready either to start working with us on a regular basis or to organize a history committee in his or her own organization. We decided to try to push ahead with interviewing because it would allow us to get started on the products of the project, it might get some people interested enough to participate further with us, and in any case it would get us out of the office and in contact with the people we were supposed to be dealing with. It was a lucky decision, and I would advise any community history workers who feel stuck to simply go out and spend some time doing interviews.

Finding people to interview turned out to be no problem. We asked everyone we met to suggest people to interview, and virtually all of them came up with suggestions. We often started by interviewing our initial contact people at unions or senior centers, then asking them to arrange interviews with other members, relatives, or friends. In effect, we utilized the networks we had or were establishing.

For most people a reference from a friend, relative, or acquaintance probably made a big difference in our acceptability. Many people said that they didn't really know anything and there was no reason to interview them. We tried to emphasize that they did indeed know things that were important to us, that we were interested not just in the union, but also in life on the job and in the neighborhoods. In the end more than three-quarters of those we approached for interviews ultimately agreed. Those who would not talk with us no doubt had a variety of reasons for the decision; apparently some were suspicious that the project was a racket, and oft-burned immigrant radicals feared exposure.

Setting up the interviews was a tedious process. Some people were hard to reach on the phone, others would put us off, and required repeated calls—perhaps in part to test the seriousness of our interest. Without a reminder call the day before, few people remembered our appointments, and even with such calls we had to tolerate a fair number of no-shows. Ultimately we had to accept that we were low on people's list of priorities. It is hard to see why we should have been any higher.

After our first twenty or thirty interviews, we began to see the limitations of our initial approach. We were very strong in those areas where we had initial contacts, such as unionized workers and the Lithuanian community. And we were strong with people who were more like ourselves: I had far more interviews with men than with women, for example.

To compensate for this, we began to put extra effort into reaching a wider cross-section of the Valley's working class. Moving outside our networks meant more work and more anxiety with less reward, since it required dealing with people with whom we had less in common. But with persistence we found the people in the categories we were weak in and then asked them to suggest others. A visit to a priest attached to the Catholic parish that served the Puerto Rican community brought us an introduction to the first Puerto Rican to work in the Waterbury brass mills. A plea to a union organizer brought us to a black woman union activist whose mother had been one of the first black women to work at the Scovill Manufacturing Company.

At the outset of the project, we had been told the anthropologist's adage: "Behind every great ethnographer lies a great informant." Looking for that "great informant" was far from my original idea of how to do community history. But there are indeed "natural historians" who have an interest in and talent for the history around them; finding them is largely a matter of chance. Two of the best were uncles of people who wandered into our office in response to a newspaper article on the project. (The only generalization I can make is that natural historians tend to be overrepresented on past and present union education committees.) Over the course of our project we found quite a few, and they not only were exciting to talk with but gave our products a depth of insight that could never have been achieved without them.

Doing open-ended historical interviews with people who are not used to any public role posed a major challenge.[2] For me, respect is the alpha and omega of good interviewing technique. You have to regard your source as someone who is at least your equal, and someone from whom you have a great deal to learn. People are very sensitive to condescension and contempt. Many academic interviewers who study working-class communities in fact feel themselves superior to those they study. Their subjects are well aware of this, but the interviewers think that they are reticent because they are inarticulate or generally suspicious.

When people agree to be interviewed, they are exposing the meaning of their lives. They should only be asked to do so if you are willing to respect it, both in your personal interaction with them and in the way you use what they give you. They need to know that they will not be forced into areas they find embarrassing or uncomfortable, and that you will be sensitive enough to back away from such areas before they have to say, "I'd rather not talk about that."

We regarded the people we were interviewing as experts on the part of the world they had lived in. We were genuinely interested in what they had to tell us. This helped us overcome the feeling that many people had that "I don't really have much that you would be interested in" or "I don't remember too much about the old days." Feelings of inadequacy were often more important in inhibiting people's participation in interviews than anxiety about what might be revealed.

We did do a few group discussions and interviews, and the staff learned a good deal from the back-and-forth responses. But they turned out to be rather difficult to manage because everyone wanted the floor at the same time. Even with several staff members trying to respond, the results tended to be rather unsatisfying for all. When elderly participants were hard of hearing, the problems were aggravated. And the tapes of such sessions proved extremely difficult to transcribe. Meetings with groups can still be valuable for a community history project, but we suggest that they be regarded more as a community activity than as a form of group interview.

The worker-community participation aspect of our project was frankly experimental. A series of ambitious proposals called for community meetings, history committees, and the like. We had decided not to solicit participation ahead of time because we could not guarantee the funding that would allow the project to go ahead. We had no assurance that even a single person would be interested in working with the project in any way. The task of generating community involvement was difficult in itself and was almost bound to engender insecurity, tension, and self-doubt in the staff as we sat isolated in our office and tried to do something nobody really knew how to do.

One of the first things we learned was to limit initial requests for participation. Asking someone who had never thought about it to organize a history committee in his or her union local was totally inappropriate: such a person had neither the skills, nor the interest, nor the self-confidence to do so. But asking someone to be interviewed, to set up an interview with an acquaintance or family member, or to go through the box of old family photographs with one of us was a reasonable request that was likely to get a positive response.

We initially defined the project as a way we could help people in the community tell their own history. Thus, we offered to help people do things: collect the history of their own organization, set up a history committee, or learn how to operate video equipment. We rapidly learned that most people defined participation very differently: as them helping us. I believe now that our initial approach was rather arrogant, and that theirs was more realistic. Ideally, people in the community might have decided that this was *their* project and we were there merely to help; but that was unlikely, since we had initiated the project. Short of that, people's definition of their participation as "helping us" allowed them to feel the "pride of the giver." Perhaps this made our expertise, education, and sanction from the outside society less intimidating.

We learned very rapidly that we would not instantly see mass interest and participation in the project. People were glad to let us talk briefly at a meeting of their organization, for example, but nobody offered to set up a history committee. We rapidly shifted from the idea of committees to the concept of a liaison person who would connect us to various groups.

The strategy that we eventually evolved was to build an informal support network around the project. We made a point of calling people we had met and asking for their opinions or help. Occasionally we would ask someone to go on an interview with us, make a contact, or otherwise take part. This process was time-consuming, but its cumulative effect was substantial. More and more people became interested in working with the project. A local black poet who read about us in the newspaper and walked into our office one day eventually became a paid part-time participant. A union activist who initially had set up an interview for us later ran an "old photo contest," publicized the project up and down the Valley, and did interviews for the project on her own. Another volunteer made excellent maps showing ethnic succession for the book.

People participated for a variety of reasons. Some, particularly those who had been active in unions and ethnic organizations, felt that they had been part of something that was historically significant and worth preserving. Some already had a special interest, such as a particular neighborhood or ethnic group, and hoped to learn more about it by working with us. A few, particularly the labor and community activists, had social messages that they felt we could help pass on to coming generations. Some were history buffs who enjoyed this kind of activity for its own sake. Some people were proud of their lives and of what they could remember, or simply enjoyed reminiscing about old times.

Ultimately, over two hundred people were involved with the project in one way or another. They contributed their stories, helped line up interviews, donated photographs, set up photographic sessions, and helped in many other ways. As originally planned, we established a Community-Labor Advisory Panel, whose twenty-five members included both those who had most actively participated in the project and representatives of local labor, community, and cultural organizations whose input we felt was important. As we completed rough versions of the book and documentary, dozens of people, especially members of the panel, reviewed them and gave us their comments. This participation certainly made the results far different than they would have been if we historians and media professionals had turned out products on our own. But the forms of participation were very different from those we had initially envisioned. Instead of formal "history committees" in unions and community organizations or volunteers working regularly in our office, participation took the form of a myriad of fluid, informal contacts with people who helped the project in numberless specific ways.

We started distributing *Brass Valley,* a heavily illustrated book composed primarily of oral history materials, in 1983. The book received substantial coverage in the local newspapers, and we gave talks about it and sold copies in local clubs and libraries. It was for sale in union halls and downtown department stores as well as in local history museums. (In the future we hope to sell it in variety stores, restaurants, and other community outlets as well as at local cultural events.) It made enough of an impact locally that I was occasionally stopped by strangers on the street or in the library and asked about it.

So far as we can judge, reaction to the book was very positive. Many people bought it as a Christmas present, especially for older relatives and for family members who had moved away from the area. It seems to have been taken as a kind of collective family album in a community where almost everyone has a relative who worked in the brass industry. Many, many people told me that they found in it pictures of relatives. One family told me that they spent Christmas together going through it. Management people who had roots in the local community liked it despite its labor orientation. We received occasional criticism for overemphasizing immigrant workers instead of the Yankee entrepreneurs who were really responsible for the achievements of the brass industry; a couple of people quarreled with our handling of internal political conflict in the labor movement; and many readers complained that we slighted the particular department where they themselves had worked. Although its long-term impact on consciousness would be difficult to judge, many local people definitely recognized themselves in the book and were pleased to have their experiences represented.

Brass Valley, a feature-length color videotape, was completed in 1984.[3] We showed it first to a special audience of those who had been involved one way or another in the project, and then in union halls, history museums, senior organizations, and elsewhere in the Naugatuck Valley. Local reactions to the movie were strongly positive. People were very impressed that it treated their often maligned communities with respect. Many who had worked in the factories identified strongly with the portrayal and said that we had told the truth about their experience in a way that they had never seen on television or in other media. Several people said that they had lived in the community all their lives but had never had the pieces of its history put together for them before. One elderly woman told us that her husband had worked in the brass mills all his life, but that she had never understood what he went through and the effect his work must have had on him until she saw the movie. Some people with an orientation toward the local business community regarded the movie as strongly pro-labor, whereas some union officials (though none, so far as I know, in the Naugatuck Valley) regarded the movie as unsympathetic to labor.

After a major press build-up, the movie was shown statewide on Labor Day evening on all the stations of the Connecticut public television system. Several people told me that they heard the program being discussed at work the next morning. On a follow-up program a few days later, "Brass Valley Counter-Point," John Driscoll, head of the Connecticut State Labor Council AFL-CIO, and I discussed some of the issues raised by the movie, particularly its presentation of political division within the Naugatuck Valley unions in the 1940s (a struggle in which he was a major actor) and its general portrayal of the labor movement.

The movie *Brass Valley* remains available in the Naugatuck Valley through the Brass Workers History Project, the Connecticut Humanities Council, and the United Auto Workers; we hope that local groups will continue to show it for years to come. We are currently developing a curriculum guide for the movie and planning a series of workshops for teachers in the Naugatuck Valley and elsewhere in Connecticut to help them introduce a labor history unit into local school courses. I have continued to talk to community groups and have been conducting interviews for a social history of the working people of Waterbury since World War I. Another spin-off of the Brass Workers History Project is an effort to collect ethnic folk music in the Waterbury area.

Perhaps the greatest lesson we have to pass on to people engaged in similar projects is that participation takes time—plenty of it. We might have found it much easier to develop community participation if we had had a staff person doing interviews and making community contacts for a year before we put on a full staff that was sprinting to finish elaborate products within grant deadlines. A project with one person working half-time for six years might have more success than one with three people working full-time for a year. For our experience shows that with persistence, labor/community participation in doing history really can work.

WILL "FRUITS" TAKE OVER?

Is our nation turning into a "fruit bowl?" Homosexuals grow more blatant every day. They took over in Germany! Can it happen in the U.S. too?

History's Gay Ghetto:

The Contradictions of Growth in Lesbian and Gay History

"I want you to see that there is a passion in what we do."
Joan Nestle, Lesbian Herstory Archives Founder, to Judith Schwarz, 1977

In June 1975, the New York Lesbian Herstory Archives collective proclaimed in its first newsletter: "For us, there is excitement and joy in sharing the records of our lives, and our Archives will be as living as the material we can collect and you can send us."[1] This sense of the living intensity of historical work has been sustained over the past decade in the astonishing proliferation of lesbian and gay history archives, projects, slide shows, and publications. The appearance of Jonathan Katz's pioneering *Gay American History* in 1976 inspired a bevy of researchers to dig out records of the lesbian and gay past in conventional libraries and manuscript collections, while institutions like the Lesbian Herstory Archives provided a model for subsequent efforts to collect materials from previously untapped sources.[2] Slide shows such as Allan Berube's "Lesbian Masquerade" (an account of the lives of women who "passed" as men in nineteenth-century San Francisco, produced with the San Francisco Lesbian and Gay History Project) began to make the rounds of major U.S. cities in 1979, playing to large and enthusiastic audiences at community centers, churches, bars, and organizational meetings.[3] Long-term research projects requiring sustained energy and commitment were also undertaken by individuals and groups such as the Buffalo Oral History Project, which designed an ambitious, continuing study of that city's working-class lesbian community before 1970.[4]

News of this activity has been carried to the lesbian and gay communities via the gay press. Newspapers and periodicals, such as Boston's *Gay Commu-*

BY LISA DUGGAN

281

nity News and Toronto's *Body Politic,* have promoted historical awareness as an integral part of the building of gay politics and community. In fact, the growth of lesbian and gay history overall has depended on the passionate energy generated by the gay liberation and lesbian-feminist movements. Lesbian and gay historical work thus has much in common with other community-based history movements generated by the social activism of the 1960s and 1970s—women's history, black history, labor history, and social history more generally. In the context of vital political movements, the political meaning of historical understanding becomes suddenly manifest, and historical work is received with an enthusiasm very far indeed from the emotional pall of the deliberately depoliticized history classroom or museum hall.

Lesbian and gay historical work has also had a special history of its own. Its subject matter is to some extent taboo in most mainstream settings, and its practitioners are saddled with a pariah status even more constraining than the culturally marginal position of leftists and feminists. This unique situation has led to a series of contradictory effects. On the one hand, lesbian and gay historians have been crippled by exclusion from the funding sources and institutional supports available to other academic and community historians. The work itself has also suffered from this intense ghettoization—it has been confined almost entirely to lesbian and gay authors and audiences. On the other hand, the stigmatization of lesbian and gay history and historians has led, ironically, to some unusual strengths. Lesbian and gay history is strongly rooted in a political community upon which it is dependent for support. The practice of historical research fostered in this context is highly democratic and innovative. Necessity has been the source of invention—lesbian and gay historical researchers have exhibited a methodological imagination, material resourcefulness, and social diversity that are rare in the practice of history.

The great bulk of work in lesbian and gay history has been undertaken outside the university, in community settings. This has remained true even as lesbian and gay historians and their work have gained a small foothold in academic institutions over the past few years. John Boswell of Yale, John D'Emilio of the University of North Carolina at Greensboro, and Lillian Faderman of the University of California at Fresno, among others, have made major contributions to the growing body of published work in lesbian and gay history.[5] Most lesbians and gay men employed on academic faculties are still closeted, however, and lesbian and gay subjects are still considered the kiss of death for an academic career. Therefore, by necessity, the primary locations for research have developed in the community, where two major institutions have been created—the independent archive and the history project.

Lesbian and gay archives have sprung up throughout North America and Europe since the mid-1970s (see the Resource List that follows the notes to this chapter). Though these institutions have a variety of structures and funding sources, most subsist on volunteer labor and individual contributions. Some collect only local materials; others have a national or even international scope. The range is from a few boxes of materials stored in someone's home to a large, structured organization like the Canadian Gay Archives in Toronto, which has organized international conferences and put out a number of publications, including a useful guide entitled *Organizing an Archives: The Canadian Gay Archives Experience*.[6] Archives collect a wider range of materials than more traditional repositories. The majority have a small library of published works, emphasizing materials likely to be missing from mainstream libraries, such as lesbian pulp novels of the 1950s. Most also collect letters, diaries, and unpublished manuscripts as well as political materials, including flyers, posters, buttons, tapes of conferences and speeches, and photographs of events. Some focus on special collections, such as the records of organizations (One Institute Library) or individuals (Harvey Milk Archives). Visitors to archives include browsers, serious researchers, and even occasional visitors hoping to make contact with the local lesbian or gay community.

The dependence of gay archives on volunteers and community fundraising means that their continuing existence reflects, and in part creates, a high level of grassroots commitment to historical archiving. But most also suffer from chronic underfunding and a shortage of useful archival technology and trained personnel. Acquisitions also tend to be haphazard, and cataloguing incomplete. Coordination among archives is at present nonexistent.

History projects have popped up and dissolved, in recurring cycles of interest, in most urban areas in the United States. Some projects, such as the one in New York, have collected sources, fostered exchange of information among members, and supported individual researchers. The New York Lesbian and Gay Historical Society began in the late 1970s as a support circle for individuals engaged in lesbian or gay history research. Eventually, a smaller Lesbian History Project evolved out of the larger group and engaged in collective research about New York City's lesbian bars during the 1950s and lesbian-theme theater productions of the 1920s and 1930s. Eventually both groups disbanded, leaving behind at the Lesbian Herstory Archives voluminous files for possible successors.[7]

Other projects, such as those in San Francisco and Boston, have produced major presentations based on local, collective research. The slide show "Our Boston Heritage," which chronicles over a century of lesbian and gay history in that city, was produced and presented throughout the United States by a collective of women and men who met and shared their original research over a period of years. The slide show provides accounts of the lives of noted lesbian and gay Bostonians, such as the poet Amy Lowell, but it also chronicles collective experience. The growth of a gay subculture, the social organization of bar culture, the pattern of police persecution, and the birth of gay liberation and lesbian feminism are presented through a text and visual images.[8] These projects, usually undertaken without outside funding, require extraordinary commitment, especially from those members who work full-time and are politically active in addition. Not surprisingly, many projects have short lives.

Archives and history projects involve both academic and community-based researchers—an integration of effort that is unusual in the historical profession. Both categories of researchers keep in touch informally as well as through a formal network, newsletters, and conferences. A few years ago the Lesbian and Gay Researchers Network, a nonacademic group composed primarily of independent historians, merged with the Committee on Lesbian and Gay History, an affiliate of the American Historical Association. This organization puts out a newsletter and provides a structure for the sharing of resources and information.[9] This integration of community and university researchers extends beyond the U.S. borders. The Canadian Gay Archives and the *Body Politic* sponsored international conferences of lesbian and gay historians in Toronto in 1982 and 1985, while a 1983 conference held in Amsterdam, "Among Women, Among Men," brought together Europeans and North Americans from a wide variety of disciplines.[10] Though the Toronto gatherings attracted a stronger contingent of community researchers than the university-sponsored meeting in Amsterdam, all the conferences included activists, researchers, and theoreticians from many different backgrounds.

One of the knottiest contradictions in the development of the lesbian and gay history movement is the double impact of gay invisibility. Though historians have often neglected or distorted the experiences of minority groups and deprived classes, only lesbians and gay men have had their existence systematically denied and rendered invisible. The work of lesbian and gay historians makes this actively hidden past visible, and so creates enormous excitement. The simplest historical narrative about gay life is often received by lesbian and gay audiences as a profound affirmation of membership in a community with a shared past. On the other hand, lesbian and gay life is *still* invisible in many social and geographic areas. Exposure can cause individuals to lose material and social supports. Many hesitate to undertake research, or even to attend a gay event. Even those who are not gay-identified fear being "suspected" and so keep their distance from gay subjects. This dynamic greatly restricts the field for the creation and dissemination of lesbian and gay history. Thus, gay invisibility both makes historical work particularly exciting and ghettoizes it.

Because of the risks involved in being identified as lesbian or gay, gay history researchers are drawn exclusively from the ranks of those who are politically committed and willing to be "out" in public. Within these limitations, though, the recruitment of researchers is remarkably democratic. For instance, the Boston Area History Project included at its founding individuals ranging in age from the early twenties to the mid-fifties, from poor, working-class, and middle-class backgrounds, and from "old gay," contemporary gay rights, and feminist movement cultures. The group included an insurance underwriter, a student, a printer, a housecleaner, a secretary, a teacher, and a trained historian. As Chris Czernick explained in an article on the Boston Project in *Gay Community News,* "This exchange, or integration of skills and orientations, pushes all of us to truly listen to each other, to think more provocatively, to approach our research more creatively, and to conceptualize our history more honestly and accurately."[11]

This democratic practice has its limits, however. Though people of both genders are involved in the projects and archives, research in gay men's history remains more developed than that in lesbian history. And most projects' memberships cross but do not erase class lines. But the most stubborn barrier to a fully democratic historical practice has been the racial barrier. Most project and archive memberships are overwhelmingly white and English-speaking. Some white researchers have focused their individual projects on the history of gay people of color—Eric Garber's slide show on Harlem gay life and J. R. Roberts' bibliography of material on black lesbians, for instance.[12] Some activist groups of lesbians or gay men of color, though not history projects per se (such as Asian Lesbians of the East Coast and the Committee for the Visibility of the Other Black Woman), have focused attention on historical work.[13] But these efforts so far constitute a kind of ghetto-within-the-ghetto of lesbian and gay history.

The major problems built into this community-based practice of historical research are, of course, money and time. Those researchers not supported by academic jobs or student stipends find the material support for their work hard to come by. Historians such as Jonathan Katz and Judith Schwarz have had to shelve highly valued research projects in order to take draining full-time jobs, and fellow researchers and devoted audiences have deeply felt the loss.

But the democratic recruitment of researchers, in spite of its difficulties and limits, has had an enormously positive influence, not only on the nature of supporting institutions like archives and projects, but also on the very methods and sources used for research. The Lesbian Herstory Archives, for instance, is not a sterile repository of materials for use by researchers, but a kind of community center where political and social groups meet in an environment that creates a sense of a shared and meaningful past. This archive's aggressive collection of current cultural, political, and personal materials also helps to generate an awareness that present accomplishments are creating a history that can shape the future.[14]

The democratic basis of research has not only helped connect historical scholarship with current concerns; it has also been indispensable in uncovering the source materials for the writing of gay and lesbian history. The problems of sources and methods for researching a group that is not just anonymous but actively hidden go far beyond those normally encountered in graduate school. Knowing where to look for sources, understanding the need for confidentiality, having some sense of the coded meanings of words and gestures, require not just training and intelligence but also diversity of experience among researchers. The Buffalo Oral History Project, for instance, found the ordinary techniques of oral history insufficient because of the interviewees' need for secrecy. Members of the project drew on experience as well as imagination in developing new techniques for generating contacts and eliciting information under these conditions. More recently, they have broadened their project's efforts to cross racial lines, drawing on the experience of project members of differing racial backgrounds.

The collective nature of much lesbian and gay historical work and the need to innovate and learn from experience have created an unusually high level of communication and cooperation among researchers. A strong informal sense of ethics about the use of colleagues' sources and the proper crediting of others' insights and information has developed. Difficulties do arise, however, as when the makers of the gay history documentary *Before Stonewall* used without proper credit unpublished material shared with them by gay historians, causing the historians to withdraw from the project.[15]

The democratic, collective nature of much lesbian and gay history has also had an impact on the form of finished work. History projects have tended to generate slide talks, lectures, radio shows, and theater presentations rather than articles and books. These forms are both more and less accessible to popular audiences. A slide tape, for instance, may be more enjoyable, immediate, and understandable than many articles, but anyone can copy an article at the public library, whereas relatively few will see any given slide tape.

The impact of community-based history on the content of finished work is less immediately clear. The quality of lesbian and gay historical work is enormously variable, and the problems of method and theory span a wide spectrum, whether the work is academic or not, and whether it is collectively or individually produced.

Much lesbian and gay history suffers from an excessive focus on "famous figures." Enormous energy is expended on the Parisian lesbian salons of the 1920s, for instance, as well as on the lives and romantic and sexual intrigues of well-known writers and artists. At its best, such work analyzes the impact of lesbian or gay identity on a small group or an individual, while making connections to the broader social meaning of that identity in a particular time and place. At its worst, a focus on the rich and famous degenerates into historical gossip about who slept with whom, and who wore what where. A concentration on the well-known is limiting and narrows the class and racial parameters of research. Researchers continue to be drawn to the study of the well-known, however, partly because of the greater availability of sources about famous figures, and partly out of a desire to show that "we were there" among the most respected figures in western culture.

But analytical and theoretically grounded studies coexist with these celebratory works. The class, race, and gender content of research is constantly subjected to critical scrutiny. Lesbian and gay historians can expect support and encouragement from their colleagues, but they must also be prepared to be held accountable for the content of their work. At its best, such criticism is useful and enormously productive. Eric Garber's early presentations of his research, for instance, met with great enthusiasm as well as constructive criticism. Some black members of his audience pointed out that his analysis tended to focus on white gays in black Harlem rather than on Harlem's own black gay community. Garber's subsequent research benefited greatly from these early criticisms, and his emphasis shifted to reflect them. Leila Rupp's review of the work of John D'Emilio and Jonathan Katz, published in the lesbian issue of *Signs,* is another example of friendly, useful criticism—this time a lesbian's critique of the work of gay men. [16]

This critical community has also fostered work with important theoretical implications. In fact, historians have developed much of the theoretical work underlying and supporting the gay movement, in part because many gay activists had strong roots in the New Left, which emphasized a historical analysis of present political realities. Lesbian and gay historians have asked questions about the origins of gay liberation and lesbian feminism and have come up with some surprising answers. Rather than finding a silent, oppressed gay minority in all times and places, historians have discovered that gay identity is a recent western historical construction. Jeffrey Weeks, Jonathan Katz, and Lillian Faderman, for example, have traced the emergence of lesbian and gay

identity in the late nineteenth century.[17] Similarly, John D'Emilio, Allan
Berube, and the Buffalo Oral History Project have described how this identity
laid the basis for organized political activity in the years following World War
II.[18]

The work of lesbian and gay historians has also demonstrated that human
sexuality is not a natural, timeless "given" but is historically shaped and
politically regulated. Their work has serious implications for the history of
sexuality and the history of gender relations, the family, social movements,
and cultural change and conflict. But the ghettoization of lesbian and gay
history limits its impact on other fields of historical research. Few historians
outside the lesbian and gay ghetto read or see lesbian and gay history. Historical research and social theory are thereby impoverished.

Enthusiastic audiences across the country have greeted this diverse work in
lesbian and gay history. Slide shows in some senses "create" an audience for
gay history. They are presented as social and political events and are often
attended by people otherwise unacquainted with gay history. Different portions of the audience often have different, and sometimes conflicting, expectations. Some lesbians and gay men translate their need for a sense of pride
into a desire for respectability, and so expect lesbian and gay history to provide them with a "cleaned up" version of the past. The "yuppie" segments of
the audience are especially embarrassed by images of gay male transvestites
and street hustlers, or by images of "butch" and "femme" lesbians. This
segment of the audience sometimes complains that such images are "negative" because they are not conventionally respectable. Other lesbians and gay
men translate a need for pride and self-validation into the opposite expectation: they want to see the whole range of lesbian and gay life reflected in
historical work, including the underground or culturally oppositional sub-
cultures within the gay community.

This division in the audience is partly a class difference: upwardly mobile
professionals project their desire for respectability onto the past, while working-class, ethnic, black, and hispanic groups wish to see their own experiences reflected without apology. The division is also political. The more conservative "civil rights" wing of the gay movement emphasizes respectability
and tends to define a "positive" role model as a well-dressed, prosperous
white professional in the present as well as in the past. The more radical wing
of the gay and lesbian-feminist movements, on the other hand, emphasizes
inclusion and presents political and cultural criticism of dominant class- and
gender-based expectations for individual and mass behavior. Audience reception of work by lesbian and gay historians thus outlines the divisions in the

lesbian and gay community at the same time that it helps to define and unify that community.

Occasionally lesbian and gay history is presented outside the arena of the "gay liberation ghetto." For example, when lesbians and gay men are fighting for a civil rights law or battling discriminatory legislation, such as the defeated Briggs initiative in California, which would have made it illegal to "advocate" homosexuality in the public schools, the cultural and intellectual resources of lesbian and gay communities are mobilized to make a public case.[19] In these circumstances the requirements of political expediency—expressed as the need for the most "positive" and publicly acceptable images of lesbians and gay men—and the need for a theoretically sophisticated, inclusive, and critical history can clash. The best history does not always seem to make the best propaganda. Nonetheless, some historians are struggling to combine complex historical analysis with pro-gay public policy efforts. John D'Emilio's affidavit, filed in the U.S. Court of Appeals in a Texas gay rights case, is one example of a successful attempt to combine these two goals.[20]

The major questions before lesbian and gay historians are these: How do we continue to grow? How do we break down the barriers that keep us underfunded and ghettoized, while maintaining our vital roots in the political communities that give us our strength? How do we continue to democratize, to more fully represent the multiple lesbian and gay communities, without fragmenting our work or sacrificing institutional cohesion? How do we learn the practice of critical historical inquiry in the context of a community under attack and in need of uplift and protection?

The answers to these questions have as much to do with the political future of the lesbian and gay movement as they do with historical practice per se. Right now, that future seems quite fragile. The past few years have seen increasing attacks on the basic rights of lesbians and gay men, and this repressive trend will probably continue for some years to come, eroding our gains and putting us on the defensive. At the same time, further gains continue to accrue, even in mainstream settings. The Lesbian Herstory Archives received foundation funding for a computer system; Allan Berube was awarded a grant for independent historical research; the University of Chicago Press has made a continuing effort to publish gay and lesbian history. And even the ghettoized and limited accomplishments of the recent past represent a historical watershed.

The successes and limitations of the lesbian and gay history movement also have implications for community and public history efforts in general. On the positive side, lesbian and gay historians have demonstrated what can be accomplished with very slender resources when historical work is closely connected to the community being studied. They have also shown some potential for a more democratic historical practice in community settings and have forged new ways of combining theoretically sophisticated research with a political commitment to the needs of an oppressed group. On the negative side, the experience of lesbian and gay history projects and archives shows the fragility of community-based efforts without more stable institutional supports. Many do not survive; even those that do have a limited impact on the historical consciousness of a broader public. The challenge for lesbian and gay history is essentially the same as that for community and public history more generally—how can historical work be made more acceptable to the mainstream, while retaining its emotional impact and political edge?

Feminism, Film, and Public History

In the mid-1970s, not long after feminist historians began to write the history of women, feminist filmmakers began to film it. One of the first efforts to create a public history of working women was *Union Maids,* directed by Julia Reichert, Jim Klein, and Miles Mogelescu and released in 1976. Lyn Goldfarb and Lorraine Gray's *With Babies and Banners* (1978) and Connie Field's *The Life and Times of Rosie the Riveter* (1980) soon followed. All three have not only proven to be classroom favorites but have also reached nonacademic audiences through community showings, theatrical distribution, and television airings. Responding to the popular interest in women's history sparked by the feminist movement, these films have brought the story of American labor militancy to a broader public and shown some of the links between women, labor, and the struggle for racial justice.

Because they have won such a strong following, it is appropriate to look at the issues raised by the use of documentary film in public history generally, and by these films particularly. Film has the advantage of flexibility and accessibility for filmmakers bent on reaching a wide audience with alternatives to mainstream history. But the use of film poses a number of challenges. All documentary filmmakers confront problems of fundraising, distribution, and the translation of factual material into visual forms that are both informative and entertaining.[1] Many, in addition, feel the need to consider the intellectual and political issues raised by radical and feminist historiography and film criticism. Although film critics and filmmakers are more concerned with questions of form and historians with those of content, the difference is one of degree rather than of kind. Members of both groups share a commitment to demystifying the past and fostering a critical consciousness in the public.

BY SONYA MICHEL

293

Yet these two goals can put them at cross-purposes, for experimental film techniques often go down badly with popular audiences. With this in mind, the makers of radical public history documentaries have tended to be less formally experimental than other independent filmmakers, focusing primarily on content and apparently assuming that a suitable film style would arise more or less naturally from the subject matter itself. But this approach often lapses into an updated form of socialist realism, with all of its attendant problems. To the extent that they move beyond this, the three films under review here succeed in transforming the conventional left documentary film into a vehicle for a new kind of public history. Before evaluating their strengths and weaknesses, let us look more closely at the challenge posed by a radical cultural critique.

In response to the thrust of Marxist cultural criticism, radical filmmakers and critics have long been concerned with the problem of ideology. They have been critical of the ways in which mass culture reinforces the hegemony of the dominant class, but they have also understood that socialist realism cannot dissolve false consciousness by simply asserting "the truth." Rather, they have attempted to understand how the medium of film serves to reproduce ideology—how it works on its audience—so that they may devise ways to offset this effect; they have sought to learn how an audience comes to question what is presented to it, so that they can create films that foster not certainty but a critical consciousness.[2] In this sense the problem of radical filmmakers is similar to that faced by radical historians and teachers who believe that they have their own insights to communicate but also want their students to learn to reach independent conclusions through a critical process.

The filmmaker's project is both easier and more difficult. Easier insofar as film is a "lazier" medium than books, essays, or lectures—viewers need not read or take notes; they can just sit back and let it all happen to them.[3] But more difficult because filmmakers must then compensate for the propensity of film to generate a sense of reality (and hence credibility) through its immediacy, sensuousness, and naturalizing tendencies. While producers of mass culture movies exploit this propensity, certain radical filmmakers and critics have attempted to counteract it. In documentary films, this effort has taken the form of montage, cinema verité, and, most recently, the self-reflexive techniques inspired by Berthold Brecht and pioneered cinematically by Jean-Luc Godard.[4]

Self-reflexive films continually interrogate themselves and undermine their own potential to make a seamless, self-confirming statement. By exposing the conditions of production, such films demystify their origins and point to the filmmakers' role in the production of meaning. They use a variety of techniques such as multiple discourses, disrupted sequences, slowed or speeded-up pace, nonmatching sound tracks and visuals, and unanticipated shot angles to jar the perceptions of the spectator and denaturalize what occurs on the screen. The spectator is forced to play an active role not only in interpreting the film but in constructing its very meaning by piecing together disparate, incomplete, incongruous or contradictory images and sounds.[5] Although the filmmaker controls the selection and arrangement of audiovisual elements, the spectator is finally responsible for creating cinematic meaning.

One of the chief objections raised against this film style is that it often surpasses the ability, not to say the willingness, of the audience to do its part. Instead of raising critical consciousness, it may evoke derision. Feminist film critics and filmmakers have been particularly sensitive to this objection, for they are faced with a dilemma. On the one hand, feminist politics call for democratic, antielitist practice in art as in everything else. On the other hand, feminist film theory at its most radical rejects conventional discourse as "phallocentric" and calls for the construction of an entirely new cinematic language—a project that, like any form of avant-garde art, tends to exclude to the extent that it succeeds.[6] One student of feminist films proposes to resolve this dilemma by constructing an audience along with the new language.[7] This can be done through extra-cinematic means, such as reviews, critical essays, and panel discussions of film theory, but such efforts presuppose a self-conscious, highly motivated—probably academic—audience. More practical, and more to the point for public history filmmakers, would be a process of immanent education through the use of increasingly sophisticated techniques in films that, intentionally or not, form a series and thus create their own public.[8]

The three films under review here may be said to comprise such a series, not because they were actually designed to do so, but because they attract a common audience through shared subject matter. While all three contribute to the same branch of public history, each has a distinct focus. *Union Maids* treats the history of women in the trade union movement, primarily in the 1930s; *Babies and Banners* recreates the role women played in the United Auto Workers' sit-down strike of 1937; *Rosie the Riveter* illuminates the experience of women in the industrial work force during World War II. The three films share form as well as content: they all employ a technique that has been labeled, somewhat disparagingly, as "talking heads"—that is, people speaking into the camera—but do so in a way that the film critic Julia Lesage has identified as particularly feminist.[9] Lorraine Gray has said that in *Babies and Banners* she sought an "in-the-kitchen atmosphere" where "women talk to each other over a cup of coffee and get down to the real nitty-gritty of what their feelings are."[10] This technique becomes progressively more complex in the three films, so that viewers who see all of them will not only learn a great deal of history but also become more critical watchers of films. Nevertheless, there are problems in all three that illustrate some of the difficulties inherent in turning history into cinema.

The "talking-head" technique links these films to two separate epistemological codes or sources—that of oral history and that of the consciousness-raising group. Lesage, in an essay on feminist documentaries, notes that "the structure of the consciousness-raising group becomes the deep structure [of these films] repeated over and over." This effect is the result of the fact that the filmmakers identify closely with their subjects, participate (sometimes with their subjects) in the women's movement, and make films with feminist intentions. In each of the three films discussed here, the filmmakers are seen or heard at some point. This acknowledgment of their presence serves several purposes. First, it deconstructs the question of "authorship" of the film, and thus any illusion that the subjects are simply speaking spontaneously. At the same time, according to Lesage, it creates or recreates the sense of mutual discourse, of having one's experience validated by telling it to someone else who is interested in hearing it—a phenomenon central to feminism and a frequent by-product of oral history.[11] In addition, the dialogue between filmmaker and subject establishes the subject as an expert on her own experience.

Lesage contends that the effect of women's telling their stories goes beyond mere "talking heads" in another important sense: a sound track full of women's voices not only lets us hear strong women tell about their lives but, even more important, demonstrates that some women have deliberately altered the rules of the game of sexual politics.[12] Thus, they constitute themselves not only as subjects—as actors in their own lives—but simultaneously as actors in history and in feminist politics, *and* as subject/actors in cinema.

Once women are so constituted, their discourse becomes privileged in the film; that is, we are led to believe what they have to say and to credit it over competing views. Of the three films, *Rosie* makes the most sophisticated use of this hierarchy of discourse. In several sequences, Field intercuts clips from *March of Time* propaganda films depicting women's wartime industrial work as safe, pleasant, and harmonious with testimony from her subjects detailing workplace hazards, racial and sexual discrimination, problems and other hardships. Even without the subjects' critical commentary, alert viewers might be predisposed to discredit the propaganda clips, for their saccharine tone betrays a euphemistic intent; the hierarchy of discourse in the film only confirms their doubt.

From a historian's point of view, however, these privileged subjects can become problematic if a film relies on them as sole or even primary informants. Although oral history subjects are frequently both engaging and uniquely informative, their accounts of historical events or periods can be partial, fragmentary, idiosyncratic, and sometimes deliberately or unintentionally misleading. Precisely because of their position within the situations they are describing, participants seldom regard events with the dispassion required for historical analysis or interpretation.[13]

The writer can overcome this difficulty more gracefully than the filmmaker. Writing, a historian can incorporate material from oral history interviews in an interpretive article or provide a synthetic introduction to an unbroken oral history narrative, thus granting an individual narrative its due while situating it within a range of historical discourses. But it is clumsy, not to say condescending, for a filmmaker to cut from the "talking head" of a historical actor to that of an "expert."[14] Rather, the documentarist must devise cinematic techniques for locating informants' testimony both critically and circumstantially within a larger historical context.

The three films discussed here illustrate some of the ways this can be done. All use montages of contemporary footage (and, in the case of *Rosie,* mass media graphics as well) to depict both the general mood of the country and the specific events or phenomena being discussed by the subjects. Such sequences provide a sense of the texture of the period—the look of the material culture—as well as the atmosphere of working-class life: plant interiors, machinery, assembly lines; picket lines, the faces of bosses and policemen. Yet all of these are external. When the subjects describe their responses and feelings, they not only add a dimension of intimacy to the account, but they implicitly set up an interrogation of the public by the private—often of the male perspective by the female.

It seems legitimate to ask how representative the chosen subjects are. Codes of journalistic interviewing ordinarily lead an audience to conclude that unless some specific identification is made, the people being questioned about a particular event are typical of the population involved. Filmmakers must come to terms with this phenomenon of implicit typicality in selecting their subjects, especially when making public history films. This task raised different issues in each of the documentaries discussed here.

The women in *Babies and Banners,* apparently chosen at random from those who had belonged to the Women's Emergency Brigade in the 1937 sit-down strike at General Motors, were supposedly representative in age, race, and marital status of Brigade members. Yet Lillian Hatcher, the only black woman in the film, was married to a man who actually worked at Chrysler, not GM. The film is dominated by Genora Dollinger, who was clearly a leader in 1937 and still is in the 1977 confrontation with the UAW on behalf of women's issues. She seems to be well known to the other women being interviewed, suggesting that perhaps they were part of an inner leadership group. If this was the case, their account of the Brigade would take on a certain cast—legitimate enough, if it were made clear. But since Gray and Goldfarb never clarify their principles of selection, the status of their subjects' accounts remains in question.[15]

There is a better match between selection and intention in *Union Maids*. Two of the three women who relate their experiences had been interviewed by Staughton and Alice Lynd for their book, *Rank and File*.[16] Their self-described commitment and life-long activism lend these women a certain celebrity, an implicit atypicality—an impression that is reinforced by their near-total silence on certain issues, like work-family tensions and sex-role conflicts, that usually crop up in working women's accounts of their experiences. But since they never claim to describe the general experience of women in the 1930s or even that of most female labor activists, they do not create a false impression that their lives were typical. Accepting this qualification means, however, that the filmmakers must also accept a certain limitation in the scope of their project and its potential for inspiring identification by large numbers of women with similar experiences.

Rosie seemingly seeks the opposite effect, presenting women who, although few in number, vary in many ways. Its filmmakers interviewed some 700 women and then chose five to be filmed, ostensibly because they represented the whole population of working women (or at least the sample interviewed). But the results are somewhat misleading. Of the five, three are black, one Jewish, one white Protestant; three worked in California, one in the Midwest, and one in New York. Although there was a substantial amount of war industry all over the country (the South is the one area notably missing), the geographic distribution is not as far off as the racial balance: although black women were disproportionately represented in the work force both before and during the war, they still made up only about 11 percent of the total female work force at its peak in 1944.[17] All five women apparently were or had been married (one was a widow), four had children, and all were working-class. Even though wartime employment drew more married women into the work force than ever before, there was still a sizable percentage of single women whose experience is not represented here. Nor do we learn how the many middle-class "Rosies" dealt with wartime challenges.

By concentrating on married, working-class women, Field apparently intended to dispel the myth that the wartime work force consisted primarily of middle-class women who did not need jobs and were more than willing to give them up when the war was over. She shows how this impression was created at the time by using *March of Time* clips in which several women attested that it was not only their patriotic duty but their heartfelt desire to yield their jobs to deserving veterans as soon as the war ended. (At a screening of *Rosie,* one of the women featured in it, Lola Weixel, wryly commented that since many of the jobs came into being with the growth of defense industries, they had not belonged to men before the war—and did not exist after it.) Although a 1944 Women's Bureau survey contradicts the notion that these sentiments were predominant (75 percent of the women interviewed wanted to continue working after the war), a significant number of women *did* want to go home, and their consciousness should have been explored as well.[18]

The lack of critical context for the oral histories becomes even more problematic when we turn to the films' treatment of the political dimension of working women's experience. Providing only the testimony of their subjects, all three leave the impression that much of women's activism occurred in a political vacuum. In *Babies and Banners,* for example, all the women were wearing red berets, but while several mention receiving training and organizing assistance from both the Communist and Socialist parties, they neither affirm nor deny membership in either. One is left wondering how the long history of sectarian tensions in the UAW played itself out in the Brigade.[19] Similarly, the political affiliations of the three subjects in *Union Maids* are never fully clarified, although Kate Hyndman brings out newspaper articles from the 1950s redbaiting her. In *Rosie* two of the subjects delimit the political topography of the 1940s: Lola Weixel obliquely refers to herself as a "working person" with "progressive ideas"; not surprisingly, she led efforts to organize her welding shop for the United Electrical Workers. Her euphemisms contrast markedly with an anecdote related by Lyn Childs: when her shipyard boss accused her of being a "commie," she unhesitatingly affirmed that if sticking up for a fellow worker meant being a commie, then by golly, she was!

Such indirection suggests that many of the people interviewed in these films may have been reluctant to discuss their political pasts openly. Yet at least one "union maid," Stella Nowicki, had already related her activities as a member of the Young Communist League and the Communist Party in *Rank and File.* This indicates that perhaps the filmmakers, not the subjects, chose to omit information about the left. Whatever the reasons, all three films leave a rather confused impression of the links between the left and the labor movement, a connection that is a central concern of twentieth-century labor historians. The dilemma for filmmakers who rely on oral history subjects for the content of their work is to avoid reproducing political mystification while respecting and safeguarding the privacy of their subjects.

From a feminist perspective, these films raise a different set of questions about the politics of film: how are women presented on the screen? According to one school of thought, any cinematic representation of women within patriarchal culture inevitably constitutes them as objects of desire.[20] Lesage disagrees with this position, arguing that it is possible to "decolonize women's sexuality," to overcome objectification through the presentation of female subjectivity, especially with regard to their own sexuality and physicality.[21] The films considered here tend to confirm Lesage's contention.

All the subjects are women in their late fifties or older; according to the patriarchal code governing female sexuality, these women are almost automatically desexualized on the basis of age alone.[22] But by discussing issues of sexuality in their pasts, they resexualize themselves, this time in a particularly feminist way that simultaneously calls attention to the narrowness of the patriarchal code and evokes their sexuality from a subjective point of view. This process is paralleled on the visual level, reaching a high degree of complexity in *Rosie*. Field sets up a tripartite interrogation of women's visual representation: the mass-culture iconography of the 1940s, illustrated by propaganda film clips and magazine graphics; candid photographs of the subjects and other women taken during the period; and images of the subjects today. The subjects first appear in the present, commenting on their wartime experience; they are established as individuals—as historical actors—before we see them as young women. Timed otherwise, these images might have the effect of validating the patriarchal code of female beauty (only attractive young women are worth attending to—and even then are not to be taken seriously), but as assembled here, they interrogate the code by making viewers aware of the changes in physical appearance that inevitably occur over time.

The film also draws attention to the relationship between women and mass culture. The wartime photographs indicate that each woman in her own way followed fashion and maintained a conventionally "feminine" appearance (at least off the job) while working in a defense plant. Such behavior is ordinarily regarded as evidence of the dominant influence of mass culture—women under the influence of advertising and marketing. Feminine style, moreover, is usually associated with fragility and vulnerability. Yet the recollections of these women affirm their actual strength and independence during this period. The contradiction between their testimony and the connotations of style suggests that women followed fashion from choice. Wanita Allen comments that while some people saved as much as they could (memories of the Depression were still vivid), she spent money on anything she could find; her voice is heard over a photograph of herself sitting in a night club, a fur stole draped prominently over one shoulder and a sparkling smile on her lips. For Allen, spending money on expensive clothing and jewelry was an outward sign of her new-found economic independence. She was not a "conspicuous consumer" in Thorstein Veblen's sense, for she was not parading her husband's wealth but rather enjoying the fruits of her own labor.

In providing this sort of insight into the meanings of women's wartime jobs, *Rosie* marks another point in the progression of films about women and work, a broadening of their scope. *Union Maids* followed the contours of conventional labor history, fitting women into previously established categories. Yet even while it was doing so, the film implicitly challenged and transformed these categories. Its three subjects established beyond question that women had a crucial role in day-to-day shopfloor struggles in the 1930s (struggles previously presumed to have been waged only by men). For workers, management, and the labor movement alike, it was not immaterial that these militant actions were undertaken by *women*. The union maids, however, tell us little about the relationship of work and politics to their personal lives. Except for brief references to their childhoods, they give the impression of having spent their entire lives at work or in union activities. Moreover, they maintain an almost Victorian silence on the question of sexuality and the labor struggle. While it is important to affirm women's identity as workers and as activists, it would seem to be a capitulation to a sexist form of economism to assume that women in these roles have the same experience as men. By focusing only on discrimination against women by management, *Union Maids* cannot account for the ways in which family life and patriarchal ideology and culture also subordinate women within the work force.

Babies and Banners took the analysis one step further, although its focus on a single event precluded a full exploration of the relationship between union activism and the rest of women's experience and gave only scant attention to women as workers in their own right. Its chief contribution was to expose the union's role in perpetuating male domination, showing how it encouraged social as well as occupational divisions between the sexes. Flint, as one Brigade woman acerbically describes it, was a town of churches and bars— churches to console the women while their men lined the bars. A double standard was clearly at work: women who dared to enter union halls risked their reputations, but the union was not above using women as buffers between all-male picket lines and the police, relying on the latter's deference to the "fair sex." (Ironically, as the film shows, the women were not as defenseless as they appeared; they were armed with blackjacks fastened by garters under their sleeves!) Once the UAW strike had been won, however, male domination was reinvoked, and the Women's Emergency Brigade was dispersed and sent home.

The film attempts to show that the Brigade had unintended consequences; once organized, its members developed a new sense of themselves and felt more important. As one woman put it, the red beret they all wore became "the symbol of a new woman who was ready to make sacrifices and could be counted on"; another felt that the actions of the Brigade gave men a "different outlook on the ordinary housewife." But it is unclear whether this new consciousness produced major changes in these women's lives at home, at work, or in the UAW. Attempting to bring the struggle up to date, the film concludes with Genora Dollinger's impassioned speech at the 1977 reunion commemorating the fortieth anniversary of the strike. She recalls the courage of the Women's Emergency Brigade, and challenges the union to support the Equal Rights Amendment and allow women greater representation within its ranks. There is a suggestion here that Dollinger's latter-day feminism is a direct outgrowth of her Brigade activities, but the film fails to bear this out. Instead it appears to engage in a bit of retrospective mythmaking.

Rosie expands the framework of working women's history in several directions. It explores labor market segregation by sex and race, showing that women were generally given inferior job assignments in defense industries, with black women relegated to the menial sweeping and cleaning jobs that had been held by black men before the war. The film makes no direct comment on unions' policies toward women either during the war on in the postwar demobilization of labor. However, the job segregation experienced by its subjects in defense industries and their subsequent employment histories (all five women returned to lower-paid, unskilled or semiskilled work, mainly in the pink-collar sector) stand as mute testimony to trade union failures to challenge a job market structured by capitalist patriarchy.[23]

Both the subjects and creators of *Rosie* seem to have understood that working women's experience is not constituted by the worker-management-union triangle alone, but that personal and social issues also intervene and must be explored simultaneously. More than its predecessors, this film attempts to provide a fuller view of women's work in its personal context. Lola Weixel's account of doing the housework after a full day of welding, while her brother-in-law lay on the couch listening to jazz records, vividly illustrates the "double day" put in by most female war workers. Margaret Wright provides another version, telling how she returned home after finishing the night shift in time to wake her children, bathe and feed them, do the laundry, and fix a meal for her husband, who worked days. There is visible emotion in Lyn Child's face as she describes leaving her small daughter with her mother when she came to Oakland to work in the shipyard because a lack of housing and child care facilities made it impossible to keep the child with her. Wanita Allen also criticizes child care services, arguing that they were probably available only to middle-class women and inconveniently located (especially given gas and tire rationing) at that.

A frequent theme in wartime articles about female employment is the opposition some women had to face from their husbands. The four married women in *Rosie* had all worked before the war and recall no tension between themselves and their men; defense jobs were not only accepted but actually celebrated, since they brought in much higher wages. All the women, however, note their regret over losing satisfying and lucrative wartime jobs. Finally, both the narratives and images from contemporary footage and graphics testify to the increasing importance of female camaraderie and homosexuality during the war, phenomena that developed as women's isolation in the home (either as housewives or domestic workers) was broken down through their concentration in industry.[24]

The overall effect of wartime work on women's personal lives was, then, ambiguous: on the one hand, it produced greater strains on them and their families; on the other, it fostered individual self-confidence and group self-consciousness. Both tendencies were, of course, to play themselves out in the postwar decades. With its subtle exploration of these issues, *Rosie the Riveter* has much to contribute to current discussions among historians about the effects of the two world wars on European and American women.

Yet all three films leave many questions unanswered. They tend to lack specificity: dates, names, and places are either absent or hard to determine; connections between events are unclear. In some cases, omissions or misrepresentations were, apparently, deliberate. Lyn Goldfarb has been quoted as saying that "there was always a tension between what was historically accurate and what was visually best. We felt obligated to set the record straight, but we also wanted to be appealing."[25] Daniel Leab, reviewing *Babies and Banners* in *Labor History,* criticizes the film for numerous inaccuracies, concluding that it is "bad history," but then *defends* it as "splendid 'agit-prop,' an excellent look at the past from a feminist perspective, a consciousness-raising document of the first order. The film well deserves all the accolades it has received . . . as a film."[26] Leab's casual willingness to trade historical documentary for "agit-prop" is disturbing. Such cynicism legitimizes films that simply replace one ideology with another, "correctness" being determined by politics instead of historical accuracy. Only viewers with prior knowledge will be any the wiser.

The effect of such films is quite different from that of films in which contradictions and gaps are immanent, films that, by themselves, stimulate critical consciousness and provoke viewers to consider the issues raised and seek further. Of the three considered here, *Rosie* comes closest to meeting this standard through its use of contemporary footage in conjunction with oral history and its sophisticated interrogation of female imagery. Incorporating the feminist interview techniques that made *Union Maids* and *Babies and Banners* so appealing, it takes the feminist documentary film one step further.

But some filmmakers question whether these techniques go far enough— whether it is even possible to make documentaries that do not reproduce all the problems of socialist realism. One of these is Jill Godmilow, director of *Far from Poland* (1984). Godmilow set out to make a documentary about the female Gdansk shipyard worker whose protest against working conditions— legend has it—sparked the Solidarity movement. In the process of making the film, however, Godmilow came to question not only her own project but the entire documentary enterprise. She did not want to produce a modern epic with idealized, larger-than-life worker-heroes. Instead, she turned *Far from Poland* into a "deconstruction" of documentary. Audiences who expect the film to be a stirring tribute to the Poles leave the theater disappointed; the film has not been a popular success. Although not pleased by the public response, Godmilow is also not surprised, for she had chosen *not* to tell "the moving story of the origins of Solidarnosc" that everyone wanted to see. After one recent showing, she commented that she no longer believes in documentary films and will never make another one.[27] (She is now working on a fiction film about Gertrude Stein.) Should other radical filmmakers follow Godmilow's lead in renouncing documentaries? Perhaps not. But they cannot ignore the concerns she has expressed, for no political movement will be well served by a cinema that hopes to teach "history" through socialist or feminist realism.

ROBERT BROWNING,

POET, AND ONE OF ENGLAND'S IMMORTALS, WAS OF NEGRO DESCENT. THIS STRAIN WAS INHERITED FROM HIS GRANDMOTHER, MARGARET TITTLE, WHO WAS A NATIVE OF JAMAICA, WEST INDIES. BROWNING'S FATHER WAS SO DARK IN COLOR THAT ONCE WHEN HE WENT TO SIT AMONG THE WHITE PEOPLE IN JAMAICA, THE BEADLE OF THE CHURCH ORDERED HIM TO TAKE HIS PLACE AMONG THE COLORED PEOPLE. THOMAS CARLYLE WAS SO IMPRESSED BY ROBERT BROWNING'S DARK SKIN THAT HE MADE MENTION OF IT AND ATTRIBUTED IT TO HIS WEST INDIAN STRAIN.

Geo LEE

OCTAVE REY,

A NEGRO, POLICE CAPTAIN OF NEW ORLEANS FROM 1868 TO 1877 HAD A PRODIGIOUS MEMORY. HE NOT ONLY KNEW EVERY OFFENDER BUT THE NAME OF EVERY MAN, WOMAN, AND CHILD IN THE CITY. **REY** WHO WAS HERCULEAN BUILD, GRACEFUL PROPORTIONS, AND COURTLY MANNERS, BECAME ONE OF THE ATTRACTIONS OF THE CITY DESPITE HIS COLOR. WHEN HE DIED IN 1902 NEW ORLEANS GAVE HIM A SPLENDID PUBLIC FUNERAL. REY WAS ALSO STATE SENATOR.

ZAID BIN HARITH,

A **NEGRO** SLAVE, WHO ROSE TO BE MOHAMET'S GREATEST GENERAL AND HIS ADOPTED SON, SHOWED HIS DEVOTION TO MOHAMET BY GIVING UP TO HIM HIS WIFE, **ZAINAB**, "THE MOST BEAUTIFUL WOMAN IN ISLAM." MOHAMET, CALLED AT **ZAID'S** HOME ONE DAY WHEN HE WAS AWAY AND SAW **ZAINAB**, HE WAS SO SMITTEN BY HER BEAUTY AND GENTLENESS THAT HE BECAME HELPLESS. **ZAID** HEARING OF HIS MASTER'S INFATUATION VOLUNTARILY YIELDED HER AND SHE BECAME ONE OF MOHAMET'S WIVES.

IN 1730 THE **NEGROES** AND THE POOR **WHITES** OF MARYLAND UNITED AND TRIED TO SEIZE THE GOVERNMENT BUT WERE DEFEATED. THEIR OBJECT WAS THE ABOLITION OF ALL DEBTS.

A Faithful Witness:

Afro-American Public History in Historical Perspective, 1828–1984

Afro-American public history arose out of the twin desire to foster the black community's self-esteem and to challenge both popular and academic white racism. Like Euro-American public history, Afro-American presentations have emphasized the exemplary individual, the laudatory accomplishment, and an ideology of success. But unlike most Euro-American public history, Afro-American public history has had an oppositional quality because it chronicled the history of a community at odds with the American status quo. Black people saw themselves as a "chosen" but oppressed people who would eventually be liberated. This interpretation of the Afro-American past included stories of liberation struggles, tropes about freedom and salvation, and explicit and implicit critiques of Euro-American history.

In the past century and a half, attempts to define Afro-American public history have been characterized by several interrelated and persistent questions. First, what is Afro-American history? Is it the history of African traditions in America or the evidence of Afro-American achievement and assimilation there? Should it focus on black "heroes" or the common folk? Can it be treated separately from mainstream American history? Second, how should the Afro-American story be presented? Are public celebrations, exhibitions, heroic narratives, or academic monographs the best medium? Third, who should be the primary audience for Afro-American history? How has the class status of the historians and their audience shaped the history that has been presented and consumed? Should Afro-American history also have a white audience?

BY JEFFREY C. STEWART
and FATH DAVIS RUFFINS

Generations of black public historians have answered these questions differently. Afro-American history has been shaped by both intellectuals—a class broadly conceived as including elite academicians, self-trained historians, public school teachers, and political activists—and the mass black audience. Afro-American public history thus reflects the changing racial strategies and cultural ideologies of the black community, from integrationism to nationalism. But what has bound together successive generations of Afro-American public historians has been their opposition to the status quo and their reliance on a tradition of Afro-American debate and self-expression.

Afro-American public history has also been powerfully shaped—indeed defined—by its black audience, which has changed profoundly in the last 150 years. Before the Civil War, when 90 percent of blacks were enslaved in the rural South, the history disseminated through northern and urban literary societies found its audience primarily among a small urban working class and a tiny elite of professionals and merchants. Not until after the Great Migration of 1915 to 1930 did a large black working class emerge and become the primary audience for African and Afro-American histories written by popular historians like Joel Rogers. Negro History Week activities tapped a different component of that northward migration, a smaller but influential black middle class comprising small business men and women (the entrepreneurial bourgeoisie) and teachers, doctors, social workers, and librarians (the educational bourgeoisie). The latter group became the bulwark of Carter Woodson's Association for the Study of Negro Life and History as well as the black historical museums of the 1960s. At the same time, the new black urban underclass that emerged after the World War II migration and exploded in the urban rebellions of the mid-1960s became a new audience for black public history.[1]

Thus, the combined impact of different generations of black intellectuals, diverse black audiences, and occasional white sponsorship, especially in moments of social crisis, has forged a distinctive but changing Afro-American public history. This essay explores the shifting form and content of that history as well as the complex social forces that continue to shape it.

In the first era of Afro-American public history (1825–1900) an improvement ideology dominated black efforts to define their historical mission in America. Motivated by racism, segregation, and a sense of distinct destiny in America, Afro-Americans founded separate churches, improvement and literary societies, and benevolent associations to elevate the moral and intellectual faculties of free blacks. The notion of "improvement" carried with it the assumption that Afro-Americans would succeed in American society only by assimilating Euro-American culture. Not until the late nineteenth century did any black intellectual challenge this assumption. Thus, in the early 1800s Afro-American historical efforts were aimed at providing a besieged minority population with a heroic past defined in conventional terms. Groups such as the "Reading Room Society," founded in 1828, collected books, sponsored debates, and presented lectures in which a popular history of Africa was invoked to inspire Afro-American achievement.[2] Maria W. Stewart, for example, told her listeners at Boston's African Masonic hall in 1833 that "history informs us that we sprung from one of the most learned nations of the whole earth; from the seat, if not the parent of science, yes, poor despised Africa was once the resort of sages and legislators of other nations . . . and the most illustrious men of Greece flocked thither for instruction."[3]

But Maria Stewart used this history to exhort the "African" in America to political and social activism, as well as to individual achievement. She and other black elite spokespersons invoked black history to stimulate self-assertion in their audience, calling on free blacks in the North to fight for their citizenship rights. They also used history to refute the American Colonization Society's recommendation that blacks be returned to Africa because of their lack of cultural achievement.[4]

The earliest audience for this history was the free black community in the urban North. In such cities as Philadelphia, New York, Boston, and Washington, D.C., free "people of color" had established stable black communities by the late eighteenth century that maintained separate churches, lodges, and schools, in part because of northern discrimination. Although a tiny entrepreneurial elite led these communities, most northern free blacks were not wealthy. The Afro-American history audience encompassed poor but pious ministers and schoolteachers, clerks and cooks, and even valets and housekeepers of wealthy white families.[5]

Still, consciousness of class distinctions shaped the presentation of Afro-American history in the antebellum North. Improvement ideology represented the entrepreneurial elite's belief that racial prejudice was caused—at least in part—by genuine deficiencies among black people.[6] Stewart and her fellow lecturers believed that their unlettered free Negro working-class audience could best refute racism by pointing to the moral respectability, intellectual sophistication, and "correct" behavior of the black elite. Stewart's history rationalized the elite's assimilationist strategy by arguing that learning, science, and achievement were not white values but a forgotten African tradition. By creating institutions, holding meetings, and attending lectures, often in formal attire, the black elite created a model of assimilated behavior for both white critics and the unlettered masses.

This assimilationist strategy infused the first published work of Afro-American history, William C. Nell's *The Colored Patriots of the American Revolution* (1854), an evocation of black exploits and achievements in the American Revolution. A "Black Brahmin" as well as an activist who helped desegregate Boston's public schools in the 1850s, Nell was the archetypical nineteenth-century Afro-American public historian: like Anglo-American gentlemen historians of the period, Nell saw himself as charged with a holy mission to draw attention to the strengths of his race, but like other ethnic historians of the period, Nell believed that he preserved a neglected history. In his words, he served as a "faithful witness" of the "true history" of Afro-Americans, which, once known and disseminated, would stimulate self-esteem and self-assertion among his own people and prove to whites that Afro-Americans deserved all the benefits of American citizenship.[7]

The Civil War gave improvement ideology a new lease on life, with millions of newly emancipated southern blacks revealed as in desperate need of "uplift." White philanthropists, among them General Samuel Chapman Armstrong who founded Hampton Institute, built educational institutions to help blacks improve themselves intellectually and to create economic opportunities.[8] The most popular theme in post–Civil War Afro-American public history was the celebration of Afro-American heroes, most notably Frederick Douglass. As a former slave who became one of the most famous and influential men in America, Douglass exhibited all the traits that Afro-American public history extolled. Here was the emblematic self-made man who showed that self-improvement was possible for Afro-Americans. When he died in 1895, his second wife, Helen Pitts Douglass, a white woman, enlisted the aid of elite Afro-Americans to preserve his Anacostia home at Cedar Hill. Calling the house a "Black Mount Vernon," she was instrumental in the formation of the Frederick Douglass Memorial and Historical Association. Over the next sixty years, preservation of the Douglass Home became a major activity for such groups as the National Association of Colored Women.[9]

Like the Douglass Home, the first Afro-American historical collections— most notably those of Lewis Tappan and Jesse Moorland at Howard University—emphasized the similarity of blacks to other Americans and the veneration of mainstream American cultural values. Moorland's collection, like the earlier literary societies, ostensibly preserved the history of all Afro-Americans but, in fact, neglected the cultural history of the masses and collected instead the autobiographies and narratives of exemplary individuals.[10] Similarly, the late nineteenth-century historical societies—for example, the American Negro Historical Society (1897) and the New York Society for Historic Research (1890)—preferred to gather materials about Negro influences in Europe than to uncover evidence about American slavery.[11]

But in the late nineteenth century, new voices challenged the aggressively assimilationist cultural ideology implicit in most improvement strategies. For example, the Museum at Hampton was established in 1868 to uplift students through contact with world culture. But when Cora Mae Folsom became museum curator shortly after 1880, she began collecting historical objects for a different purpose: to promote self-knowledge among black and Indian students. Together with William Sheppard, Folsom amassed a collection of historical and anthropological objects that presented an African alternative to the ideology of self-improvement through assimilation.[12]

As a young man educated early in the Reconstruction period, Sheppard imbibed the post–Civil War missionary idea that Afro-Americans should "improve" the barbarian Africans. But when Sheppard went to Africa in 1890 to bring Christianity and European civilization to his unenlightened brethren, he discovered a complex and sophisticated Africa in the early phases of European colonization. Sheppard amassed a large collection of African artifacts from the Kuba peoples of the Congo and sold it to the Hampton Museum in 1911. Although Sheppard continued to believe in the need for education and advancement, he rejected the notion that wholesale assimilation of Euro-American values was necessarily an improvement for black people. Instead, Sheppard taught that identification with Africa was crucial to creating an Afro-American identity.[13]

Before the twentieth century, few shared Sheppard's respect for African culture: most black public historians, like the black elite generally, accepted Social Darwinist notions about the "backwardness" of unlettered Africans and Afro-Americans. They ignored black folk culture and applauded its disappearance. But by the turn of the century, new voices began to proclaim the importance of the African inheritance as well as the unique qualities of the Afro-American vernacular culture—a culture unmistakably derived from the formerly enslaved masses of southern black people. Members of this group founded the Boston Society for the Collection of Negro Folklore in the 1890s to preserve a heritage that, they saw, was fast disappearing.[14] W. E. B. Du Bois was an unusual scholar who drew attention to Afro-American folk culture. Like William C. Nell, Du Bois was on a preservation mission. But what he wished to preserve was not primarily evidence of heroic actions by the assimilated elite but the unique "sorrow songs"—spirituals sung by slaves—of nineteenth-century Afro-American folk culture. As a result, he laid the foundation for other scholars to collect and preserve the myths, jokes, toasts, and tales of southern black vernacular culture.[15]

Still, Du Bois reflected the nineteenth-century Afro-American elite's ambivalence toward the Afro-American masses. Though a political radical—an early Pan-Africanist and later a Marxist—Du Bois was a true inheritor of Brahmin elite culture. Men and women like him began to be crowded out of their old neighborhoods and churches by the floodtide of southern migration in the early twentieth century. These migrants jarred the sensibilities of the northern Afro-American elite. Intellectuals could not completely abandon the notion that the masses needed improvement, not only in terms of education and technical skills, but also in terms of cultural style and manners. The elite maintained its social distance from the masses even as its members extolled their indigenous folk virtues.

Yet the rigid racial prejudice and evolving segregation of the North ensured that black intellectuals like Du Bois could not leave the masses behind. As *The Souls of Black Folk* (1903) chronicled, the black scholar-advocate was forced to confront the Afro-American folk culture by teaching in rural southern schools and segregated colleges, writing for independent black newspapers, and creating a history that spoke to the needs of the Afro-American mass public. As a result, independent black institutions, including cultural organizations and museums, benefited directly from an infusion of intellectual talent, even though these intellectuals carried with them ambivalent and contradictory notions about the value of Afro-American culture.

D uring the first decades of the twentieth century, such young Afro-American intellectuals as Du Bois and Carter G. Woodson emerged from white universities to face an unprecedented tide of Jim Crow segregation, disenfranchisement, and white terror. A racist academic history flourished, which—from the "Teutonic" George Bancroft to the "scientific" William Dunning and his followers at Columbia University—lent credibility to popular notions of black inferiority. In addition, the popular histories of Thomas Dixon, Claude Bowers, and many others depicted Reconstruction as a moment of unparalleled violence, depravity, and corruption, for which Negroes were to blame. D. W. Griffith's *The Birth of a Nation* (1915), further inscribed on the popular mind the idea that the Negro had to be kept down if civilization in the United States was to be preserved.[16]

At the same time, crises in race relations galvanized the concern of white liberals. After the vicious Springfield riot of 1908, in which whites burned and looted the black section of the city of Lincoln's birth, William Walling, a southern liberal, convened a small conference of white leftists that eventually led to the formation of the National Association for the Advancement of Colored People (NAACP) in 1910. That same year the National Urban League was formed to assist black migrants to northern cities. Like other Progressives, the black and white founders of the NAACP and the Urban League believed that society could solve its problems through voluntary organizations. They also believed that racism was a moral evil, like political corruption or alcoholism, that could be rooted out by education and the exercise of political and legal power. In this context of Progressive era voluntarism and optimism, Carter G. Woodson founded the Association for the Study of Negro Life and History (ASNLH) in 1915.[17]

The ASNLH was a cultural adjunct of the NAACP and the Urban League, and its program paralleled their reform strategy. Woodson wanted to use Negro history to combat white racism and build black self-esteem. During the association's first ten years, Woodson focused its efforts on correcting the errors and biases of contemporary white scholarship, rather than disseminating popular histories. He began collecting primary sources that were eventually placed at the Library of Congress, founded the respected *Journal of Negro History* and Associated Publishers, Inc., and wrote several scholarly works of his own. Woodson also encouraged white scholars to join his Executive Council and solicited money and endorsements from white foundations and organizations. Despite that white presence, ASNLH gave black scholars, who were excluded from white professional organizations, a forum and a sense of community. In these early years of operation, the annual meetings of the association included schoolteachers, ministers, and businesspeople from the black middle class along with scholars. Yet the ASNLH resembled nineteenth-century literary and historical societies in that it catered more to the elite—the "talented tenth," in Du Bois's terminology—than to the black masses.[18]

No sooner had Woodson founded the ASNLH than the wartime Great Migration permanently altered the Afro-American history audience. From 1915 to 1930 millions of blacks migrated from the rural South to such cities as New York, Chicago, Pittsburgh, and Cleveland to take jobs in war industries. Significant class divisions emerged in these northern cities as the elite was inundated by a Southern-born peasantry and a middle class of doctors, ministers, and entrepreneurs who followed their clientele northward. Marcus Garvey tapped the latent racial nationalism of these migrants with a blend of self-improvement ideology and religious millennialism that enabled him to build the largest black mass movement of his time. Garvey linked the Afro-American public to its African heritage and argued that blacks from both the American South and the West Indies were all part of one oppressed, transplanted race victimized by white imperialism.[19]

The new urban black working and middle-classes became the backbone of Garvey's Universal Negro Improvement Association (UNIA) and the most important new audience for Afro-American history in the 1920s. At UNIA meetings participants encountered popular books, essays, and pamphlets that told of black contributions to world history and of a great, civilized Africa that had blossomed before European contact. Such self-trained Afro-American historians as Joel A. Rogers, James Webb, and George Wells Parker refuted white claims that Europeans were the sole creators of "civilization." For the black masses gathering in the cities from diverse social and geographic backgrounds, these histories of a glorious African past provided an untainted common heritage. Race histories aided the rite of passage for the rural black people who had left the South with great hopes for redemptive freedom in the North, only to encounter urban crowding, unemployment, and white racist violence.[20]

One of the most remarkable of these popular historians was Drusilla Houston, an Oklahoma City schoolteacher, who spent years in libraries poring over ancient history books in order to reconstruct the influence of black Ethiopians on Egyptian, Greek, and Mediterranean culture. In *Wonderful Ethiopians of the Ancient Cushite Empire* (1926), she pioneered the study of the influence of indigenous African peoples on world civilization. Houston's insistence on the primacy of Ethiopians in the making of modern civilization kept her and other black popular historians from reaching a white audience. Her work succeeded with its black mass audience precisely for the reasons that the white audience would have found it distasteful: her history directly challenged pervasive Eurocentric and white-supremacist notions of the development of civilization.[21]

But lack of formal training and academic credentials remained the Achilles heel of the Afro-American popular historians of the 1920s. Houston's was essentially a nineteenth-century history of the ancient world with one difference: the Ethiopians rather than the Europeans were the solitary authors of civilization. Houston seems to have been unaware of Columbia University anthropologist Franz Boas's theory that civilization is the product of the interaction of diverse races and that nonwhite cultures should not be evaluated in terms of European standards or achievements. Academically trained black writers such as Alain Locke, Zora Neale Hurston, and Langston Hughes used

Boas' ideas to show that Afro-Americans possessed a distinct folk culture rooted in the rural South and flowering anew in the urban North—a culture that black popular historians ignored. Indeed, Houston, Joel A. Rogers, and Arthur Schomburg, the black bibliophile, abhorred "lower-class" forms of popular culture such as jazz. These popular historians had not broken with nineteenth-century improvement ideology; their black history accepted a European cultural framework.

No lay historian felt more intensely the disadvantage of not having a college degree than Arthur Alfonso Schomburg. Born in Puerto Rico in 1874, he migrated to Brooklyn and on a bank clerk's salary bartered, brokered, and bought thousands of books, essays, and primary source documents in black history. Schomburg was part of the old historical society establishment, serving as a book purchaser and lecturer for the Yonkers Negro Historical Society and later as president of the American Negro Academy. Evidence of Negro influence in Europe fascinated Schomburg, and as a Puerto Rican, he pioneered in the study of Caribbean and South American black history. But his most important contribution was his vast and amorphous collection, which he directed first in his Brooklyn home and then at the 135th Street Branch of the New York Public Library, which purchased his collection in 1926 with a $10,000 Carnegie Foundation grant. Ironically, as his biographer, Elinor Sinnette, points out, this black pride collection was purchased by white philanthropists who were "far removed from the Harlem community and the concerns of black identity."[23]

Still the purchase of Schomburg's collection helped make the 135th Street Branch Harlem's cultural center, the scene, for example, of Harlem street historian Hubert Harrison's weekly lectures on Afro-American history as well as exhibitions of African and Afro-American art. James Baldwin recalls the Schomburg Branch in the 1930s as a refuge from the constricted ghetto for intellectually oriented Harlemites. It was an early model of what black museums would become in the 1960s—a community institution where people from different groups and classes could interact, exchange ideas, and redefine their collective mission.[24]

It was left to Carter G. Woodson, however, to develop a viable economic base for black historical institutions that was fully independent of white philanthropy. During the 1920s Woodson realized that the ASNLH had left out an important clientele for black history—the black masses. Association meetings had, of course, always included a limited number of ministers, doctors, and teachers. But scholarly papers on black history failed to evoke broad-based support. Impressed by Garvey's success in creating a mass movement for black pride, Woodson decided to direct more of the ASNLH's energies toward providing programs on black history to the general public. In 1926 he founded the association's Home Study Department and Lecture Bureau, which engaged scholars with graduate degrees to teach extension courses and offer public lectures on Afro-American history. He also devised Negro History Week, his most successful strategy for publicizing black history. That celebration took place in February between the birthdays of Abraham Lincoln and Frederick Douglass and consisted of lectures, speeches, and discussions on topics of Negro history. The association served as a clearinghouse for Negro History Week observances, producing and distributing books, pamphlets, bibliographies, and photographs to school boards, newspapers, and community organizations, which designed and implemented their own programs.[25]

Negro History Week was an instant success in part because it was launched during the peak of the Harlem Renaissance, the black literary arts movement that spread rapidly through northern cities in the 1920s. Afro-American history played an important role in the effort to celebrate a distinctive black cultural identity and educate whites to the humanity of blacks. Negro history, wrote Schomburg in his essay for Alain Locke's anthology *The New Negro* (1925), was essential to the self-confident identity of the "New Negro." But unlike Harlem Renaissance projects, which often appealed to a predominantly white or elite audience, Woodson presented Negro History Week activities in black schools, churches, and social clubs. Although the popular historians continued to attract the black masses, Woodson reached a wider spectrum that included the black masses, the old Negro middle class of the premigration urban North, and the new Negro middle class recently arrived from the South.[26]

Woodson captured a new audience for Afro-American public history because he moved beyond exhibiting historical materials in "societies" and libraries and took that history directly to the people in local churches and schools. His most important advance was working with schoolteachers, many of whom were more willing to promote a Negro history produced by a professional association such as Woodson's than one produced by such self-trained historians as Hubert Harrison and Arthur Schomburg. Woodson successfully cultivated a new audience, the educational bourgeoisie of the urban North, who were becoming more concerned with professionalism and found in Negro History Week a way to participate in the decade's consciousness-raising experiment in cultural self-appreciation.[27]

By broadening his association to include public history, Woodson more effectively engaged the black audience; but he had not given up his intention of reaching a white audience. His goal was not a Negro history per se, but rather "a history influenced by the Negro," and he sought to have Negro History Week observed in both white and black and northern and southern school systems.[28] His most successful efforts, however, came within the black community. In February 1930, for example, Woodson and Lorenzo Greene, a graduate student, organized a "Monster Mass Meeting" in Washington, D.C. This politically oriented Negro History Week celebration brought together three Afro-American congressmen: Oscar De Priest, the Chicagoan then serving in Congress, and two Reconstruction era representatives—John R. Lynch of Mississippi and Thomas E. Miller of South Carolina. Organized in one month with funds raised by subscription to the event, the celebration attracted more than 2,000 Afro-Americans during the Great Depression to hear speeches by the congressmen that blended Reconstruction revisionism with contemporary political criticism.[29] Lynch, for example, "characterized as honorable the records made by the Negro in congress and carefully discriminated between the actual facts of history and the perversion of it by propagandists who for more than three generations have been trying to discredit the Negro through slander."[30] When Oscar De Priest took the podium, he used the past to criticize the American present: "It is worse than a crime to witness in the United States the gross intolerance which exists in a country famed for its foundation on the rock of liberty. To think that millions of citizens are disenfranchised of the Constitution is appalling."[31]

By bringing forth black Reconstruction congressmen who were largely unknown to the Afro-American audience, this event contradicted the larger society's claim that blacks were unfit for political office. Woodson and Greene, moreover, established the historical continuity of the black political perspective and provided a revisionist interpretation of Black Reconstruction that was years ahead of mainstream academic history.[32] This celebration not only stimulated black racial pride, but also challenged the black community to fight for its civil rights by invoking the memory of its earlier political activism.

Greene and Woodson were able to present this critique of Reconstruction historiography because their celebration was financed by a community whose historical consciousness was at odds with mainstream history and its financial supporters. They advertised the event and raised funds for it by speaking in black churches, schools, and fraternal associations in the Washington area. A testimonial dinner with the names of contributors listed on the program gave visibility and prestige to those who supported the venture. At every stage they involved the community and encouraged an identification with the celebration.[33]

The popularity of this politically explicit public history event suggests the new mood of the Afro-American public of the early 1930s. Suffering hardship during the Depression, the Afro-American community was increasingly concerned with the economic and political situation of blacks in America and the Afro-American role in American political history. Woodson and Greene had captured the mood of a public that desired a more directly political critique of the American status quo in public history celebrations. Such inexpensive forms as Negro History Week allowed local black communities to express their political needs without having to rely on white funding.

Public history events became even more important to the survival of the ASNLH after 1933, when white foundations stopped funding its activities. Starting in the mid-1920s, white foundations demanded that Woodson affiliate his association with a Negro college or university, but Woodson refused: his own negative experience at Howard University in early 1920 had convinced him that black colleges could not be trusted, because they were controlled by meddlesome white trustees. With the end of white support, Woodson obtained funding from Negro fraternities, sororities, college professors, secondary school teachers, women's clubs, churches, and mail carrier groups.[34]

Pruning back the association's scholarly work, Woodson concentrated his resources on projects that served this new supporting public. He encouraged black teachers' groups to take courses and buy books from the association. And he began publishing books directed at general and high school readers. According to his biographer, Jacqueline Goggin, he began the *Negro History Bulletin* in 1937 specifically because "public school teachers, clubs, and church organizations frequently solicited general information on black history."[35] By 1937 the ASNLH had turned from producing scholarly refutations of white racist historiography to publishing educational works for a predominantly Afro-American audience of teachers, ministers, and students. Although Woodson had begun the association with the goal of creating a history that was nonracist and directed at all Americans, he now produced popular history for an increasingly segregated black audience.

Woodson's contribution to Afro-American public history was to develop a credible Afro-American history that was not dependent on white funding and support. He succeeded by creating a financial network among the emerging educational bourgeoisie of the 1920s; but he also reached the black masses with a history that was both scholarly and reflective of their viewpoint. Woodson's Afro-American history appealed across class lines because he was both a man of the masses and a member of the bourgeoisie: though the son of a poor sharecropper, he had made himself a member of the black middle class and shared its traditional values. His decision to ground his movement in the black public was not only a response to a lack of white funding but also a conscious affirmation of nationalism and self-improvement. Separating his movement from the scholarly and white mainstream allowed him the independence to develop creative and innovative black public history.

D uring the Great Depression, the nationalism of Afro-American public history came under attack from many Afro-American intellectuals who saw a purely racial analysis as inadequate in view of the economic crisis of the 1930s. This critique emerged in the midst of a struggle among intellectuals affiliated with the Communist Party, the federal government, and white philanthropic foundations who believed that the Afro-American masses would be the avant-garde of any revolutionary change in America. The involvement of the Communist Party and the federal government helped bring concern for Afro-American history into the radical white community, creating a degree of interaction and discussion between white and black intellectuals that had not existed before. Although Communist and government projects diversified Afro-American public history and made it more critical of the American experience, few of these efforts succeeded in attracting a mass audience among blacks. Ironically, the works of self-trained historians continued to be the most popular form of black history consumed in the 1930s.

At the NAACP's 1933 conference in Amenia, New York, on the contemporary crisis of Negro America, younger intellectuals, such as E. Franklin Frazier, Ralph Bunche, and Abram Harris, attacked older leaders, such as Du Bois, for maintaining that the "Negro problem" could be solved in isolation. These "Young Turks," as they were called, argued that class was as important a factor in black life as race and that black and white workers had to unite in a common struggle against capitalism. They called on black leaders and intellectuals to focus on the plight of the masses and abandon their bias toward the middle class.[36]

The black masses demonstrated their discontent with segregation through the Harlem Race Riot of 1935, the first "modern" race riot and a major rebellion against institutional racism and economic exploitation operating within the black community itself. Harlem residents destroyed white-run local businesses, leading black and white liberals to believe that the Depression might spark a violent black rebellion. Moreover, the riot called into question the ability of older black intellectuals to capture the new mood of the black masses. Du Bois's *Dusk of Dawn* (1940), which called on blacks to accept segregation and build an autonomous black society in the ghetto, seemed to confirm the Young Turks view that such leadership had become anachronistic. Earlier in 1935 Alain Locke had received Carnegie Foundation money to publish the works of Ralph Bunche, Sterling Brown, and Eric Williams in paperback "Bronze Booklets" that sold for twenty-five cents and condensed technical discussions of race-relations, literature, and Caribbean history into easily read narratives for an adult education audience. But these books did not enjoy wide circulation. Other attempts to reach the mass audience included Howard University English professor Benjamin Brawley's unsuccessful scheme to publish biographies of Frederick Douglass, Sojourner Truth, and other "Negro heroes" for popular consumption. Black scholars who wished to publish for the mass audience and who were viewed as "safe" by white foundations and the federal government found opportunities in the 1930s that had previously eluded them; but these efforts were not successful in engaging the attention of the masses of black people in the 1930s.[37]

Coinciding with the Harlem riot of 1935 was the establishment of the New Deal's Works Progress Administration (WPA). WPA administrators realized that some concessions to black cultural projects were necessary to maintain the agency's legitimacy. Almost immediately, the WPA's Federal Writers' Project (in collaboration with Fisk University) began collecting interviews with former slaves in nearly twenty states, thus providing employment for such black scholars as Zora Neale Hurston. Growing acceptance of Boas' notion of cultural relativism led the WPA to employ Hurston (a former student of his) in 1935 to collect Afro-American music and folklore from the turpentine camps and jook joints, from women in rural homes, and from hoodoo priests and conjure men and women in Louisiana and Florida.[38]

But the thrust of the Young Turks criticism of existing Afro-American racial strategies was not a demand for employment for historians interested in collecting black culture but rather a call for black intellectuals to explore and develop an economic critique of American capitalism and its systematic exploitation of the black masses. In 1937 Lawrence Reddick, a young black historian, focused this economic critique specifically on the Negro history movement.[39] According to Reddick, "Negro history" perpetuated a narrow focus on race and a sentimentalized gospel of success that he caricatured in the following synopsis of a typical Afro-American public history text: "Brought over in 1619, he [the Negro] was soon inducted into the fields of the South. Led by the Republican Party, war was waged to preserve the Union and to free the slaves. Reconstruction was a horror which stirred up ill will. Since that time, life has been hard, but talented Negroes through hard work and high faith have leaped over all hurdles to success. Conditions are becoming better and better. If we will but work a little harder, save a little more, establish a few more businesses and 'get educated,' we will some day receive our rightful place at the table of democracy, praise God from whom all blessings flow!"[40]

Reddick argued that Afro-American history should break with its "Polyanna optimism" and its amateur authors. Trained scholars would provide a larger critique of the place of blacks in American society, focusing on the masses rather than the "professional classes."[41] Whereas Reddick centered his criticism on the American gospel of success inscribed in Afro-American public history, a white labor journalist, Benjamin Stolberg, attacked Negro public history for promoting race "chauvinism" and perpetuating an ethnic consciousness that kept the black proletariat from uniting with their white working-class brethren. Both Reddick and Stolberg believed that Afro-American public history uncritically presented racism, rather than economic oppression, as the major obstacle inhibiting black success in America.[42]

Ironically, it was a public history project sponsored by the federal government that came closest to realizing what Reddick, Stolberg, and other leftist critics of Afro-American public history had in mind. Hallie Flanagan, director of the Federal Theatre Project (FTP), encouraged the black playwright Abraham Hill to write a play chronicling American Negro history. But Hill's strong script (written with John Silvera) for *Liberty Deferred* (1938) proved to be too controversial. In one scene a lynching victim with a rope around his neck inscribes the gruesome details of his murder in a giant "Book in the Sky." In another a white man comfortably sips a mint julep while bidding on a procession of black bodies in a slave auction. Hill's explicit images were too charged even for the leftist FTP, which was to face congressional investigations for communist infiltration in the late 1930s. Even though it had already been advertised, FTP officials canceled its production of *Liberty Deferred*.[43]

In view of the hysterical right-wing claims that Communists were responsible for perverting the FTP, one might have expected truly radical Afro-American public history to come from events sponsored directly by the American Communist Party. Generally speaking, however, the Party's Negro history celebrations of the late 1930s were relatively traditional in form and content. In the early 1930s the Party had fiercely criticized black nationalist movements in Harlem and Afro-American culture generally as impediments to working-class unity. But with the turn to the Popular Front Against Fascism in 1935 and the decision to make common cause with liberals and socialists, the Party dropped its criticism and attempted to woo middle-class black intellectuals by encouraging prominent black scholars to lecture on "Negro contributions to American culture" at Communist Party retreats.[44]

The Party embraced Afro-American history during the Popular Front period for roughly the same reasons that the earlier Negro progressives had: it hoped that Negro history would further the coalition of black and white workers both by attracting blacks to the Party and by educating whites out of their racism. This position logically committed the Party to disseminating Afro-American history to a white as well as a black audience. In practice, however, Party-sponsored Negro history programs remained confined to blacks. One of these was the Frederick Douglass Historical and Cultural League. In November 1939 the Afro-American Communists Richard Moore and Ben Davis obtained Party sponsorship for the league, which, according to Mark Naison, "aimed to distribute Douglass's writings to popularize the 'historical and cultural heritage of the Negro people' and to 'set forth the true role of the Negro in world history, ancient and modern.' "[45]

Marxism was a form of integration that allowed black intellectuals to argue with white intellectuals over the history of American racism and black strategies for combatting it. But Marxism also allowed black intellectuals to assimilate a western intellectual tradition that valued criticism, especially self-criticism, and thus enabled them to break the "gag rule" on criticism of black institutions. Leftists, whether black or white, provided a long-overdue critique of the ideological biases, banal forms, and inaccuracies of "Negro history." An uncritical racial nationalism had become outdated among the black intellectual elite of the 1930s.

However, this criticism alienated the Marxists from the black community, which felt that these Young Turks were attacking their special history and limited resources. Blacks had learned from popular histories and Negro History Week activities that they had a glorious tradition and a heroic African past, and that they could make it if they tried. When Marxist intellectuals attacked the celebratory form of black history, as well as its ideology of upward mobility and racial nationalism, they separated themselves from the internal values of the community. The large following of Noble Drew Ali and the popularity of the "Don't Buy Where You Can't Work" campaigns in the 1930s suggest that many blacks retained a nationalist ideology even while they simultaneously embraced the decade's new class analyses.[46] Nationalism was only one of the values flouted by many black Marxists, who saw the Party as an avenue of escape from a provincial black community. As a result, these radicals were unable to mobilize their community to support their new version of Afro-American history.

Moreover, these critics failed to create alternative means of supporting black history. The suppression of *Liberty Deferred,* the boldest attempt yet to present a radical Afro-American public history, revealed a basic problem: Afro-American public history relied on the autonomous black community's support in the first place because mainstream American public institutions would not support a black history that was oppositional in its basic message. National white support in the 1930s went only so far: projects to collect slave folklore would receive funding; explicit exposés of slavery's economic bases would not. The limits of Afro-American public history were set more by its patrons than by its producers.

Young black intellectuals were in the unenviable position of attacking the ideology of the black middle class—a major audience for an autonomous Afro-American public history. In organizations like the ASNLH, school-teachers, librarians, and other black professionals possessed considerable power to shape the content of the history they consumed. During the Great Depression, the black middle class retained its faith in race uplift, self-reliance, and eventual success under American capitalism.[47] As late as 1940, even Woodson advocated a similar "bootstrap" philosophy as a solution to contemporary black problems.

Moreover, as noted above, the new intellectuals did not enjoy a large audience among the black masses, the other significant public for Afro-American history. The books that flourished in the 1930s and the 1940s were by Afro-American popular historians like Joel A. Rogers. *The World's Greatest Men and Women of African Descent* (1931), *A Hundred Amazing Facts About the Negro: With Complete Proof, A Shortcut to the World History of the Negro* (1934), and *Sex and Race: Negro-Caucasian Mixing in All Ages and All Lands* (1940), all written by Rogers, were bestsellers, yet they ignored the coherent sociological analyses favored by Reddick and Stolberg in favor of "proving" that many heroes of European civilization had actually been black. Similarly, Rogers' popular *Pittsburgh Courier* column, "Your History," provided captioned illustrations of famous blacks in a style imitative of Ripley's "Believe It or Not."[48]

Stolberg's claim that popular black histories were responsible for the persistence of nationalism, success ideology, and hero worship among the masses was partly true: Rogers' books were popular because they did not challenge his community's values but instead reinforced them. Rogers gave back to the community what it wanted to hear: white people had lied about black history, and there had been many more black "successes" than was generally known. Whereas the Marxists criticized the black community's basic values, Rogers reflected those values so uncritically that he could not move that community to a higher level of political consciousness. Neither the Marxists nor Rogers succeeded in politically mobilizing the black community of the 1930s through public history.

Marxist-oriented Afro-American public history projects were limited by both federal censorship and leftists' ambivalence toward the mass audience they sought to cultivate. Just as Du Bois's 1903 eulogy to the folk culture of the black masses was colored by an elitist romanticizing of "the folk," so too "armchair Marxists" of the 1930s found it easier to theorize about the desires and interests of the masses than to actually create forms that engaged that audience. Nevertheless, leftists, whether white or black, brought to Afro-

American public history a badly needed debunking of the errors, exaggera-
tions, and hero worship that characterized much of "Negro history." As a
result, such hagiography would never again be entirely free from intellectual
scrutiny.

Afro-American public history reached a turning point in the 1930s. The
WPA, the Communist Party, and the debate over Afro-American public history brought together for the first time white and black intellectuals to criticize
the black perspective on American history. After the "crisis of capitalism," a
small but growing white public of radicals and liberals would influence the
course of Afro-American history writing.

W orld War II brought Afro-American history for the first time to
a large white audience, in part because a war against fascism
showed policy-makers the national security implications of ra-
cial segregation. The most remarkable contribution to Afro-
American public history in this period was a U.S. Army film, *The Negro
Soldier*, which unintentionally became a propaganda film for integration.
Generally speaking, however, Afro-American public history took a backseat
during the 1940s and 1950s, as such black scholars as E. Franklin Frazier,
Kenneth Clark, Allison Davis, and John Hope Franklin pursued scholarly
"Negro studies" that for the first time reached a white audience. These scholars succeeded in affecting white opinion because they assimilated the values
of social science professionalism, worked on integrated team research projects with prominent white social scientists, and placed black themes within a
scholarly analysis of American life. Yet the cost of integration was the abandonment of Woodson's and Rogers' black history public. Some, moreover,
produced a sociology that described black life as pathological and denigrated
the notion of a distinct Afro-American culture. By the mid-1950s there were
two Afro-American histories: a scholarly history that was increasingly integrated into the white academic establishment, and a public history that remained a racially autonomous movement in a predominantly segregated black
urban community.

World War II placed American racism under an international spotlight and
forced the federal government to confront American racist practices and their
propaganda implications for war mobilization. Nazi propagandists argued that
Afro-Americans had no reason to fight for a racist America. At the same time,
the NAACP and other organized groups lobbied the U.S. government to integrate the armed forces and the entire war effort. When the army began to

experience morale problems among its black soldiers, it commissioned film-maker Frank Capra to make *The Negro Soldier* (1944), hoping that the film would build black enthusiasm for the war and reduce criticism of army segregation.[49]

The young black writer Carlton Moss, who also acted the title role, wrote the script, which recounted the history of Afro-American participation in American wars from the Revolution to World War I and the contributions made by blacks in science, athletics, and the arts. The film also depicted contemporary opportunities for advancement to higher rank so unrealistically that army officials feared that the film would spark riots when shown to black servicemen. But Negro servicemen applauded the film. Professionally pho-tographed, tastefully presented, this depiction of Afro-Americans in heroic roles elevated black self-esteem precisely in the ways that Woodson and other public historians had first attempted in the 1920s and 1930s.[50]

What particularly surprised the army was the response of white soldiers, who overwhelmingly approved of the film and recommended that it be shown to civilian audiences, which the army consented to do after numerous cuts were made. The prospect of facing a common enemy reduced racial antag-onism among white servicemen, who may have been reassured by the film's visual evidence of black heroism. But more important, World War II, accom-panied by forced migration, an expanded need for industrial labor, and the use of such social engineering techniques as "propaganda" films, transformed traditional values and the traditional "place" American society had assigned to blacks as well as women. *The Negro Soldier* marked the beginning of a shift in white attitudes (and subtly furthered that shift) toward greater accep-tance for nonstereotyped images of blacks in American life.[51]

Conventional Negro history appealed to the army because of its conser-vative ideology: a recounting of the heroic black past was less threatening than a direct political challenge to the status quo. But what the Army learned was that it was impossible to appropriate the medium of Afro-American pub-lic history without accepting its subversive content: Afro-American public history was rooted in a perspective at odds with the status quo. The postwar climate of opinion not only forced the army to desegregate, but also forced Hollywood to abandon traditional black stereotypes and to produce films, such as *Home of the Brave* in 1949, which owed some of their success to the pioneering influence of *The Negro Soldier*.[52]

The Negro Soldier symbolized the beginning of a new phase in Afro-Amer-ican public history—its integration into the mainstream of American culture. The 1940s witnessed the rise of integration as the official ideology of liberal social science in America. During World War II, most of the young black intellectuals who had taken up Marxism in the 1930s separated themselves from leftist politics and became integrationists. The war had created a patriotic incentive for integrationism as well as a demand for black social science talent. Moreover, the increased professionalization of black scholars, many of whom attended prestigious white universities, combined with the rise of an integrationist sociology in such universities to give them legitimacy.

Perhaps the most important team project to integrate Afro-American scholars into the social science mainstream was Gunnar Myrdal's Carnegie Corporation–financed study, which produced the widely influential book *An American Dilemma* (1944). Relying on the work of such black scholars as Ralph Bunche and E. Franklin Frazier, Myrdal boldly championed integration and attacked the Negro history movement for its "distortion in the emphasis and the perspective given the facts: mediocrities have been expanded into 'great men'; cultural achievements which are no better—and no worse—than any others are placed on a pinnacle."[53] Myrdal's work also helped to introduce a new sociology of race relations that deemphasized Afro-American culture and helped to establish a new generation of black scholars (epitomized by E. Franklin Frazier) who themselves criticized the notion of African survivals in black American life and sought to incorporate the discussion of blacks within a larger examination of American social processes.[54]

This integrationist movement found its clearest and most powerful expression in Afro-American history with the publication of John Hope Franklin's landmark study, *From Slavery to Freedom*. Franklin's book was a turning point in Afro-American historiography: it was the first academic text to thoroughly integrate black history into American political history and the first, as one reviewer noted, to narrate Afro-American history with "that objectivity which the best historical scholarship requires." After the publication of *From Slavery to Freedom* in 1947 and the death of Woodson in 1950, there would be two Afro-American histories: a scholarly tradition of "objective" Afro-American history produced by professional historians in the academy and a popular tradition of "partisan" history produced by lay historians whose Negro history events, celebrations, and books made up a separate record of black accomplishment.[55]

Franklin was a transitional figure in Afro-American historiography. He continued the older tradition of participation in the ASNLH, Negro History Week activities, and popular writing projects, but his scholarly work was designed to gain academic respectability for Negro history rather than to respond directly to the needs and concerns of the black masses. Franklin opened a wedge for a new generation of black scholars who would go on to attain teaching positions in white colleges and universities in the 1960s and who were able to realize Woodson's Progressive dream of influencing public policy through scholarship. But a division of labor emerged between Afro-American public history and scholarly history, the latter being produced by scholars—in white or black colleges and universities—who wrote increasingly for an academic audience. A rift between the scholars and the black public began to emerge in the ASNLH in the early 1960s, in part because no new scholar emerged with Woodson's abilities as an administrator, fundraiser, and financial manager, and in part because the organization lost the participation of some leading scholars whose professionalization demanded involvement in mainstream historical associations.[56]

The diminished role of scholars cost Afro-American public history some of its vitality. As the educational bourgeoisie, with its close ties with ministers and business leaders in segregated black communities, began to assert itself in the ASNLH, the scholarly quality of Negro History Week activities declined: Negro History kits, for example, in the late 1950s and early 1960s presented local black doctors as "Negro heroes," surely a step backward from the history disseminated under Woodson. At the same time, less direction from the national office meant that local groups of lay people were able to organize Negro History Week celebrations that reflected local political and cultural needs, and in the consumer ethos of the 1950s, these events defined black success as entrance to the professional class. Afro-American public history, especially that associated with the ASNLH, became more decentralized, a development that spurred the emergence of new and alternative public history institutions—namely, the historical museums of the 1950s and 1960s.[57]

During the 1960s a new synthesis emerged that combined all the earlier elements of Afro-American public history, making it an activist history dedicated to mobilizing the black community by raising its consciousness of its unique history and destiny. The black intellectuals of the 1960s—older leftists, younger civil rights activists, community leaders, and members of the educational bourgeoisie—founded numerous cultural institutions that reflected the emerging black ideological militancy and cultural authority. Dominated largely by an integrationist ideology in the early years of 1955 to 1965, this activist Afro-American public history turned nationalistic after 1965, fostering a critique of both the American status quo and black accommodation to it. Unlike the 1930s radicals, the black intellectuals of the 1960s developed connections with the church and other traditional black institutions and affirmed the value of Afro-American culture. Such intellectuals also engaged the black masses: when the black underclass rioted in the mid-sixties, for example, black intellectuals took their history to the streets. These riots, along with the civil rights movement, raised the consciousness of white America, brought a mass white audience to Afro-American public history, and stimulated corporate and government funding of Afro-American public history projects.

For the first time positive images of blacks and Afro-American culture entered the mainstream of American culture. By the late 1970s Afro-American history was part of most American public and academic institutions. Just as important, separate black museums and cultural organizations were established in this period. This activist history had successfully realized Woodson's dream of promoting positive images of blacks through history and establishing black institutions to keep alive the sense of black pride in an oppressed community.

The civil rights movement influenced Afro-American public history in a number of ways. The movement radicalized both older members of the educational bourgeoisie and younger students by teaching them to respect the ideas and beliefs of poorer black folk. Whereas both the NAACP and the ASNLH pioneered a racial strategy for the bourgeoisie, who as teachers, ministers, and other professionals assumed a paternalistic attitude toward poor blacks, the civil rights movement's direct action wing taught volunteers to view themselves as "facilitators" and to help local communities lead their own fights. Moreover, Student Nonviolent Coordinating Committee (SNCC) organizers committed themselves to remaining in a community and working through such institutions as the black church; they affirmed the indigenous values of the community even as the movement changed them.[58]

The civil rights movement defined history as a tool for community empowerment. In SNCC's Mississippi "freedom schools," students learned "the history of the black liberation movement" along with political skills. The direct action wing of SNCC and the Congress of Racial Equality (CORE) thus defined a new Afro-American public history: history should be used to mobilize the community, and the people themselves should be encouraged to record, to study, and to exhibit their own view of history apart from what scholars and academics defined as "accurate" history.

This activist ideology led some black volunteers in the movement to found historical museums as a way to practice radical cultural politics and to link themselves firmly to the urban black community. For example, Byron Rushing became the director of the Museum of Afro-American History in Boston, after working with CORE and the Boston College/Urban League Joint Center for Inner City Change. Similarly, the Afro-American Cultural Arts Center in

Minneapolis combined community organizing with collecting and exhibiting art and history. Its low-paid staff resembled a cell in a grassroots political organization, bound together by a "commitment to the black community." Dr. Charles Wright organized a new museum in Detroit after returning from the Selma marches, where he had served on SNCC's Medical Support Committee for Human Rights and come to see historical education as a key to mobilizing the northern black community. Wright's museum collections and exhibitions argued that the "true history" of Afro-Americans began in Africa and that blacks remained a revolutionary people who had not been "broken," as academic scholars had claimed, by the "mark of oppression."[59]

Not only did civil rights activists repudiate the view of black communities as pathological, but some also rejected both the improvement ideology of Woodson's generation and the integrationist ideology of Franklin's and Frazier's generation. Most of the black historical institutions that emerged in the 1950s, such as Margaret Burroughs' Ebony Museum of Negro Culture in Chicago (1961), the Elma Lewis School for the Arts in Boston (1950), and the San Francisco Negro Historical and Cultural Association (1956) had had an explicitly integrationist orientation. The organizers of the museums had seen art museums and historical societies as relatively safe ways (in the shadow of McCarthyism) to practice interracial radical politics, although Burroughs and Lewis seem to have anticipated the mid-1960s black pride movement in their conviction that art and history should teach racial self-appreciation.[60]

In the mid-sixties SNCC and CORE rejected integrationism and ousted their white members, amid charges that whites were unable to relate to poor blacks in a "facilitator" role. Sharing this perspective and frustrated with white-dominated institutions, young black intellectuals began to foster black nationalist organizations and public institutions. They also embraced African traditions and a colonialist interpretation of American history, as evidenced in such magazines as *Black Scholar* and *Third World* (later *First World*). This interpretation of Afro-American and American history was relatively new and had grown out of contacts between African and American activists at schools like Howard University and in the civil rights movement. Separatist religious groups like the Nation of Islam (the Black Muslims) gained popularity among the younger members of the black middle class, as Malcolm X used the history of slavery to argue for separation from the "white beast." At the same time, academic historians developed a body of work that reinterpreted Afro-American history, validating the African connections. In this new history, Afro-Americans were not merely the victims of oppression but rather a people who had created and maintained a distinctive culture with many demonstrably African-linked elements. In 1965, for example, Leroi Jones (later Amiri Baraka) published a history of black Americans called *Blues People,* which asserted that Afro-Americans not only had a distinct history but had evolved new cultural forms and modes of communication.[61]

While cultural nationalism gained strength among young black people and social historians in the 1960s, these views directly challenged and angered some members of the traditional educational and entrepreneurial black bourgeoisie. Young radicals from SNCC, for example, criticized older civil rights organizations such as the NAACP, the Urban League, and even the Southern Christian Leadership Conference for their integrationist and assimilationist ideology. They charged that the methods and models of these older organizations implied that Afro-Americans should mimic white behavior. Similarly, they attacked such middle-class publications as *Ebony* for its advertisements for skin bleaching creams, its articles on conspicuous consumption, and its eulogies of black doctors and other professionals as "Negro heroes." A bitter battle erupted in the ASNLH in 1968 as an alliance of younger and older radicals forced the ASNLH to drop "Negro" from its name and to become the Association for the Study of Afro American Life and History (ASALH).[62]

Not surprisingly, the new museums of the period called themselves Black, African, or Afro-American. Often located in the heart of urban black neighborhoods, the museums headed by Burroughs, Wright, Rushing, and Lewis enjoyed increased attendance in the mid-1960s as many blacks responded to the black pride movement by developing an interest in African art, music, and clothing that could generally be found only at these institutions. Moreover, cultural nationalism, but emphasizing loyalty to independent black institutions, increased attendance by both adults and children, as many working- and middle-class parents brought their children to black museums and art centers for educational purposes.[63]

Yet the ghetto riots of the middle and late 1960s challenged the belief of Afro-American public historians that their efforts to reach "the people" were actually effective. From the Watts riot of 1965 to the nationwide rioting in 1968, leaderless urban rebellions disturbed even seasoned black radicals, who saw in them a degree of self-destructive violence that threatened even the nationalistic concept of black power. For Afro-American public historians, the riots were stark evidence that a new and volatile audience existed—the black underclass—which, unlike the black working- and middle-class public, had probably never attended a Negro History Week (or after 1968, a Black History Month) celebration.

In response, some black intellectuals took to the streets. Charles Wright purchased a trailer and toured the city in his mobile museum during the long and bloody Detroit riots of 1967, believing that "if you can't bring the people to the museum to understand their own history, you should take the news to them." In 1968 Wright changed the name of his Detroit museum to the International Afro-American Museum of Detroit, in part to obtain the acronym "I AM," as in "I am somebody." Popularized by Jesse Jackson, the slogan "I am somebody" derived from Martin Luther King's belief that the black community needed a sense of "somebodiness" or collective self-worth to meet the challenges of black life in the twentieth century. The urban riots of the 1960s seemed to confirm the judgment that such a sense of self-worth was desperately needed in the black ghettos of the North, South, and West.[64]

In the aftermath of the riots, many indigenous Afro-American public history efforts that had been unsupported before 1968 enjoyed an avalanche of government and corporate funds. For example, Wright's Detroit museum secured city funding for an annual arts festival. Eventually he installed permanent exhibitions on African and Afro-American history; by 1984 the museum had received more than $2 million from the city to construct new quarters.[65] Money poured into black historical and cultural institutions partially because it was easier to spend money on a cultural institution than to finance an economic reconstruction of inner city ghettos.

Many new museums were established in this climate of white concern. Although the secretary of the Smithsonian Institution, S. Dillon Ripley, announced a desire to create a "black museum" in 1965, so that minorities would feel that the Smithsonian was "their" institution, this populist idea did not reach fruition until September 1967 after one of the worst summers of urban rioting. With John Kinard, a black minister, poverty program worker, and community organizer as its director, the innovative Anacostia Neighborhood Museum of Washington, D.C., was established by the Smithsonian. In addition to landmark exhibits such as "Out of Africa," Anacostia developed programs that responded to the needs and interests of its wide community audience. "The Rat: Man's Invited Affliction," for example, created by Zora Felton, combined a history of the animal, information on how to protect oneself and one's property from it, and a cage of live rats! Here was an exhibition that spoke directly to the daily struggle of this urban community.[66]

The strength of the Afro-American museums and cultural organizations founded during the 1960s and 1970s lay in their redefinition of what a museum was supposed to be. Rather than holders of precious artifacts, stored and exhibited in isolated splendor, Afro-American historical museums became cultural centers, providing outlets for many separate and sometimes contradictory impulses in local black communities. Black-supported museums such as Burroughs' Du Sable museum in Chicago fostered a "living environment" and fulfilled social and entertainment functions as well as presenting historical artifacts and art. Dance, musical, and performance programs were common in black museums. Elma Lewis' National Center of Afro-American Artists, for example, combined performance art with exhibition space.[67]

The notion that the black community should be encouraged to create its own liberationist culture, inspired by the freedom schools, in turn inspired the black museums and cultural centers of the 1960s. For example, the Du Sable Museum encouraged local black communities to create their own history through oral history projects, retention and collection of family documents, and storytelling. Museums and cultural organizations of the civil rights era synthesized educational, historical, and artistic impulses in an activist commitment to stimulating the community to make its own history and culture.[68]

One of the ironies of this period is that a great deal of the money from white funding sources went to organizations that advocated separation from white America. In New York, for example, leaders of the black community persuaded the wealthy white members of the Junior Council for the Museum of Modern Art to provide funds for the Studio Museum of Harlem, which immediately began an ambitious exhibition program that supported explicitly cultural-nationalist and even separatist politics. Most institutions funded by private and governmental sources ultimately made the transition from the radical political rhetoric of the 1960s to become conventionally organized public institutions with much more conservative goals in the 1970s and 1980s.[69]

While militant separatist rhetoric flourished, Afro-American public history also gained access to a white mass audience in the 1970s through mainstream museums, visual media, and local school systems. Such prestigious institutions as the Brooklyn Museum, the Field Museum in Chicago, the Los Angeles County Museum of Arts, the National Portrait Gallery, and the National Museum of History and Technology sponsored new exhibitions in this period that emphasized Afro-American contributions to American social and cultural history. During the late 1960s and early 1970s, Hollywood and the television networks produced numerous documentaries, feature-length movies, and television specials on black historical themes. Black history was also institutionalized in the public schools in the early 1970s through special assemblies and lectures during the month of February and through new textbooks that stressed the black contribution to American culture. Whereas angry black students had stormed onto white university campuses in the 1960s to demand an Afro-American history relevant to the black community, by the mid-1970s observances of Black History Month had become regular calendar events in most major white universities across the nation. When the nation celebrated the Bicentennial in 1976, some "Bicentennial Minutes" on television dramatized the role of little-known "black heroes." By 1980, for the first time in

American history, a positive image of the black past had become a fixture in public expressions of American culture.[70]

The single most important public history event of the 1970s, however, was the incredibly successful television mini-series based on Alex Haley's *Roots*. It adapted the older narrative concept of Afro-Americans as a heroic and chosen people to the history of a single, ordinary black family. Although "Roots" endorsed uplift and upward mobility, its more important message was the continuity of the Afro-American experience from its origins in an African past through the travail of slavery into a more tolerant American present. For many black as well as white Americans, "Roots" offered a disturbing education in the history of slavery; many angered blacks were forced to admit, "I didn't know slavery was that bad." For whites, "Roots" confirmed what the radical rhetoric of the 1960s had announced—that much of American history had been a tragic hell for a people whose only salvation seemed to be in the heroism displayed by ordinary people, white as well as black.

The influence of social history on Afro-American public history, however, was never as strong as that of celebratory "Negro heroes," perhaps because the latter type of history confirms both Afro-American and Euro-American values. The establishment of the birthday of Martin Luther King, Jr., as a holiday in 1984 exemplified this "integration" of black and white valuations of historical narrative. In an era of retrenchment in civil rights, the birthday of King—who had dedicated himself to bringing together the black and white communities—remains a symbol of white and black cooperation and community. Whereas such militant black leaders as Malcolm X used a black nationalist history, King invoked a distinctively American belief in freedom and justice that grew in part out of Euro-American history. Quoting the Founding Fathers and Abraham Lincoln, King's sermons and speeches interpreted contemporary American race relations as a betrayal of past American ideals. King's birthday became a national holiday precisely because his life affirmed an interpretation palatable to the broadest spectrum of the American public: the American system works if black and white Americans dedicate themselves to realizing its highest ideals.[71]

By contrast, Afro-American museums and other cultural organizations established in the civil rights era affirm a more nationalistic and critical interpretation of Afro-American and American history. Tied by practice to the experience of the contemporary black community and by ideology to Afro-American vernacular culture, most Afro-American museums and public history programs present evidence that alternatives to the predominant American way of life survive in the Afro-American community.

Moreover, such independent black museums as the Rhode Island Black Heritage Society, begun in 1975 by Rowena Stewart, have become innovators in the historical profession by establishing close connections with academics, museum professionals, and the local black community. By 1980 Stewart had developed an innovative collecting method that involves oral histories, public meetings and discussions, research by scholars, and exhibitions, all designed to include the local community. A new Afro-American public history is being created today in which the activist demand that the people be allowed to interpret their own history is fused with sophisticated scholarship and museum presentation.[72]

A fro-American public history arose out of the desire to promote a positive racial identity among blacks, to preserve a history in danger of being lost, and to challenge the racist stereotypes and myths pervasive in American popular culture. For most of its two hundred years, Afro-American public history has been supported by a black audience, since black history and historians were excluded from mainstream public and academic institutions before the 1940s. Thus, Afro-American public history has tended to serve the external and internal needs of the black community. Afro-American public history has played a role in both the cultural self-defense of the black community and the debate over the merits of integration and separation.

Afro-American public history has tended to prosper during periods of social change when Afro-Americans have found in history a means of coping with social upheaval and integrating new segments of the black population into the community. During the 1830s, for example, improvement societies developed a historical consciousness that not only helped to refute racist stereotypes but also helped to integrate runaways and other freedmen into a free northern black community. During the early twentieth century, black scholars used history to combat scientific racism, at the same time that black popular historians produced a literature that tapped the vernacular cultural nationalism of newly arrived southern migrants and eased their integration into a northern Afro-American identity. Woodson completed the process of binding together the northern urban black community by promoting history among a newly emergent black middle class and the black masses. Afro-American public history has also played an important role in eras of racial retrenchment: public celebrations of Afro-American history have kept alive a sense of hope and dignity in hard times, resuscitating a downtrodden minority with the conviction that eventually liberation from oppression would be achieved.

Afro-American public history has also prospered from the involvement of Afro-American intellectuals—especially academically trained black professionals. It has done less well when large numbers of black intellectuals have shunned association with Afro-American public history either because of Marxist criticism, as in the 1930s, or because of social science professionalization, as in the 1940s and 1950s. The alienation of trained black scholars left the field of Afro-American public history to popular historians, whose "Negro heroes" approach had become anachronistic by the 1950s.

Out of the civil rights movement, however, came a new type of activist intellectual, who identified with and worked in the black community and was committed to challenging and empowering that community to change the status quo. Activist Afro-American historians founded museums and other cultural organizations to cement their relationship to that community, and these institutions became arenas in which the black middle and working classes could explore their heritage. By joining and sponsoring institutions outside the academy, Afro-American public historians were able to realize the SNCC maxim that the role of the intellectual is to give voice to the community.

The civil rights movement and the urban rebellions spawned a political ferment that changed American culture. Communist Party and WPA involvement in the 1930s allowed Afro-American public history to reach a tiny, radical white audience; World War II birthed a historical film on Afro-American bravery that briefly challenged prevailing stereotypes of black behavior. But these ventures were ephemeral compared with the explosion of media attention given to Afro-American history in the sixties. The dream of older Negro progressives of disseminating a positive image of blacks through scholarly and public history was realized. Whereas mainstream public history institutions totally ignored black history twenty-five years ago, today these same institutions, although not fully integrated, are making an effort to promote Afro-American public history as an integral part of their overall programs. The establishment of Martin Luther King's birthday as a national holiday symbolizes this new era of public recognition of Afro-American history.

Today we find Afro-American history presented to the public in two kinds of historical institutions. Black history has been "integrated" into American public institutions at the same time that the number of autonomous Afro-American museums and cultural organizations has increased. Afro-American public history now contains two histories—an integrationist history, newly arrived and aimed primarily at an educated, academic, "successful" public of whites and blacks, and a nationalist history, dominant in the pre-1975 era and aimed primarily at a nonacademic, black working- and middle-class public that views itself as an oppressed minority in America. The first type evolved and remains to fight racism in our culture; the latter evolved and remains to keep alive the sense of pride and the liberationist ethos that exists in the still-segregated black communities.

Yet, a new synthesis is beginning to emerge, an Afro-Americanist interpretation of American history, which incorporates the early, autonomous Afro-American public history and the more recent integrationist history. Despite the integrationist idea that black institutions would or should wither away in the aftermath of integration, Afro-American public institutions have continued to grow and flourish, becoming a permanent landmark on our shared cultural landscape.

BOSTON, NOVEMBER·1980·

Story by Harvey Pekar
Art by Kevin Brown

HARVEY, NICE TO FINALLY MEET YOU.

MARTY?

MARTY'S FRIEND, SAL, STOPPED BY A SHORT TIME LATER AND WE CONTINUED OUR DISCUSSION.

SAL AND I HAVE BEEN WORKING WITH THESE OLD UNION PEOPLE IN LYNN, MASS. PEOPLE WHO WORKED IN THE SHOE INDUSTRY. I WAS RECENTLY INVOLVED IN SETTING UP A REUNION FOR THEM. WE'RE BOTH INTO ORAL HISTORY AND THE EVENT WAS ORGANIZED AS A WORKSHOP. THERE WERE DISCUSSION GROUPS WHERE PEOPLE TALKED ABOUT THIER PAST UNION ACTIVITIES.

IT'S INTERESTING THAT A NUMBER OF WORKERS WHO ARE NOW STRIKING AT A G.E. PLANT IN LYNN ATTENDED THE MEETING; GOOD TO SEE FRATERNIZATION BETWEEN THE OLDER AND YOUNGER WORKERS...

WHAT I LIKED ABOUT MARTY AND SAL WAS THAT THEY HAD REAL WARMTH, REAL EMPATHY FOR PEOPLE. I'D KNOWN A LOT OF RADICALS AND AGREED WITH THEM ON A LOT OF ISSUES, BUT NOT ALL WERE REAL NICE PEOPLE. SOME WERE ARROGANT, POWER-HUNGRY, EVEN DISHONEST. SOME DIDN'T REALLY CARE THAT MUCH, EXCEPT IN AN ABSTRACT WAY, ABOUT THE POOR PEOPLE THAT THEY SAID THEY WERE TRYING TO HELP.

Engaging in People's History:

The Massachusetts History Workshop

In 1978 three activist historians formed the Massachusetts History Workshop to experiment with a participatory approach to people's history. For nearly a decade historians influenced by the student and antiwar movements and by black and women's liberation politics had engaged in various popular history projects ranging from the publication of pamphlets and journals to the organization of community history forums, all designed to reach a wider audience outside the universities. At the same time the History Workshop movement emerged in Britain when students of trade union history began publishing local history pamphlets and holding workshops that brought together academics, activists, and workers with common interests in the past. The British History Workshop aimed to bring "the boundaries of history closer to people's lives" and to make the past more relevant to working people. It championed collective projects that challenged "the intellectual division of labor" in historical work and encouraged working people to participate in presenting and writing history.[1]

The Massachusetts History Workshop adopted the same goals and carried on the work begun by activist historians in the United States during the late 1960s. We organized three workshops for historians, workers, and activists, focusing on Lynn shoemakers, Lawrence textile workers, and Boston clerical workers, and produced three popular history booklets based on the oral history testimony of the working people who participated. We also organized a cultural event in Cambridge, featuring songs, poems, and stories about surviving and organizing in hard times, and a public event at Faneuil Hall in Boston commemorating the founding of the Women's Trade Union League. In addition, our workshop group has provided a meeting place for activist

BY JAMES GREEN

historians, especially nonacademics. More recently, we have tried to provide a kind of people's history service for institutions, groups, and labor unions that might otherwise overlook historical education or turn to commercial outfits specializing in "public history." We see the Workshop as part of the trend toward public history, but we prefer to call our efforts "people's history" because we reject the mainstream approach, which presents professional historians as experts who do history *for* the public. We want to work *with* the public in a democratic, participatory way and help organize projects that will enable people to do their own history.[2]

This essay describes the activity of the Massachusetts History Workshop and the political context from which it emerged between 1968 and 1978. Though the making of people's history in the United States and Britain occurred in the highly charged political climate created by the protest movements of that decade, what follows is not addressed only to veterans of those movements. Radical historians in this country and in Britain have taken the lead in the democratic people's history movement, but this kind of history includes a broad range of people. The intense agitational quality of movement-inspired history in the late 1960s has ebbed. Activists recognize more than ever the need to produce history that really represents the collective memory of communities and work groups. People's history today attracts not just leftist historians but also other historians who want to take history out of the academy, to affect popular historical consciousness and to do history with working people who have been denied access to their own past by schools, employers, and the media. Ultimately, engaging in people's history may provide political empowerment as well as cultural enrichment and a deeper understanding of social and personal change.

T he roots of people's history lie in the politics of protest. Social movements struggling for radical change have always called up popular histories of oppression and resistance, and within these struggles historians and intellectuals have usually joined other activists in an interrogation of the past and its meaning for the present and future. The traveling lecturers of the Farmers' Alliance, one of the largest mass movements in U.S. history, soon produced histories of the rural cooperative crusade.[3] And in 1886, at the labor movement's greatest moment of solidarity, George McNeill, who had helped organize the Eight Hour League and the Knights of Labor, edited a stunning example of movement history, *The Labor Movement: The Problem of Today*. This remarkable compilation included McNeill's own history of the labor movement and the eight-hour-day crusade, Henry George's history of the land question, and accounts of various trades unions by the unions' leaders.[4] These activists saw no boundaries between agitating, organizing, lecturing, and writing history.

The same spirit prevailed in the Debsian socialist movement. Countless writers produced historical works that organizers used in their recruiting. For example, Oscar Ameringer, the best-known of these socialist writers, used his famous booklet, *The Life and Deeds of Uncle Sam: A Little History for Big Children,* at the large socialist summer encampments that provided a kind of evangelical setting for movement-building in the Southwest.[5] Later, Communist writers created a remarkable range of popular industrial, social, and political histories influenced by strong partisan positions. Much of the Communists' labor history degenerated in the 1920s and 1930s into factionalism, attributing the problems of labor to "leadership sellout." Labor history has been highly contested terrain ever since, with historians of various partisan views contending for influence. Notable works include Richard O. Boyer and Herbert Morais' widely read *Labor's Untold Story,* sympathetic to the Communist Party, and the less well known *Labor's Giant Step* by Art Preis of the Trotskyist opposition.[6]

Throughout the twentieth century writers inspired by social movements have been influenced by our three greatest people's historians, W. E. B. Du Bois, Charles Beard, and Mary Ritter Beard. The young New Left historians of the 1970s deeply appreciated these three independent radical historians even as they criticized the Old Left for its narrowness.[7] In the manner of the Beards and Du Bois, the Federal Writers' Project of the Works Progress Administration enlisted thousands of paid workers and community volunteers during the late 1930s to interview people, including former slaves, about their working lives and to produce people's history through the "American Guide Series." The Writers' Project was urged to avoid partisan or leftist politics, but many of the writers were activists in various social movements of the 1930s, and the *Guides* were still criticized for their radical approaches to U.S. history.[8]

In the 1960s the civil rights and black power movements revived the study of Afro-American history and culture, created "freedom schools" in the South and later "liberation schools" in the cities, and agitated for black studies in colleges.[9] The student and antiwar movements of the era also generated popular history in the form of pamphlets and articles in publications like *Studies on the Left* and *Radical America.* The latter was founded in 1967 at the University of Wisconsin to recover the history of earlier protest and resistance and to support radical graduate students attempting to create a new democratic history.[10] Meanwhile, the study of women's history contributed to the con-sciousness raising that emerged from the feminist movement.[11]

These social movements affected the scholarly work taking place in univer-sities; they also influenced the staid proceedings of professional history asso-ciations, like the 1969 meeting of the American Historical Association (AHA), during which shouting and fisticuffs punctuated a debate over a reso-lution condemning the U.S. invasion of Vietnam. At the same meeting the Radical Historians' Caucus defended the academic freedom of leftist teachers, demanded the democratization of the profession, and called for a history "from the bottom up" that would be more responsive to people and move-ments outside the academy.[12]

The historian Staughton Lynd personified these various trends. Both Yale University and Roosevelt University fired him for political reasons, the for-mer after his peace trip to Hanoi. After being blacklisted, Lynd continued to work as a historian for the movement. He ran for president of the AHA in 1969 and remained active in the Radical Caucus. His greatest contribution to people's history came after he left academic life: in Gary and other south Chicago steel towns, he and Alice Lynd collected oral histories of veteran union militants. In 1969 his article "Guerilla History in Gary" threw down a bold challenge to historians: support workers in writing their own history.[13]

The next year Lynd helped organize a community forum in East Chicago, Indiana, which became a model for many later activities. Entitled "Labor History from the Point of View of the Rank and File," it featured organizers of the Congress of Industrial Organizations who described both the vigor and the suppression of 1930s militancy. As an extension of this forum, Lynd formed the Gary Writers' Workshop, which developed and published a highly creative alternative to the 1971 United Steel Workers' contract based on the demands of midwestern rank-and-file groups. The connection between histor-ical work and activism was clear: the knowledge of how rank and filers built the union and struggled to keep it democratic informed attempts to restore rank-and-file control in the 1970s.[14]

Oral history was the medium that linked activist history and labor militants, giving the Lynds a way to meet workers and later providing the basis for a critical history of the steelworkers' union. The Lynds' oral histories, pub-lished first in *Radical America* and then as *Rank and File* in 1973, contributed to another important medium in people's history, the movement-oriented doc-umentary film. Interviews with three women organizers in the Lynds' book became the basis for the film *Union Maids,* one of many excellent visual projects linking oral history, photographic documents, and activist politics. A number of similar projects united activist historians with labor and community groups to do people's history.[15]

As the student and antiwar movements declined during the early 1970s, activists within the universities found themselves increasingly cut off from protest movements and from the social problems and concerns of workers.[16] This separation seemed particularly acute to those who ended up in elite universities. As a first-year faculty member at Brandeis University, I became convinced that activist historians could form real connections with other activists only by leaving the university for alternative institutions like free schools, publishing groups, and organizing collectives.[17]

The most exciting people's history had been created by movement-inspired historians who deliberately took their research out of the academy. In addition to the Lynds' *Rank and File,* I was impressed by two other projects. After working in the civil rights movement and writing for the *Texas Observer,* Lawrence Goodwyn began to research the history of populism. He studied the suppression of the powerful interracial People's Party in Grimes County, East Texas, gaining access to the black side of the oral tradition through contacts in the civil rights movement. Goodwyn's article, "Populist Dreams and Negro Rights," and his subsequent work on populism are activist history motivated by a concern for rebuilding a mass democratic movement.[18] When radical historians in the Boston area organized public workshops in the early 1970s, two Harvard students played tapes of an elderly Alabama cotton farmer's description of his life, including his years in the Sharecroppers' Union of the 1930s. Like Goodwyn, Dale Rosen and Ted Rosengarten wanted to find a black version of the union's history. When they met Ned Cobb in 1969, he recognized them as "his people" and knew why they had come because they looked like movement folks, like the union organizers who came into rural Alabama in the early 1930s to organize a sharecroppers' union. In their first meeting, the historians asked him why he joined the union, and Ned Cobb spoke for nine hours. Rosen and Rosengarten published Cobb's account of a "shootout" with a union-busting posse in *Radical America,* and the full narrative appeared in 1973 as *All God's Dangers: The Life of Nate Shaw.*[19]

During the early 1970s a demand for people's history in a popular form emerged from newer kinds of activism. A typical product of this impulse was the Southern Conference Educational Fund's *Appalachian People's History Book.*[20] Veterans of the student and antiwar movements remained active in various workplace, community, and women's groups. Furthermore, rank-and-file insurgency hit many of the major international labor unions and evoked a new kind of activist-oriented labor history, such as Lynd's articles on the Steelworkers.[21] When I joined the *Radical America* editorial collective in 1972, I was immediately asked to write a popular overview article on worker militancy in the 1930s for an issue featuring two movement-oriented articles: Ned Cobb's account of the attack on the Alabama Sharecroppers' Union and Staughton Lynd's essay on the missed opportunity to create a rank-and-file steelworkers' movement in 1935.[22]

The Institute for Southern Studies began publishing a magazine called *Southern Exposure* in 1973. An early issue of the journal, "No More Moanin': Voices of Southern Struggle," epitomized an era of people's history. The editors wrote that they were searching for "that part of Southern history that is usually ignored or distorted, the history of people fighting for the right to lead decent productive lives." They did not intend "to romanticize the past, but rather to place our own work and lives within an historical context." The issue relied heavily on oral history to present a participants' view of the Southern Tenant Farmers' Union, an autoworker sit-down strike in Atlanta, Tennessee coal-mining wars, and slavery as reflected in the Writers' Project slave narratives. Sue Thrasher, a southern movement activist and editor of the magazine, later recalled that her interest in the working-class and progressive history of the South "necessarily involved oral history" because the voice and memory of working people was absent from standard historical accounts.[23]

During the mid-seventies, however, the political situation changed. The energies that had been channeled into the antiwar movement were not easily redirected, and activist historians found it increasingly difficult to maintain a movement orientation. The economic crisis discouraged the wildcat strikes and rank-and-file insurgencies that had been so common in the early 1970s. Left groups whose members had taken industrial jobs became discouraged and fragmented along sectarian lines. Even the women's movement seemed stymied. The Coalition of Labor Union Women, a promising initiative of feminists and union members, seemed moribund by 1975, stripped of its early movement orientation. Veterans of the black and women's liberation movements concentrated on defending hard-won rights, as did many active in the labor movement. Historians and intellectuals reacted accordingly. *Socialist Revolution* changed its name to *Socialist Review* and published less about movement-building and more about theory. *Radical America* continued to publish labor and women's history articles by movement-oriented historians, but with less missionary zeal and a reduced sense of relevancy, focusing less on spontaneous moments of resistance and possibilities for alternative politics and more on the obstacles to working-class unity.[24]

As a result, people's history in the late 1970s and the 1980s lost some of its initial movement orientation, if not its political motivation, and moved closer to traditional organizations and institutions. The possibility of securing funding for people's history projects under the Carter-era National Endowment for the Humanities (NEH) rapidly advanced this institutional orientation. The symbolic populism of the Carter administration filtered through the NEH and encouraged historians to participate with community and labor groups in celebrating ethnic and racial pride and the struggles of the women's, labor, and even leftist movements. This kind of populist orientation was sometimes uncritically romantic; some local history projects celebrating ethnic roots, community pride, and family survival stressed cultural solidarity and autonomy instead of class exploitation and group conflict. As David Gerber has pointed out, the populist history of the 1930s had seen immigrants and ethnics "as vital components of a diverse American proletariat which shared, for all its subcultural fragmentation, common needs and a common history of economic hardship," whereas the local and community history of the 1970s deemphasized the exploitation of immigrant and black labor and focused on the more subtle social ostracism suffered through the painful process of assimilation.[25]

If the NEH helped lead movement-oriented historians into uncritical populism, the Endowment's academic requirements presented an opposite problem of elitism and scholasticism. On the face of it, the need to involve academic humanists in all projects seemed to contradict the NEH's openness to people's history. In practice, however, NEH projects allowed many university-based historians to work with activists and make history more accessible to the public; they also offered isolated history professors a rare chance to engage the public in a dialogue about the past. Some historians found the demands of people's history and the realities of community politics in tension with their ideas about good history, but that tension was often creative. Many scholars with an activist orientation found in these projects an opportunity to begin a democratic dialogue about the past and to develop a new sort of relationship with working people outside the academy.

The shift away from agitational people's history did not mean that a movement orientation entirely disappeared. For example, Working Women developed a history curriculum to address the problems of women office workers and the movement to organize clerical workers that emerged in the 1970s, thereby earning the condemnation of the right-wing Heritage Foundation. Other historians worked closely with unionists in labor history societies formed in Illinois, West Virginia, Pennsylvania, Vermont, and elsewhere during the 1970s. In Rhode Island historians and unionists formed a Labor History Forum that featured veteran labor militants in well-attended community meetings. When the Radical Historians' Caucus became a national group called the Mid-Atlantic Radical Historians Organization in 1973 and started publishing the *Radical History Review,* collectives of historians formed around the country. Most of them concentrated on intellectual activity, but in

Rhode Island the collective combined public forums with historical research, some of which appeared in a special 1978 issue of the *Radical History Review* on "Labor and Community Militance" in the state. This publication, like the pamphlet "Vermont's Untold Story," was funded by a leftist collective. Like the NEH-funded *Boston's Workers,* these people's histories have been used by labor studies classes and union training sessions and read by individual labor leaders, union members, and activist newcomers.[26] This kind of work was activist history inspired in part by rank-and-file movements of miners and auto workers and various union reform efforts that continued into the late 1970s and early 1980s. Though popular labor history enhanced labor studies courses and gave historians access to union activity, including steward and leadership training, it had the limitations of the printed medium in a visual age. As funding for full-scale documentary films ebbed, many experimented with less-expensive videotape projects. Historians also began to seek more enduring connections to existing institutions like labor unions, not only to obtain funding, but to make their work more accountable to the people they hoped to address.

In this context and with some of these concerns, Marty Blatt, Susan Reverby, and I organized the Massachusetts History Workshop in 1978. We had been involved with earlier activist efforts and knew of precedents like the Gary Writers' Workshop, the Rhode Island Labor History Forum, and the Illinois Labor History Society, and we were also inspired by the British History Workshop movement. When I spent a year in England in 1975 and 1976, I was impressed by the movement-sense of the History Workshop; its national network had a coherence that we lacked in the United States, while depending less on academic historians and not at all on government funding. The Workshop provided direction and support for activist historians, many of them workers, outside the universities. The actual workshops attracted a good mix of university scholars, activists, and worker-historians and seemed to be approaching Staughton Lynd's goal of making participatory democracy a model for doing history.

H istory Workshop originated in 1967 at Ruskin College, Oxford, a school for trade unionists. The Workshop "was an attempt to create, within a very limited compass, an alternative educational practice, to encourage Ruskin students—working men and women, drawn from the labor and trade union movement—to engage in research and to construct their own history as a way of giving them an independent critical vantage point in their reading," according to Ruskin tutor Raphael Samuel.[27]

Since the examination system at Ruskin was based entirely on traditional readings, the workers who engaged in research in primary sources seemed to be involved in a kind of "subversive educational activity." Between 1970 and 1974 they produced thirteen History Workshop pamphlets based on original research in working-class history; typical titles were "Pit Life in County Durham" by Dave Douglass and "The Children's Strikes of 1911" by Dave Marson. It was, as Samuel said, "an attempt to build historical interpretation from the accumulated reflections of working men and women." This History Workshop approach has been unjustly criticized for relying entirely on the subjective feelings and memories of workers, but worker historians did not simply record experience; they reflected upon it and interpreted it. Their tutor thought these first-time historians enthusiastic but not naive; they had no illusions that the facts spoke for themselves.[28]

In addition to the pamphlets, the History Workshop organized yearly gatherings at Ruskin that were more overtly political, often responding directly to contemporary events. The workshops were indeed "tense with political expectancy," electrified by "a search for . . . political belonging." With respect to the labor movement, the Workshop took its stand "on the side of self-management," and "in labor history its main focus of attention was on rank-and-file movements, and the more spontaneous forms of working-class action, such as insurrections and strikes."[29] The History Workshop's approach to people's history seemed very movement-oriented as late as 1976, when I attended Workshop Number 10, an inspiring meeting devoted entirely to workers' education. The sessions were intended to be open and informal and to avoid "the treadmill of academic controversy." Worker-historians participated actively, demonstrating that the History Workshop had helped to "enlarge the constituency of historical writers and researchers" and to show "in practice that the career historians had no monopoly on writing and research."[30]

Indeed, History Workshop 10 impressed me with the exceptional advantages British historians enjoyed in creating a democratic and participatory working people's history. Worker-historians from Ruskin College and other places found in the Workshop a context for mutual support and constructive criticism. Labor education flourished, notably in the local activities of the Workers' Education Association, which brought many activist-historians together with workers in extra-mural teaching situations free of the worst aspects of university elitism and scholasticism.

In the United States, however, workers' education still seemed to be thoroughly dominated by anticommunist liberals in the universities and by cautious bureaucrats in the unions. Furthermore, labor education in this country tended to focus on "nuts and bolts" courses in collective bargaining and grievance procedure, with an occasional dash of the old institutional labor history. For example, the United Auto Workers' once-independent educational activities had been reduced to "thought control and indoctrination" by the 1950s, according to an experienced UAW labor educator. During the 1970 auto strike against General Motors, the UAW's effort to revive the militant spirit of the 1930s failed to overcome the harmful effects of bureaucratic education.[31] Veterans of the student and antiwar movements who wanted to become involved in labor education during the early 1970s found it difficult to proceed. In Massachusetts a few union organizers met with historians and other activists to form a chapter of Workers' Education Local 189, recently expelled from the American Federation of Teachers for opposing the policies of its president, Albert Shanker. The chapter sponsored a few labor history and folk song events, and the historians involved compiled a bibliographical pamphlet on New England labor history, but the chapter collapsed when the key union organizer left. At that point, none of the members were actually doing direct labor education work with union members. The movement historians were still searching for a way to make contact with more working people and to make some impact on the labor movement.

By contrast, the British History Workshop built upon a very strong labor education tradition (with an impressive socialist strain) and operated within a trade union culture that valued history. When the History Workshop published the first issue of its journal in 1976 (boldly labeled "a journal of socialist historians"), congratulatory advertisements from major national trade unions filled its pages. Clearly, the *Radical History Review* could not achieve anything like this kind of formal support from the AFL-CIO. Labor history even penetrated the mass media in the United Kingdom, notably in an amazing six-part docudrama called "The Days of Hope" in which a socialist scriptwriter traced the lives of three characters who were radicalized by events between the Easter Rising in 1916 and the General Strike of 1926.

I did not leave England with the view that a History Workshop was impossible in the United States or that the British efforts were without their problems. To some extent British labor history was a captive of the Trade Union Congress and the Labour Party. Socialism was traditional, co-opted to some extent by the official labor movement. Furthermore, even with the connections provided by workers' education, some British academics had trouble relating to workers, reading long-winded scholarly papers at History Workshop meetings. At times class differences between academics and workers seemed even more deep-seated in Britain than in the United States. Indeed, within a few years some tensions erupted within the Workshop between academics and worker-historians and between socialist labor historians and feminists.

At History Workshop 13 in 1979, the last to be held at Ruskin College, worker-students rebeled at the abstract debates over history and theory conducted by star intellectuals in rather obscure language, sparking a sharp debate between theoretically oriented Marxist historians and popularly oriented people's historians. Ken Worpole, an activist and advocate of community-based history and worker-autobiography, pointed to the "uneasy" relationship between the "flourishing" Federation of Worker Writers and Community Publishers and the group around the *History Workshop Journal.* An obsession with theory threatened to isolate workers' history from its "originating constituency." Debates about history and theory in the *Journal* were "impenetrable to anyone other than full-time academic historians," Worpole charged. History Workshop gatherings, once integrated with other "new forms of community politics," had tended to become more isolated from working people by 1979. And many of the activists who organized them "went into the academic sphere rather than returning to local history initiatives" begun in the early 1970s.[32] The British activist-historians, even with the exceptional advantages they enjoyed, had to face many of the same dilemmas we faced in the United States.

Moreover, we had certain resources and opportunities missing in the United Kingdom. Socialist discourse in Britain seemed to invite theoretical disputation and sectarian wrangling and to overwhelm more practical and more democratic discussions of how to do people's history. In the United States, historians actually engaged in people's history avoided this kind of wrangling like the plague. Furthermore, socialist debate in Britain tended to exclude other critical political perspectives. Feminism, populism, and cultural nationalism (even anarcho-syndicalism) enriched the blend of critical ideas influencing radical history in the United States and opened up new approaches to people's history.

In Britain the History Workshop developed a growing but tense relationship with the women's movement that ultimately led editors to change the movement publication's name in 1982 to a "journal of socialist and feminist historians." British feminists like Anna Davin worked actively to free people's history from the male-dominated concerns of traditional Marxist labor historians. Activist-historians in the United States lacked strong ties to the labor movement, but they often had more contact than their British counterparts with community and women's groups. Moreover, feminist historians and students of black and ethnic history brought a greater sensitivity to investigations of the role of gender, race, and nationality in U.S. people's history.[33] In sum, the possibilities for applying some of the History Workshop's methods to the ongoing work of activist-historians here seemed exciting, but engaging in people's history in New England would certainly mean something different from what it meant in Britain.

I n 1978 I learned that Marty Blatt, an activist historian, had started working on a museum exhibit entitled "Life and Times of Shoe City: The Shoe Workers of Lynn" at the Essex Institute in Salem, Massachusetts. Several historians—Paul Faler, Alan Dawley, and John Cumbler—influenced by the new social and cultural history pioneered by E. P. Thompson and Herbert Gutman, had chosen to write about the class-conscious shoe workers of Lynn because of their own involvement in the movements of the 1960s and their interest in uncovering radical traditions for the labor movement. Susan Reverby, a historian who had organized around health care and working women's issues, joined Marty Blatt and me in discussing the formation of a Lynn history workshop. She recruited Mary Blewett and Libby Zimmerman, whose research concerned women workers in and around Lynn. The Essex exhibit provided an excellent opportunity for organizing a workshop. The Institute had a sizable grant from the NEH and found itself in the awkward position of mounting an exhibit on Lynn shoe workers in the bourgeois, commercial town of Salem. The curator, Ann Farnham, was quite open to the idea of bringing the project back to Lynn. And Marty Blatt was already collecting oral histories and artifacts for the exhibit, so he was well placed to make contact with people who could support and participate in the workshop.[34]

Seventy former Lynn shoe workers attended our first History Workshop at the Hibernian Hall, near the giant General Electric River Works, where some of the workers were on strike. A few of these strikers attended the gathering, along with various historians and activists, but the shoe workers predominated. Some of the stitchers and cutters had not seen each other since they had been together "at the bench" in the waning days of the "shoe game" in Lynn. They gathered to talk, to celebrate their history, and to recreate the spirit of an old-time union meeting. We intentionally downplayed the formal role of the historians and stressed the free lunch, sociability, and the air of a family reunion, in large part because of the good advice of Jennie Stankiewicz, a

staff member of the old United Shoe Workers local. She enthusiastically created interest in the workshop among union pensioners and even organized a
car pool on the day of the workshop.

After a sign-in, coffee, and greeting session, Paul Faler, who had studied
the skilled artisans of Lynn, led a discussion of the labor process. Workers
emphasized the pride they took in their work, whether they were male cutters
or female stitchers, and in the industry that made Lynn the number one shoe-
making city in the country. Many who moved on to work at General Electric
remembered the lax discipline of the "shoe game" as much more humane.
Several women commented in group discussions that the shoe shops offered
better social relations and more fun than school ever had. Workers seemed
preoccupied with the decline of Lynn's shoe industry. This perspective also
appeared in an oral history booklet produced later by Workshop member Sal
Salerno and a group of Lynn high school students. "Voices of a Generation"
reflected a collective sense of loss about Lynn's past and the memory of earlier experiences of difficulty, solidarity, and community.

After lunch, Alan Dawley and John Cumbler, who have both written on
Lynn's militant union tradition, led a discussion on the city's labor movement. Dawley began the afternoon by passing out large reproductions of a
lithograph of women stitchers leading a parade through the snow during the
great 1860 shoe strike. It was not difficult to tap into the oral tradition of union
democracy and militancy in Lynn. A hot discussion ensued in which the Boot
and Shoe Workers Union, a now-defunct AFL business union, was denounced as the "manufacturers' union." Margaret DeLacey, an organizer for
the more militant United Shoe Workers, bitterly recounted what she had been
told about the AFL union's initial sellout in 1903, before she was born. Mae
Young, an 84-year-old CIO organizer, gave a moving speech about what the
union struggle had meant to her. Though blind and slow-moving, Mae spoke
in a sharp, clear voice and instantly recreated the feeling of an old union
meeting. It was one of those moments workshop organizers hope to create,
when the *feeling* of past struggles is revived.

The retired workers clearly enjoyed our first history workshop, and for us
the meeting reaffirmed the importance of historical memory in working people's lives. It enhanced our confidence about engaging in public history; it
encouraged us to make further contacts with unions and other groups in industrial communities; and it convinced us that under the right circumstances
workers would join with historians to share a common interest in history.

But our next project, which involved retired textile workers in Lawrence,
Massachusetts, was not as successful. A grant from the state humanities foundation provided a much larger budget than we had at Lynn. And we recruited

two organizers who were familiar with "immigrant city": Susan Porter Benson taught labor education classes for the Amalgamated Clothing and Textile Workers Union and Sarah Nordgren collected oral history for the Merrimack Valley Textile Museum. But despite our greater resources, the results were less satisfying than they were in Lynn because only about twenty workers attended and the event lacked the enthusiasm and collective engagement of our first effort.

We decided to feature historians more prominently in the Lawrence workshop, and David Montgomery gave a spirited introduction, describing important struggles in the city's history. The moderators, discouraged by the low turnout, faded out of the discussion, and it was dominated by two elderly organizers, one of whom was the colorful Angelo Rocco, a ninety-two-year-old lawyer who had been prominent in the leadership of the 1912 "Bread and Roses" strike. This was history with a capital *H*, exciting and entertaining, but not the kind of interior look at workers' lives we had enjoyed in Lynn. In fact, the discussion of family and community scheduled for later in the day did not develop as planned.

We were discouraged about the low turnout of textile workers, though we knew that a terrible rainstorm hurt our chances and learned later that a history workshop meeting held in Bradford, England, the sister woolmaking city to Lawrence, had also "failed to attract working-class people."[35] We were even more disturbed by the feeling of unease that prevailed in a gathering in which academics and activists vastly outnumbered workers. Nonetheless, people still talked in small groups during the afternoon, and historians elicited some interesting oral history, which Martha Coons wove together skillfully into an attractive booklet commemorating the event. The success of the booklet among retired textile workers across the country and the good press we received for attempting the event partly compensated for our disappointment with the low turnout and the breakdown of the program.[36]

In the post-workshop discussions we identified many practical changes that we would make in future workshops—for example, including workers in the planning and organizing process. We also questioned the wisdom of mobilizing for a one-time event in a community in which we were outsiders. We agreed that a workshop would be more effective either as part of a continuum of events—as in the case of Lynn—or as the beginning of a longer-term process.

We were also concerned with political and historical issues raised by the Lawrence workshop. Several of the workers questioned the value of history, especially union organizer Dan Downey, who said that most elderly people would rather forget the past, "forget the clubbings of 1912, the jailings of 1919, and the clubbings again in 1931." Downey also asked us who was going to write Lawrence history so that younger people would know what had happened. Our response was inadequate. We presented ourselves simply as historians eliciting oral testimony, not as professionals who intended to rewrite history, though, indeed, some of us meant to do just that. In retrospect, we should have been more affirmative and answered, yes, we are going to write workers' history, but it will be better if we can include your memories.

An observer and friendly critic, Tom Leary, also suggested that we should have taken on the other hard question about why people should not forget the past. In the future, he suggested, it might be helpful to distribute a few blatantly offensive quotations about workers from a high school textbook or business publication to show why workers' own memories are important. "Worker participation in any booklets or documentaries would be a further bonus," Leary added, "though the latter expectation may be a foredoomed extrapolation from the English model given the difference in the level of U.S. class consciousness and the educational policy of our unions."[37] In some ways the Lawrence workshop forced us to step back from our initial enthusiasm for a participatory people's history, but we did not give up hope that workers in Massachusetts could participate in doing their own history. Indeed, we had not yet taken on the difficult but exciting task of working with them in actually planning, organizing, and producing an event and the publication that followed. Workers in Lawrence contributed their memories, but as in most oral history projects, they did not join the historians in presenting and interpreting the past. The political challenge of doing collaborative people's history remained before us. With these thoughts in mind, we proposed our third workshop to the state humanities foundation and received a $9,000 grant to organize a meeting of women clerical workers in Boston and to work with them to produce a booklet about their history. This time workers and activists would be involved with historians from start to finish.

Boston had been the scene of significant office-worker agitation, starting with founding of 9 to 5 in 1973 and carrying on through the difficult and unsuccessful drives to organize workers at Harvard and the Massachusetts Institute of Technology, the founding of Union Local 925, and the 1979 victory of Boston University clerical and technical workers represented by District 65. Some of the city's office workers had been affected by this agitation, notably 9 to 5's campaign to show how a business cartel held down women's wages. Some consciousness raising also took place through history courses sponsored by Working Women and through publications like Jean Tepperman's *Not Servants, Not Machines,* and Margery Davies' *Radical America* pamphlet on the feminization of office work. Many of the younger activist workers had college educations, and some had participated in the antiwar and feminist movements.[38] We hoped a history workshop would further the consciousness raising and perhaps contribute to organizing efforts.

We hired Carol Yourman, who had been active in the Boston University union drive, to organize our workshop. She was very familiar with women's and workers' history and strongly committed to office organizing. Her skill and energy helped make the workshop our greatest success. Yourman suggested that oral history interviews with older and retired clerical workers could involve these women in the workshop from the start. She recruited about a dozen younger activist clerical workers to conduct the interviews according to a format she developed with workshop historians. The oral history project, which began in January 1982, created enthusiasm and a sense of involvement in the workshop for the younger women doing the interviews and for the older women giving testimony. It also served to meet a goal unattained in previous workshops: putting a younger generation of workers in touch with an older generation. Oral history provided a perfect vehicle for passing along traditions, experiences, and lessons, giving retired workers a sense that their stories really mattered and would be welcomed by young people at the workshop. Finally, the project contributed substantially to the second goal of our effort: to involve clerical workers in researching, writing, designing, and distributing an account of their own history.

The workshop itself took place during National Secretaries Week in April 1982 and was a big success. Held at the University of Massachusetts–Boston under the title "They Can't Run the Office Without Us: Women Look at Sixty Years of Clerical Work," the meeting attracted over two hundred women and a few men. There was a good mix of older and retired women and younger office workers, many of them with experience in union organizing.

The morning session set the tone for the whole day. Margery Davies discussed the feminization of clerical work, and three women spoke about different aspects of their work lives. Eleanor Coughlin gave a wonderful talk about historical changes in government and union offices. The "hideous regimentation" of the early days had faded somewhat, but, she added in a sentence that became the headline of a *Boston Herald* story the next day, "The salaries haven't changed. We're still the lowest part of the totem pole." She also explained how contact with the young oral historians convinced her that—as a worker—she had something significant to say about historical change. The opening session energized the gathering and helped stimulate the small-group discussions, carefully organized so that each group contained a mix of older and younger workers. As a result of this planning and thoughtful work by each group leader, we actually achieved the elusive goal of intergenerational sharing and communication. The report-back session proved engaging and at times inspiring as women commented on what this experience meant to them.

The afternoon session was equally successful and added the energy of historical controversy to the workshop. Women's historian Sharon Hartman Strom offered a clear feminist criticism of unions' failure to organize clerical workers.[39] Ann Prosten, who headed the left-led CIO office workers' union in Boston during the 1930s, responded by explaining the problems unions faced in organizing white-collar and blue-collar workers together. The head of the Boston University union gave a strong speech on what the union meant to its members and a 9 to 5 leader explained how many office workers had found tactics other than unionization to pressure employers. Though the session presented a strong case for unionization, it also examined the historic limitations of unions and explored alternatives.

Many people responded to our request for volunteers to work on a historical study of office workers in Boston. In the months that followed, we divided into work groups and began the difficult but exciting process of writing history collectively. In many ways our numbers (eight people in the history research and writing group plus ten people working on graphics and design) proved an advantage, especially in transcribing and organizing the results of our oral history interviews. But writing history by committee also presented some problems and tested the limits of our participatory model.

Among the people who worked on the history committee, only one had worked as a professional historian and three others had some graduate training in history. The rest worked in offices and had union experience; they had written leaflets and newspaper articles but not historical narrative. We tried to create a mutually supportive process for the actual writing, but some writers were too busy or too inexperienced to complete their drafts. Our grant provided payments to our organizer and the academic humanists, but not to those who participated in the writing group. This made it difficult for workers to put in much time on the project; as the deadline for a funding cutoff approached, the academic with the most experience in writing history hastily wrote two of the chapters and turned them over to the editors.

Still and all, clerical workers performed the bulk of the work on the booklet: all of the oral history interviews, transcribing, photo research, design, production, and editing, and most of the actual writing. Over a hundred people contributed to the final product. In the end, the project represented a fairly successful collaborative effort in which workers themselves researched and interpreted their own history. Maximum attention was devoted to making the book accessible and relevant to office workers; the oral histories became the basis of a narrative written in a voice workers would recognize.

There was little disagreement between the historians and workers about the process of working together or the need to make the presentation popular, but differences over language and interpretation did arise. For example, a historian and an editor who had organized clerical workers debated over the process of deskilling identified and analyzed by Harry Braverman and Margery Davies.[40] The editor argued that the notion of deskilling belittled the experience of the clerical workers she knew, who thought of themselves as quite skilled. The historian at first argued for a long view that revealed the capitalist managerial strategy of separating conception from execution in the labor process, but in the end had to admit that the oral histories revealed mainly positive, self-respecting memories of office work. The tension between subjective experience and historical analysis was resolved by describing the changes that management attempted to make in office work without using the term *deskilling*. Susan Porter Benson's work on department store clerks and Margery Davies' own comments on secretaries in small offices revealed that Braverman's model of the deskilled male craftsman could not be readily applied to women's experience.[41] The book examines changes in the organization of office work as well as the effects of scientific management and mechanization, yet it is still, as Davies put it in a pre-publication comment, "imbued with an impressive spirit of self respect which office workers have for themselves and their work."

They Can't Run the Office Without Us appeared in January 1985, eighty pages long with over fifty illustrations and a title borrowed from the 1982 workshop.[42] The book took two and a half years to complete, and its production encountered many problems, mainly related to time and money. The success of the project was probably due most of all to the fact that the history seemed so directly relevant to workplace organizing; the search for a usable past energized clerical workers and office organizers to explore history.[43] Early responses to the book, including a favorable review in the *Boston Globe*'s "Living with Work" column, have justified their efforts. The clerical and technical workers' union at Yale University, fresh from its historic 1985 strike victory, used the book for their steward training and internal organizing. Workshop members have also used it in steward training for telephone company clerical workers, and plans are now being made to distribute the book to other unionized office employees.

After nearly eight years of activity, the experience of the Massachusetts History Workshop suggests some practical considerations for others who would engage in democratizing people's history.

First, the British History Workshop model can be applied to the United States. The lack of class consciousness among North American workers and the weakness of labor education are not insurmountable obstacles to collaborating with workers. The lack of contact between historians and workers is more the result of institutional and cultural segregation than of cultural or political antagonism. Rank-and-file workers have not been particularly suspicious of our attempts at collaborative historical work, though politically preoccupied union officials sometimes are. We have enhanced our credibility with the workers by producing free or low-cost pamphlets about local work groups and their history. There are, of course, limits to the print medium, and we hope to experiment with videotapes and dramatic performances, but these engaging forms of people's history are more costly and more difficult to produce. Second, we have learned something about actually organizing public history events. Our successes have come from engaging organizers to work on the projects with local people for a period of months. We also discovered that oral history can be more than a method of gathering historical recollections; it can be used as a way of involving workers in public history events and publications. Third, we have learned to use our resources more effectively by working closer to home, by seeking alternatives to federal and state humanities funding, and by trying to serve existing organizations and institutions.

The resources for doing people's history in Massachusetts have expanded in recent years. One of our members is now working through the Massachusetts Office of Labor to integrate workers' history into the state's heritage parks and public school curricula. Revivals of the Workers' Education Organization and the Coalition of Labor Union Women signal a renewed interest in workers' education. These groups, as well as the new Massachusetts Labor Support Project, create both an interest in and a demand for working people's history. Moreover, the crisis of organized labor in the past decade has led AFL-CIO officials to call for a revival of labor-history education in unions and public schools.[44]

In 1983 we decided to test this new situation by organizing, with the official sponsorship and support of the state AFL-CIO, an event to commemorate the eightieth anniversary of the founding of the Women's Trade Union League. A newly created women's committee of the state labor council helped us to gain an endorsement and a modest contribution from the council as well as from a surprising range of local unions, like the glaziers, pipefitters, and airline mechanics. We also received funds from History Workshop supporters, women's groups, and a leftist foundation. The result, presented at Faneuil Hall in Boston, was a curious hybrid event sponsored by organized labor as well as by the left and the women's movement. It was a lively, successful meeting attended by over two hundred, but it was not without its tensions: the state labor council president told the crowd how much he had done for women, and

the feminist historian and novelist Meredith Tax emphasized how little unions
had done for women and how much remained to be accomplished. These
contrasts embarrassed some people, but they arose inevitably as a result of our
effort to make a claim on both the labor and women's movements. We gained
financial support and enhanced credibility from both unionists and feminists,
drawing upon the skills of union staff members such as Susan Phillips, who
designed a beautiful poster and program, and at the same time involving
women's movement groups such as the outstanding Word-of-Mouth drama
group, whose members dressed like WTUL organizers, sang songs, performed skits, and gave soap-box speeches as people entered the hall. In sum,
as organizers we used people's history as a way of bringing political education
on an important issue (women's role in the labor movement) to a much broader public audience than we had ever reached before.[45]

As History Workshop activities attracted more attention, history enthusiasts
asked to join our group. Open meetings attracted ten to fifteen people, mainly
graduate students, activists, and union staffers who wanted to do history for
political reasons and who did not face the career pressures of university-based
historians. At the same time, we shifted to smaller, more manageable projects
closer to home. For example, in the summer of 1982 we received funds from
the Cambridge Arts Council to organize an outdoor cultural event as part of
the city's summer River Festival. "Hard Times and Workers' Lives: Songs,
Stories and Poems about Organizing and Carrying On" took place in a local
park and attracted about a hundred people.

A second focus of the group is to provide support for the historical work
members are doing outside the academy. This means becoming engaged in
ongoing public history projects even though they may be motivated by political and cultural concerns different from our own. We do not present ourselves
as historians for hire or as expert consultants like the American History Workshop and other commercial history groups, but rather as activist historians
eager to support institutions and groups who want to enable people to do their
own history. For example, one of the people who attended our meetings
worked at the Lowell Public Library, which had received an NEH grant to
present family histories of various immigrant groups. A local history teacher
and a park guide were hired to organize work groups of people from each
nationality to collect oral histories and then construct a typical family history
for each group. We offered methodological and practical advice even though
the project ignored some of our questions about Lowell's history. We did
have a chance to raise some issues based on our understanding of family and
ethnic history, but in the end it was not our project: we were supporters and
advisors rather than organizers and directors.

The History Workshop approach holds out the promise that history can be a cultural resource in movement-building, but doing people's history is not simply a matter of using the past for agitational purposes. We have rejected the professional models of academic and public history in favor of a democratic approach that challenges the current division of labor in producing history. We cannot replace those models with an elitist view of activists bringing historical consciousness to forgetful workers. By applying a democratic yardstick to our work we were compelled to listen to our co-workers and respond to their ideas about the project. Invariably, our projects improved when we did so. Listening carefully also means hearing things that can be offensive or disturbing—myths, prejudices, and inaccuracies in the way people see things—but these subjective feelings are the stuff of people's history, and activist historians must view this engagement with popular historical memory as a central goal of their work. Unless we hear what people think about the past, we cannot begin to have a democratic dialogue in which we are given an opportunity to ask why people think as they do. Nor can we begin to create the kind of trusting, mutually rewarding relationships in which people will ask us what we think about the past and why we think that way.

Engaging in people's history through such a democratic dialogue and participatory process can educate all concerned and create a new kind of history that is neither academic nor anecdotal, but that draws upon subjective historical memories and popular interpretations along with more scholarly forms of analysis and interpretation.[46] Whatever form the ultimate product takes, the process of engaging in people's history can be an empowering democratic experience of a kind difficult to find in our society.[47] Perhaps this process can even be seen as a kind of rehearsal for the political education and consciousness raising that take place spontaneously within mass social movements. It happened in the populist and socialist movements, in the black and women's liberation movements; it surely took place in the early labor movement as well as in the Solidarity insurgency in Poland and in the ongoing black workers' movement in southern Africa.[48] And this sort of dialogue about the meaning of a people's history must be part of a revived labor movement or any insurgencies that capture the popular imagination.

★ Notes ★

Chapter 1

1. This essay originated in a talk delivered in October 1979 at the SUNY–Buffalo Law School, as part of an unusual symposium. Marcel Ophuls had joined the Law School's faculty and students as a Mitchell Lecturer for a week focused on his documentary films, a body of work that explores the meeting ground of law, ethics, politics, and morality as found in some of the focal points of modern history—the Holocaust and the Nuremberg trials, the Nazi occupation of France, and the conflict in Northern Ireland. At the end of several days of screening and informal discussion, there was a public symposium featuring M. Ophuls. The discussion focused in particular on *The Memory of Justice,* the film most relevant to its American law school audience.

Because readers may not have a viewing of Ophuls' long, complex movie fresh in mind, and many may not have seen it at all, I have recast my remarks in more general terms. Toward the end, however, I will return to a brief discussion of The Memory of Justice, in part as a way of repaying a considerable intellectual debt, since so much of my own thinking about documentary and oral history was crystallized, well before the Mitchell lectures, by Ophuls' films and the human spirit animating them.

2. The 1972 campaign is the rule-proving exception. With the stage set for a major ideological confrontation, somehow the play was canceled: McGovern came to seem a simpleton or worse, only partly because of his own errors. Efforts to produce a referendum on the war foundered on the hardly coincidental emergence of McGovern's credibility and image problems. Accordingly, to most Americans there seemed to be no "real" or "serious" alternative to Nixon, and therefore no deeper choices to be made about the war or anything else.

3. New York: Oxford University Press, 1978.

4. These remarks were made in a conversation. For a fuller elaboration of their author's perspective, readers are referred to Chinweizu, *The West and the Rest of Us: White Predators, Black Slavers, and the African Elite* (New York, 1975). This is a

361

remarkable book—a comprehensive synthesis of colonial African history, a devastating critique of the neocolonial corruption of most postindependence African institutions, and a world history from an African vantage—a furious and relentlessly incisive "victims'-eye view" of the inexorable expansion of the West and its usual historical rationalizations.

5. I have discussed some of these points in "The New York State Labor History Association's Fourth Annual Meeting: A Participant's Critique," *International Labor and Working-Class History,* 16 (Fall 1979), 51–55.

6. See my essay "Oral History, Documentary, and the Mystification of Power: A Case Study Critique of Public Methodology," prepared for the Fifth International Oral History Conference, Barcelona, March 1985 (publication pending).

7. Studs Terkel, *Hard Times: An Oral History of the Great Depression* (New York, 1970); *All God's Dangers: The Life of Nate Shaw,* comp. Theodore Rosengarten (New York, 1971); and Brass Workers History Project, *Brass Valley: The Story of Working People's Lives and Struggles in an American Industrial Region,* Comp. and ed. Jeremy Brecher, Jerry Lombardi, and Jan Stackhouse (Philadelphia, 1982).

8. See my "Oral History and *Hard Times:* A Review Essay," *Oral History Review* (1979), 70–80.

9. See Rosenberg's review essay, "The Shadow of the Furies," *New York Review of Books,* Jan. 20, 1977, 47–49, and Ophuls' extensive, eloquent reply, *New York Review of Books,* March 17, 1977, 43–45. Also see Dorothy Rabinowitz's review, "Ophuls: Justice Misremembered," in *Commentary,* Dec. 1976, 65–67.

Chapter 2

Acknowledgments: I would like to thank Jean-Christophe Agnew, Susan Porter Benson, Steve Botein, Stephen Brier, Alan Brinkley, Josh Brown, Jane Caplan, Peter Dimock, Deborah Kaplan, Warren Leon, Nick Salvatore, Michael Wallace, and Jon Wiener for helpful comments on this article. I also want to thank Byron Dobell, Jack Garraty, Barbara Klaw, and Richard Snow for talking with me about *American Heritage* and allowing me to examine some materials from the magazine's files without imposing any restraints on my use of this information. The Allan Nevins papers are quoted with the permission of the Rare Books and Manuscript Library, Columbia University.

1. U.S. Congress, Senate, Committee on the Judiciary, *The Attempt to Steal the Bicentennial: The Peoples Bicentennial Commission: Hearings Before the Subcommittee to Investigate the Administration of the Internal Security Act,* 94th Cong., 2d sess., 1976, 3, 24.

2. "*American Heritage* Starts Trade Book Division," *Publishers Weekly,* July 15, 1968, 33. On "product line" see, for example, advertisements in the Dec. 1980 issue, and on tours, see *McGraw-Hill Annual Report 1971* (New York, 1972), 9. On television, see Val Adams, "Civil War Series Planned on C.B.S.," *New York Times,* Jan. 6,

1959; and *TV Guide,* Oct. 24, 1959, 12–15; Feb. 20, 1960, 12–14; Nov. 17, 1973, 16–17; Jan. 19, 1974, 30–32. *American Heritage* recently discontinued its catalogue sales operation, which was not doing well.

3. See, for example, David D. Van Tassel and James A. Tinsley, "Historical Organizations as Aids to History," in William B. Hesseltine and Donald R. McNeil, eds., *In Support of Clio: Essays in Memory of Herbert A. Kellar* (Madison, 1958), 138; Walter Muir Whitehill, *Independent Historical Societies* (Boston, 1962), xi, 514–16; John Higham, *History: Professional Scholarship in America* (rev. ed., Baltimore, 1983), 80–84.

4. This and the following paragraph are based on Allan Nevins, *The Gateway to History* (1938; rev. ed., Chicago, 1963), 8; "The Reminiscences of Allan Nevins," Oral History Research Office, Columbia University, 1963, 170; F. E. Dayton to Allan Nevins, Sept. 1, 1938, Box 86, Archives of the American Historical Association, Division of Manuscripts, Library of Congress (hereafter cited as AHA MSS); "Retrospect of 1954," in Allan Nevins Diaries, Box 32, Allan Nevins Papers, Rare Book and Manuscript Library, Columbia University (hereafter cited as Nevins MSS); Conyers Read to James P. Baxter, Sept. 14, 1938, Sept. 22, 1938, and Memo of Sept. 21, 1938, Box 86, AHA MSS. On Nevins, see Richard M. McMurry, "Allan Nevins," in Clyde N. Wilson, ed., *Twentieth Century American Historians* (Detroit, 1983), 326; Ray Allen Billington, "Allan Nevins, Historian: A Personal Reminiscence," in Billington, comp., *Allan Nevins on History* (New York, 1975), ix–xxvii.

5. Merk to Members of the Council of the American Historical Association, Dec. 12, 1938, Box 113, AHA MSS; "Reminiscences of Nevins," 173; *Annual Report of the American Historical Association for the Year 1939* (Washington, D.C., 1939), 32.

6. Nevins, "Retrospect of 1954"; "Reminiscences of Nevins"; Nevins, "What's the Matter with History?" *Saturday Review of Literature,* Feb. 4, 1939, 3–4, 16.

7. McMurry, "Nevins," 316; Nevins, "What's the Matter," 16; Nevins, "An Idea Whose Time Has Come," *New York Times,* Oct. 18, 1959, sec. 11 (advertisement). On *Saturday Review* and "adult education in the value of books," see Joan Rubin's excellent article, "Self, Culture, and Self-Culture in Modern America: The Early History of the Book-of-the-Month Club," *Journal of American History,* 71 (1983), 782–806. The phrase "democratic public" comes from Nevins' address to the AHA: "Not Capulets, Not Montagus," *American Historical Review,* 65 (1960), 256.

8. Nevins, "Retrospect of 1954"; U.S. Bureau of the Census, *Historical Statistics of the United States, Part 1* (Washington, D.C., 1975), 169 (hereafter cited as *Historical Statistics*).

9. Becker to Nevins, Feb. 2, 1939, Box 49, Nevins MSS; Read to Becker, Jan. 25, 1939, Box 114, and Read to Baxter, Sept. 14, 1938, Box 86, both AHA MSS.

10. Nevins, "Retrospect of 1954"; *Publishers Weekly,* Feb. 10, 1951, 858, and May 12, 1951, 949. On the benefits of running no advertisements, see "The Reminiscences of James Parton," Oral History Research Office, Columbia University, 1959, 18–19. For *Milestones* prospectus, see Box 69, Nevins MSS.

11. "History at the Grass Roots," *Time,* Nov. 26, 1951, 59–60; "Historical Heritage," *Newsweek,* Apr. 21, 1952, 104–5; On the AASLH, see Van Tassel and

Tinsley, "Historical Organizations," 136–38; George Rollie Adams, "AASLH," *History News*, 37 (Sept. 1982), 12–18. On earlier magazines issued by historical, patriotic, and genealogical societies, see Frank Luther Mott, *A History of American Magazines*, 5 vols. (Cambridge, Mass., 1957), vol. 3, 258–63, IV, 137–40. One of the objections raised to the Nevins project in 1938 came from the head of the Wisconsin Historical Society, who worried that it would "destroy all of the historical quarterlies in the country." Nevins, "Retrospect of 1954."

12. S. K. Stevens, Editorial Statement, *American Heritage* (hereafter cited as *AH*), 1 (Sept. 1949), 1. In a later issue of the magazine, AASLH Vice President Clifford Lord commented similarly: "You cannot know what makes the American community click and be either a good Fascist or a good Communist. And that is important. . . . We must know and understand the basic genius of the American experiment, if we are to be able to defend it and to publicize it to the four corners of this round world": *AH*, 4 (Summer 1953), 1.

13. On the UAW, see Victor Reuther, "UAW," *AH*, 2 (Summer 1951), 42–43. See issues of *AH*, 1949–54.

14. "History at the Grass Roots"; "Historical Heritage"; "Reminiscences of Parton," 13.

15. "Reminiscences of Parton," 14–15.

16. Kouwenhoven to Nevins, June 14, 1954; Parton to Nevins, June 18, 1954. On negotiations with SAH: Rudolf Clemen to Nevins, June 6, 1954; James Parton to Nevins, June 15, 1954; Parton to Clemen, June 16, 1954; Clemen to Nevins, June 18, 1954; Clemen to Nevins, June 22, 1954; S. K. Stevens to Nevins, June 22, 1954; all in Box 69, Nevins MSS. Nevins' role in the founding of the magazine can be traced in his correspondence from 1954 (Box 69) and diaries for that year (Box 32).

17. Parton to Nevins, Aug. 5, 1954, Box 69, Nevins MSS; *New York Times Book Review*, Oct. 17, 1954, 27. (The promotional letters are in the same box of Nevins' correspondence.)

18. *New York Times Book Review*, May 6, 1951, 9.

19. Nevins to Catton, Aug. 22, 1954, Box 69, Nevins MSS; Nevins, "Retrospect of 1954"; Nevins Diary, Jan. 2, 1956, Box 32, Nevins MSS.

20. Nevins, "Retrospect of 1954"; Nevins quoted in Edward N. Saveth, "What Historians Teach About Business," *Fortune*, April 1952, 48; Nevins, "Should American History Be Rewritten? Yes," *Saturday Review*, Feb. 6, 1954, 48; "Reminiscences of Nevins," 249–50.

21. Nevins, "Retrospect of 1954"; "Reminiscences of Oliver Jensen," Oral History Research Office, Columbia University, 1959, 13; "Reminiscences of Parton," 16, 23. The actual dollar figure for *AH*'s start-up capital varies in different accounts from $62,000 to $69,000.

22. William Harlan Hale, "The Boom in American History," *Reporter* 12 (Feb. 24, 1955), 43; *Historical Statistics*, I, 169; Nevins Diary, Sept. 14, 1954, Box 32, Nevins MSS.

23. Printed promotional materials prepared ca. spring 1959, *American Heritage* office files, New York City (hereafter cited as "promotional materials"); *Historical*

Statistics, I, 116, 289–92, 380–81; *New York Times,* Oct. 18, 1959, sect. 11. A 1956 survey found similar results: *"American Heritage* Grows," *History News,* 12 (Dec. 1956), 15. The "executive-managerial-proprietor" category apparently included professionals, who composed one-third of the audience in the 1956 survey. Current visitors to Colonial Williamsburg show a similarly upper-middle-class profile, which may suggest that an interest in "formal" American history is generally strong among the well-to-do, or may simply reflect the cost of visiting museums and buying magazines. Michael Wallace, "Visiting the Past: History Museums in the United States," in this volume, p. 137.

24. Promotional materials.

25. "Reminiscences of Parton," 20; "Reminiscences of Jensen," 7–23; Nevins Diary, June 14, 1954, June 20, 1954; "Reminiscences of Nevins," 248. The AASLH did receive substantial royalty payments over the years. Between 1954 and 1969 *AH* paid $750,000 to AASLH and SAH. When financial hard times hit *AH* in the 1980s, it sought to break the royalty agreement with the AASLH, which sued but then settled out of court. Oliver Jensen, "An Anniversary," *AH,* 21 (Dec. 1969), 3; Gerald George, "From the Director," *History News,* 39 (March 1984), 4.

26. For Nevins' involvement with the magazine see, for example, Nevins Diary, Nov. 2, 1955, Dec. 30, 1955, Jan. 17, 1956, Jan. 16, 1957; Nevins to Catton, Sept. 2, 1954, Box 69, Nevins MSS; Billington, *Allan Nevins,* xxii; "Reminiscences of Jensen," 23. Nevins retained a connection to *AH* even after he retired from Columbia in 1958 and moved to the Huntington Library in California.

27. "Reminiscences of Jensen," 1–14; interview with Barbara Klaw, April 17, 1984, New York City; "Jensen, Oliver O(merod)," *Current Biography 1945* (New York, 1945), 302–4. Catton remained an active presence on the magazine after he became senior editor. Between 1964 and 1966 Thorndike is listed as editor in chief; after 1966 he is listed as chair of the editorial committee, but this title refers to his role in the publishing company and not the magazine. Thorndike and Jensen are still senior editors of *AH*. Parton, however, appears to have completely severed his ties to the magazine; between 1979 and 1981 he was even associated with a competitor, *American History Illustrated.* The Time-Life influence on the magazine also came from art director Irwin Glusker, picture editor Joan Patterson Mills, and promotional writer Frank Johnson. "Reminiscences of Jensen," 14; *"American Heritage* the Product of Resourceful Planning," *Publishers Weekly,* Sept. 3, 1955, 904–7.

28. On Catton, see Carol Reardon, "Bruce Catton," in Wilson, *Twentieth Century American Historians,* 98–102. On the choice of Catton as editor, see Nevins Diary, June 21, 1954; Nevins, "Retrospect of 1954"; Parton to Nevins, June 18, 1954, Box 69, Nevins MSS.

29. Bruce Catton, "What They Did There," *AH,* 6 (Dec. 1954), 3–4; Catton, *The Warlords of Washington* (New York, 1948), 309. Catton was listed as a "staff contributor" to the *Nation* until November 1955, shortly after that magazine gave *American Heritage* perhaps the only negative review it received. See Kenneth Rexroth, "Advertisers Anonymous," *Nation,* 181 (Oct. 29, 1955), 358–59. Later biographical sketches of Catton ignore his earlier political commitments.

30. Oliver Jensen, "The Peales," *AH,* 6 (April 1955), 40–51; "T. R. Writes His Son," *AH,* 10 (Dec. 1958), 128; former staff member to author, April 11, 1984.

31. "Dear Reader," Dec. 29, 1958, Box 69, Nevins MSS; and in *AH:* Clay Perry, "Big Guns for Washington," 6 (April 1955), 12–15, 102; Esther M. Douty, "The Greatest Balloon Voyage Ever Made," 6 (June 1955), 10–13, 106–7; Fairfax M. Downey, "The Tragic Story of the San Patricio Battalion," 6 (June 1955), 20–23; Lucius Beebe, "The Overland Limited," 15 (Dec. 1963), 54–57, 87; John Nelson Culbertson, "A Pennsylvania Boyhood," 18 (Dec. 1966), 80–88; Marshall Fishwick, "The Pepys of the Old Dominion," 11 (Dec. 1959), 4–7, 117–19; Timothy Severin, "The Preposterous Pathfinder," 19 (Dec. 1967), 56–63.

32. "Catton, (Charles) Bruce," *Contemporary Authors,* new revision series (Detroit, 1982), vol. 7, 109; *New York Times,* Aug. 29, 1978. On same impulse in Nevins, see "Reminiscences of Nevins," 143.

33. "Reminiscences of Jensen," 9, 16; "Jensen, Oliver O(merod)," 303; "Parton Paper," *History News* 13 (Feb. 1957), 26. A story that Jensen once commissioned from a German prison camp official with the title "Everything Was Gemütlich in the Prison Camps" proved too breezy for some Jewish staff members and sparked a staff revolt: Dora Jane Hamblin, *That Was the Life* (New York, 1977), 276. Jensen's political and social inclinations as well as his journalistic background probably influenced his work on the magazine. A conservative who preferred the nineteenth century, he drenched his own articles (frequently about steamboats), as well as the magazine in general, in a nostalgic yearning for a nonexistent American past.

34. Thomas E. Cooney, "The Author," *Saturday Review,* Oct. 27, 1956, 14; McMurry, "Nevins," 324. On historical memory under advanced capitalism, see Wallace, "Visiting the Past," p. 137. On the survival of oral and folk traditions among nonelites, see, for example, Gladys-Marie Fry, *Night Riders in Black Folk History* (Knoxville, 1975); William Lynwood Montell, *The Saga of Coe Ridge: A Study in Oral History* (Knoxville, 1970).

35. *New York Times Book Review,* Oct. 17, 1954, 27.

36. Bruce Catton, "The Wind in the Wires," *New York Times,* Oct. 18, 1959, sec. 11. On the "liberal consensus," see Godfrey Hodgson, *America in Our Time* (New York, 1976), passim. Kennedy, himself the ostensible author of the best-selling history book of the postwar period (*Profiles in Courage*), wrote the foreword to *AH*'s sixteen-volume supermarketed history of the United States, Robert G. Athearn, *The American Heritage New Illustrated History of the United States,* 16 vols. (New York, 1963).

37. Russell H. Bastert, "The New American History and Its Audience," *Yale Review,* 46 (1956), 258.

38. Promotional materials; "*American Heritage* Grows." Random House's Landmark book history series for children sold 4 million copies in the early fifties, and *AH* created its own "Junior Library" series: Hale, "Boom," 42; "Heritage Begins Children's Series," *History News* 15 (Sept. 1959), 105. *Business Week* noted the particular appeal of *AH* for lawyers and children: "Magazines with the Book Look," July 1, 1961, 38.

39. See, for example, in *AH,* Henry Steele Commager, "The Constitution: Was It an Economic Document?" 10 (Dec. 1958), 58–61, 100–103; David Donald, "Why They Impeached Andrew Johnson," 8 (Dec. 1956), 20–25, 102–3; James G. Randall and R. N. Current, "Excerpt from *The Last Full Measure,*" 6 (June 1955), 65–88; Oscar Handlin, "A Liner, a U-Boat, and History," 6 (June 1955), 40–45, 105. Among the other leading historians who appeared in the first fifteen years of *American Heritage* were Samuel Eliot Morrison, Perry Miller, and Arthur Schlesinger, Jr. On the historical profession in the 1950s, see Jesse Lemisch, *On Active Service in War and Peace: Politics and Ideology in the American Historical Profession* (Toronto, 1975); Higham, *History,* 212–32.

40. Allan Nevins, "Henry Ford: A Complex Man," *AH,* 6 (Dec. 1954), 54–59. On Nevins and business historiography, see Harvey Wish, *The American Historian: A Social-Intellectual History of the Writing of the American Past* (New York, 1960), 321–50.

41. Hale, "Boom," 113, 116; William L. Neumann, "Historians in an Age of Acquiescence," *Dissent,* Winter 1957, 64–69. On philanthropy by businessmen, see Allan Nevins' introduction to "The Memoirs of Frederick T. Gates: The Man Who Gave Away Rockefeller's Millions," *AH,* 6 (April 1955), 66–70; Caroline E. Werkley, "Mister Carnegie's 'Library,'" 21 (Feb. 1970), 65–68; Joseph Frazier Wall, "What Princeton Really Needed," 21 (June 1970), 91–92.

42. "Primitive in the Park," *AH,* 6 (Oct. 1955), 52–55; Oliver E. Allen, "The Lewis Albums," *AH,* 14 (Dec. 1962), 65–80.

43. James Taylor Dunn and Louis C. Jones, "Crazy Bill Had a Down Look," *AH,* 6 (Aug. 1955), 61–63, 108. On women in *AH,* see, for example, Thomas H. Johnson, "The Great Love in the Life of Emily Dickinson," 6 (Apr. 1955), 52–55; Martha Bacon, "The Parson and the Bluestocking," 13 (Dec. 1961), 12–15, 88–91; Martha Bacon, "Miss Beecher in Hell," 14 (Dec. 1962), 28–31, 102–5; Mary R. Maloney, "General Reynolds and 'Dear Kate,'" 15 (Dec. 1963), 62–65; Anita W. Hinckley, "A Gibson Girl Romance," 17 (Dec. 1965), 106–11. Native Americans were the major exception to *AH*'s neglect of "minorities"; they were, of course, heavily represented. Emblematic of the magazine's coverage of class conflict was a comment in a sidebar to an article on Andrew Carnegie, which discussed the Homestead Steel Strike: "The truth was that had Carnegie been on the ground when the strike broke, trouble might never have started, for the men worshiped him": Robert L. Reynolds, " '(The Works Are Not Worth One Drop of Blood,' " *AH,* 12 (Aug. 1960), 109.

44. Walter Muir Whitehill, "Promoted to Glory . . . .: The Origin of Preservation in the United States," in Albert Rains, et al., eds., *With Heritage So Rich* (New York, 1966), 43, as quoted in Wallace, "Visiting the Past," p. 137.

45. Catton, "Reading, Writing and History," *AH,* 6 (Oct. 1955), 108–9.

46. "Reminiscences of Jensen," 22; "Reminiscences of Parton," 19–20.

47. Close to Nevins and Rudolf A. Clemen, Aug. 30, 1954; Catton to Close, Sept. 7, 1954, both Box 69, Nevins MSS.

48. Nevins, "What's the Matter," 16.

49. "Reminiscences of Parton," 16; "*American Heritage* the Product of Resourceful Planning," 904–7.

50. Steve Botein to author, Aug. 23, 1984; former staff member to author, April 11, 1984.

51. "Culture Is Their Business," *Time*, Feb. 17, 1958, 46. Interview with John A. Garraty, April 18, 1984. Josh Brown provided a number of helpful comments that have influenced my discussion of *AH*'s use of visual materials. That *AH* recently won two National Magazine Awards indicates the continuing professionalism and editorial talent of the staff and the high regard for the magazine within the publishing industry.

52. "When the Old Streets Talked," *AH*, 6 (June 1955), 46–49; Arnold Whitridge, "Eli Whitney: Nemesis of the South," *AH*, 6 (April 1955), 5.

53. See *AH:* 6 (Aug. 1955), 28, 29; 6 (Oct. 1955), 6; 7 (April 1956), cover, 12; 8 (June 1957), 58; 19 (Aug. 1968), 47; 20 (Oct. 1969), 31. Some of the illustrations are engravings "after Chappell." See the similar lack of dating of works by twentieth-century Belgian-American painter Edward P. Buyck: 7 (Feb. 1956), 26–27; 20 (Oct. 1969), 29.

54. Maxine Hong Kingston, "San Francisco's Chinatown," *AH*, 30 (Dec. 1978), 36–47. Recently, former *AH* editor Geoffrey C. Ward has published (in *AH*) some thoughtful comments on the use "of old pictures selectively to portray a relentlessly cheerful American past that never was." He does not indicate, however, that such criticisms are pertinent to *AH* itself: "Notes on a Wisconsin Ego Trip," 35 (Feb.–March 1984), 8.

55. The respondents to the survey also argue passionately against any plans to "cheapen" or "change" the magazine, by which they mean following the path taken by *AH*'s companion publication, *Horizon*, which had earlier gone to softcovers, advertising, and more "relevant" contents. A large number noted that they had dropped their subscriptions to *Horizon* in response to those changes. The sixty or so survey forms that I examined (through the courtesy of *AH*) were not a complete or representative sample of those who responded; rather, they present the views of the magazine's most loyal readers.

56. David McCullough, "The Lonely War of a Good Angry Man," *AH*, 21 (Dec. 1969), 97–113; Charlton Ogburn, Jr., "Catastrophe by the Numbers," ibid., 114–17.

57. Early reader surveys found that about two-thirds of *AH* subscribers were male: "*American Heritage* Grows"; promotional materials. On the class dimensions of conservation, see Jim O'Brien, "Environmentalism as a Mass Movement: Historical Notes," *Radical America*, 17 (March–June 1983), 7–27. For example, "Audubon Society members polled in 1976 had an average income of $35,700; 85 percent of them had gone to college" (19).

58. John Brooks, "A Clean Break with the Past," *AH*, 21 (Aug. 1970), 4–7, 68–75; Richard Hofstadter, "America As a Gun Culture," *AH*, 21 (Oct. 1970), 4–11, 82–85; William P. Jones to Editor, *AH*, 21 (Feb. 1970), 117. I used the subscription figures presented annually in the magazine, as required for second-class mailing status. Paid circulation in the fall of 1967 was 341,000; by 1968 it was 293,800; it dropped to 258,000 in 1969, 241,800 in 1970, and 217,200 in 1971.

59. Daniel T. Chapman, "The Great White Father's Little Red Indian School," *AH*, 22 (Dec. 1970), 48–53, 102; Elizabeth N. Layne, "Carlisle's Legacy: Another Point of View," ibid., 102.

60. Genovese participated in a symposium entitled "Is History Dead?" *AH*, 28 (Dec. 1976), 90. On Josephy, see *Contemporary Authors*, 1st revision (Detroit, 1976), vols. 17–20, 386; Emma Mitchell New, "Years Came Along One After the Other . . . *AH*, 28 (Dec. 1976), 4–7; Carl Solberg, "The Tyranny of Oil," ibid., 8–13, 78–83; Lawrence Lader, "The Wallace Campaign of 1948," ibid., 42–51.

61. Stephen W. Sears, "'Shut the Goddam Plant!'" *AH*, 33 (April–May 1982), 49–64; "Rosie the Riveter Remembers," *AH*, 35 (Feb.–March 1984), 94–103; Eric Foner, "The New View of Reconstruction," *AH*, 34 (Oct.–Nov. 1983), 78–84. Dobell also worked at Time-Life, the great nesting ground for *AH* editors, where he was senior editor of Time-Life Books and of the revived *Life*. When he was hired, Dobell announced plans to put more emphasis on the twentieth century: "New Editor at American Heritage Magazine," *New York Times*, Jan. 21, 1982.

62. Sears, "'Shut the Goddam Plant!'" 64; "Letter from the Editor: Storytelling," *AH*, 33 (April–May 1982), 3.

63. In its first two years under Dobell, the magazine tilted further in more "serious" and contemporary directions. On EPCOT see Michael Wallace, "Mickey Mouse History: Portraying the Past at Disney World," *Radical History Review*, 32 (1985), 33–57. On textbooks, see Frances FitzGerald, *America Revised: History Schoolbooks in the Twentieth Century* (Boston, 1979).

64. Philip H. Dougherty, "American Heritage to Accept Ads," *New York Times*, June 11, 1982.

65. Samuel P. Reed, "Letter from the Chairman," *AH*, 31 (Aug. 1980), 3.

66. Interview with Byron Dobell, April 17, 1984, New York City; Reed, "Letter from the Chairman," 3; "McGraw-Hill to Add Heritage," *New York Times*, April 19, 1969; "McGraw-Hill Sells Engelhard Heritage Unit," Jan. 14, 1976; *McGraw-Hill Annual Report 1969* (New York, 1970). The magazine was subsequently bought from Englehard Hanovia Inc. by its president, Samuel P. Reed. Reed is the grandson of Samuel F. Pryor, former chairman of the executive committee of Remington Arms, as well as son-in-law of Charles W. Englehard, the "multimillionaire precious metals industrialist and race horse owner," who was sometimes identified as the model for "Goldfinger," the villain of the James Bond novel written by Englehard's friend Ian Fleming (*New York Times*, June 11, 1982; March 3, 1971, 46). One reader from Wisconsin, who wrote rather extensive comments in response to the 1979 questionnaire, may have articulated what many *AH* readers were thinking in this period. After praising the magazine as "a bright spot in modern historical writing" and criticizing it for "an occasional tendency to descend into the arena of present-day controversy," he wrote: "I would be very sorry to see you either shift to a more flimsy format (I keep my copies forever—I have eight feet of them) which would not last well nor stand well on the shelf, and I would also dislike a more deluxe edition, which would be beyond my purse, and the luxury of which might well be wasted, or lead you into the sort of editorial excesses which brought about the demise of HORIZON. . . . In conclusion, I

do want to say that the distribution of this questionnaire strikes me as a sign of trouble. People who are justifiably confident of their competence do NOT feel it necessary to ask their customers how they are doing. Possibly, alerted, you can correct this element of self-doubt, an element happily missing in your earlier work."

67. Reed, "Letter from the Chairman," 3; *AH* generously supplied me with data on their current subscribers. All but 3 percent of subscribers are over 21. I used age distribution figures for 1980 to make the comparison. See Andrew Hacker, *U/S: A Statistical Portrait of the American People* (New York, 1983), 30. According to the publisher's figures, mail subscriptions have risen from 111,626 in 1982 to 124,887 in 1984. The increase in circulation is actually slightly higher (114,913 to 133,266) because newsstand sales have grown faster than subscriptions. Current promotion efforts through direct mail and cable television appear to be pushing subscriptions still higher but are, of course, also raising costs. Despite the rise in subscriptions and growing advertising revenues, the magazine continues to lose money, and it is rumored to be up for sale again.

68. Edwin McDowell, "A New Look for American Heritage," *New York Times,* Dec. 31, 1984.

69. Quoted in Geoffrey C. Ward, "Letter from the Editor: An Anniversary Note," *AH,* 31 (Dec. 1979), 4.

70. Nevins, "What's the Matter," 4. Interestingly, the AHA has now reversed the position it took back in 1938 and has been trying to set up its own popular history magazine.

71. Eric Breitbart, "The Painted Mirror: Historical Re-creation from the Panorama to the Docudrama" in this volume, p. 105. One recent example of the heroic, narrative mode in left documentary film is *The Good Fight,* a film about the Abraham Lincoln Brigade and the Spanish Civil War.

72. Quoted in Jesse Lemisch, "History, Complete With Historian," *New York Times Book Review,* Nov. 19, 1972, 71. On historical narrative, see Marjorie Murphy, "Telling Stories, Telling Tales: Literary Theory, Ideology, and Narrative History," *Radical History Review,* 31 (1984), 33–38; Hayden White, "The Question of Narrative in History," *History and Theory,* 32 (1984), 1–33; Lawrence Stone, "The Revival of Narrative: Reflections on a New Old History," *Past and Present,* 85 (Nov. 1979), 3–24. Interestingly, the decline in college history majors seems to have paralleled closely the decline in *AH* sales. For figures on history majors, see Higham, *History,* 236.

Chapter 3

Acknowledgments: Thanks to Susan Porter Benson, Stephen Brier, Joshua Brown, Barbara Melosh, Roy Rosenzweig, and Robert Westbrook for their thoughtful comments on earlier versions of this essay. Special thanks to Jean-Christophe Agnew and Ben Chitty for their suggestions, encouragement, and humor.

1. Cited in Walter Rideout, *The Radical Novel in the United States, 1900–1954* (Cambridge, Mass., 1956), 280.
2. See Howard Fast, *Literature and Reality* (New York, 1950), 9.
3. "My Decision," *Mainstream,* 10 (March 1957), 28.
4. Aljean Harmetz, "'Freedom Road': The Long Haul to TV," *New York Times,* Oct. 28, 1979, 33.
5. Donald Newlove, "Three Novels," *New York Times Book Review,* Oct. 2, 1977, 22.
6. "Pictures of the Homeland: The Legacy of Howard Fast," *Radical America,* 17 (Jan.–Feb. 1983), 51.
7. Jennifer Durning, "Behind the Best Sellers," *New York Times Book Review,* Dec. 11, 1977, 48.
8. Cited in Edwin McDowell, "Behind the Best Sellers," *New York Times Book Review,* Nov. 22, 1981, 50.
9. For an illuminating discussion of these problems within the historical potboiler, see Joshua Brown, "The Great American (Marxist) Novel," *Radical History Review,* 31 (1984), 5–21, especially 15–18.

Chapter 4

Acknowledgments: My thanks to Jeanie Attic, Kate Pfordresher, Janet Francendese of Temple University Press, and the editors of this volume for their editorial assistance and cogent criticism. In particular, Milton Meltzer's knowledge of history and children's history books, as well as his editorial suggestions, aided this greenhorn as he trudged through a new-found land. And thanks, of course, to Gideon and Daniel Brown, my resident experts in the field, who first motivated me to explore children's books for the *Radical History Review.*

1. Arthur Schlesinger, Jr., "Advice from a Reader-Aloud-to-Children," *New York Times Book Review,* Nov. 25, 1979, 3, 94, takes a very different tack. He dismisses the new children's fiction as didactic: "Why read the moderns when there is the great treasure house of children's classics, stories that form the landscape of every civilized person's mind?" After critical responses to Schlesinger's article noted the racism in many of the classic works he recommended—including the Doctor Dolittle books—Schlesinger asserted that the problems were located solely in the books' illustrations (a gross distortion), and even then dismissed the impact of such material: Jan. 13, 1980, 37. For the less complacent, the Council on Interracial Books for Children publishes a newsletter that analyzes racial and sexual stereotypes in children's books, both "classics" and "moderns" (1841 Broadway, New York, N.Y., 10023).
2. Joseph Lelyveld, "The Enduring Legacy," *New York Times Magazine,* March 31, 1985. See also Michael Frisch, "The Memory of History," in this volume.
3. Book Industry Study Group Survey cited in Edwin McDowell, "Trade Paperbacks Reshaping Book Publishing," *New York Times,* April 22, 1985. See also Eric

Breitbart, "The Painted Mirror: Historical Re-creation from the Panorama to the Doc-udrama," in this volume. Whatever one might think of the mini-series "Roots," it was the chronicle of Kunta Kinte and his descendants that formed most youngsters' (and adults') understanding of slavery, not the many scholarly studies of the institution that have appeared in the last generation.

4. For example, *Cobblestone: The History Magazine for Young People; Roots,* published by the Minnesota Historical Society.

5. Betsy Hearne, "Bad Children's Books Drive Out Good," *New York Times Book Review,* Feb. 3, 1985, 24; Geraldine DeLuca and Roni Natov, "Interview with Milton Meltzer," *The Lion and the Unicorn,* 4 (Summer 1980), 97; Ann Durrell, "If There Is No Happy Ending: Children's Book Publishing—Past, Present, and Future" (pt. 2), *Horn Book Magazine,* April 1982.

6. "Art and Text—and Context," *Horn Book Magazine,* April 1984, 158; Hear-ne, "Bad Children's Books," 24. Hearne notes that the 1984 Editor's Choice selec-tions in the children's section of *Booklist,* the review journal of the American Library Association, featured twice as many notable picture books as works of either fiction or nonfiction.

7. For Edwardian glamor in the guise of children's edification, see John S. Good-all, *An Edwardian Season* (New York, Macmillan, 1979). For juvenile treatments of ancient Egypt following the Tutankhamun show, see Miriam Schlein, *I, Tut: The Boy Who Became Pharaoh,* illus. Erik Hilgerdt (New York: Four Winds Press, 1979), which is as shallow as its silly title implies. In contrast, Aliki's *Mummies Made in Egypt* (New York: Crowell, 1979) details the religious basis and craft of mummifica-tion and avoids the preoccupation with "Tut."

8. "The perfect picture book is an art form in which two separate disciplines, literature and art, merge to create a new, integrated whole": Ava Weiss, "The Artist at Work: The Art Director," *Horn Book Magazine,* May–June 1985, 269. Unfortunate-ly, beyond genuflections to creativity and "taste," Weiss fails to discuss qualitatively the relationship of art and text.

9. Less prevalent than the rural idyll is the inverted image of an urban golden age, good-old-days when streets were clean, children well-behaved, and people in general quaint and unthreatening. The dustjacket of Betty Baker's *My Sister Says* (New York: Macmillan, 1984) claims that its tale of two little girls traipsing through the New York waterfront of the 1850s is based on careful research, but neither its saccharine pictures (by Tricia Taggart) nor its text reflect any sense of a particular time or a specific urban location.

10. Loeper can write compellingly about the past once he wipes the gauzy cobwebs from his eyes. His more recent *Going to School in 1876* (New York: Atheneum, 1984) is a delightful, far-ranging, and critical survey of what the educational experience (or lack of it) was like one hundred years ago.

11. The fascination with a disembodied technology is most evident in Macaulay's *Underground* (Boston: Houghton Mifflin, 1976), which investigates the root system underlying the city today—without showing the people living in that city or building or maintaining the systems that support it.

12. See, as a recent example, David Adler, *Our Golda: The Story of Golda Meir,* illus. Donna Ruff (New York: Viking, 1984).

13. Jean Fritz, "George Washington, My Father, and Walt Disney," *Horn Book Magazine,* April 1976, 191–98.

14. Judith Sloane Hoberman, "Recycling the Red, White, and Blue: The Bicentennial and Books for Children," *Harvard Educational Review,* 46 (August 1976), 471.

15. A similarly fascinating correction to the rural idyll can be found in William Kurelek's autobiographical *A Prairie Boy's Winter* (Boston: Houghton Mifflin, 1973) and *A Prairie Boy's Summer* (Boston: Houghton Mifflin, 1975). Another version of the agrarian myth portrays Native Americans as either noble or malevolently mysterious. A welcome corrective is David and Charlotte Yue's dense *The Tipi: A Center of Native-American Life* (New York: Knopf, 1984).

16. Jonathan Cott, *Pipers at the Gates of Dawn: The Wisdom of Children's Literature* (New York, 1983), pp. xviii–xxii.

17. The publication of new hardcover historical fiction does not contradict earlier comments about the curtailed library market and the emergence of the adult-oriented picture book. Fiction hardcover titles quickly go out of print, no longer sustained by institutional sales. Worn-out or lost books are simply not reordered by budget-weary libraries. At the same time, paperback publishers—in a reversal of previous policy— are now loath to reprint even prize-winning fiction titles. Their goal is commercial sales, and with the continued expansion of chain stores, the bookdealers they cater to are interested in mass appeal and fast turnover, favoring bestsellers and gimmick books and refusing to maintain backlists of slow-moving, if venerated, children's book titles. See Chris Goodrich, "Avon Isn't Calling Anymore: Most Paperbacks Are in Chains," *Nation,* 240 (May 4, 1985), 523–25, and Hearne, "Bad Children's Books."

18. Penelope Lively, "Children and Memory," *Horn Book Magazine,* Aug. 1973, 401.

19. Anna Davin, "Historical Novels for Children," *History Workshop Journal,* 1 (Spring 1976), 155–56. Cott notes the explicitly didactic tone in classical children's literature, which in some cases carries an implicitly antiauthoritarian, challenging message: *Pipers at the Gates of Dawn,* xvii.

20. Michael Kammen, *A Season of Youth: The American Revolution and the Historical Imagination* (New York, 1978), 165–68, 206–8, 216; Christopher Collier, "Johnny and Sam: Old and New Approaches to the American Revolution," *Horn Book Magazine,* April,1976, 132–38; Hoberman, "Recycling the Red, White, and Blue," 470.

21. Hoberman, "Recycling the Red, White, and Blue," 471–72; Ann Durrell, "If There Is No Happy Ending" (pt. 1), *Horn Book Magazine,* Feb. 1982, 28; pt. 2, April 1982, 146–47. See Kammen, *A Season of Youth,* chap. 6, passim, for trends in fictional portrayals of the American Revolution.

22. There are important exceptions to the consensual rule in children's historical fiction in the 1950s, notably the work of Dorothy Sterling, and in particular *Captain of the Planter: The Story of Robert Smalls* (New York: Doubleday, 1958). As for more

recent works, the themes mentioned by no means exhaust the topics covered in the field, which has gone beyond American to European, African, and Asian history, although the American context far outweighs the others. For Native Americans see, among many other works, Jamake Highwater, *Anapao: An American Indian Odyssey* (Philadelphia: Lippincott, 1977) and *Legend Days* (New York: Harper & Row, 1984), Elizabeth George Speare, *The Sign of the Beaver* (Boston: Houghton Mifflin, 1983), and Luke Wallin, *In the Shadow of the Wind* (Scarsdale, N.Y.: Bradbury Press, 1984); for Asians, less well represented, see Bette Bao Lord, *In the Year of the Boar and Jackie Robinson,* illus. Marc Simont (New York: Harper & Row, 1984). Highwater and Lord represent another important development—minority authorship of books about minorities. The transformation of the field of juvenile historical fiction has not been total: vacuous costume dramas continue to be churned out. See, for the Revolution, Avi, *The Fighting Ground* (Philadelphia: Lippincott, 1984); Betty Baker, *The Night Spider Case* (New York: Macmillan, 1984) is a silly turn-of-the-century adventure book set in an antiquarian New York City.

23. Pat Aufderheide, "Interview with Natalie Davis," *Radical History Review*, 28– 30 (Sept. 1984), 138. See Hoberman, "Recycling the Red, White, and Blue," 474, for *Johnny Tremain* versus *My Brother Sam Is Dead*. For all her insights into the strengths and weaknesses of new juvenile accounts of the American Revolution, Hoberman is more eager to debunk the great men and present the pluralism of experience than to foster a larger understanding of America's past—to note, for example, that slaves were there, rather than that slavery was a complicated and varied institution.

24. Davin, "Historical Novels for Children," 165. See also Steven Marcus, "Awakening from the Nightmare? Notes on the Historical Novel," in *Representations: Essays on Literature and Society* (New York, 1975), 161–82. See also Kammen, *A Season of Youth,* 219–220, for literary distortions of the American Revolution that support a conservative world view.

25. For observations on the presentation of history and the question of alternative narrative forms, see Joshua Brown, "The Great American (Marxist) Novel," and Marjorie Murphy, "Telling Stories, Telling Tales: Literary Theory, Ideology, and Narrative History," *Radical History Review*, 31 (Dec. 1984). Also see Roy Rosenzweig's compelling remarks on presentation in "Marketing the Past," in this volume.

26. See also James Lincoln Collier, *Why Does Everybody Think I'm Nutty?* (New York: Grosset & Dunlop, 1971), where a child enters an "imaginary" medieval city. The extraordinary novels of Virginia Hamilton, notably *The House of Dies Drear* (New York: Macmillan, 1968), are set in the present, yet, as in novels that use the time travel convention, the contemporary is made comprehensible through a larger understanding of its historical roots (Afro-American history and slavery).

27. Historians' attentiveness to textbooks should not be overstated either. Scholars, in their roles as authors and teachers, may consider college texts, but, Frances FitzGerald eloquently argues, they have little involvement in or concern for the production of secondary-school history books. The gap between academic historiography and the content of junior and senior high school textbooks is vast and shocking. See

America Revised: History Schoolbooks in the Twentieth Century (Boston, 1979), 43, 89.

28. Milton Meltzer, "Where Do All the Prizes Go? The Case for Nonfiction," *Horn Book Magazine,* (Feb. 1976), 18–21; Milton Meltzer, "The Possibilities of Nonfiction: A Writer's View," *Children's Literature in Education,* 11:3 (1980), 111. The ideological character of the term "literature" is artfully dissected by Terry Eagleton in *Literary Theory: An Introduction* (Minneapolis, 1983), esp. 1–16. See also the historical development of the term in Raymond Williams, *Keywords: A Vocabulary of Culture and Society* (New York, 1976), 150–54.

29. Meltzer, "Where Do All the Prizes Go?" 17, 20–21.

30. Recently reprinted and diluted Landmark titles include Richard Tregaskis, *Guadalcanal Diary* (New York: Random House, 1955), and Willial L. Shirer, *The Rise and Fall of Adolf Hitler* (1961). See also Katherine B. Shippen, *Alexander Graham Bell Invents the Telephone* (1952), and Wyatt Blassingame, *Underwater Warriors* (1964).

31. As in the case of historical fiction, there were important exceptions to the rule in the early 1960s—for example, Milton Meltzer's three-volume *In Their Own Words* (New York: Crowell, 1964, 1965, 1967), revised and updated in one volume as *The Black Americans: A History in Their Own Words* (New York: Crowell, 1984). For more recent publications on black history, see Eloise Greenfield and Lessie Jones Little, *Childtimes: A Three-Generation Memoir* (New York: Crowell, 1979); for Native Americans, Peter Nabokov, ed., *Native-American Testimony: An Anthology of Indian-White Relations, First Encounter to Dispossession* (New York: Crowell, 1979); for women, Linda Grant De Pauw, *Founding Mothers: Women of America in the Revolutionary Era* (Boston: Houghton Mifflin, 1975), and Janet Harris, *Thursday's Daughters: The Story of Women Working in America* (New York: Harper & Row, 1977). FitzGerald, *American Revised,* 38–42, chronicles the impact on textbooks of the events of the 1960s.

32. Jo Carr, "The Literature of Fact," *Horn Book Magazine,* Oct. 1981, 523. See also her *Beyond Fact: Nonfiction for Children and Young People* (Chicago, 1982); Edward Barrett, "Writing the Literature of Fact," *The Lion and the Unicorn,* 6 (1982), 91–96; Meltzer, "Where Do All the Prizes Go?" 21–22.

33. For comments on social history and the narrative, see Murphy, "Telling Stories, Telling Tales." Two examples of the academic debate are Lawrence Stone, "The Revival of Narrative: Reflections on a New Old History," *Past and Present,* 85 (Nov. 1979), 3–24, and E. J. Hobsbawm, "The Revival of Narrative: Some Comments," *Past and Present,* 86 (Feb. 1980), 3–8. For a cogent analysis of a current historiographic controversy that derives from this debate, see Jon Wiener, "Footnotes to History," *Nation,* 240 (Feb. 16, 1985), 180–83.

34. Meltzer, "The Possibilities of Nonfiction," 114; see also Barrett, "Writing the Literature of Fact," 94.

35. For a similar approach, see Milton Meltzer, *A Book of Names: in which custom, tradition, law, myth, history, folklore, foolery, legend, fashion, nonsense, symbol, taboo help explain how we got our names and what they mean* (New York: Crowell,

1984). See also Meltzer, *All Times, All Peoples: A World History of Slavery*, illus. Leonard Everett Fisher (New York: Harper & Row, 1980), and *The Terrorists* (New York: Harper & Row, 1983); Jules Archer, *You Can't Do That To Me! Famous Fights for Human Rights* (New York: Macmillan, 1980). Frances FitzGerald, *America Revised*, 157–159, notes that children's textbooks often approach controversial issues as "problems" to avoid addressing conflict in history. These "social problem" books do not manifest this form of intellectual cowardice.

36. Two series of similarly exemplary biographies of women, usually focusing on people who played important roles in American history but are neglected by standard texts and curricula, are the twenty-five titles of Women of America, published for young adults by Crowell until 1978 (including biographies of Abby Kelly Foster, Lydia Maria Child, Emma Goldman, Mary Elizabeth Lease, Frances Wright, and Ida Tarbell), and Viking Press's newly launched Women of Our Time, a series for young readers (including Dorothea Lange, Betty Friedan, Mary McLeod Bethune, Eleanor Roosevelt, and—a nice departure—Diana Ross).

37. DeLuca and Natov, "Interview with Milton Meltzer," 98–99.

38. See DeLuca and Natov, "Interview with Milton Meltzer," 100, for fascinating insights into the craft of writing sophisticated history for young people. Some of the titles included in the Living History Library are John Anthony Scott, *Trumpet of a Prophecy: Revolutionary America, 1763–1783;* Marion Starkey, *Lace Cuffs and Leather Aprons: Popular Struggles in the Federalist Era, 1783–1800;* Leonard Falkner, *For Jefferson and Liberty: The United States in War and Peace, 1800–1815;* Douglas T. Miller, *Then Was the Future: The North in the Age of Jackson, 1815–1850;* John Anthony Scott, *Hard Trials on My Way: Slavery and the Struggle Against It;* Milton Meltzer, *Bound for the Rio Grande: The Mexican Struggle, 1845–1850;* James M. McPherson, *Marching Toward Freedom: The Negro in the Civil War, 1861–1865;* Steven Jantzen, *Hooray for Peace, Hurrah for War: The United States During World War I;* Milton Meltzer, *Brother, Can You Spare a Dime? The Great Depression, 1929–1933.*

39. FitzGerald, *America Revised*, 15–16.

40. DeLuca and Natov, "Interview with Milton Meltzer," 102. Although these books do not encounter censorship problems, as many children's textbooks do, the conservative backlash has affected the acquisition policies of many secondary school systems and created an unhealthy atmosphere for the adoption of alternative histories in general (FitzGerald, *America Revised*, 29–38).

41. On the possibilities and limitations of "counterpublic" educational institutions, see Terry Eagleton, *The Function of Criticism: From The Spectator to Post-Structuralism* (London, 1984), 110–15.

Chapter 5

Acknowledgments: I want to thank Clive Bush, Jeanne Chase, V. F. Perkins, and seminar participants at the universities of Warwick and East Anglia and New York University for comments on earlier drafts of this essay.

1. See Roger Bromley, "Natural Boundaries: The Social Function of Popular Fiction," *Red Letters,* no. 7 (n.d.), 34–60, and *On Ideology,* Working Papers in Cultural Studies, no. 10 (Birmingham, England, 1977).

2. See the discussion in J. A. Place, *The Western Films of John Ford* (Secaucus, N.J., 1974), 42–57, and Andrew Sarris, *The John Ford Movie Mystery* (London, 1976), 89–90.

3. For a discussion of the cultural image of the Revolution, see Michael Kammen, *A Season of Youth: The American Revolution and the Historical Imagination* (New York, 1978). Kammen inaccurately suggests that since films about the Revolution are generally derived from novels, they need no separate study. See pp. 143–44.

4. "John Ford's *Young Mr. Lincoln*" (a collective text by the editors of *Cahiers du Cinéma*). *Screen,* 13 (Autumn, 1972), 5–44.

5. Cf. Peter Wollen, *Signs and Meaning in the Cinema* (London, 1972), 74–115; James Monaco, *How to Read a Film* (New York, 1977), 318; and François Truffaut, "Une Certaine Tendence du Cinéma Français," *Cahiers du Cinéma,* 6 (1954), 15–29.

6. Walter D. Edmonds, *Drums Along the Mohawk* (Boston, 1936; reprint ed., New York, 1976).

7. Edmonds, *Drums* (1976), ix.

8. Cf. Jesse Lemisch, "Listening to the 'Inarticulate': William Widger's Dream and the Loyalties of American Revolutionary Seamen in British Prisons," *Journal of Social History,* 3 (1969), 1–29.

9. For Sir William's biography, see Milton W. Hamilton, *Sir William Johnson, Colonial American: 1715–1763* (Port Washington, N.Y., 1976).

10. Cf. Adam Gordon to Sir William Johnson, July 2, 1765, *The Papers of Sir William Johnson,* ed. Milton W. Hamilton (Albany, 1962), Vol. 13, 375–76; "Journal of Warren Johnson," June 20, 1760–July 3, 1761, ibid., (Albany, 1957), vol. 12, 773; Joseph Chew to an unspecified addressee in London, January 25, 1776, British Library, manuscript division, Add. MS. 29327; *The Minute Book of the Committee of Safety of Tryon County,* ed. J. Howard Hanson and Samuel Ludlow Frey (New York, 1905).

11. Roland Barthes, *Mythologies* (St. Albans, 1976), 109–59.

12. John E. O'Connor, "A Reaffirmation of American Ideals: *Drums Along the Mohawk,*" in John E. O'Connor and Martin A. Jackson, eds., *American History/American Film: Interpreting the Hollywood Image* (New York, 1979).

Chapter 6

1. Dolf Sternberger, *Panorama of the Nineteenth Century* (New York, 1977), chap. 1. See also Helmut and Alison Gernsheim, *L. J. M. Daguerre* (New York, 1956). Daguerre, one of photography's pioneers, was also a master of the Diorama and the Panorama.

2. Hugo Munsterberg, *The Photoplay,* reprint ed. (New York, 1974), 56.

3. Jay Leyda, *Films Beget Films* (New York, 1964), 13.

4. Quoted in George C. Pratt, *Spellbound in Darkness* (New York, 1966), 511. This idea of the movie screen as a "squre hole" through which one sees reality is a recurring theme in film history. In a recent advertising campaign for Eastman Kodak, the director Michael Cimino (*The Deer Hunter, Heaven's Gate*) was quoted as saying: "Everything we do is aimed at demolishing the barrier of the screen's two-dimensional plane. We have to remove the camera—erase the frame. . . . We want to remove all the factors that threaten the audience's belief that they are participating, that they are there."

5. Joseph Patterson, "The Poor Man's Elementary Course in Drama," *Saturday Evening Post,* Nov. 23, 1907 (quoted in Pratt, *Spellbound,* 46).

6. A. William Bluem, *Documentary in American Television,* (New York, 1969), 192.

7. *On Location,* Jan.–Feb. 1980, 83–88.

8. Ibid.

9. Raymond Williams, *Television: Technology and Cultural Form* (New York, 1975), 59.

10. Editorial, *New York Times,* Jan. 10, 1985.

11. *Emmy Magazine,* Summer 1979.

12. Ibid.

13. *New York Times,* Dec. 31, 1980.

14. Editorial, *New York Times,* Feb. 10, 1985.

15. *USA Today,* November 9, 1984.

16. Ibid.

17. Christopher Lasch, *The Culture of Narcissism* (New York, 1979), 16.

18. Gernsheim and Gernsheim *Daguerre,* 68.

Chapter 8

Acknowledgments: My thanks—as much for their patience as for their invaluable assistance—to Sue Benson, Steve Brier, Ted Burrows, Janet Corpus, Vicki de Grazia, Susan Henderson, Mike Merrill, Roy Rosenzweig, Alan Wolfe, and the New York MARHO Collective.

1. Cited in David Lowenthal, "The American Way of History," *Columbia University Forum,* 9:3 (Summer 1966), 28.

2. Charles B. Hosmer, Jr., *Presence of the Past: A History of the Preservation Movement in the United States Before Williamsburg* (New York, 1965), 35–37; Richard Caldwell, *A True History of the Acquisition of Washington's Headquarters at Newburgh by the State of New York* (Salisbury Mills, N.Y., 1887), 21.

3. Hosmer, *Presence,* 42–43.

4. Grace King, *Mount Vernon on the Potomac: History of the Mount Vernon Ladies' Association of the Union* (New York, 1919), 22; Mount Vernon Ladies' Association, *Historical Sketch of Ann Pamela Cunningham, "The Southern Matron," Founder of the "Mount Vernon Ladies' Association"* (Jamaica, N.Y., 1903), 20. On

the Washington cult see Hosmer, *Presence,* 44–46; George B. Forgie, *Patricide in the House Divided: A Psychological Interpretation of Lincoln and His Age* (New York, 1979), 168–99; Michael Kammen, *A Season of Youth: The American Revolution and the Historical Imagination* (New York, 1978), 252 and passim.

5. Hosmer, *Presence,* 39; Kammen, *A Season of Youth,* 59–60.

6. Laurence Vail Coleman, *Historic House Museums* (Washington, D.C., 1933), 20.

7. John Higham, *Strangers in the Land: Patterns of American Nativism, 1860– 1920* (New Brunswick, N.J., 1955), 45–63; Wallace Evans Davies, *Patriotism on Parade* (Cambridge, Mass., 1955), 46.

8. Barbara Miller Solomon, *Ancestors and Immigrants: A Changing New England Tradition* (New York, 1956), 29–30; Hosmer, *Presence,* 55, 66–70, 73, 88–89, 122, 126–27; Davies, *Patriotism,* 44–73; Margaret Gibbs, *The DAR* (New York, 1969), 32–76.

9. Hosmer, *Presence,* 55; Davies, *Patriotism,* 79–82.

10. Lewis Mumford, *Sticks and Stones: A Study of American Architecture and Civilization* (New York, 1924), 123–54.

11. Hosmer, *Presence,* 237–59; Matthew Josephson, *The Robber Barons: The Great American Capitalists, 1861–1901* (New York, 1934), 332–46.

12. Hosmer, *Presence,* 138–39; Kammen, *A Season of Youth,* 219.

13. See, for example, Herbert Gutman, *Work, Culture, and Society in Industrializing America* (New York, 1977).

14. Solomon, *Ancestors and Immigrants,* 87.

15. The ancestral societies continued their efforts, however. By 1930 there were over four hundred house museums, the bulk of them patriotic enterprises of the older sort. Coleman, *House Museums,* 20.

16. James Warren Prothro, *The Dollar Decade: Business Ideas in the 1920s* (Baton Rouge, 1954), 4, 191.

17. Hosmer, *Presence,* 153–93.

18. Higham, *Strangers,* 248; John B. Rae, ed., *Henry Ford* (Englewood Cliffs, N.J., 1969), 5; William Greenleaf, *From These Beginnings: The Early Philanthropies of Henry and Edsel Ford, 1911–1936* (Detroit, 1964), 96.

19. Walter Karp, "Greenfield Village," *American Heritage,* 32 (Dec. 1980), 101–2.

20. Ibid., 102–3; Geoffrey C. Upward, *A Home for Our Heritage: The Building and Growth of Greenfield Village and Henry Ford Museum, 1929–1979* (Dearborn, Mich., 1979), 1–21.

21. Roger Butterfield, "Henry Ford, the Wayside Inn, and the Problem of 'History is Bunk,' " *Proceedings of the Massachusetts Historical Society,* 76 (1965), 57–66; David L. Lewis, *The Public Image of Henry Ford: An American Folk Hero and His Company* (Detroit, 1976), 225–26; James Brough, *The Ford Dynasty: An American Story* (New York, 1977), 161; Karp, "Greenfield Village," 102.

22. Walter Muir Whitehill, *Independent Historical Societies* (Boston, 1962), 466; Greenleaf, *From These Beginnings,* 71–112; Karp, "Greenfield Village," 104.

23. Upward, *Home,* 21–58.

24. Lewis, *Public Image,* 278–81.

25. Keith Sward, *The Legend of Henry Ford* (New York, 1948), 259–75; Allan Nevins and Frank Ernest Hill, *Ford: Expansion and Challenge, 1915–1933* (New York, 1957), 504–5.

26. R. Douglas Hurt, "Agricultural Museums: A New Frontier for the Social Sciences," *History Teacher,* 11:3 (May 1978), 368–69; Nathan Weinberg, *Preservation in American Towns and Cities* (Boulder, Colo., 1979), 18–19; Edward P. Alexander, *Museums in Motion: An Introduction to the History and Functions of Museums* (Nashville, 1979), 10.

27. William Adams Symonds, *Henry Ford and Greenfield Village* (New York, 1938), 183.

28. See Karp, "Greenfield Village," for an alternative interpretation.

29. Raymond B. Fosdick, *John D. Rockefeller, Jr.: A Portrait* (New York, 1956); Alvin Moscow, *The Rockefeller Inheritance* (Garden City, N.Y., 1977).

30. Fosdick, *Rockefeller,* 356–57.

31. Cabell Phillips, "The Town That Stopped the Clock," *American Heritage,* 11 (Feb. 1960), 22–25; Fosdick, *Rockefeller,* 282–300; Rutherford Goodwin, *A Brief and True Report Concerning Williamsburg in Virginia* (Williamsburg, 1936); *Colonial Williamsburg: The First Twenty-Five Years, A Report by the President* (Williamsburg, 1951), 7–18.

32. Colonial Williamsburg, *The President's Report* (Williamburg, 1962), 32. Hereafter, all presidents' reports will be cited as *PR*.

33. Testimony before the House Committee on Mines and Mining, in *New York Times,* April 7, 1914, 2; Graham Adams, *The Age of Industrial Violence, 1910–1915* (New York, 1966).

34. John D. Rockefeller, Jr., "The Genesis of the Williamsburg Restoration," *National Geographic Magazine,* April 1937, 401; Moscow, *Rockefeller,* 104–6; Manfredo Tafuri and Francesco Dal Co, *Modern Architecture* (New York, 1979), 232. See E. R. Chamberlin, *Preserving the Past* (London, 1979), 43–50.

35. *The Public Papers and Addresses of Franklin D. Roosevelt,* 1938 vol. (New York, 1941), 158–61.

36. Thomas F. King, Patricia Parker Hickman, and Gary Berg, *Anthropology in Historic Preservation: Caring for Culture's Clutter* (New York, 1977), 22; Wolf Von Eckardt, "Federal Follies: The Mismanaging of Historic Preservation," *Historic Preservation* (Jan.–Feb. 1980), 2 (hereafter cited as *HP*); Weinberg, *Preservation,* 24; Edward Francis Barrese, "The Historical Records Survey: A Nation Acts to Save Its Memory" (Ph.D. diss., George Washington University, 1980).

37. King, Hickman, and Berg, *Anthropology,* 23, 202–4; Ronald F. Lee, "The Preservation of Historic and Architectural Monuments in the United States," *National Council for Historic Sites and Buildings Newsletter,* 1 (Dec. 1949), 2 (hereafter cited as *NCHSB Newsletter*).

38. Whitehill, *Independent Historical Societies,* 386–90, 469–70; Frank Stella, et al., *New Profits from Old Buildings; Private Enterprise Approaches to Making Preser-*

vation Pay (New York, 1979), 247–48; Merrimack Valley Textile Museum, *The Housing of a Textile Collection, Occasional Report No. 1* (North Andover, Mass., 1968), 7–12.

39. My interpretation is based on a 1980 visit and an examination of old exhibits.

40. Richard M. Candee, "Old Sturbridge Village: From Model Village to Village Model," paper presented to Society of Architectural Historians, April 1975; A. B. Wells, *Old Quinabaug Village* (Sturbridge, Mass., 1941), 4.

41. Lee, "Preservation," 8.

42. *CW News, Fiftieth Anniversary Issue* (November 27, 1976), 4.

43. *Colonial Williamsburg: The First Twenty-five Years,* 10, 12, 18; Thomas Wertenbaker, "Historic Restorations in the United States," *NCHSB Newsletter,* 1 (Sept. 1949), 9.

44. Kenneth Chorley, "Historical Preservation—Issues and Problems, 1948," *NCHSB Quarterly Report,* 1 (March 1949), 2; Colonial Williamsburg and the College of William and Mary, *They Gave Us Freedom* (Williamsburg, 1951), 5.

45. Daniel J. Boorstin, "Past and Present in America: A Historian Visits Colonial Williamsburg," *Commentary,* Jan. 1958, 4; Edward P. Alexander, "Historical Restorations," in William B. Hesseltine and Donald R. McNeil, eds., *In Support of Clio: Essays in Memory of Herbert A. Kellar* (Madison, 1958), 195; Edward P. Alexander, *The Museum: A Living Book of History* (Detroit, 1959), 13; Kenneth Chorley, *The New Commonwealth of the Intellect* (London, 1958), 23–24.

46. Boorstin, "Past and Present," 3, 5–6. In 1969 Boorstin was appointed to the board of Colonial Williamsburg.

47. These developments are discussed in the presidents' reports of the 1950s. Bush is quoted in *PR* (1955), 14.

48. *PR* (1959), 37; *PR* (1955), 13; *CW News, Fiftieth Anniversary,* 10; CW, *Proceedings of the Presentation of the Williamsburg Award by the Trustees of Colonial Williamsburg to the Rt. Hon. Sir Winston S. Churchill at Drapers' Hall, London, December 7, 1955* (Williamsburg, 1957).

49. Weinberg, *Preservation,* 30.

50. Peirce F. Lewis, "The Future of the Past: Our Clouded Vision of Historic Preservation," *Pioneer America,* 7 (July 1975), 1–20.

51. Ada Louise Huxtable, "Dissent at Colonial Williamsburg," *New York Times,* Sept. 22, 1963; Ada Louise Huxtable, "Lively Original Versus Dead Copy," *New York Times* May 9, 1965; Lowenthal, "American Way," 31; Walter Muir Whitehill, "Promoted to Glory . . .": The Origin of Preservation in the United States," in Albert Rains, et al., eds., *With Heritage So Rich* (New York, 1966), 43.

52. Carl Feiss, "Preservation of Historic Areas in the United States," *HP,* 16:4 (1964), 145; Lowenthal, "American Way," 31.

53. America the Beautiful Fund, *Old Glory: A Pictorial Report on the Grass Roots History Movement and the First Hometown History Primer* (New York, 1973), 63; on the Society for the Preservation of Weeksville and Bedford-Stuyvesant History, see *HP,* 31 (March–April 1979), 23; Joe Louis Mattox, "Ghetto or Gold Mine—Hold On to That Old House," *American Preservationist,* 1 (Feb.–March 1978), 4.

54. Personal visit and interview with museum staff and university historians.

55. Not all did, however. See George L. Wrenn, III, "What Is a Historic House Museum?" *HP*, 23 (Jan.–March 1971), 55–57.

56. Hurt, "Agricultural Museums," 367–75; James Deetz, "The Changing Historic House Museum—Can It Live?" *HP*, 23 (Jan.–March 1971), 51–54; Darwin P. Kelsey, "Old Sturbridge Village Today," *Antiques* (1979); 826–43; G. Terry Sharrer, "Hitching History to the Plow," *HP*, 32 (Nov.–Dec. 1980), 42–49.

57. See, for example, Wrenn, "Historic House Museum," 55–56; David Lowenthal, "Past Time, Present Place: Landscape and Memory," *Geographical Review*, 65 (Jan. 1975), 1–36; Lewis, "Future of the Past," passim; Frank Barnes, "Living History: Clio—or Cliopatria," *History News*, 29 (Sept. 1974), 202. Thomas J. Schlereth's excellent survey presents the new consensus in summary form: "It Wasn't That Simple," *Museum News*, 56 (Jan.–Feb. 1978), 36–44.

58. Alvin Toffler, *Future Shock* (New York, 1970), 390–91.

59. CW, *Official Guidebook*, 7th ed. (Williamsburg, 1979), x–xi; Gary Carson, "From the Bottom Up," *History News*, 35 (Jan. 1980), 7–9; Shomer Zwelling, "Social History Hits the Streets: Williamsburg Characters Come to Life," *History News*, 35 (Jan. 1980), 10–12; James R. Short, "Black History at Colonial Williamsburg," *Colonial Williamsburg Today*, 2 (Winter 1980), 10–11; Alexander, *Museums in Motion*, 210–11.

60. Alexander, *Museums in Motion*, 222. The disconnection of past and present generated peculiar but instructive difficulties. At Williamsburg, Rockefeller had stopped time just before that junction at which artisanal production succumbed to capitalist social relations. Williamsburg craft workers went through actual apprentice programs and had to have a masterpiece approved by other masters around the country and by Colonial Williamsburg, Inc. One problem with this system was that the craft workers could not, as the real ones did, develop their art; they had always to produce in the same style. This inhibition was enhanced by CW's desire to sell their pewter candlesticks and silver bowls as commodities. Indeed, when the old methods failed to keep up with demand, a modern factory was set up (not, of course, in the historic area), which churned these products out. And when the master silversmiths said that they wanted the profits from such sales—their forebears, after all, had *owned* their finished products—CW briskly reminded them of the facts of capitalist life: despite their wigs and shoppes, they were employees. The silversmiths departed from CW in a huff to set up their own company.

61. J. H. Plumb, *The Death of the Past* (Boston, 1970), 30.

62. See Raymond Williams' excellent discussion and deployment of this kind of analysis in *Politics and Letters* (London, 1979), 324–29, and *The Country and the City* (New York, 63, 1973), 22–34, 120–26.

63. Attendance at CW went from 166,251 in 1947, to 708,974 in 1967, to over 1,200,000 in 1976. Greenfield Village passed the 1,000,000 mark in 1960 and hit 1,701,559 in 1973; and Mount Vernon drew over a million visitors in 1975. William T. Alderson and Shirley Payne Low, *Interpretation of Historic Sites* (Nashville, 1976), 22; Tony P. Wren, "The Tourist Industry and Promotional Publications," *HP*,

16 (May–June 1964), 111; Eleanor Thompson, "Mt. Vernon, America's Oldest Preservation Project: Past Accomplishments, Present Status, Future Prospects" (precis), *Journal of the Society of Architectural Historians,* 35 (Dec. 1976), 264; Lewis, *Public Image,* 280.

64. An unpublished 1979 Williamsburg survey found that 64 percent of their visitors had total family incomes over $25,000, and 17 percent had incomes over $50,000; 54 percent had some graduate credit or a graduate degree.

65. Wren, "Tourist Industry," 111, 112.

66. John Berger, *About Looking* (New York, 1980).

67. See Walter LaFeber, "The Last War, the Next War, and the New Revisionists," *democracy* 1 (Jan. 1981), 93–103; and Paul Berman, "Gas Chamber Games: Crackpot History and the Right to Life," *Village Voice,* (June 10–16, 1981, 1ff.

Chapter 9

1. David Lowenthal, "The Place of the Past in the American Landscape," in David Lowenthal and Martyn J. Bowden, eds., *Geographies of the Mind: Essays in Historical Geosophy* (New York, 1976), 89–117; David Lowenthal, "The American Way of History," *Columbia University Forum,* 9:3 (Summer 1966), 27–32.

2. On historicist architectural allusions see Paul Goldberger, *The Skyscraper* (New York, 1981), 39, 44, 53.

3. Cadwallader Colden, *Memoir, at the Celebration of the Completion of the New York Canals,* cited in Lowenthal, "The Place of the Past," 93.

4. On the Brahmins, see Michael Wallace, "Visiting the Past," in this volume, p. 137, and Barbara Miller Solomon, *Ancestors and Immigrants: A Changing New England Tradition* (New York, 1956).

For a comparison with the emergence of a bourgeois preservation lobby in England, see Michael Bommes and Patrick Wright, " 'Charms of Residence': The Public and the Past," in Richard Johnson, et al., *Making Histories: Studies in History Writing and Politics* (Minneapolis, 1982), 273–75.

5. Thomas F. King, Patricia Parker Hickman, and Gary Berg, *Anthropology in Historic Preservation: Caring for Culture's Clutter* (New York, 1977), 10–19.

6. Ibid.; Oscar Gray, "The Response of Federal Legislation to Historic Preservation," *Law and Contemporary Problems,* 36:3 (Summer 1971), 312; Ronald F. Lee, *The Antiquities Act of 1906* (Washington, D.C., 1970).

7. Charles B. Hosmer, Jr., *Presence of the Past: A History of the Preservation Movement in the United States Before Williamsburg* (New York, 1965), 306–12; Charles B. Hosmer, Jr., *Preservation Comes of Age: From Williamsburg to the National Trust, 1926–1949* (Charlottesville, 1981), 232–34; Patrick Gerster and Nicholas Cords, eds., *Myth and Southern History* (Chicago, 1974).

8. Hosmer, *Preservation Comes of Age,* 234–36; Edward D. Campbell, *The Celluloid South: Hollywood and the Southern Myth* (Knoxville, 1981).

9. Nathan Weinberg, *Preservation in American Towns and Cities* (Boulder, Colo., 1979), 39; Hosmer, *Preservation Comes of Age,* 232–74.

10. M. Christine Boyer, *Dreaming the Rational City: The Myth of American City Planning* (Cambridge, Mass., 1983).

11. Hosmer, *Preservation Comes of Age,* 290–306; Jacob H. Morrison, *Historic Preservation Law* (Washington, D.C., 1965), 12, 157–58.

In San Antonio a 1921 flood led consulting engineers from Boston to propose paving over the San Antonio River. In response, local affluent and well-connected women founded the San Antonio Conservation Society and in 1924 convinced the city that the river was an asset (with the aid of a puppet show about preservation as the "goose that laid golden eggs"): John Pastier, "After the Alamo," *Historic Preservation,* 35 (May–June 1983), 40–47 (hereafter cited as *HP*).

12. On this movement, see Wallace, "Visiting the Past," p.137.

13. On professionals, see Magali Sarfatti Larson, *The Rise of Professionalism* (Berkeley, 1977); Boyer, *Dreaming the Rational City;* Pat Walker, ed., *Between Labor and Capital* (Boston, 1979).

14. Boyer, *Dreaming the Rational City,* 46–56.

15. King, Hickman, and Berg, *Anthropology,* 22–24; Wolf Von Eckardt, "Federal Follies: The Mismanaging of Historic Preservation," *HP,* 32 (Jan.–Feb. 1980), 2; Weinberg, *Preservation,* 24; Hosmer, *Preservation Comes of Age,* 509–62.

16. On the 1935 act: King, Hickman, and Berg, *Anthropology,* 23, 202–4; Ronald F. Lee, "The Preservation of Historic and Architectural Monuments in the United States," *National Council for Historic Sites and Buildings Newsletter,* 1 (Dec. 1949), 2; Hosmer, *Preservation Comes of Age,* 562–76. On the Branch of History: ibid., 580–99.

17. Hosmer, *Preservation Comes of Age,* 626–49.

18. For European parallels, see Eric Hobsbawm and Terence Ranger, eds., *The Invention of Tradition* (Cambridge, England, 1983).

19. On the "modernist" tendencies of capitalist development in the 1920s, see Susan Buck-Morss, "Benjamin's Passagen-Werk: Redeeming Mass Culture for the Revolution," *New German Critique,* no. 29 (Fall 1984), 211–40; Richard Wightman Fox and T. J. Jackson Lears, eds., *The Culture of Consumption* (New York, 1983).

20. See the prescient talk by Ronald F. Lee, chief historian of the National Park Service, "The Effect of Postwar Conditions on the Preservation of Historic Sites and Buildings," cited in Hosmer, *Preservation Comes of Age,* 818.

21. On the growth coalition: John H. Mollenkopf, "The Postwar Politics of Urban Development," in William K. Tabb and Larry Sawyers, eds., *Marxism and the Metropolis* (New York, 1978), 117–51; Alan Wolfe, *America's Impasse: The Rise and Fall of the Politics of Growth* (New York, 1981), 83, 96. On the popularity of suburbanization: Mark I. Gelfrand, *A Nation of Cities: The Federal Government and Urban America, 1933–1965* (New York, 1975), 149–50, 155, 217–18, 350–51.

22. Martin Anderson, *The Federal Bulldozer: A Critical Analysis of Urban Renewal, 1949–1962* (Cambridge, Mass., 1964), 54, 65; Charles Abrams, *The City Is*

the Frontier (New York: Harper & Row, 1965), 133; Wolfe, *America's Impasse*, 94–96; Weinberg, *Preservation*, 30. For the prestige of the new, the impact of planned obsolescence on popular taste, and general reflections on the emergence of a facsimile culture, see James Marston Fitch, *Historic Preservation: Curatorial Management of the Built World* (New York, 1982).

23. Hosmer, *Preservation Comes of Age*, 809–65; David Finley, *History of the National Trust for Historic Preservation, 1947–63* (Washington, D.C., 1965). For differences over the line such propagandizing should take, see *NCHSB Quarterly Report*, 1 (March 1949), 1–6.

24. Elizabeth D. Mulloy, *The History of the National Trust for Historic Preservation, 1963–1973* (Washington, D.C., 1976), 11–13, 26–27. (The council remained in existence until 1953, when it merged with the Trust.)

25. To Ronald F. Lee, chief historian of the National Park Service and secretary of the National Council, "professionalization" meant getting away from the kinds of "local lore and legendary anecdotes purveyed by commercial guides." Interpretation, he thought, should be done "by trained historians and museum curators in a manner commensurate with the dignity and significance of the nation's historical heritage": Lee, "Preservation," 8–9. In this period Colonial Williamsburg joined with the National Park Service and the American University to present seminars on the preservation and interpretation of historic sites and buildings, and Cooperstown inaugurated a similar seminar in American history and culture: Lee, "Preservation," 7–8.

26. Additional historic zoning districts were created in this period. On Georgetown's construction by local bankers, lawyers, architects, and diplomats interested not in saving homesteads but in investing in planned redevelopment, see *NCHSB Quarterly Report*, 2 (1950), 91; Edward F. Gerber, "Historic Georgetown, Inc.: The Economics Involved in Preservation," *Urban Land*, 34 (July–Aug. 1975), 14–26. Society Hill, Capital Hill, and Historic Annapolis soon followed: Mulloy, *National Trust*, 12; Gelfand, *Nation of Cities*, 185.

27. On Jacobs: Weinberg, *Preservation*, 30; Abrams, *The City Is the Frontier*. Mollenkopf notes that there were major community protests in the 1960s in Boston, Cambridge, and San Francisco: "Postwar Politics," 141.

28. Quotation is from Joyce Brothers, in *HP*, 17 (May–June 1965), 113–14. On this critical group generally, a good introduction is Peirce F. Lewis, "The Future of the Past: Our Clouded Vision of Historic Preservation," *Pioneer America*, 7 (July 1975), 1–20. See also Jane Jacobs, *The Death and Life of Great American Cities* (New York, 1961); Herbert Gans, *The Urban Villagers* (New York, 1962); Ada Louise Huxtable's collection of essays, *Will They Ever Finish Bruckner Boulevard?* (New York, 1970).

29. Mulloy, *National Trust*, xi.

30. Alan Wolfe (*America's Impasse*) sees the poor taking to the streets, starting in 1964, in a rage at urban renewal, highway construction, and the rise of the medical-industrial complex. Mollenkopf notes that virtually all riot areas were sites of major renewal efforts; Newark was a notable example: "Postwar Politics," 142–43. See also

Gelfand, *Nation of Cities,* 215; Bernard J. Frieden and Marshall Kaplan, *The Politics of Neglect: Urban Aid from Model Cities to Revenue Sharing* (Cambridge, Mass., 1975), 33.

31. Hosmer, *Presence of the Past,* 262, 268, 293; Laurence Vail Coleman, *Historic House Museums* (Washington, D.C., 1933), 23; Warren James Belasco, *Americans on the Road: From Autocamp to Motel, 1910–1945* (Cambridge, Mass., 1979).

32. Tony P. Wren, "The Tourist Industry and Promotional Publications," *HP,* 16 (May–June 1964), 111–13; William T. Alderson and Shirley Payne Low, *Interpretation of Historic Sites* (Nashville, 1976), 22.

33. New York State: Morrison, *Preservation Law,* 54. Figures for 1964: Wren, "Tourist Industry," 112. Daniels: Jonathan Daniels, *Life Is a Local Story* (Nashville, 1964), quoted in Wren, "Tourist Industry," 111; Walter Muir Whitehill, *Independent Historical Societies* (Boston, 1962), 461.

34. Wren, "Tourist Industry," 113–14. This was a widespread phenomenon. For discussions of Santa Barbara, Annapolis, Newport, Natchez, and a variety of western towns, see Whitehill, *Independent Historical Societies,* 551, and his chapter on "Mammon and Monuments"; "Annapolis," *American Preservation,* 1 (Oct.–Nov. 1977), 27 (hereafter cited as *AP*); Hosmer, *Preservation Comes of Age,* 359, 371.

35. On Savannah and for quotation from July 1975 *Fortune,* see Leopold Adler, II, "Preservation as Profitable Real Estate in Savannah," in National Trust for Historic Preservation, *Economic Benefits of Preserving Old Buildings,* (Washington, D.C., 1975), 143–47; see also Carol Matlack, "Savannah," *AP,* (Feb.–March 1979), 11–24; Weinberg, *Preservation,* 95–107.

San Antonio businessmen also saw the light. About to embark on a new round of development, they changed course and spent hundreds of thousands of dollars to landscape parkways and restore Spanish missions. Recalling the 1924 campaign, a spokesman reported that San Antonio was "beginning to recognize that to destroy those things that set it apart from other cities is to kill the goose that laid the golden egg": Wren, "Tourist Industry," 114.

To these big-city converts were added hosts of small-town Main Street shopkeepers, driven to the wall by competition from the highway-linked malls: Anderson, *Federal Bulldozer,* 68; Gelfand, *Nation of Cities,* 195, 338–39, 361.

36. Ada Louise Huxtable, "Lively Original Versus Dead Copy," *New York Times,* May 9, 1965, reprinted in Huxtable, *Bruckner Boulevard,* 211–12. See also Lowenthal, "American Way," 27.

37. Ada Louise Huxtable, *Kicked a Building Lately?* (New York, 1976), 234.

38. Sidney Hyman, "Empire for Liberty," in Albert Rains, et al., eds., *With Heritage So Rich* (New York, 1966), 1; Whitehill, "The Right of Cities to Be Beautiful," in Rains, *Heritage,* 55; Gelfand, *Nation of Cities,* 187, 192, 318.

39. John Greenya, "The Quiet Power of Gordon Gray," *HP,* 35 (Sept.–Oct. 1983), 26–29.

40. The text of the act can be found in King, Hickman, and Berg, *Anthropology,* 205. See also Mulloy, *National Trust,* 68–85; Robert R. Garvey and Terry Brust

Morton, *The U.S. Government in Historic Preservation: A Brief History of the 1966 Historic Preservation Act and Others* (Washington, D.C., 1975).

41. Heywood T. Sanders, "Urban Renewal and the Revitalized City: A Reconsideration of Recent History," in Donald B. Rosenthal, ed., *Urban Revitalization* (Beverly Hills, Calif., 1980), 103–26; Gelfand, *Nation of Cities,* 361–67, 374; Frieden and Kaplan, *Politics of Neglect,* 33–34.

42. Wolfe, *America's Impasse,* 103–5; Gelfand, *Nation of Cities,* 361, 374.

43. Bernard J. Frieden and Arthur P. Solomon, *The Nation's Housing: 1975–1985* (Cambridge, Mass., 1977); Frieden and Kaplan, *Politics of Neglect,* 267; Raymond A. Rosenfeld, "Who Benefits and Who Decides: The Uses of Community Development Block Grants," in Rosenthal, *Urban Revitalization,* 211–35; John Ross, "Impacts of Urban Aid," in Rosenthal, *Urban Revitalization,* 158–64; Advisory Committee on Historic Preservation, *Report to the President and Congress* (Washington, D.C., 1980), 20–22; Phyllis Myers, "Urban Enterprise Zones: UDAG Revisited?" *HP,* 33 (Nov.–Dec. 1981), 13, 60–61.

44. Phillip L. Clay, *Neighborhood Renewal: Middle-Class Resettlement and Incumbent Upgrading in American Neighborhoods* (Lexington, Mass., 1979), 3–15, 20; Mollenkopf, "Postwar Politics," 128; James Henry Johnson, Jr., "Incumbent Upgrading and Gentrification in the Inner City: A Case Study of Neighborhood Revitalization Activities in Eastown. Grand Rapids" (Ph.D. diss., Michigan State University, 1980), 23.

45. Johnson, "Incumbent Upgrading," 24. For my speculations about how the popularity of the old is generated by the sterility of the new, see "Visiting the Past," p. 137.

46. Chester Hartman, Dennis Keating, and Richard LeGates, *Displacement: How to Fight It* (Berkeley, 1982), 1–25.

47. Advisory Council on Historic Preservation, *Report to the President and the Congress of the United States (1979)* (Washington, D.C., 1980), 1–3, (hereafter cited as ACHP, *Report for 1979*). In 1979 a redeveloper sued the Historic Alexandria Foundation (Virginia) for refusing to give him historical plaques for his houses; real estate agents had told him that the plaques would add $10,000 to each property (Ibid.).

48. Amy Singer, "When Worlds Collide," *HP,* 36 (July–Aug. 1984), 39; Jason Berry, "The 'Upgrading' of New Orleans," *Nation* (September 23, 1978), 271. For similar gentry imperialism in East Capitol Hill, see Peter Thomas Rohrbach, "The Poignant Dilemma of Spontaneous Restoration," *HP,* 22 (Oct.-Dec. 1970), 4–7; On Savannah, see Matlack, "Savannah," *AP,* 2 (Feb.–March, 1979), 22.

49. Carrie Johnson, "The Preservation Movement Looks at Itself," *HP,* 32 (Nov.–Dec. 1980), 33; ACHP, *Report for 1982,* 39. By 1981 New York City's Landmarks Preservation Commission had designated forty-one historic districts. Five were in Harlem, but in most cases the designation roped off gentry quarters like Gramercy Park, Brooklyn Heights, Greenwich Village, and the Upper East Side. The commission regulated 15,000 buildings, 2 percent of the city's housing stock: *New York Times,* September 20, 1981, p. 56.

50. Phyllis Meyers and Gordon Blinder, *Neighborhood Conservation: Lessons from Three Cities* (Washington, D.C., 1977); *New York Times*, September 20, 1981, p. 56; *AP*, 1 (Feb.–March 1978), 71.

51. Lewis, "Future of the Past," 18.

52. America the Beautiful Fund, *Old Glory: A Pictorial Report on the Grass Roots History Movement and the First Hometown History Primer* (New York, 1973), 37–39. This book contains dozens of other local stories, but this remains another area badly in need of further research. Worth exploring are episodes of community resistance in New Haven's Wooster Square, Baltimore's Fells Point, and New York's Soho. On developer wariness: National Trust, *Economic Benefits*, 76.

53. On the National People's Action: *AP*, 1 (Oct.–Nov. 1977), 26. A study by the New World Foundation found two thousand active neighborhood self-help groups: *AP*, 3 (May–June 1980), 7–8. On the National Commission on Neighborhoods: *AP*, 1 (April-May 1978), 4–5, and James Barry, "The National Commission on Neighborhoods: The Politics of Urban Revitalization," in Rosenthal, *Urban Revitalization*, 165–87. On the fund: *AP*, 1 (Aug.–Sept. 1978), 5. On antiredlining actions see Richard Hula, "Housing, Lending Institutions and Public Policy," in Rosenthal, *Urban Revitalization*, 77–99; William K. Tabb, *The Long Default: New York City and the Urban Fiscal Crisis* (New York, 1982), 96–97.

54. David Morris and Karl Hess, *Neighborhood Power: The New Localism* (Boston, 1975); Myers and Binder, *Neighborhood Conservation*. Restrictive covenants were one of the oldest devices for "preserving" property values; it had always been considered acceptable to block the free market on racist grounds.

55. On the AIA statement: Lachlan F. Blair and John A. Quinn, eds., *Historic Preservation: Setting, Legislation, and Techniques* (Urbana, Ill., 1977), 13. On the traditional movement's reaching out to neighborhoods: ACHP, *The National Historic Preservation Program Today* (Washington, D.C., 1976), 3. In 1977 James Biddle, president of the National Trust, called neighborhood conservation a major issue for preservationists: *AP*, 1 (Feb.–March 1978), 3, 71; *AP*, 2 (Oct.–Nov. 1978), 76–77; *New York Times*, March 2, 1980, sec. 8, 1; Arthur P. Ziegler, Jr., *Historic Preservation in Inner City Areas: A Manual of Practice* (Pittsburgh, 1971), 8, 17–18; Rohrback, "Poignant Dilemma," 4–10; *Wall Street Journal*, February 6, 1961; "Savannah," *AP*, 2 (Feb.–March 1979), 22; Paul J. Goldberger, "The Dangers in Preservation Success," in National Trust, *Economic Benefits*, 159–60.

56. Rohrback, "Poignant Dilemma," 7.

57. Ibid.; Joe Louis Mattox, "Ghetto or Gold Mine—Hold On to That Old House," *AP*, 1 (Feb.–March 1978), 3; *AP*, 1 (Feb.–March 1978), 71.

58. Weinberg, *Preservation*, 110; Biliana Cicin-Sain, "The Costs and Benefits of Neighborhood Revitalization," in Rosenthal, *Urban Revitalization*, 53–55; Andrea Kirsten Mullen, "Preservation in the Black Community: A Growing Commitment," *HP*, 34 (Jan.–Feb. 1982), 39–43; "Weeksville Rediscovered and Restored," *Metropolis: The Architecture and Design Magazine of New York* (July–Aug. 1984).

59. Raymond P. Rhinehart, "Preservation's Best Interests," *Preservation News,* Oct. 1976, 5 (hereafter cited as *PN*); Andrea Kirsten Mullen, "A Black Preservationist Speaks Out," *HP,* 35 (Nov.–Dec. 1983), 12–13.

60. Ziegler, *Historic Preservation,* v. On a black community's refusal to let whites in, and the consequent capital boycott, see Weinberg, *Preservation,* 109–10.

61. "Savannah Landmark: A New Type of Landlord," *AP,* 2 (Feb.–March 1979), 16–17; George McMillan, "Staying Home in Savannah," *HP,* 32 (March–April 1980); Adler, "Preservation as Profitable Real Estate," 143–47, 190; Michael D. Newsom, "Blacks and Historic Preservation," *Law and Contemporary Problems,* 36 (1971), 423–31.

62. *AP,* "Editorial," 3 (May–June 1980), 3; Hartman, Keating, and LeGates, *Displacement,* 164.

63. ACHP, *Report for 1980,* 9; Frank Stella, *New Profits from Old Buildings* (New York, 1979), 2. Preservation journals for mass audiences were also launched in this period: ACHP, *Report for 1980,* 10.

64. Gordon Gray, Trust president, quipped: "I only regret that I have but one staff to give to my country": *AP,* 2 (Oct.–Nov. 1978), 50. On new legislation, see King, Hickman, and Berg, *Anthropology,* 41–63; Mulloy, *National Trust,* 94–108.

65. *A Report by the US Historic Preservation Team of the US–USSR Joint Working Group on the Enhancement of the Urban Environment. May 25–June 14, 1974* (Washington, D.C., 1975), 8–15 and passim; ACHP, *National Historic Preservation,* 59–62, 79–97. On lobbyists and Preservation Action, see Jane Holtz Kay, "The National Trust," *AP,* 2 (Oct.–Nov. 1978), 74; *AP,* 1 (Oct.–Nov. 1977), 8; *Preservation Action Alert,* 1 (Jan. 1976), 1 (hereafter cited as *PAA*); Steve Weinberg, "Lobbying Congress . . . The Inside Story," *HP,* 34 (Jan.–Feb. 1982), 17–18. The Advisory Council claimed that "the most vital energy resource for this country is its sense of purpose. That sense of purpose, of national identity and destiny, is nourished by symbols from our past, reminders of our unique experiences and goals": ACHP, *National Historic Preservation,* 1; see also Mulloy, *National Trust,* xv.

66. Nellie L. Longsworth, "After 200 Years—What?" in Blair and Quinn, *Historic Preservation,* The expanded council included all cabinet members except the secretary of labor. Amendments added in 1980 required federal agencies to minimize harm to landmarks to the "maximum extent possible": ACHP, *Report for 1982.*

67. On the Tax Act see Longsworth, "After 200 Years," 4; Gregory E. Andrews, ed., *Tax Incentives for Historic Preservation* (Washington, D.C., 1980); *PAA,* 1 (Oct. 1976), 3.

68. Frank B. Gilbert, "Assessing the Grand Central Decision," *HP,* 32 (Sept.–Oct. 1980), 39; England: Graham Ashworth, "Contemporary Developments in British Preservation Law and Practice," *Law and Contemporary Problems,* 36 (Summer 1971), 348–61.

69. Morrison, *Preservation Law,* 20–21.

70. Ibid., ix; Joseph L. Sax, "Takings Private Property and Public Rights," *Yale Law Journal,* 81 (1971), 149–86; Malcolm Baldwin, "Historic Preservation in the

Context of Environmental Law: Mutual Interest in Amenity," *Law and Contemporary Problems,* 36 (Summer 1971), 432–41; "Aesthetic Zoning: Preservation of Historic Areas," *Fordham Law Review,* 29 (1961), 729–40; Ellen L. Kettler and Bernard D. Reams, Jr., *Historic Preservation Law: An Annotated Bibliography* (Washington, D.C., 1976), iii.

71. Gilbert, "Assessing Grand Central," 38–39; Frank Greve, "David Bonderman, Esq., Preservation's Unsentimental Hero," *HP,* 35 (Jan.–Feb. 1983). Cf. Ada Louise Huxtable's comments in *New York Times,* July 9, 1978, sec. 2, 21.

It should be kept in mind that the districts the decision upheld were for the most part elite enclaves. It is interesting to speculate on whether the simultaneous legal affirmation of suburban zoning, environmental and aesthetic regulation, and historic preservation represents the efforts and interests of an upper-middle-class stratum who in the middle to late sixties developed a cultural resistance to unrestrained growth, which was now increasingly associated with lower-class expansion. For analogous thoughts on the suburban desire to protect investment through exclusionary zoning ("Bang the bell, Jack, I'm on board") see Bernard J. Frieden, *The Environmental Protection Hustle* (Cambridge, Mass., 1979); Roger Alcaly and David M. Mermelstein, eds., *The Fiscal Crisis of American Cities* (New York, 1977), 63, 73; Mollenkopf, "Postwar Politics," 125.

72. ACHP, *Report for 1979,* 2; Cicin-Sain, "Costs and Benefits." Note that to the degree that the careless culture of planned obsolescence was a function of cheap energy, which in turn was related to American imperial power, liberation and nationalist movements in the Third World helped force a reconstruction of American preservation consciousness.

73. Bernard J. Frieden and Arthur P. Solomon, *The Nation's Housing: 1975–1985* (Cambridge, Mass., 1977; ACHP, *Report for 1980,* 15; ACHP, *Report for 1982,* 23; Clay, *Neighborhood Renewal,* 15. On 1976: ACHP, *Report for 1979,* 2.

74. Booz, Allen, Hamilton study: *New York Times,* March 2, 1980, sec. 8, 1. The 38 percent figure for rehabilitation comes from Paul Edward Parker, Jr., "Preservation Can Make a Profit," *HP,* 31 (Sept.–Oct. 1979), 23.

75. Jonathan Walters, "Main Street Turns the Corner," *HP,* 33 (Nov.–Dec. 1981), 36–45.

76. Robert Campbell, "Lure of the Marketplace: Real-Life Theater," *HP,* 32 (Jan.–Feb. 1980), 46–48; Arthur M. Skolnik, "A History of Pioneer Square," in National Trust, *Economic Benefits,* 15–19; Clay, *Neighborhood Renewal,* 12–13.

77. Jonathan Walters and Sace Davis, "The Boom in Born-Again Buildings," *HP,* 36 (Aug. 1984), 18–19; Terrence Maitland, "Corporate Takeovers," *HP,* 33 (Sept.–Oct. 1981), 42–48; Parker, "Preservation Can Make a Profit," 22–23. On Lowell see Ron LaBrecque, "New Industry for Mill City, USA," *HP,* 32 (July–Aug. 1980), 32–39. On Providence, Savannah, and New York, see *New York Times,* April 7, 1980; "Savannah," 11–25; Roberta Brandes Gratz and Peter Freiberg, "Has Success Spoiled SoHo?" *HP,* 32 (Sept.–Oct. 1980), 9–15.

78. *New York Times,* August 13, 1981.

79. Mulloy, *National Trust,* 173; Kay Holmes, "Learning About the Real World," *HP,* 32 (July–Aug. 1980), 2–3; Marsha Glenn, "Academic Programs in Historic Preservation: An Up-to-Date Survey of the Field," *Journal of the Society of Architectural Historians,* 35 (Dec. 1976), 265; King, Hickman, and Berg, *Anthropology,* 43; National Trust for Historic Preservation, *Annual Report, 1976–1977* (Washington, D.C., 1977), 14–15.

80. Frank Stella, *New Profits from Old Buildings: Private Enterprise Approaches to Making Preservation Pay* (New York, 1979), 3–21 and passim (this is an authoritative study commissioned by the corporate elite); Charles N. Tseckares, "Adaptive Office Space in Old Buildings," in National Trust, *Economic Benefits,* 76; Parker, "Preservation Can Make a Profit," 22–23.

81. Stella, *New Profits,* 2; Parker, "Preservation Can Make a Profit," 23; ACHP, *Report for 1982,* 23.

82. *PN,* Nov. 1981; *PN,* April 1981; Leonard Curry, "Finding Shelter in Old Buildings," *HP,* 32 (March–April 1980), 27–31; "Preservation Movement Comes of Age," *New York Times,* Oct. 7, 1979, and Oct. 14, 1979, sec. 8, 1.

83. John Sower, "Financing and Developing Large Commercial Preservation Projects," in National Trust, *Economic Benefits,* 133; National Association of Building Owners and Managers 1980 report, "Renaissance in Office Buildings" (How to Convert Old Office Buildings into Luxury Apartments): ACHP, *Report for 1980,* 12.

84. Robertson E. Collins, Foreword to Weinberg, *Preservation,* xi–xii.

85. National Trust for Historic Preservation, *Annual Report 1975–1976* (Washington, D.C., 1976), 1; National Trust, *Annual Report 1976–1977,* 10, 13, 19, 38; ACHP, *Report for 1980.* 9. Only two union organizations signed on, the AFL-CIO and the International Union of Bricklayers and Allied Craftsmen: ibid.

86. National Trust, *Annual Report 1976–1977,* 19.

87. *PAA,* 5 (Jan. 1980), 1–2; Curry, "Finding Shelter," 30; *PAA,* 3:5, 4:2, 5:2. Deregulation moves were afoot at the state level too. For antipreservationist arguments in Waterbury, Connecticut ("Waterbury is not a historic city. It's a city for surviving"), see Elise Vider, "The City That Said 'No,' " *HP,* 32 (Sept.–Oct. 1980), 52. In New York, St. Bartholomew's Church, blocked from constructing a highrise, led a move in the legislature to overturn landmarks legislation on the grounds that it violated the First Amendment guarantee of freedom of religion: *New York Times,* Jan. 31, 1984.

88. *New York Times,* August 12 and 13, 1980.

89. Jeanie Wylie, "A Neighborhood Dies So GM Can Live," *Village Voice,* July 8–14, 1981, 1, 11–13; "Corporate Domain," *Nation,* (April 4, 1981), 389; Richard Hodas, "Neighborhood and Factory Could Coexist," *HP,* 33 (Jan.–Feb. 1981); Hartman, Keating, and LeGates, *Displacement,* 147–49. A film—*Poletown Lives!*— is available from Information Factory, 3512 Courville, Detroit, MI 48224.

90. Corinne L. Gilb, "Detroit Must Move Forward," *HP,* 33 (Jan.–Feb. 1981), 47–49.

91. *Preservation Action Alert, Historic Preservation, and Preservation News* for 1981–1985; Steve Weinberg, "Super List," *HP,* 34 (July–Aug. 1982), 10–17; Myers, "Urban Enterprise Zones," 12ff.; *New York Times,* September 24, 1983.

92. Weinberg, "Lobbying Congress," 19–25; *PN,* June 1981.

93. *PAA,* (Aug. 1983), 8; *PN,* May 1981; *HP,* 37 (June 1985), 4.

94. Lee A. Daniels, "New Tax Breaks Spurring Preservation," *New York Times,* May 23, 1982, sec. 8, 1; Walters and Davis, "Born-Again Buildings," 18–19; *PN,* Jan. 1984, 3; Andre Shashaty, "The Deal Makers," *HP,* 35 (May–June 1983), 14; *PN,* March 1985, 1.

95. Goldberger, "The Dangers in Preservation Success," 159–61. For similar warnings about the current coziness, see Peter Brink, "A Bottom Line?" *AP,* 1 (Dec. 1977–Jan. 1978), and Peirce Lewis ("We can hardly complain of barbarism if we deliberately lie down with barbarians"), "Future of the Past," 16.

96. Carl Abbott, "The Facadism Fad: Is It Preservation?" *HP,* 36 (Oct. 1984), 42–47. The vogue for "post-modern" architecture, which amounts to putting historicist flourishes on the façades of new structures, bears an interesting resemblance to façadism proper.

97. On the Times Square hotel: *PN,* Jan. and Sept. 1981; *New York Times,* Feb. 12, 1982.

98. Giuseppe Campos Venuti, "The Conservation of the Architectural Heritage As a Means of Stimulating and Diversifying Economic Activity at the Regional and Local Levels," *Council of Europe Symposium No. 6* (Strasbourg, 1978).

99. On a particularly brutal displacement of a thousand blacks and Puerto Ricans in Hartford, Connecticut, in 1981 by Aetna Life, see *PN,* Sept. 1981. For the estimate that 2.5 million Americans are forced to move from homes and neighborhoods from all causes each year (the official government figure is 1.4 million involuntarily displaced), see Hartman, Keating, and LeGates, *Displacement,* 3, 5.

100. Huxtable, *Kicked a Building Lately?* 234.

101. John Kenneth Galbraith warned that "[P]reservationists must never be beguiled by the notion that we can rely on natural economic forces or that we can rely on the market. If we do, a large number of important art objects, artifacts and buildings will be sacrificed. The reason is that the market works on a short-time dimension, and the people who respond to the market are different from those who ultimately gain from conservation or preservation": "Preservationists Will Reap What They Sow . . . Eventually," *HP,* 32 (Sept.–Oct. 1980), 29.

Note also the conclusion of Bommes and Wright, based on the English experience, that "capitalist property relations can only be preserved if they are reproduced through new accumulative cycles," which in turn "necessitates the constant transformation of social relations in accordance with the needs of capital." The ensuing widespread change and actual demolition leads to conflict with the preservation lobby. Bommes and Wright, "'Charms of Residence,'" 275.

102. Quoted in Philip Langdon, "Plain Talk About Displacement," *HP,* 32 (March–April 1980).

103. On a larger land-use package, see the summary of Planners Network ideas in Peter Dreier, "Dreams and Nightmares: The Housing Crisis," *Nation* (Aug. 21–28, 1982), 141–44.

104. The most imaginative preservation efforts in the world have been undertaken in Bologna, where sociocultural engineering aims at preserving both people and places. See Campos Venuti, "The Conservation of the Architectural Heritage"; Fitch, *Historic Preservation*, 40–41, 67.

Chapter 10

Acknowledgments: We are grateful for the critical comments of Susan Porter Benson, Pat Cooper, Gary Kulik, Judith Smith, and Bruce Tucker, for the thoughts of Sarah Simmons Dickson and Anna Kornbluh on Barbie, and for typing by Rosemary Weaver.

1. Blanche Wiesen Cook, "The Historical Denial of Lesbianism," *Radical History Review*, 20 (Spring/Summer 1979), 60–65.

2. Sylvia Van Kirk, *"Many Tender Ties"*: *Women in Fur Trade Society, 1670–1870* (Winnipeg, 1980).

3. James C. Mohr, *Abortion in America: The Origins and Evolution of National Policy, 1800–1900* (New York, 1978).

4. Inez Haynes Irwin, *Angels and Amazons* (New York, 1934), 393.

5. For a discussion of social feminism, see J. Stanley Lemons, *The Woman Citizen: Social Feminism in the 1920s* (Urbana, Ill., 1973).

6. "The Barbie Mystique," *ISM on the Move*, Nov.–Dec. 1984, 10.

7. Attendance at "Barbie" from Susan Jean Dickey, curator of the exhibit at the Indiana State Museum, letter to Barbara Melosh, October 9, 1985.

8. For a discussion of the importance of recognizing a separate women's culture based on female experience and identity, see Estelle Freedman, "Separatism as Strategy: Female Institution Building and American Feminism, 1870–1930," *Feminist Studies*, 5 (1979), 512–29.

Chapter 11

Acknowledgments: This article could not have been written without the gracious cooperation of the historians who agreed to be interviewed for it and who commented on it. I also wish to thank Paul Mattingly, Judith Walkowitz, and the editors of this volume for their criticisms of earlier drafts.

1. Richard Marks (pscud.), telephone interview with the author, Nov. 21, 1984.

2. David R. Smith, "An Historical Look at Business Archives," *American Archivist*, 45 (Summer 1982), 274.

3. Richard Forman, "History Inside Business," *Public Historian,* 3 (Summer 1981), 45–49.

4. Smith, "Historical Look," 274.

5. Harold P. Anderson, "The Corporate History Department: The Wells Fargo Model," *Public Historian,* 3 (Summer 1981), 25–29; and William Strobridge, telephone interview with the author, Nov. 14, 1984.

6. Fred Jones (pseud.), telephone interview with the author, Nov. 15, 1984.

7. Deborah Gardner, *Marketplace: A Brief History of the New York Stock Exchange* (New York, 1982).

8. Gardner, *Marketplace; Finding Aid: NYSE Union Records* (unpublished inventory, New York Stock Exchange Archive, no date).

9. New York Stock Exchange Archive.

10. Forman, "History Inside Business," 59–60.

11. See articles in several pamphlets: the History Department, "Old Sacramento: Spirit of Gold Rush Days," "Wells Fargo: Service to Sacramento," "Wells Fargo Express: Old Sacramento Agency," "The Telegraph—A Vital Link for California," "Good Old Block," "Stagecoach Keeps On Rolling," and "The Current Staff—The Tradition Lives On," in *Wells Fargo Express: Old Sacramento Agency,* 4th ed. (San Francisco, n.d.); Wells Fargo History Department, *The History Department* (San Francisco, n.d.); and Anderson, "Corporate History Department."

12. The History Department, *Wells Fargo & Company: A Brief History* (San Francisco, n.d.), 23.

13. Charles Phillips, "History's Hired Hands: Plain Talk About Writing Business Histories," *History News,* 39 (May 1984), 10. See Herbert S. Parmet, *Two Hundred Years of Looking Ahead: Commemorating the Bicentennial of the Founding of the Bank of New York* (Rockville, Md., 1984).

14. James Laichas, "Business and Public History: The Insurance Industry," *Public Historian,* 2 (Spring 1980), 59; see also Barbara Benson Kohn, "Corporate History and the Corporate History Department: Manufacturers Hanover Trust Company," *Public Historian,* 3 (Summer 1981), 31–40; and George David Smith and Laurence E. Steadman, "The Present Value of Corporate History," *Harvard Business Review,* 60 (Nov.–Dec. 1981), 165–70.

15. Stephen J. Kobrin, "Political Assessment in International Firms: The Role of Nontraditional Specialists in Business Organizations," *Public Historian,* 3 (Summer 1981), 87–94.

16. Robert Pomeroy, "Introduction," *Public Historian,* 3 (Summer 1981), 6.

17. Ralph Jeffries (pseud.), telephone interview with the author, Nov. 26, 1984.

18. Stanley Engerman, telephone interview with the author, Nov. 23, 1984, and Vincent Carosso, conversation with the author, Nov. 30, 1984.

19. Tom Huertas, telephone interview with the author, Nov. 14, 1984; Carosso conversation; and Engerman interview.

20. George Smith, interview with the author, New York City, Nov. 23, 1984.

21. Susan English (pseud.), inerview with the author, New York City, Nov. 12, 1984.

22. Enid Hart Douglass, "Corporate History—Why?" *Public Historian,* 3 (Summer 1981), 78.

23. Smith and Steadman, "Present Value," 172.

24. Ibid., 167.

25. English, Huertas, Jeffries, Marks, Smith, and Strobridge interviews.

26. English, Jeffries, Jones, Marks, and Smith interviews.

27. See also W. David Lewis and Wesley Phillips Newton, "The Writing of Corporate History," *Public Historian,* 3 (Summer 1981), 172.

28. Albro Martin, "The Office of Corporate Historian: Organization and Function," *Public Historian,* 3 (Summer 1981), 16.

29. Douglass, "Corporate History—Why?" 77–78.

30. English interview; Martin, "Office of Corporate Historian."

31. English interview.

32. Forman, "History Inside Business," 58–59. On credit for authorship, see, for example, Gardner, *Marketplace,* and Parmet, *Two Hundred Years.* Gardner is identified as the author on the last page of the book; Parmet's name is on the binding and first page. In contrast, the articles in the newspaper published by the History Department of Wells Fargo Bank have no by-lines.

33. Phillips, "History's Hired Hands," 11–14.

34. Smith interview.

35. Laichas, "Business and Public History," 58–59.

36. Marks interview.

37. Smith interview.

38. English interview.

39. Strobridge interview.

40. Kohn, "Corporate History," 37.

41. Martin, "Office of Corporate Historian," 13.

42. These sentiments are attributed to Judith Ryder, Deborah Gardner, and Robert Pomeroy in Candace Floyd, "The Historian in the Gray Flannel Suit," *History News,* 39 (May 1984), 9.

43. Darlene Roth, "The Mechanics of a History Business," *Public Historian,* 1 (Spring 1979), 39.

44. Martin, "Office of Corporate Historian," 14.

45. Douglass, "Corporate History—Why?" 77–78.

46. See Immanuel Wallerstein, *The Modern World System* (New York, 1974); David F. Noble, *Forces of Production* (New York, 1984); William A. Williams, *The Contours of American History* (Chicago, 1966); Eugene Genovese and Elizabeth Fox-Genovese, *The Fruits of Merchant Capital* (New York 1983); and David Gordon, *Segmented Work, Divided Workers* (Cambridge, Mass., 1982).

47. Smith interview. Pomeroy makes the same point, though quite differently in "Introduction," 6–7.

48. Roth, "Mechanics of a History Business," 36.

49. Forman, "History Inside Business," 49.

Chapter 12

An earlier version of this essay was delivered at the American Historical Association Pacific Coast Branch meeting in Eugene, Oregon, in August 1981.

1. Darlene Roth, "The Mechanics of a History Business," *Public Historian* 1 (Spring 1979), 30.

2. Darlene Roth, comments made during the first national symposium on public history, as transcribed in the *Public Historian* 2 (Fall 1979), 47.

3. Stephen D. Mikesell, "Historical Analysis and Benefit-Cost Accounting: Planning for the New Melones Dam," *Public Historian* 1 (Winter 1979), 64.

4. Thad Sitton and Claudette Harrell, "The Caldwell County Project Creating a Usable Past," *Public Historian* 1 (Spring 1979), 42.

5. Wayne D. Rasmussen, "Some Notes on Research and Public Historians," *Public Historian* 1 (Spring, 1979), 68.

6. Paul David Friedman, "Fear of Flying: Airport Noise, Airport Neighbors," *Public Historian* 1 (Summer 1979), 66.

7. Maurice Matloff, "Government and Public History: The Army," *Public Historian* 2 (Spring 1980), 49.

8. Lawrence B. de Graaf, "Summary: An Academic Perspective," *Public Historian* 2 (Spring 1980), 66–67.

9. Joan Hoff Wilson, "Is the Historical Profession an 'Endangered Species'?" *Public Historian* 2 (Winter 1980), 18.

10. Larry E. Tise, "State and Local History: A Future from the Past," *Public Historian* 1 (Summer 1979), 19–21.

11. Robert W. Pomeroy, "Historians' Skills and Business Needs," *Public Historian* 1 (Winter 1979), 8.

12. Stephen W. Grable, "Applying Urban History to City Planning: A Case Study in Atlanta," *Public Historian* 1 (Summer 1979), 48.

13. Roy Lopata, "Historians in City Planning: A Personal View," *Public Historian* 1 (Summer 1979), 40–44.

14. Larry Tise, comments made during the first national symposium on public history, as transcribed in *Public Historian* 2 (Fall 1979), 58–64.

15. Edward D. Berkowitz, "The Historian as Policy Analyst: The Challenge of HEW," *Public Historian* 1 (Spring 1979), 17–25.

16. *Public Historian* 2 (Winter 1980), 70–75.

17. *Public Historian* 2 (Spring 1980), 91–96.

18. Roth, "Mechanics of a History Business," 36.

19. Lawrence B. de Graaf, "Summary," 69.

20. Paul Israel, "Recording Bridges, HAER in California," *Public Historian* 1 (Summer 1979), 63.

21. James Laichas, "Business and Public History: The Insurance Industry," *Public Historian* 2 (Spring 1980), 59.

Chapter 13

Acknowledgments: I wish to thank W. T. Durr, former director of the Baltimore Neighborhood Heritage Project, whose generous style of leadership allowed me to explore many of the ideas presented here; Stephen Brier, Warren Goldstein, Betsy Blackmar, Roy Rosenzweig, Robert Entenmann, and Susan Porter Benson of MAR-HO, who made valuable comments on an earlier draft of this article; and especially Mary Ellen Graham, former administrator of the project, and the twelve oral historians associated with it, whose insights into what we were doing and what it all meant continually informed and focused my own thinking. Thanks also to Kathy Raab and Carolyn Ferrigno, who graciously and efficiently typed various versions of this article.

Information about the project can be obtained by writing to Dr. Durr at the Department of Sociology, University of Baltimore, Charles and Mt. Royal, Baltimore, MD 21201. The special issue of *Maryland Historical Magazine* on Baltimore neighborhoods and *Baltimore People: Baltimore Places* are available from the Maryland Historical Society, 201 W. Monument St., Baltimore, MD 21201.

Chapter 14

1. See also the appendix, "How This Book Was Made," in Brass Workers History Project, *Brass Valley: The Story of Working People's Lives and Struggles in an American Industrial Region* (Philadelphia, 1982), compiled and edited by Jeremy Brecher, Jerry Lombardi, and Jan Stackhouse; Jeremy Brecher, "How I Learned to Quit Worrying and Love Community History: A "Pet Outsider's' Report on the Brass Workers History Project," *Radical History Review,* 28–30 (1984), 187–201.

2. Our approach to interviewing is spelled out in Jeremy Brecher, *History from Below: How to Uncover and Tell the Story of Your Community, Association, or Union* (New Haven, 1986), available from Commonwork, Box 2026, New Haven, Conn., 06521–2026.

3. Distributed by Cinema Guild, 1697 Broadway, New York, N.Y., 10019.

Chapter 15

Acknowledgments: Special thanks to John D'Emilio for his help with this essay and to Susan Porter Benson for her suggestions and patience. The addresses of all of the projects mentioned in the text are included in the Resource List that follows the notes.

1. Lesbian Herstory Archives, *Newsletter,* 1 (June 1975).

2. Jonathan Katz, *Gay American History* (New York, 1976). This collection of documents revealed the wealth of gay and lesbian materials in libraries and traditional archives. The footnotes and bibliographic notes were frequently as useful as the re-

printed documents themselves. It was followed in 1983 by another impressive collection, Katz's *Gay/Lesbian Almanac* (New York, 1983).

3. This slide show has been updated and revised as "She Even Chewed Tobacco" by the San Francisco Lesbian and Gay History Project, from which it is now available. An account of its contents is in Allan Berube, "Lesbian Masquerade," *Gay Community News,* Nov. 17, 1979, 8–9.

4. The Buffalo Oral History Project has not yet published its results, but continuing reports on its work are on file with the Lesbian Herstory Archives.

5. See John Boswell, *Christianity, Social Tolerance and Homosexuality: Gay People in Western Europe from the Beginning of the Christian Era to the Fourteenth Century* (Chicago, 1980); John D'Emilio, *Sexual Politics, Sexual Communities: The Making of a Homosexual Minority in the United States, 1940–1970* (Chicago, 1983); Lillian Faderman, *Surpassing the Love of Men: Romantic Friendship and Love Between Women from the Renaissance to the Present* (New York, 1981).

6. James A. Fraser and Harold A. Averill, *Organizing an Archives: The Canadian Gay Archives Experience* (Toronto, 1980). This is available from the Canadian Gay Archives for $10 plus postage.

7. All records of the New York history projects are on file at the Lesbian Herstory Archives in New York.

8. The slide show is available frm the Boston Lesbian and Gay History Project. An account that includes much of the same material is Joseph Interrante, "From the Puritans to the Present: 350 Years of Lesbian and Gay History in Boston," in Richard Burns, Neuma Cradall, and Eric Rofes, eds., *Gay Jubilee: A Guidebook to Gay Boston—Its History and Resources* (Boston, 1980).

9. The *Newsletter* is available from the Committee on Lesbian and Gay History (see note following Resource List).

10. Proceedings of the Amsterdam conference were published by Gay Studies and Women's Studies of the University of Amsterdam, *Among Women, Among Men: Sociological and Historical Recognition of Homosocial Arrangements* (Amsterdam, 1983).

11. See Chris Czernick, "How the Boston History Project Began," *Gay Community News,* June 16, 1984, 14–17.

12. Eric Garber, "Tain't Nobody's Bizness." This slide show, available through the Committee on Lesbian and Gay History, is an account of gay life during the Harlem Renaissance. See also J. R. Roberts, comp., *Black Lesbians: An Annotated Bibliography* (Tallahassee, Fla., 1981), foreword by Barbara Smith.

13. Materials collected by these groups, and reports on their activities, are on file at the Lesbian Herstory Archives.

14. For a discussion of the politics of archiving, see Joan Nestle, "Radical Archiving: A Lesbian Feminist Perspective," *Gay Insurgent,* 4–5 (Spring 1979), 10–12.

15. John D'Emilio and Allan Berube, among others, withdrew their cooperation from this film project when their unpublished research was used without proper permission, credit, and payment.

16. Leila Rupp, review of Katz and D'Emilio, *Signs,* 9 (1984), 712–15.

17. Katz, *Gay/Lesbian Almanac;* Faderman, *Surpassing the Love of Men;* Jeffrey Weeks, *Coming Out: Homosexual Politics in Britain from the Nineteenth Century to the Present* (London, 1977); Jeffrey Weeks, *Sex, Politics and Society: The Regulation of Sexuality Since 1800* (London, 1981). See also Kenneth Plummer, *The Making of the Modern Homosexual* (London, 1981).

18. D'Emilio, *Sexual Politics;* Buffalo Oral History Project file box, Lesbian Herstory Archives; Allan Berube, "Marching to a Different Drummer: Lesbian and Gay GIs in World War II," *Advocate,* Oct. 15, 1981, 20–24. This article gives an account of Berube's slide show of the same name.

19. For an account of the campaign against the Briggs initiative, see Amber Hollibaugh, "Sexuality and the State," *Socialist Review,* 9 (May–June 1979), 55–72.

20. This affidavit recounts the contributions of gay people and their special oppression in American history. D'Emilio makes a sophisticated but extremely clear historical case for an end to the legal persecution of gay people. Affidavit of John Anthony D'Emilio in the United States Court of Appeals for the Fifth Circuit (No. 82-1590).

Resource List

Archives

Archives et Récherches Lesbiennes
65 rue St. Martin
75006 Paris, France

Archive of Homosexuality/CERES
San Francisco State University
San Francisco, CA 94132

Atlanta Lesbian-Feminist Alliance
Southeastern Lesbian Archives
P.O. Box 5502
Atlanta, GA 30307

Australian Gay Archives
P.O. Box 124
Parkville, Australia 3052

Campaign for Homosexual Equality Archives
42A Formosa Street
London W9, England

Canadian Gay Archives
P.O. Box 639, Station A
Toronto, Canada M5W 1G2

Circolo 28 Giugno
C.P. 691
40100 Bologna Centro, Italia

Florida Collection of Lesbian Herstory
P.O. 5605
Jacksonville, FL 32207

Fondazione Sandro Penna
Via Accademia delle Scienze 1
10123 Torino, Italia

Gay Alliance of Genesee Valley Library
713 Monroe Avenue
Rochester, NY 14607

Gay Archives Collective
P.O. Box 3130 M.P.O.
Vancouver, BC, Canada U6B 3X6

Gay Archives of Texas
c/o Interact Houston
P.O. Box 16041
Houston, TX 77022

Gay Community News Library
167 Tremont St., 5th floor
Boston, MA 02111

Gay Monitoring and Archive Project
c/o Julian Meldrum
10 East Avenue
Wallington, Surrey, England SM6 8PL

Gay Savoir
c/o Claude Courouve
BP 13
75961 Paris, CEDEX 20, France

Henry Gerber
Pearl M. Hart Library
Midwest Lesbian and Gay Resource Center
3225 N. Sheffield Avenue
Chicago, IL 60657

Harvey Milk Archives
c/o Castro Street Fair
3930 17th Street
San Francisco, CA 94114

Herizon Herstory Archives
77 State Street
Binghamton, NY 13901

Homosexual Information Center
6715 Hollywood Blvd., Suite 210
Los Angeles, CA 90028

Institute of Social Ethics
P.O. Box 3417, Central Station
Hartford, CT 06103

International Gay and Lesbian Archives
Natalie Barney and Edward Carpenter Library
1654 North Hudson Avenue
Hollywood, CA 90028

International Gay History Archive
P.O. Box 2, Village Station
New York, NY 10014

Irish Gay Rights Movement Library
P.O. Box 739
Dublin 4, Ireland

Kentucky Lesbian Herstory Archives
c/o Sunnybrook Wimmin's Collective
Sunnybrook, KY 42650

Kinsey Institute for Sexual Research
416 Morrison Hall
Bloomington, IN 47401

Lavender Archives
P.O. Box 2337
Philadelphia, PA 19103

Lesbian and Gay Archives of Naiad Press
P.O. Box 10543
Tallahassee, FL 32302

Lesbian and Gay Rights Resource Center
P.O. Box 11-695
Manners Street Post Office
Wellington, New Zealand

Lesbian Community Center Library
3435 N. Sheffield Ave.
Chicago, IL 60657

Lesbian Herstory Archives
P.O. Box 1258
New York, NY 10001

Lesbian Information and Documentation Archives
Centre Claudie Lesselier
48 rue Sedaire
75011 Paris, France

Lesbisch Archief Leeuwarden
Postbus 4062
8901 EB, Leeuwarden, Netherlands

Mariposa Foundation Library
1800 Highland Avenue
Hollywood, CA 90028

Midwest Gay and Lesbian Archives
c/o GAU, P.O. Box 60046
Chicago, IL 60660

Multi-Cultural Lesbian and Gay Studies Program
c/o Anna Peterson, Grahame Perry
300 Eshelman Hall
University of California
Berkeley, CA 94720

National Coalition of Black Gay Archives
P.O. Box 57236
Washington, DC 20037

NGRC Resource Center
P.O. Box 350
Wellington, New Zealand

New Alexandria Lesbian Library
P.O. Box 402
Florence, MA 01060

One Institute Library
3340 Country Club Drive
Los Angeles, CA 90019

Oregon Gay Archives
c/o PTC
320 SW Stark, Apt. 506
Portland, OR 47204

San Francisco Gay Library Project
Capp Street Foundation
294 Page Street
San Francisco, CA 94102

San Francisco Lesbian Archives
P.O. Box 1653
San Francisco, CA 94103

Southern Gay Archives
P.O. Box 2118
Boca Raton, FL 33432

Stonewall Library
Stonewall Committee
P.O. Box 2084
Hollywood, FL 33020

Suppressed Histories Archives
Max Dashu
3901-C Clarke St.
Oakland, CA 94609

Tennessee Lesbian Archives
c/o Catherine R. Moirai
Rt. 2, P.O. Box 252
Luttrell, TN 37779

Van Leeuwen Bibliotheek
Keizersgracht 10
1015 CN Amsterdam, Netherlands

West Coast Lesbian Connections
P.O. Box 23753
Oakland, CA 94623

Wilde-Stein Research Fund
c/o Women's Studies Library
Main Library
Ohio State University
1858 Neil Avenue
Columbus, Ohio 43210

Women's History Research Center
2325 Oak St.
Berkeley, CA 94708

Women's Movement Archives
P.O. Box 928, Station Q
Toronto, Canada M5W 1G2

History Projects

Buckwheat Turner
Celebrating Women
P.O. Box 251
Warrensburg, NY 12885

Boston Lesbian and Gay History Project
c/o 285 Harvard St., Apt. 102
Cambridge, MA 02139

Buffalo Lesbian Oral History Project
255 Parkside Avenue
Buffalo, NY 14214

Chicago Gay & Lesbian History Project
P.O. Box 60046
Chicago, IL 60660

Florida Collection of Lesbian History
P.O. Box 5606
Jacksonville, FL 32207

Gay History Film Project
P.O. Box 77043
San Francisco, CA 94107

Gay History Project
c/o Our History
P.O. Box 7508
Saskatoon, SAS, Canada

Lesbian and Gay History Group of Toronto
P.O. Box 639, Station A
Toronto, Canada M5W 1G2

Garcia Lorca Educational Fund
Lesbian Gay Latino History Project
1654 North Hudson Avenue
Hollywood, CA 90028

Los Angeles Gay and Lesbian Heritage Society
1654 North Hudson Avenue
Hollywood, CA 90028

Lesbian-Feminist Study Clearinghouse
Women's Studies Program
1012 Cathedral of Learning
University of Pittsburgh
Pittsburgh, PA 15260

Lesbian Heritage/DC
c/o Washington Area Women's Center
1519 P Street, NW
Washington, DC 20005

Montana Women's History Project
315 South 4th East
Missoula, MT 59801

New York Lesbian & Gay History Project
c/o Lesbian Herstory Archives
P.O. Box 1258
New York, NY 10116

Our South
Institute for Southern Studies
P.O. Box 1832
Durham, NC 27702

San Francisco Lesbian and Gay History Project
P.O. Box 42332
San Francisco, CA 94101

Women's History Research Center
2325 Oak Street
Berkeley, CA 94708
Note: The above listings appeared in the summer 1984 issue of the *Newsletter* of the Committee on Lesbian and Gay History. They are incomplete and may change. For updated information contact: CLGH, c/o John D'Emilio, Department of History, University of North Carolina at Greensboro, NC 27412. Recent information is also available in newsletters of the Lesbian Herstory Archives, the International Gay and Lesbian Archives, and the Canadian Gay Archives.

Chapter 16

Acknowledgments: I would like to thank Andrea Walsh, Anson Rabinbach, and the editors of this volume, Susan Porter Benson, Stephen Brier, and Roy Rosenzweig, for comments that helped me clarify a number of points in this review.

1. See Connie Field's comments on the need for high technical standards in radical films in "Institutional Obstacles to Creativity in Media," a round table with media workers, *Tabloid,* (Spring–Summer 1980), 48.

2. For an excellent summary of Marxist discussions of ideology, see Stuart Hall, "Culture, the Media, and the 'Ideological Effect,' " in James Curran et al., eds., *Mass Communication and Society* (London, 1977), 315–48.

3. Roland Barthes, "Rhetoric of the Image," in *Image-Music-Text,* trans. Stephen Heath (New York, 1977), 41.

4. Reviews and theoretical discussions of these issues have appeared in *Screen, Jump Cut, Cinéaste,* and other film journals since the late 1960s. For these and other discussions, see Jack Ellis, "Documentary Film Bibliography," *Jump Cut,* 23 (Nov. 1980), 30–31.

5. Hall, "Culture, the Media," 326–27; Peter Gidal, "Theory and Definition of Structural/Materialist Film," in Gidal, ed., *Structural Film Anthology* (London, 1976), 1–21.

6. For overviews see "Feminism and Film: Critical Approaches," editorial in *Camera Obscura,* 1 (Fall 1976), 3–10; Christine Gledhill, "Recent Developments in Feminist Film Criticism," *Quarterly Review of Film Studies,* 3 (1978), 457–93. A key article is Laura Mulvey, "Visual Pleasure and Narrative Cinema," *Screen,* 16 (Autumn 1975), 6–18. Lesley Stern discusses the conflicts between feminist film theory and politics in "Feminism and Cinema—Exchanges." *Screen* 20 (Winter 1979), 89–105.

7. Stern, "Feminism and Cinema," 92.

8. Producers of mass media consciously form series when they use a formula derived from one hit film or television program to clone others; but series can also be used for progressive purposes, with educational effects.

9. Julia Lesage, "The Political Aesthetics of the Feminist Documentary Film," *Quarterly Review of Film Studies,* 3 (1978), 507–23.

10. Quoted in Jayne Loader, "Flint Sit-Down Veterans Speak," *Seven Days,* Oct. 13, 1978, 32.

11. Lesage, "Political Aesthetics," 521.

12. Ibid.

13. Lesage notes that "the emphasis on the experiential . . . can sometimes be a political limitation, especially when the film limits itself to the individual and offers little or no analysis or sense of collective process leading to social change": "Political Aesthetics," 509. On the relationship between historical actors and historical knowledge, see E. P. Thompson, *The Poverty of Theory and Other Essays* (New York, 1978), 19.

14. A rather ludicrous example of such an effort may be seen in Lee Grant's *Wilmar Eight,* when a bespectacled young man with a rather pompous manner (identified as a sociologist) is consulted on the effects of a strike by eight female bank employees. His remarks were barely audible over the audience laughter when I saw the film.

15. Daniel Leab, "Writing History on Film: Two Views of the 1937 Strike Against General Motors by the UAW," *Labor History,* 21 (Winter 1979–80), 110–111. See also Susan Reverby, review of *With Babies and Banners, Radical America,* 13 (Sept.–Oct. 1979), 63–69.

16. Staughton and Alice Lynd, *Rank and File* (Boston, 1973).

17. Chester Gregory, *Women in Defense Work During World War II* (New York, 1974), 4, 144,

18. William Chafe, *The American Woman* (New York, 1972), 181.

19. Reverby, review, 64.

20. Gledhill, "Recent Developments," 458–61.

21. Simone de Beauvoir, *The Second Sex* (New York, 1961), 541–60.

23. Ruth Milkman, "Organizing the Sexual Division of Labor: Historical Perspectives on Women's Work and the American Labor Movement," *Socialist Review*, 49 (Jan.–Feb. 1980), 94–150.

24. The 1983 Hollywood film *Swing Shift*, starring Goldie Hawn, stresses this theme, particularly in the closing scene. See also John D'Emilio, *Sexual Politics, Sexual Communities: The Making of a Homosexual Minority in the United States, 1940–1970* (Chicago, 1983), chap. 2.

25. Quoted in Reverby, review, 66.

26. Leab, "Writing History," 112.

27. Conversation with the author after a showing at Harvard University, Cambridge, Mass., March 6, 1985.

Chapter 17

Acknowledgments: The authors wish to thank Paul Coates, Jacqueline Goggin, E. Curmie Price, and Paul Ruffins for their assistance.

1. For a contemporary discussion of the forces behind the initial "Great Migration" of 1915–18, see Emmett J. Scott, *Negro Migration During the War* (New York, 1920). For an excellent analysis of class formation in the aftermath of that migration, see Kenneth Kusmer, *A Ghetto Takes Shape: Black Cleveland, 1870–1930* (Urbana, Ill., 1976).

2. Dorothy Porter, "Organized Educational Activities of Negro Literary Societies, 1828–1846," *Journal of Negro Education*, 5 (1936), 558.

3. Dorothy Porter, ed., *Early Negro Writing, 1760–1837* (Boston, 1971), 130–31.

4. On cultural arguments concerning colonization, see George Frederickson, *The Black Image in the White Mind* (New York, 1971).

5. Helen Boardman, "The Rise of the Negro Historian," *Negro History Bulletin*, 8 (April 1945), 148–49. Leonard Curry, *The Free Black in Urban America, 1800–1850* (Chicago, 1981), 196 215; James Horton and Lois Horton, *Black Bostonians* (New York, 1979); Dorothy Porter, "Early American Negro Writings: A Bibliographical Study," *Papers* Bibliographical Society of America, 39 (1945), 192–368.

6. On "elevation" and improvement ideology, see Frederick Cooper, "Elevating the Race: The Social Thought of Black Leaders 1827–1850," *American Quarterly*, 24 (1972), 604–25. Emma J. Lapsansky, "'Since They Got Those Separate Churches': Afro-Americans and Racism in Jacksonian Philadelphia," *American Quarterly*, 32

(1980), 54–78, is an excellent discussion of the class consciousness and Yankee gentility of early nineteenth-century Afro-American leaders.

7. William C. Nell, *The Colored Patriots of the American Revolution, with Sketches of Several Distinguished Colored Persons: To Which Is Added a Brief Survey of the Conditions and Prospects of Colored Americans* (Boston, 1855).

8. Jeanne Zeidler, director, University Museum, Hampton University, Hampton, Va., telephone interview with Fath Davis Ruffins, December 14, 1984.

9. Jacqueline A. Goggin, "Carter G. Woodson and the Movement to Promote Black History" (Ph.D. diss., University of Rochester, 1983), 40–43; Fath Davis Ruffins, "The Historic House Museum as History Text: The Frederick Douglass Home at Cedar Hill," paper delivered to Museum Education Program, George Washington University, Washington, D.C., Oct. 9, 1984. We have benefited from conversations with Derrick Cooke, site manager, Tyra Walker, curator, and Marilyn Nickels, historian for Capitol Parks East—all members of the National Park Service—on the history of the Frederick Douglass Home at Cedar Hill.

10. Thomas Battle, curator, Manuscript Division, Moorland-Spingarn Research Center, Washington, D.C., interview with Fath Davis Ruffins, Dec. 19, 1984. Thomas Battle, "Research Centers Document the Black Experience, *History News* 36, (Feb. 1981), 8–11; Michael R. Winston, "Moorland-Spingarn Research Center: A Past Revisited, A Present Reclaimed," *New Directions* (Howard University), Summer 1974, reprint.

11. For a discussion of Afro-American historical societies, see Charles Wesley, "Racial Historical Societies and the American Heritage," *Journal of Negro History,* 37 (1952), 11–15. Also see Goggin, "Carter G. Woodson," 22–39, 46–49.

12. Zeidler interview with Ruffins.

13. On William Sheppard, see Harold G. Cureau, "William H. Sheppard, Missionary to the Congo and Collector of African Art," *Journal of Negro History,* 67 (1982), 340; Keith L. Schall, ed., *Stony the Road: Chapters in the History of Hampton Institute* (Charlottesville, 1977); William H. Sheppard, *Presbyterian Pioneers in Congo* (Richmond, Va, 1917).

14. Goggin, "Carter G. Woodson," 22.

15. W. E. B. Du Bois, *The Souls of Black Folk* (1903; reprint ed., Greenwich, Conn., 1961).

16. C. Vann Woodward, *The Strange Career of Jim Crow* (1957; reprint ed., New York, 1974), and Rayford W. Logan, *The Negro in American Life and Thought: The Nadir, 1877–1901* (New York, 1954), provide information on the rise of Jim Crow segregation, disenfranchisement, lynching, and cultural racism in the late nineteenth and early twentieth centuries. For a discussion of "Teutonic" academic history, see Dorothy Ross, "Historical Consciousness in Nineteenth-Century America," *American Historical Review,* 89 (1984), 909–28. Some of the popular fictions that passed as history in the early twentieth century are Thomas Dixon, *The Leopard's Spots: A Romance of the White Man's Burden, 1865–1900* (New York, 1902), and *The Clansman: An Historical Romance of the Ku Klux Klan* (New York, 1906), and Claude Bowers, *The Tragic Era: The Revolution After Lincoln* (Cambridge, Mass., 1920).

See Kelly Miller, *As to the Leopard's Spots: An Open Letter to Thomas Dixon* (Washington, D.C., 1905).

17. Barbara Joyce Ross, *J. E. Spingarn and the Rise of the NAACP, 1911–1939* (New York, 1972), 16–22; Langston Hughes, *Fight for Freedom: The Story of the NAACP* (New York, 1962), 20–21; Charles Flint Kellogg, *NAACP: A History of the National Association for the Advancement of Colored People* (Baltimore, 1967); Mary White Ovington, *The Walls Come Tumbling Down* (New York, 1947); Jesse Thomas Moore, Jr., *A Search for Equality: The National Urban League, 1910–1961* (University Park, Pa., 1981); Goggin, "Carter G. Woodson," 10.

18. Goggin, "Carter G. Woodson," 61–71, 93–104.

19. For a discussion of the roots of cultural nationalism in the Afro-American masses, see Sylvia M. Jacobs, *The African Nexus: Black American Perspectives on the European Partitioning of Africa, 1880–1920* (Westport, Conn., 1981), 5–13, 237–60, 269–74. For information on Marcus Gravey, see Edmund Cronon, *Black Moses: The Story of Marcus Garvey* (Madison, 1969); Tony Martin, *Race First: The Ideological and Organizational Struggles of Marcus Gravey and the Universal Negro Improvement Association* (Westport, Conn., 1976); Edwin S. Redkey, *Black Exodus: Black Nationalist and Back-to-Africa Movements* (New Haven, 1969); Wilson J. Moses, *The Golden Age of Black Nationalism, 1850–1925* (Hamden, Conn., 1978); Robert A. Hill, ed., *The Marcus Garvey and Universal Negro Improvement Association Papers,* 2 vols. (Berkeley, 1983).

20. The popular historians associated with Garvey included Joel A. Rogers, Hubert Harrison, and John Bruce. For information on Harrison and Bruce, see Hill, *Marcus Garvey Papers,* vol. 1, pp. 200 and 212–11, respectively. For information on the fate of southern migrants, see Gilbert Osofsky, *Harlem: The Making of a Ghetto: Negro New York, 1890–1930* (New York, 1966), and Claude McKay, *Harlem: Negro Metropolis* (1940; reprint ed., New York, 1968). For a discussion of early twentieth-century race riots, see William M. Tuttle, *Race Riot: Chicago in the Red Summer of 1919* (Urbana, Ill., 1970). Some popular black histories of the period were James Webb, *The Black Man as the Father of Civilization Proven by Biblical History* (Chicago, n.d. [1914?]), George Wells Parker, *The Children of the Sun* (Omaha, 1918; orig. pub. as *African Origins of Grecian Civilization,* 1917), and Joel A. Rogers, *From Superman to Man* (Chicago, 1917). We are indebted to Paul Coates, archivist in the Manuscript Division of the Moorland-Spingarn Research Center, for information on black self-trained historians.

21. Drusilla D. Houston, *Wonderful Ethiopians of the Ancient Cushite Empire* (1926; reprint ed., Baltimore, 1985).

22. For information on Zora Neale Hurston and the influence of Franz Boas on black writers and intellectuals, see Robert Hemenway, *Zora Neale Hurston, A Literary Biography* (Urbana, Ill., 1977).

23. Elinor Sinnette, "Arthur Alfonso Schomburg: Black Bibliophile and Curator: His Contribution to the Collection and Dissemination of Materials about Africans and Peoples of African Descent" (Ph.D. diss., Columbia University, 1977), 48–51, 137–38, 143–44. We have benefited from numerous conversations on Schomburg with Dr.

Sinnette. Howard Dodson, chief of the Schomburg Center for Research in Black Culture, the New York Public Library, Astor, Lenox, and Tilden Foundation, telephone interview with Fath Davis Ruffins, Dec. 21, 1984.

24. Osofsky, *Harlem,* 181; Sinnette, "Arthur Alfonso Schomburg," 138–39; *My Childhood: James Baldwin's Harlem,* Part II, Benchmark Film, 1964.

25. Goggin, "Carter G. Woodson," 190–202. We have benefited from conversations with Michael R. Winston on Carter G. Woodson.

26. Goggin, "Carter G. Woodson," 200.

27. For the reception of Negro History Week by the black press, see, for example, "Negro History Week," *New York Amsterdam News,* Feb. 9, 1927, and *New York Amsterdam News,* Feb. 15, 1928. Also see "Read Negro History," *Pittsburgh Courier,* Feb. 15, 1930.

28. Annual Report, *Journal of Negro History,* 12 (1927), 572–73.

29. Lorenzo Greene, "Preparation of My First Observance of Negro History Week with Carter G. Woodson 1930," selection from the diary of Lorenzo Greene, read at the annual meeting of the Association for the Study of Afro-American Life and History, Oct. 19, 1984; "Negro History Week Celebration," *Journal of Negro History,* 15 (1930), 128–31.

30. "Negro History Week Celebration," 129.

31. Ibid., 131.

32. For a discussion of Reconstruction historiography, see Eric Foner, "Reconstruction Revisited," *Reviews in American History,* 10 (Dec. 1982), 82–100.

33. Greene diary.

34. Goggin, "Carter G. Woodson," 273–74, 282–86.

35. Ibid., 249.

36. James O. Young, *Black Writers of the Thirties* (Baton Rouge, 1973), 3–63.

37. Morris Janowitz, "Patterns of Collective Racial Violence," in Alexander Callow, ed., *American Urban History* (New York, 1973), 563–85. Janowitz describes the Chicago race riot of 1919 and similar early twentieth-century disturbances as "communal riots," and the riots of the 1960s as "commodity riots," seeing these as involving not violence between persons or communities, but a struggle for goods by ghetto populations. He cites the Harlem riot of 1943 as having "features of the new type of rioting" (567), but so did the Harlem riot of 1935. See Claude McKay, "Harlem Runs Wild," *Nation,* 140 (April 3, 1935), 382–83. On scholarly black publications see Locke to Cartwright, January 11, 1935, Box 171, Folder C-D, Alain Locke Papers, Manuscript Division, Moorland-Spingarn Research Center, Howard University; Locke to Brawley, November 11, 1932, Box 8, Benjamin Brawley Papers, Manuscript Division, Moorland-Spingarn Research Center, Howard University.

38. For information on blacks in the WPA Writers Project, see Monty Noam Penkower, *The Federal Writers' Project: A Study in Government Patronage of the Arts* (Urbana, Ill., 1977), 66–67. For information on Hurston's participation in the project, see Hemenway, *Zora Neale Hurston,* 104–58.

39. Lawrence D. Reddick, "A New Interpretation for Negro History," *Journal of Negro History,* 22 (1937), 17–28.

40. Ibid., 23–24.

41. The phrase "Polyanna optimism" is taken from Locke's "Jingo, Counter-Jingo and Us," *Opportunity,* 16 (1938), 11, reprinted in *The Critical Temper of Alain Locke: A Selection of His Essays on Art and Culture,* ed. Jeffrey C. Stewart (New York, 1983), 262. Locke's review was an answer to a review of popular Negro histories by Benjamin Stolberg, "Minority Jingo," *Nation,* 145 (Oct. 23, 1937), 437–39.

42. Stolberg, "Minority Jingo." For a more recent discussion of this issue, see Mark Naison, "Ethnic Chauvinism vs. Ethnic Progressivism: Is Ethnicity Reactionary?" *Jewish Currents,* Oct. 1981, 4–9, 26–31.

43. Lorraine Brown, historian, Federal Theatre Project Archives, George Mason University, telephone interview with Jeffrey C. Stewart, April 10, 1985. E. Quita Craig's study, *Black Drama of the Federal Theatre Era* (Amherst, 1980), provides the most balanced analysis of the *Liberty Deferred* controversy. Although formal congressional investigation of the Federal Theatre Project took place in 1939, the project's director, Hallie Flanagan, recalled that as early as February of 1938, the project was criticized by a southern senator for producing *"Turpentine,"* a black play critical of the South. Craig, *Black Drama,* p. 112. Also see Doris E. Abramson's *Negro Playwrights in the American Theatre, 1925–1959* (New York, 1969). Abramson accepts the explanation of Emmet Lavery, director of the National Service Bureau, that poor craftsmanship was the reason the project did not produce *Liberty Deferred.* For a general account of blacks in the Theatre Project, see Ronald Ross, "The Role of Blacks in the Federal Theatre, 1935–1939," *Journal of Negro History,* 59 (1974), 38–50.

44. Mark Naison, "Communism and Harlem Intellectuals in the Popular Front: Anti-Fascism and the Politics of Black Culture," *Journal of Ethnic Studies,* 9 (Spring 1981), 1–25.

45. Mark Naison, *Communists in Harlem During the Depression* (New York, 1984), 198, 201–2.

46. Ibid., 299; Naison quotes from a letter by Angelo Herndon to John P. Davis, Nov. 30, 1939, in the National Negro Congress Papers at the Schomburg Collection in the Harlem Branch of the New York Public Library. See also John A. Davis, "We Win the Right to Fight for Jobs," *Opportunity,* 16 (1938), 232.

47. Examples of Woodson's uplift philosophy include "Some Suggestions with Respect to Business and the Depression," *Negro History Bulletin,* 3 (Jan. 1940), 37–38; "How to Get Out of the Bread Line," ibid., 58. We are indebted to Dr. Goggin for these references: see "Carter G. Woodson," 223.

48. Rogers wrote to Arthur Spingarn in 1934: "[T]here is a market and a good one for a certain type of literature among Negroes and those whites who are interested in the race question. . . . The fact is that I receive almost daily inquiries as to when the big work will appear. Were I interested in the publishing angle of it, I would have had it out long ago myself, and made money on it. Of that little book you have 500 copies were sold in 10 days to colored people over the counter of the Amsterdam News after notice had appeared of it,": Rogers to Spingarn, February 18, 1934, Box 94, Folder Rod-Rog, Arthur Spingarn Collection, Moorland-Spingarn Research Center, Howard University. In fact, Rogers had already begun publishing his own books in the 1930s,

obtaining enough revenue to continue publishing until his death in 1966. These works are still in print and in demand, and small independent reprint publishers, such as Black Classic Press, P.O. Box 13414, Baltimore, MD, still receive numerous inquiries for Rogers' work today—many, according to Paul Coates, owner of Black Classic Press, from inmates of America's prison system. For contemporary reviews of Rogers' writings, see John W. Ivy, *Crisis,* 47 (Nov. 1940), 362, and Ivy, *Crisis,* 50 (April 1943), 121, 123, 124.

49. Thomas Cripps and David Culbert, "The Negro Soldier (1944): Film Propaganda in Black and White," *American Quarterly,* 31 (1979), 616–40.

50. Ibid., 623, 627–28. Also see Daniel J. Leab, *From Sambo to Superspade: The Black Experience in Motion Pictures* (Boston, 1975), 127–28.

51. Cripps and Culbert, 630–36. See *Pittsburgh Courier,* Feb. 26, 1944: "The Negro Soldier" (editorial) and Ted Le Berthon, "White Man's Views: 'Negro Soldier' Film is Actual Portrayal of Race's Role in Wars."

52. Cripps and Culbert, *"The Negro Soldier,"* 640.

53. Gunnar Myrdal, *An American Dilemma,* vol. 2 (New York, 1944), 751. See " 'Rogers Says: Some Consider Study of Negro History As Purely 'Impertinence,' " *Pittsburgh Courier,* Feb. 12, 1944, 7, for Rogers' defense of himself and Negro history in the light of Mydral's criticisms. The black scholars who worked on the Myrdal project included Ralph J. Bunche, Doxey A. Wilkerson, Sterling Brown, J. G. St. Clair Drake, E. Franklin Frazier, Charles S. Johnson, and Ira De A. Reid.

54. On African survivals, see E. Franklin Frazier, *The Negro Family in the United States* (Chicago, 1939). Other books in the tradition of integrationist sociology include Abram Kardiner and Lionel Ovesey, *The Mark of Oppression* (New York, 1951); Lee Rainwater, *And the Poor Get Children* (Chicago, 1960); Thomas F. Pettigrew, *A Profile of the Negro American* (Princeton, 1964); and Kenneth A. Clark, *Dark Ghetto,* foreword by Gunnar Myrdal (New York, 1965). Nathan Glazer and Daniel P. Moynihan's *Beyond the Melting Pot* (1963; 2d ed., Cambridge, Mass., 1970) was the culmination of this "culture of poverty" analysis: the theory that the cultural dislocation of slavery, coupled with contemporary exclusion from Euro-American middle-class values, had created a pathologically deprived lower-class black family and community life that could only be remedied by integration. Earlier expressions of this integrationist sociology were the scholarly basis for the 1954 Supreme Court decision in *Brown* v. *Board of Education of Topeka, Kansas,* which struck down educational segregation; see Richard Kluger, *Simple Justice* (New York, 1975). Our notion of "integrationist sociology" is derived from Houston A. Baker's conception of "integrationist poetics," which he develops in *Blues, Ideology, and Afro-American Literature: A Vernacular Theory* (Chicago, 1984).

55. Quote taken from Locke's review, "Moral Pivot," *Saturday Review of Literature,* Nov. 8, 1947, 16. See Locke's "Inventory at Mid-Century: A Review of the Literature of the Negro for 1950," *Phylon* 12 (2d Quarter 1951), 185–86, reprinted in *Critical Temper,* 369, for a contemporary analysis of the significance of Woodson's death.

56. See John Hope Franklin, "Rebels, Runaways, and Heroes: The Bitter Years of Slavery," in *Life* 65 (November 22, 1968), 92–93, 108–20. Also see "Says Negro

Needs Not More History But Better History," *Philadelphia Tribune,* February 17, 1948, for Franklin's subtle redirection of the battle against white racist historical scholarship to the question of the quality of the work done by white scholars. Franklin left Howard University in 1956 to teach at Brooklyn College until 1964, when he joined the history faculty of the University of Chicago. Abram Harris, a black economist, and Allison Davis, a black anthropologist, also went to the University of Chicago, in 1946 and 1941 respectively. Telephone conversation with Nancy Corrothers of the University of Chicago Provost's Office, June 10, 1985. They were members of the first cohort of black scholars to teach at white colleges. In 1970 John Blassingame went to Yale University, and in 1962 Nathan Huggins went to California State University, Long Beach. On the split in the ASNLH after Woodson's death, we have benefited from conversations with Michael R. Winston and Robert Hall.

57. On the subject of Negro History Kits, we have benefited from conversations with Jacqueline Goggin. By "educational bourgeoisie," we mean the librarians and elementary and high school teachers in the ASNLH.

58. On SNCC and the "facilitator" role, see Clayborne Carson, Jr., *In Struggle: SNCC and the Black Awakening of the Sixties* (Cambridge, 1981). We are indebted to Howard Dodson for his insights into the 1960s civil rights movement and its significance for Afro-American history.

59. Byron Rushing, director, Museum of Afro-American History, Boston, and president, African-American Museums Association, interview with Fath Davis Ruffins, April 12, 1985; Leclair Lambert, director, African-American Museum of Art and History, Minneapolis, telephone interview with Fath Davis Ruffins, Dec. 18, 1984; Charles Wright, M.D., founder and chairman of the board, Museum of African-American History, Detroit, telephone interview with Fath Davis Ruffins, Dec. 15, 1984. (In 1969 the name of the Ebony Museum of Negro History was changed to the Jean Baptiste Pointe Du Sable Museum of African-American History to honor the black founder of the city of Chicago.)

60. Elma Lewis, founder and director of the Elma Lewis School for the Arts, Boston, telephone interview with Fath Davis Ruffins, Oct. 21, 1985; Monica Scott, executive director, San Francisco African-American Historical and Cultural Society, San Francisco, telephone interview with Fath Davis Ruffins, Dec. 16, 1984; Margaret Burroughs, founder and director emeritus, Jean Baptiste Point Du Sable Museum, Chicago, telephone interview with Jeffrey C. Stewart, Nov. 20, 1984. Also see Eugene Pieter Feldman, *The Birth and Building of the Du Sable Museum* (Chicago, 1981). In part as a result of her work for the National Conference of Negro Artists (later the National Conference of Artists) after 1959, Elma Lewis came to the conclusion that a national center was needed for the support of professional Afro-American artists. After several years of planning, she opened the National Center of Afro-American Artists in 1968, with Edmund Barry Gaither as the first director. She saw these efforts as part of a continuum with her work in the school to stimulate young and emerging black artists.

61. On colonialist interpretations of Afro-American history, see Stokely Carmichael and Charles Hamilton, *Black Power: The Politics of Liberation in America* (New York, 1967); Frantz Fanon, *The Wretched of the Earth,* trans. Constance Far-

rington (New York, 1965); and Kwame Nkrumah, *Neo-Colonialism: The Last Stage of Imperialism* (New York, 1966). On new interpretations from the cultural nationalist perspective, see Addison Gayle, Jr., *The Black Aesthetic* (New York, 1971); Le Roi Jones, *Blues People*: Negro Music in White America (New York, 1963); and Baker, *Blues, Ideology*. For Malcom X's interpretation of Afro-American history, see Malcolm Little, *Malcolm X on Afro-American History,* introduction by George Breitman (1967; reprint ed., New York, 1969), especially "Negro History Week," 14–18, and "Ancient Black Civilizations," 18–22.

62. John Harmon, executive board member emeritus, African-American Museum Association Conference, New Orleans, interview with Fath Davis Ruffins, Oct. 1, 1984.

63. Edmund Barry Gaither, director, the Museum of the National Center of Afro-American Artists, Boston, telephone interview with Fath Davis Ruffins, Dec. 18, 1984.

64. Wright interview.

65. Audley Smith, executive director, Museum of African-American History, Detroit, telephone interview with Fath Davis Ruffins, Dec. 18, 1984.

66. On the history of the Anacostia Museum: John Kinard, director, Anacostia Neighborhood Museum, Smithsonian Institution. Washington, D.C., interview with Fath Davis Ruffins, April 11, 1985; Louise Hutchinson, historian, Anacostia Neighborhood Museum, telephone interview with Fath Davis Ruffins, Dec. 18, 1984. On "The Rat: Man's Invited Affliction," Zora Felton, education officer, Anacostia Neighborhood Museum, interview with Jeffrey C. Stewart and Fath Davis Ruffins, November 13, 1984. We have also benefited from discussions with Rebecca Welch, historian, Anacostia Neighborhood Museum.

67. Burroughs interview; Lewis interview.

68. Ibid.

69. On the history of funding for black museums, Joy Ford Austin, director, African American Museums Association, telephone interview with Fath Davis Ruffins, Dec. 22, 1984. On the history of the Studio Museum of Harlem, Mary Schmidt Campbell, executive director, Studio Museum of Harlem, New York, telephone interview with Fath Davis Ruffins, Dec. 18, 1984.

70. Delores Sura, director, Institutional Sales, CBS, Telephone interview with Jeffrey C. Stewart, Nov. 14, 1984. A sampling of programs created by CBS includes: "Black Heritage: A History of Afro-Americans," narrated by John Henrik Clark; "Black History: Lost, Stolen and Strayed," narrated by Bill Cosby; "Great Americans: Harriet Tubman and the Underground Railroad"; "Tell It Like It Was," a series that included African music, art, and religion, as well as historical information on the Harlem Renaissance, Langston Hughes, and Malcolm X; "The Autoibiography of Miss Jane Pittman"; "With All Deliberate Speed: The 1954 Supreme Court Decision" with Ed Bradley. These programs remain very popular, according to Sura, as evidenced by the lucrative royalty reports. Most requests are from schools and libraries. On local school programs, Ellis Jurica, director, Bureau of Social Studies, Chicago Unified School District, telephone interview with Jeffrey C. Stewart, Nov. 28, 1984;

Maurice Sykes, director, Public Relations Department, District of Columbia School System, telephone interview with Jeffrey C. Stewart, Nov. 28, 1984; Fran Walker, director, Student Life Office, University of Pennsylvania, telephone interview with Jeffrey C. Stewart, Nov. 16, 1984. For federal recognition of black history, see "Negro History Commission," *Congressional Quarterly Almanac,* 24 (1968), 529–30. At the National Museum of History and Technology (now the National Museum of American History), such exhibitions as "We the People" (1975) and "A Nation of Nations" (1976) contained material on the Afro-American experience. The National Portrait Gallery mounted an exhibition entitled "The Black Presence in the Era of the American Revolution 1770–1800" (1973), with an extremely valuable documentary catalogue by Sidney Kaplan. The Field Museum in Chicago hosted an exhibit on black folk art in America, 1930–1980, during the summer of 1984 and, the same year, one entitled "Afro-American Insights," an exhibition of artifacts from Africa that relate to Afro-American history today: Lana Neander, Public Relations Department, Field Museum, telephone interview with Jeffrey C. Stewart, June 17, 1985. The Brooklyn Museum hosted in 1977 "Two Centuries of Black American Art," an exhibition that originated at the Los Angeles County Museum of Art and was organized by David Driskell, who also produced the catalogue for this traveling exhibition. The Brooklyn Museum has excelled at documenting the African presence: in 1978 "Nubian Africa in Antiquity: The Arts of Ancient Nubia and the Sudan" sought to show the historical and cultural connections between ancient Egypt and the rest of Africa, and in 1981 it presented an exhibition of African cultural and household objects: Missy Sullivan, Education Specialist Department, Public Programs and Media, telephone interview with Jeffrey C. Stewart, June 17, 1985.

71. For King's use of history, see King, "I Have a Dream," in Jamye C. Williams and McDonald Williams, eds., *The Negro Speaks* (New York, 1970), 213–18. Also see his *Why We Can't Wait* (New York, 1964), especially chap. 2, "The Sword That Heals," 15–31.

72. Rowena Stewart, founder and director, Rhode Island Black Heritage Society, Providence, telephone interview with Fath Davis Ruffins, Dec. 18, 1984; Cecilia Byers, director, Mann-Simms Cottage, Charleston, S.C., telephone interview with Fath Davis Ruffins, Nov. 20, 1984; Clifton Johnson, executive director, Amistad Research Center, New Orleans, telephone interview with Fath Davis Ruffins, Dec. 15, 1984.

Chapter 18

1. Editorial, *History Workshop Journal,* 1 (Spring 1976), 1.

2. Raphael Samuel, "People's History," in Raphael Samuel, ed., *People's History and Socialist Theory* (London and Boston, 1981), xiv–xxiii, and my essay review "People's History and Socialist Theory," *Radical History Review,* 28–30 (Sept. 1984), 169–86.

3. The histories of the farmers' movement by activist historians are W. L. Garvin and S. O. Daws, *History of the National Farmers' Alliance and Co-Operative Union* (Jacksboro, Tex., 1887), and W. Scott Morgan, *History of the Wheel and Alliance, and the Impending Revolution* (Hardy, Ark., 1891). Morgan, a founder of the Agricultural Wheel and an influential newspaper publisher, was a socialist voice within the farmers' movement and a liberal on racial issues. See Lawrence Goodwyn, *Democratic Promise: The Populist Movement in America* (New York, 1976), 36–37, 148, 231, 534–60, and 621, n. 17, on Garvin as a "movement historian."

4. George E. McNeill, ed., *The Labor Movement: The Problem of Today* (Boston, 1886). After the first edition, printed at a Knights of Labor Co-op, the book was published in a second edition by ten publishers in different cities. In addition to Henry George, the "associate authors" who wrote the chapters on the histories of various trade unions included P. M. Arthur, Richard Trevellick, Terence Powderly, and P. J. McGuire.

5. See new edition of Oscar Ameringer, *The Life and Deeds of Uncle Sam: A Little History for Big Children,* with an introduction by Paul Buhle (Chicago, 1984). Also see my introduction to the 1940 autobiography of Oscar Ameringer, *If You Don't Weaken* (Norman, Okla., 1983).

6. On Communist historians in the 1930s, see Paul Buhle, "American Marxist Historiography, 1900–1940," *Radical America,* 4 (Nov. 1970), 16–23. And on the relationship between leftist politics and the labor history produced by historians for the union movement, see James Green, "L'histoire du mouvement ouvrier et la gauche americaine," *Mouvement Social,* 102 (Jan.–March 1978), 9–41.

7. See Jerre Mangione, *The Dream and the Deal: The Federal Writers' Project, 1935–1943* (New York, 1972), and Monty Noam Penkower, *The Federal Writers' Project: A Study in Government Patronage of the Arts* (Urbana, Ill., 1977).

8. For an appreciation of these progressive writers by New Left historians, see Paul Richards, "W. E. B. DuBois and American Social History," and James O'Brien, "The Legacy of Beardian History," *Radical America,* 4 (Nov. 1970), 37–66 and 67–80, and Mari Jo Buhle, Ann Gordon, and Nancy Schrom, "Women in American Society," *Radical America,* 5 (July–Aug. 1971), 3–6.

9. The radical historian Vincent Harding wrote the clearest statement of the importance of history to the black liberation movement: "The Afro-American Past and the American Present," *Motive,* April 1968, reprinted in Mitchell Goodman, ed., *The Movement Toward a New America* (Philadelphia, 1970), 127–29. The clarity remains in Harding's powerful book, *There Is a River: The Black Struggle for Freedom in America* (New York, 1983), which is the best example of movement-inspired history now available.

10. On the development of New Left history in the student movement, see Paul Buhle, Introduction to "Fifteen Years of *Radical America:* An Anthology," *Radical America,* 16 (May–June 1982), 2–8.

11. On history and the feminist movement, see Edith Hoshino Altbach, ed., *From Feminism to Liberation* (Cambridge, Mass., 1971), which grew out of a 1970 issue of

Radical America edited by Altbach. In particular see her bibliographical essay on the bearing of past women's movement history on the present (253–75).

12. James Green, "Radical Historians, 1968–1978," *Radical Teacher*, 11 (March 1979), 26–27.

13. Staughton Lynd, "Guerilla History in Gary," *Liberation*, 16 (Oct. 1969), 12–15.

14. Staughton Lynd, "Personal Histories of the Early CIO," *Radical America*, 5 (May–June 1971), 49–50, and "Two Steel Contracts," *Radical America*, 5 (Sept.– Oct. 1971), 41–64.

15. James Green, "Radical Historians," p. 27.

16. See James Weinstein, "Can a Historian Be a Socialist and a Revolutionary?" *Socialist Revolution*, 1 (May–June 1970), 97–106.

17. James Green, "Intellectuals and Activism: The Dilemma of the Radical Historians," *Activist*, 1 (Fall 1970), 3–5, 28.

18. Lawrence C. Goodwyn, "Populist Dreams and Negro Rights: East Texas as a Case Study," *American Historical Review*, 86 (1971), 1435–56, and conversations with the author.

19. Dale Rosen and Theodore Rosengarten, "Shootout at Reeltown," *Radical America*, 6 (Nov.–Dec. 1972), 65–84, and conversations with Rosen and Rosengarten.

20. Suzanne Crowell, *Appalachian People's History Book* (Louisville, Ky., 1971).

21. Staughton Lynd, "The Possibility of Radicalism in the Early 1930s: The Case of Steel," *Radical America*, 6 (Nov.–Dec. 1972), 37–64.

22. Rosen and Rosengarten, "Shootout at Reeltown," and Lynd, "Possibility of Radicalism."

23. "No More Moanin': Voices of Southern Struggle," *Southern Exposure*, nos. 3–4 (1974), and Sue Thrasher "Oral History," in "Liberating Our Past," a special issue of *Southern Exposure*, no. 12 (1984), 80–81.

24. James Green, Introduction, in *Workers' Struggles, Past and Present: A "Radical America" Reader* (Philadelphia, 1983).

25. David A. Gerber, "Local and Community History: Some Cautionary Remarks on an Idea Whose Time Has Returned," *History Teacher*, 45 (Winter 1980), 15–16.

26. "Labor and Community Militance in Rhode Island," *Radical History Review*, 17 (Spring 1978); "Vermont's Untold Story" (Burlington, Vt., 1976); and James R. Green and Hugh Carter Donahue, *Boston's Workers: A Labor History* (Boston, 1979).

27. Raphael Samuel, "History Workshop Methods," *History Workshop Journal*, 9 (Spring 1980), 162–63.

28. Ibid., 163–65.

29. Ibid., 165.

30. Ibid., 168.

31. Frank Marquart, *An Auto Worker's Journal: The UAW from Crusade to One Party Union* (University Park, Pa., 1975), and William Serrin, *The Company and the Union* (New York, 1973), 189–90.

32. Ken Worpole, "A Ghostly Pavement: The Political Implications of Local Working Class History," in Samuel, *People's History and Socialist Theory*, 23, 28.

33. Samuel, "History Workshop Methods," 166, and Anna Davin, "Feminism and Labour History," in Samuel, *People's History and Socialist Theory*, 176–181. The multicultural approach of U.S. historians is well represented in Howard Zinn, *A People's History of the United States* (New York, 1980).

34. For a more detailed description, see Marty Blatt, Jim Green, and Susan Reverby, "A Reunion of Shoeworkers: The First Massachusetts History Workshop," *Radical America*, 14 (Jan.–Feb. 1980), 67–73.

35. Bob West, "Report Back on the Bradford History Workshop," *History Workshop Journal*, 10 (Autumn 1980), 187.

36. Martha Coons, ed., *Life and Times in Immigrant City: Memories of a Textile Town* (Cambridge, Mass., 1980), and Kathie Neff, "Former Mill Workers Tell of Past in Living History Workshop," *Lawrence Eagle-Tribune*, Oct. 12, 1980.

37. Letter from Tom Leary to Massachusetts History Workshop, Oct. 25, 1980.

38. Jean Tepperman, *Not Servants, Not Machines: Office Workers Speak Out* (Boston, 1976), and Margery Davies, "A Woman's Place is at the Typewriter: The Feminization of Clerical Work," *Radical America*, 8 (July–Aug. 1974), 1–28, later published as a pamphlet by the New England Free Press.

39. See Sharon Hartman Strom, "'We're No Kitty Foyles': Organizing Clerical Workers in the 1930's," in Ruth Milkman, ed., *Women, Work and Protest* (Boston, 1985), chap. 9.

40. Harry Braverman, *Labor and Monopoly Capital: The Degradation of Work in the Twentieth Century* (New York, 1974), and Margery W. Davies, *A Women's Place Is at the Typewriter: Office Work and Office Workers, 1870–1930* (Philadelphia, 1982).

41. Susan Porter Benson, "The Clerking Sisterhood: Rationalization and the Work Culture of Saleswomen in American Department Stores," in Green, *Workers' Struggles*, 101–16. On the creative tension between subjective experience and historical analysis, see Raphael Samuel, "History and Theory," in *People's History and Socialist Theory*, xix–li.

42. Available for $4.00 postpaid from the Women's Center, 46 Pleasant St., Cambridge, MA 02139.

43. See Warren I. Sussman, "History and the American Intellectual: The Uses of a Usable Past," in *Culture as History* (New York, 1985), 7–26.

44. On the decline of organized labor and the need for revived labor education in the schools, see the AFL-CIO's *The Changing Situation of Workers and Their Unions* (Washington, D.C., 1985). For a call to revive labor history in workers' education programs by adopting a History Workshop approach, see Ronald J. Filipelli, "The Uses of History in the Education of Workers," *Labor Studies Journal*, 5 (Spring 1980), 3–10.

45. See my report, "Worker Education and Labor History," *History Workshop Journal*, 14 (Autumn 1982), 168–70.

46. For a discussion of this synthesis of populist practice and critical historical analysis, see my review of the British debate in "People's History and Socialist Theory," 180–86.

47. Lawrence Goodwyn offers some spirited suggestions on how to build on those democratic experiences that really exist in "Organizing Democracy," *Democracy,* 9 (Jan. 1981), 41–60.

48. In a recent visit to the United States, the head of the black textile workers' union in South Africa said that educating new members in the history of the workers' movement was a top priority. For an example of how a leading radical intellectual read Polish history for the Solidarity movement, see Jacek Kuron, "Reflections on a Program for Action," *Polish Review,* 22 (1977), 6–63.

★ List of Contributors ★

SUSAN PORTER BENSON teaches at Bristol Community College and is a consulting editor of the *Radical History Review*. She has been a coordinator of the Amalgamated Clothing and Textile Workers Union's Threads Humanities Program, vice-chairperson of the Rhode Island Committee for the Humanities, and a frequent participant in humanities programs about women and work. Benson is also the author of *Counter Cultures: Saleswomen, Managers, and Customers in American Department Stores, 1890–1940*.

JEREMY BRECHER is the author of *Strike!* and the co-author or editor of *Common Sense for Hard Times, Root and Branch: The Rise of the Workers Movements*, and *Brass Valley: The Story of Working People's Lives and Struggles in an American Industrial Region*. He is currently completing *History from Below: How to Uncover and Tell the Story of Your Community, Workplace, or Union*.

ERIC BREITBART is a freelance writer and media producer based in New York City. He has a degree in Comparative Literature from Columbia University and studied filmmaking in Paris. He is a regular contributor to *American Film* magazine and has directed several historical documentaries, including film biographies of Frederick Winslow Taylor and Harry Truman.

STEPHEN BRIER is the director of the American Social History Project at the Graduate Center, CUNY. He recently produced and directed the project's first documentary film, *1877: The Grand Army of Starvation*. Brier has taught history at several universities, most recently the Media and History course in New York University's Public History Program. He is a contributing editor of the *Radical History Review* and one of the founders of the New York City Public History Project.

JOSHUA BROWN is director of visual research and graphic art for the American Social History Project, for which he has written scripts and directed the design of an award-winning audiovisual series depicting the U.S. working-class past. His art appears in numerous academic and popular publications. He has published articles on the presentation of history in the popular arts and consulted on various public history projects.

REGINALD BUTLER teaches colonial history at North Carolina State University. He has been a fellow at the Smithsonian Institution and worked as a research historian at the Colonial Williamsburg Foundation.

EDWARD COUNTRYMAN teaches history and film studies at the University of Warwick and is a consulting editor of the *Radical History Review*. He has written two books on revolutionary America. His essay in this volume grows from his concern with the question of how people who are interested in history but are not academic learn about the past.

LISA DUGGAN is a doctoral candidate in women's history at the University of Pennsylvania. She is a founding member of the New York Lesbian and Gay History Project and an active member of the Committee on Lesbian and Gay History. She is also an activist and writer whose work has appeared in *Gay Community News, In These Times, Ms.*, and the *Village Voice*.

GERTRUDE FRASER is writing her dissertation on rural Virginia for the Johns Hopkins University. Currently she is a fellow at the Carter G. Woodson Institute for Afro-American and African Studies at the University of Virginia.

MICHAEL H. FRISCH is chair of the American Studies Department at SUNY-Buffalo. Co-editor of *Working-Class America* (1983), he has written widely on urban, oral, and public history and participated in numerous recent documentary projects, ranging from a neighborhood history street exhibit for Philadelphia's tercentenary to the award-winning film *Small Happiness: Women of a Chinese Village*, for which he was the oral history consultant.

JAMES R. GREEN teaches history and directs the labor studies program at the College of Public and Community Service, University of Massachusetts, Boston. He is the author of *Grass Roots Socialism, Boston's Workers*, and *The World of the Worker*, and editor of *Workers' Struggles, Past and Present*. An associate editor of *Radical America* and a coordinator of the Massachusetts History Workshop, he is active in various labor education and strike support efforts.

BARBARA MELOSH is associate curator of the Medical Sciences Division of the National Museum of American History, Smithsonian Institution, and assistant professor of English and American Studies at George Mason University. Her most recent publication in public history, urging serious historical reviews of museum exhibits, appeared in the Organization of American Historians *Newsletter*, 13 (May 1985).

SONYA MICHEL has served as consulting scholar to the People's Film Series, sponsored by the Rhode Island Committee for the Humanities, and to the Massachusetts and New Hampshire Humanities Programs in Libraries. She has conducted oral history interviews among the Jewish population of Rhode Island and frequently lectures on American Jewish history. She teaches at Harvard University.

PRISCILLA MUROLO is a graduate student in American Studies at Yale University and a member of the editorial collective of the *Radical History Review*. She has spoken to many non-academic audiences about the past and future of women who work in offices. She is currently completing a dissertation on the development of working women's group consciousness in the United States between 1880 and 1930.

TERENCE O'DONNELL is on the staff of the Oregon Historical Society and is also adjunct professor in Persian Studies at Portland State University. From 1978 to 1982 he was the Historical Society's coordinator for the Oregon Historical Society–Portland State University M.A. Program in Public History.

ROY ROSENZWEIG, associate professor of history and director of the Oral History Program at George Mason University, has consulted for many museums and community history projects and has produced and written historical documentary films. Rosenzweig is currently writing a book on the public presentation and perception of the past in the United States and co-editing (with Warren Leon) a volume on history museums. He is also the author of *Eight Hours for What We Will: Workers and Leisure in an Industrial City*.

FATH DAVIS RUFFINS is a historian at the National Museum of American History, Smithsonian Institution. She was project director of a new permanent hall, *After the Revolution: Everyday Life in America, 1780–1800*, and also curated the traveling version of that exhibition. From 1976 to 1979, she was the administrator of the W. E. B. DuBois Institute for Afro-American Research at Harvard University.

LINDA SHOPES is writing a dissertation on Baltimore cannery workers. She has taught in the American Studies Department at the University of Maryland Baltimore County and is currently working with the Touring Baltimore Project. Shopes has also written elsewhere about the theoretical issues confronting public historians, most recently in the *International Journal of Oral History* (November 1984).

CHRISTINA SIMMONS teaches American history and women's studies at Raymond Walters College, University of Cincinnati. She has written on twentieth-century sexual ideology and on women in day care and social welfare. She worked in the 1970s with the Providence MARHO group in presenting public history forums and has frequently spoken on women's history to a wide range of community groups.

JEFFREY C. STEWART, assistant professor of history and black studies at Scripps College of the Claremont Colleges, produced and acted in *Waiting for Lefty* and lectured on and assisted in the production of "Harlem Renaissance" as part of the *On Campus* television series for WNBC in Los Angeles. He has coordinated lectures, exhibitions, and performances to celebrate Black History Month at the Claremont Colleges.

DANIEL J. WALKOWITZ is co-director of the Graduate Program in Public History at New York University. He supervised the translation of his book, *Worker City, Company Town,* into a 90-minute docudrama, *The Molders of Troy.* Since then he has worked as a producer and consulted on various film projects, museum programs, and community history projects. He is currently writing a book about New York City social workers.

MICHAEL WALLACE is editorial coordinator of the *Radical History Review* and a director of the New York City Public History Project. He teaches history at John Jay College and has written a series of essays on popular historical consciousness.